Self, Others and the State

Criminal responsibility is now central to criminal law, but it is in need of re-examination. In the context of Australian criminal laws, *Self, Others and the State* reassesses the general assumptions made about the rise to prominence of criminal responsibility in the period since around the turn of the twentieth century. It reconsiders the role of criminal responsibility in criminal law, arguing that criminal responsibility is significant because it organises key sets of relations – between self, others and the state – as relations of responsibility. Detailed studies of decisive moments and key developments since the turn of the twentieth century, and original explorations of relations of responsibility, expose the complexity and dynamism of criminal responsibility and reveal that it is the means by which matters of subjectivity, relationality and power make themselves felt in the criminal law.

Arlie Loughnan is Professor of Criminal Law and Criminal Law Theory at the University of Sydney, and Co-Director of the Institute of Criminology, University of Sydney. She is the author of *Manifest Madness: Mental Incapacity in Criminal Law* (2012).

The Law in Context Series

Since 1970 the Law in Context series has been at the forefront of the movement to broaden the study of law. It has been a vehicle for the publication of innovative scholarly books that treat law and legal phenomena critically in their social, political and economic contexts from a variety of perspectives. The series particularly aims to publish scholarly legal writing that brings fresh perspectives to bear on new and existing areas of law taught in universities. A contextual approach involves treating legal subjects broadly, using materials from other social sciences, and from any other discipline that helps to explain the operation in practice of the subject under discussion. It is hoped that this orientation is at once more stimulating and more realistic than the bare exposition of legal rules. The series includes original books that have a different emphasis from traditional legal textbooks, while maintaining the same high standards of scholarship. They are written primarily for undergraduate and graduate students of law and other disciplines, but will also appeal to a wider readership. In the past, most books in the series have focused on English law, but recent publications include books on European law, globalisation, transnational legal processes and comparative law.

Books in the Series

Acosta: *The National versus the Foreigner in South America*
Ali: *Modern Challenges to Islamic Law*
Alyagon Darr: *Plausible Crime Stories: The Legal History of Sexual Offences in Mandate Palestine*
Anderson, Schum & Twining: *Analysis of Evidence*
Ashworth: *Sentencing and Criminal Justice*
Barton & Douglas: *Law and Parenthood*
Beecher-Monas: Evaluating Scientific Evidence: An Interdisciplinary Framework for *Intellectual Due Process*
Bell: *French Legal Cultures*
Bercusson: *European Labour Law*
Birkinshaw: *European Public Law*
Birkinshaw: *Freedom of Information: The Law, the Practice and the Ideal*
Broderick & Ferri: *International and European Disability Law and Policy: Text, Cases and Materials*
Brownsword & Goodwin: *Law and the Technologies of the Twenty-First Century: Text and Materials*
Cane & Goudkamp: *Atiyah's Accidents, Compensation and the Law*
Clarke & Kohler: *Property Law: Commentary and Materials*

Collins: *The Law of Contract*
Collins, Ewing & McColgan: *Labour Law*
Cowan: *Housing Law and Policy*
Cranston: *Legal Foundations of the Welfare State*
Darian-Smith: *Laws and Societies in Global Contexts: Contemporary Approaches*
Dauvergne: *Making People Illegal: What Globalisation Means for Immigration and Law*
Davies: *Perspectives on Labour Law*
Dembour: *Who Believes in Human Rights? Reflections on the European Convention*
de Sousa Santos: *Toward a New Legal Common Sense*
Diduck: *Law's Families*
Estella: *Legal Foundations of EU Economic Governance*
Fortin: *Children's Rights and the Developing Law*
Garnsey: *The Justice of Visual Art: Creative State-Building in Times of Political Transition*
Ghai & Woodman: *Practising Self-Government: A Comparative Study of Autonomous Regions*
Glover-Thomas: *Reconstructing Mental Health Law and Policy*
Gobert & Punch: *Rethinking Corporate Crime*
Goldman: *Globalisation and the Western Legal Tradition: Recurring Patterns of Law and Authority*
Haack: *Evidence Matters: Science, Proof, and Truth in the Law*
Harlow & Rawlings: *Law and Administration*
Harris: *An Introduction to Law*
Harris, Campbell & Halson: *Remedies in Contract and Tort*
Harvey: *Seeking Asylum in the UK: Problems and Prospects*
Herring: *Law and the Relational Self*
Hervey & McHale: *European Union Health Law: Themes and Implications*
Hervey & McHale: *Health Law and the European Union*
Holder & Lee: *Environmental Protection, Law and Policy: Text and Materials*
Jackson & Summers: *The Internationalisation of Criminal Evidence: Beyond the Common Law and Civil Law Traditions*
Kostakopoulou: *The Future Governance of Citizenship*
Kreiczer-Levy: *Destabilized Property: Property Law in the Sharing Economy*
Kubal: *Immigration and Refugee Law in Russia: Socio-Legal Perspectives*
Lewis: *Choice and the Legal Order: Rising above Politics*
Likosky: *Transnational Legal Processes: Globalisation and Power Disparities*
Likosky: *Law, Infrastructure and Human Rights*
Lunney: *A History of Australian Tort Law 1901–1945: England's Obedient Servant?*
Maughan & Webb: *Lawyering Skills and the Legal Process*
McGlynn: *Families and the European Union: Law, Politics and Pluralism*
Moffat: *Trusts Law: Text and Materials*
Monti: *EC Competition Law*
Morgan: *Contract Law Minimalism: A Formalist Restatement of Commercial Contract Law*
Morgan & Yeung: *An Introduction to Law and Regulation: Text and Materials*

Nicola & Davies: *EU Law Stories: Contextual and Critical Histories of European Jurisprudence*
Norrie: *Crime, Reason and History: A Critical Introduction to Criminal Law*
O'Dair: *Legal Ethics: Text and Materials*
Oliver: *Common Values and the Public–Private Divide*
Oliver & Drewry: *The Law and Parliament*
Picciotto: *International Business Taxation*
Probert: *The Changing Legal Regulation of Cohabitation, 1600–2010*
Reed: *Internet Law: Text and Materials*
Richardson: *Law, Process and Custody*
Roberts & Palmer: *Dispute Processes: ADR and the Primary Forms of Decision-Making*
Rowbottom: *Democracy Distorted: Wealth, Influence and Democratic Politics*
Sauter: *Public Services in EU Law*
Scott & Black: *Cranston's Consumers and the Law*
Seneviratne: *Ombudsmen: Public Services and Administrative Justice*
Seppänen: *Ideological Conflict and the Rule of Law in Contemporary China*
Siems: *Comparative Law, 2nd Edition*
Stapleton: *Product Liability*
Stewart: *Gender, Law and Justice in a Global Market*
Tamanaha: *Law as a Means to an End: Threat to the Rule of Law*
Turpin & Tomkins: *British Government and the Constitution: Text and Materials*
Twining: *General Jurisprudence: Understanding Law from a Global Perspective*
Twining: *Globalisation and Legal Theory*
Twining: *Human Rights, Southern Voices: Francis Deng, Abdullahi An-Na'im, Yash Ghai and Upendra Baxi*
Twining: *Jurist in Context*
Twining: *Rethinking Evidence: Exploratory Essays*
Twining & Miers: *How to Do Things with Rules*
Ward: *A Critical Introduction to European Law*
Ward: *Law, Text, Terror*
Ward: *Shakespeare and Legal Imagination*
Wells & Quick: *Lacey, Wells and Quick: Reconstructing Criminal Law*
Zander: *Cases and Materials on the English Legal System*
Zander: *The Law-Making Process*

International Journal of Law in Context: A Global Forum for Interdisciplinary Legal Studies

The International *Journal of Law in Context* is the companion journal to the Law in Context book series and provides a forum for interdisciplinary legal studies and an intellectual space for ground-breaking critical research. It publishes contextual work about law and its relationship with other disciplines including but not limited to science, literature, humanities, philosophy, sociology, psychology, ethics, history and geography. More information about the journal and how to submit an article can be found at http://journals.cambridge.org/ijc

Self, Others and the State

Relations of Criminal Responsibility

ARLIE LOUGHNAN
University of Sydney

CAMBRIDGE
UNIVERSITY PRESS

CAMBRIDGE
UNIVERSITY PRESS

University Printing House, Cambridge CB2 8BS, United Kingdom
One Liberty Plaza, 20th Floor, New York, NY 10006, USA
477 Williamstown Road, Port Melbourne, VIC 3207, Australia
314–321, 3rd Floor, Plot 3, Splendor Forum, Jasola District Centre, New Delhi – 110025, India
79 Anson Road, #06-04/06, Singapore 079906

Cambridge University Press is part of the University of Cambridge.

It furthers the University's mission by disseminating knowledge in the pursuit of education, learning, and research at the highest international levels of excellence.

www.cambridge.org
Information on this title: www.cambridge.org/9781108497602
DOI: 10.1017/9781108596367

First published 2020

Printed in the United Kingdom by TJ International Ltd. Padstow Cornwall

A catalogue record for this publication is available from the British Library.

Library of Congress Cataloging-in-Publication Data
Names: Loughnan, Arlie, author.
Title: Self, others and the state : relations of criminal responsibility / Arlie Loughnan.
Description: Cambridge, United Kingdom ; New York, NY, USA : Cambridge University Press, 2020 | Series: Law in context | Includes bibliographical references and index.
Identifiers: LCCN 2019029335 | ISBN 9781108497602 (hardback) | ISBN 9781108497602 (ebook)
Subjects: LCSH: Criminal liability--Australia.
Classification: LCC KU3878 .L68 2020 | DDC 345.94/04--dc23
LC record available at https://lccn.loc.gov/2019029335

ISBN 978-1-108-49760-2 Hardback

For my family, with love

Contents

Acknowledgements

This book was made possible by an Australian Research Council (ARC) Fellowship *Responsibility in Criminal Law* (Grant No. DE130100418) held at the University of Sydney. I would like to thank the ARC, and my colleagues at Sydney Law School – Andrew Dyer, Tanya Mitchell, Joellen Riley, David Rolph, Rayner Thwaites, Kevin Walton and Kim Weatherall – for the support they provided to me while I was working on this book.

While writing the book, I held Visiting Fellowships at the University of Cambridge, University College London and the University of Melbourne. I would like to thank my hosts at these institutions – Henry Mares, Ian Dennis and Gerry Simpson – for their warm hospitality. I was also able to present my research to various audiences, including at the London School of Economics, the National University of Singapore, the University of New South Wales, the University of Technology, Sydney, the University of Toronto and the University of Western Australia, and I benefited from the discussions that ensued.

I am grateful to Thomas Crofts, Jesse Elvin, Lindsay Farmer, Mark Finnane, Nicola Lacey, Tanya Mitchell and Kevin Walton for generously giving their time to read parts of this book and providing valuable comments on draft chapters. I would like to thank Peter Cane, Markus Dubber, Matthew Dyson, Jeremy Gans, Shaun McVeigh, Ngaire Naffine, David Omerod and Peter Rush for helpful conversations at crucial junctures. Thanks, too, to Alexandra Chappell, Umeya Chaudhuri, Natalie Czapski, James Monaghan, Mikah Pajaczkowska-Russell, Hae Soo Park and Louisa Vaupel for excellent research assistance. I would also like to thank Michelle Daly, Sirinporn Lub-Ubolkeao and Patrick O'Mara from the University of Sydney Library. A special thank you is reserved for Sabine Selchow, for the many enthusiastic exchanges on the ideas presented here and for being my first reader.

The editorial team at Cambridge University Press, including Finola O'Sullivan, Marianne Nield and Adam Hooper, has been wonderful to work with and I appreciated all assistance offered to me. Constructive suggestions were provided by each of the three referees consulted by Cambridge; I thank them and the editors of the *Law in Context* series – William Twining, Bronwen Morgan and Maksymilian Del Mar.

Parts of this book draw from the following articles: 'Consorting, Then and Now: Changing Relations of Responsibility' (2019) 45(2) *University of Western Australia Law Review* 8–36; 'Women's Responsibility for Crime: Dynamics of Change in Australia since the Turn of the Twentieth Century' (2018) 5(2) *Law & History* 137–64; 'The Meta-Significance of Criminal Responsibility' (2017) 4(1) *Critical Analysis of Law* 31–41; and '"The Very Foundations of Any System of Criminal Justice": Criminal Responsibility in the Australian Model Criminal Code' (2017) 6(3) *International Journal for Crime, Justice and Social Democracy* 8–24. I thank the editors and publishers of these journals for allowing me to reuse the materials.

Table of Cases

(All Australian cases unless otherwise indicated)

Ansari *v.* The Queen (2010) 241 CLR 299

Attorney-General for the State of South Australia *v.* Brown (1960) 44 Cr App R 100 (Privy Council)

Auld *v.* Purdy (1933) 50 WN (NSW) 218

Australian Capital Television *v.* Commonwealth (1992) 177 CLR 106

Bank of England *v.* Vagliano Brothers [1891] AC 107

Beer *v.* Toms, Ex parte Toms (1952) 46 QJPR 102

Berry *v.* Ritchie [1932] [Vol. IV] NZLR 357 (New Zealand)

Birrell *v.* Astor [1940] VLR 180

Boughey *v.* The Queen (1986) 161 CLR 10

Brealy *v.* Buckley [1934] Argus LR 371

Brennan *v.* The King (1936) 55 CLR 253

Bryan *v.* White [1962] Tas SR 113

Byrne *v.* Shearer [1959] VR 606

Canino *v.* Samuels [1968] SASR 303

Clarke *v.* Nelson; ex parte Nelson [1936] QWN 17

Codd *v.* Lewis (1944) 38 QJPR 135

Codd *v.* Wall (1944) 38 QJPR 141

CTM *v.* The Queen (2008) 236 CLR 440

Cubillo *v.* Commonwealth (No. 2) (2000) 103 FCR 1

Dias *v.* O'Sullivan [1949] SASR 195

Dietrich *v.* The Queen (1992) 177 CLR 292

Director of Public Prosecutions *v.* Majewski [1977] AC 443 (England)

Director of Public Prosecutions *v.* Smith [1963] AC 220 (England)

Director of Public Prosecutions (Cth) *v.* Poniatowska (2011) 244 CLR 408

Director of Public Prosecutions (WA) *v.* McGarry [No. 9] [2016] WASC 306

Duncan *v.* Ellis (1916) 21 CLR 379

Erlich *v.* Leifer & Adass Israel School Inc [2015] VSC 499

Ex parte Finney; Re Miller & Anor (1936) 50 WN (NSW) 190

Ex parte King; Re Blackley (1938) 38 SR (NSW) 483

Ferrier *v.* Wilson (1906) 4 CLR 785

Forster *v.* Director of Public Prosecutions (NSW) [2017] NSWSC 458

Gabriel *v.* Lenthall [1930] SASR 318
Green *v.* R (1997) 191 CLR 334
Guider *v.* Walker [1933] VLR 413
Hardgrave *v.* The King (1906) 4 CLR 232
He Kaw Teh *v.* The Queen (1985) 157 CLR 523
Jago *v.* District Court of New South Wales (1989) 168 CLR 23
Jan *v.* Fingleton (1983) 32 SASR 379
JGE *v.* The Trustees of the Portsmouth Roman Catholic Diocesan Trust [2012] 4 All ER 1152 (England)
Johanson *v.* Dixon (1979) 143 CLR 376
Jolly *v.* Salvitti [1974] VR 484
King *v.* Mullen (1938) 59 CLR 124
Kruger *v.* Commonwealth (1997) 190 CLR 1
Kuczborski *v.* Queensland (2014) 254 CLR 51
Lange *v.* ABC (1997) 189 CLR 520
Lavallee *v.* The Queen 55 CCC (3d) 397 (1990) (Canada)
Lee *v.* The Queen (2007) 71 NSWLR 120
Lee Fan *v.* Dempsey (1907) 5 CLR 310
Leeth *v.* The Commonwealth of Australia (1992) 174 CLR 455
Liberato *v.* The Queen (1985) 159 CLR 507
Mabo *v.* State of Queensland (No. 1) (1988) 166 CLR 186
Mabo *v.* State of Queensland (No. 2) (1992) 175 CLR 1
MacDonald *v.* The King (1935) 52 CLR 739
Mancini *v.* Director of Public Prosecutions [1942] AC 1
McClelland *v.* Symons [1951] VLR 157
Mraz *v.* R (No. 2) (1956) 96 CLR 62
Mullen *v.* The King [1938] St R Qd 97
Muller *v.* Murphy; ex parte Murphy [1935] St R Qd 85
NSW *v.* Lepore (2003) 195 ALR 412
Osland *v.* R (1998) 197 CLR 316
O'Connor *v.* Johnston (1903) 23 NZLR 183 (New Zealand)
Palmer *v.* The Queen [1971] AC 814
Parker *v.* R (1963) 111 CLR 610
Patterson *v.* Harrison [1957] Argus LR 1195
Peters *v.* The Queen (1998) 192 CLR 493
Piro *v.* Foster (1943) 68 CLR 313
Polyukhovich *v.* Commonwealth (1991) 172 CLR 501
Porter *v.* Bryan [1963] Tas SR 41
Prince Alfred College Incorporated *v.* ADC (2016) 258 CLR 134
Proudman *v.* Dayman (1941) 67 CLR 536
R *v.* Anunga (1976) 11 ALR 412
R *v.* Babsek [1998] QCA 116
R *v.* Barlow (1997) 188 CLR 1
R *v.* Bonnor [1957] VR 227

Singh *v.* R [2012] NSWSC 637
Soderman *v.* The King (1936) 55 CLR 192
South Australia *v.* Totani (2010) 242 CLR 1
Stapleton *v.* The Queen (1952) 86 CLR 358
Tajjour *v.* New South Wales; Hawthorne *v.* New South Wales; Forster *v.* New South Wales (2014) 254 CLR 508
Tesco *v.* Nattrass [1972] AC 153 (England)
The King *v.* Mullen (1938) 59 CLR 124
The Queen *v.* Robyn Kina [1993] QCA 480
The Queen *v.* Secretary [1996] NTCCA 18
Thomas *v.* R (1937) 59 CLR 279
Toonen *v.* Australia (1994) Communication No. 488/1992, U.N. Doc CCPR/C/50/D/488/1992 (United Nations)
Trustees of the Roman Catholic Church for the Archdiocese of Sydney *v.* Ellis [2007] NSWCA 117
Vallance *v.* The Queen (1961) 108 CLR 56
Viro *v.* The Queen (1978) 141 CLR 88
Wainohu *v.* New South Wales (2011) 243 CLR 181
Widgee Shire Council *v.* Bonney (1907) 4 CLR 977
Wilson *v.* Giles [1966] SASR 361
Woolmington *v.* Director of Public Prosecutions [1935] AC 462 (England)
Zecevic *v.* Director of Public Prosecutions (Vic) (1987) 162 CLR 645

Table of Statutes

AUSTRALIA

Aboriginals Ordinance 1918 (Cth)
Aborigines Act 1905 (WA)
Aborigines and Torres Strait Islander Act 1965 (Qld)
Anti-Terrorism Act (No. 2) 2004 (Cth)
Australia Act 1986 (Cth)
Charter of Human Rights and Responsibilities Act 2006 (Vic)
Child Welfare Act 1939 (NSW)
Child Welfare Act 1954 (Vic)
Child Welfare Ordinance 1957 (ACT)
Children, Youth and Families Act 2005 (Vic)
Children's Court Act 1906 (Vic)
Civil Liability Legislation Amendment (Child Sexual Abuse Actions) Act 2018 (WA)
Commonwealth of Australia Constitution Act 1900 (Cth)
Corporations Act 2001 (Cth)
Crimes Act 1900 (NSW)
Crimes Act 1914 (Cth)
Crimes Act 1928 (Vic)
Crimes Act 1949 (Vic)
Crimes Act 1958 (Vic)
Crimes (Amendment) Act 1951 (NSW)
Crimes (Amendment) Ordinance No. 2 1990 (ACT)
Crimes Amendment (Abolition of Defensive Homicide) Act 2014 (Vic)
Crimes Amendment (Consorting and Organised Crime) Act 2012 (NSW)
Crimes (Criminal Organisations Control) Act 2009 (NSW)
Crimes (Domestic and Personal Violence) Act 2007 (NSW)
Crimes (Homicide) Act 2005 (Vic)
Crimes (Homicide) Amendment Act 1982 (NSW)
Crimes (Summary Offences) Amendment Act 1979 (NSW)
Crimes and Other Acts Amendment Act 1974 (NSW)
Criminal Code Act 1899 (Qld)

Criminal Code Act 1901 (Qld)
Criminal Code Act 1902 (WA)
Criminal Code Act 1913 (WA)
Criminal Code Act 1924 (Tas)
Criminal Code Act 1983 (NT)
Criminal Code Act 1995 (Cth)
Criminal Code Act Compilation Act 1913 (WA)
Criminal Code Amendment (Abolition of Defence of Provocation) Act 2003 (Tas)
Criminal Code and the Offenders Probation and Parole Act Amendment Act 1971 (Qld)
Criminal Code Bill 1994 (Cth)
Criminal Law Amendment Act 1891 (Qld)
Criminal Law Amendment Act 1892 (Qld)
Criminal Law Amendment Act 1894 (Qld)
Criminal Law Amendment (Homicide) Act 2008 (WA)
Criminal Law Amendment (Simple Offences) Act 2004 (WA)
Criminal Law and Evidence Act 1891 (NSW)
Criminal Law Amendment Act 1883 (NSW)
Criminal Law Consolidation Act 1935 (SA)
Criminal Organisations Act 2009 (Qld)
Criminal Organisations Control Act 2012 (Vic)
Criminal Organisations Control Amendment (Unlawful Associations) Act 2015 (Vic)
Criminal Procedure Act 1986 (NSW)
Director of Public Prosecutions Act 1983 (Cth)
Evidence Act 1995 (Cth)
Evidence Further Amendment Act 1876 (NSW)
Financial Transactions Reports Act 1988 (Cth)
First Offenders Probation Act 1894 (NSW)
Human Rights Act 2004 (ACT)
Immigration (Guardianship of Children) Act 1946 (Cth)
Immigration Restriction Act 1901 (Cth)
Infant Life Protection Act 1904 (NSW)
Justices Act 1886 (Qld)
Justices Act 1850 (NSW)
Justices Act 1902 (NSW)
Justice Fines Act 1899 (NSW)
Legal Identity of Defendants (Organisational Child Abuse) Act 2018 (Vic)
Limitations of Actions Amendment (Child Abuse) Act 2015 (Vic)
Marriage Act 1961 (Cth)
Masters and Servants Act 1840 (NSW)
National Crime Authority Act 1984 (Cth)

National Crimes Commission Act 1982 (Cth)
Neglected Children and Juvenile Offences Act 1905 (NSW)
Northern Territory Aboriginals Act 1906 (SA)
Northern Territory National Emergency Response Act 2007 (Cth)
Ordinance Relating to Aboriginals 1918 (NT)
Pacific Islands Labourers Act 1901 (Cth)
Police Act 1892 (WA)
Police Offences Act 1890 (Vic)
Police Offences Act 1928 (Vic)
Police Offences Act 1935 (Tas)
Police Offences Act 1957 (Vic)
Police Offences (Amendment) Ordinance 1983 (ACT)
Police Offences (Consorting) Act 1931 (Vic)
Police Regulation Act 1862 (NSW)
Privy Council (Limitation of Appeals) Act 1968 (Cth)
Privy Council (Appeals from the High Court) Act 1975 (Cth)
Proceeds of Crime Act 1987 (Cth)
Road Traffic Act 1934–39 (SA)
Royal Commissions Act 1902 (Cth)
Royal Commissions Act 1923 (NSW)
Seat of Government Supreme Court Act 1933 (Cth)
Serious and Organised Crime (Control) Act 2008 (SA)
Serious Crime Control Act 2009 (NT)
State Children's Act 1895 (SA)
Statute of Westminster Adoption Act 1942 (Cth)
Summary Offences Act 1953 (SA)
Summary Offences Act 1966 (Vic)
Summary Offences Act 1970 (NSW)
Summary Offences Act 1923 (NT)
The Offenders Probation Act 1886 (Qld)
The Vagrants, Gaming and Other Offences Act 1931 (Qld)
Vagrancy Act 1902 (NSW)
Vagrancy Act 1966 (Vic)
Vagrancy (Amendment) Act 1929 (NSW)
Vagrancy (Repeal) and Summary Offences (Amendment) Act 2005 (Vic)
Vicious Lawless Association Disestablishment Act 2013 (Qld)
War Precautions Act Repeal Act 1920 (Cth)
Welfare Ordinance 1953 (Cth)
Welfare Ordinance 1953 (NT)

CANADA

Criminal Code of Canada 1893

ENGLAND

Australia Act 1986
Colonial Laws Validity Act 1865
Criminal Evidence Act 1898
Criminal Justice Act 1855
Empire Settlement Act 1922
Homicide Act 1957
Infanticide Act 1922
Infanticide Act 1938
Jervis Acts 1848
Offences Against the Person Act 1861
Prisoners Counsel Act 1836
Statute of Westminster 1931
Theft Act 1968
Vagrancy Act 1824

NEW ZEALAND

Criminal Code Act 1893
Police Offences Amendment Act 1901
Police Offences Act 1884
Supreme Court Act 2003

Abbreviations

AC	Appeal Cases Law Reports
A Crim R	Australian Criminal Reports
All ER	All England Law Reports
ALR	Australian Law Reports
Argus LR	Argus Law Reports
CCC	Canadian Criminal Cases
CLR	Commonwealth Law Reports
Cox CC	Cox's Criminal Cases
Cr App R	Criminal Appeal Reports
FCR	Federal Court Reports
KB	Law Reports, King's Bench Division
Legge	Legge's Supreme Court Cases (New South Wales)
NSWLR	New South Wales Law Reports
NSWSC	Supreme Court of New South Wales
NTCCA	Court of Criminal Appeal (Northern Territory)
NZLR	New Zealand Law Reports
QB	Law Reports, Queen's Bench Division
QBD	Law Reports, Queen's Bench Division
QCA	Queensland Court of Appeal
Qd R	Queensland Reports
QJPR	Queensland Justice of the Peace Reports
SASR	South Australian State Reports
SR (NSW)	State Reports (New South Wales)
St R Qd	Queensland State Reports
Tas SR	Tasmanian State Reports
VLR	Victorian Law Reports
VR	Victorian Reports
VSC	Supreme Court of Victoria
WASC	Supreme Court of Western Australia
WN (NSW)	New South Wales Weekly Notes

Introduction

Criminal responsibility is having a brilliant career. With its dual dimensions – as both the basis on which individuals are called to account for criminal conduct, and the form or structure of the criminal law – criminal responsibility is now central to the criminal law. Responsibility has come to occupy this position in criminal law over the course of the twentieth century. At the turn of the twentieth century, lawyers, scholars and reformers were concerned with a range of matters, including the organisation of the criminal law and its mode of expression – as common law, legislation or code – but, by the turn of the twenty-first century, the myriad of concerns with the criminal law – including its organisation and its mode – were each refracted through the lens of criminal responsibility. In the intervening period, criminal responsibility became key to the self-definition of the criminal law, and the language of criminal responsibility became the language of the criminal law, spoken by scholars, judges, legislators, reformers and others. As a result, in the current era, criminal responsibility is not just one topic of study among many, but seems to hold the clue to understanding the criminal law as a whole.

There is a general story told about this rise to prominence of criminal responsibility. In broad terms, and at some risk of caricature, this story runs along these lines: the centrality of criminal responsibility to criminal law in the current era represents the maturation of the law of crime, with criminal responsibility providing an internal guiding line allowing criminal law to be measured against itself. In Lindsay Farmer's words, criminal responsibility has become central to 'the law's reflexive account of itself', that is, to the criminal legal story about the criminal law.[1] In this general story, the era of mature criminal law dates from the middle of the twentieth century, when, aided by the scholarship of leading legal theorists, such as H. L. A. Hart at Oxford, and by major, hybrid academic-practice law reform projects, such as the *Model Penal Code* in the United States, criminal responsibility came to represent the normative heart of the law of crime.[2] In this mid-century

[1] L. Farmer, 'The Obsession with Definition: The Nature of Crime and Critical Legal Theory' (1996) 5 *Social & Legal Studies* 57–73, 68.

[2] Regarding H. L. A. Hart, see H. L. A. Hart, *The Concept of Law*, 3rd ed. (Oxford: Oxford University Press, 2012 [first published 1961]); H. L .A. Hart, *Punishment and Responsibility:*

moment, the history of criminal responsibility – its absence from the early modern criminal law, and its gradual and uneven emergence only from the eighteenth century – ended, and the present began. In the present, the story of criminal responsibility is usually told as a legal-philosophical tale, in which the main preoccupations are the (ever greater) refinement of principles of criminal responsibility (by reference to moral and political theoretical precepts), and the critique of substantive systems of criminal law for their failures to adhere to these principles.

But there is reason to think a critical account of criminal responsibility principles and practices in the twentieth century will reveal a different story. While not associated with the seismic changes of previous eras – in which, for instance, one mode of criminal trial gave way to another – the twentieth century has seen important developments that have impacted on criminal responsibility. The growth of the administrative state, the massive expansion of the criminal law, and the radical restructuring along horizontal lines of relationships between individuals, along with other developments, have influenced criminal responsibility. In this period, strong public and political discourses about responsibility for crime have impacted on responsibility in criminal law, what individuals are responsible for has changed, and the relation between state responsibility and individual responsibility has shifted in important ways. Over about the same time, criminal responsibility has come to be accorded strong symbolic value in the legal order and the wider social order of which it is part. As a result, criminal responsibility – which has been labelled 'primarily a legal artefact'[3] – carries with it particular significance, and this is vital to our understanding of it.

This book has two main aims: in the context of Australian criminal laws, it reassesses the general story of the rise to prominence of criminal responsibility over the twentieth century, paying close and careful attention to the intricacies of developments in criminal responsibility within this period, and it reconsiders the role and significance of criminal responsibility in criminal law, arguing that criminal responsibility is significant as it organises keys sets of relations – between self, others and the state – as relations of responsibility. My analysis generates two main insights that correspond with the two aims of the book. First, it reveals the gradual and distinctive way in which criminal law came to be organised around criminal responsibility, and what this makes

Essays in the Philosophy of Law, 2nd ed. (Oxford: Oxford University Press, 2008); see also N. Lacey, *A Life of H.L.A. Hart: The Nightmare and the Noble Dream* (Oxford: Oxford University Press, 2006). Regarding the *Model Penal Code*, see American Law Institute, *Model Penal and Correctional Code: Official Draft and Explanatory Notes* (adopted 24 May 1962). (Philadelphia, PA: The American Law Institute, 1985); for analysis, see M. D. Dubber, 'Penal Panopticon: The Idea of a Modern Model Penal Code' (2000) 4(1) *Buffalo Criminal Law Review* 53–100.

3 L. Farmer, *Making the Modern Criminal Law: Criminalization and Civil Order. Series: Criminalization* (Oxford: Oxford University Press, 2016), pp. 165, 170.

possible and what it precludes. Second, it exposes the complexity and dynamism of the relations of responsibility that subtend criminal responsibility principles and practices, substituting the still-dominant account of criminal responsibility as singular, general and universal, for an account of criminal responsibility characterised by multiplicity, specificity and variation across the criminal law field.

Introducing Criminal Responsibility

Criminal responsibility now attracts significant attention both inside and outside the legal academy, but the term of criminal responsibility is not always used in the same way, so it is worth introducing the subject matter of this book – and my approach to it – with some care. While criminal responsibility may be used as if it were a loose, non-technical term – to provide a rough synonym for criminal liability – or to denote specific doctrines of criminal law such as non-age or mental incapacity, it has a more precise meaning in criminal law scholarship and in this book. I assess the scholarship on criminal responsibility in detail in Chapter 2, where I also present my own account of the role and significance of criminal responsibility, but, here, in advance, I briefly introduce the topic of criminal responsibility.

Criminal responsibility has two dimensions. These are sometimes collapsed into each other, but it is worth separating them. In its first dimension, criminal responsibility relates to responsibility attribution – the practice of assigning responsibility to someone or something for particular behaviour. Responsibility attribution is the way in which human and non-human subjects are held accountable for their conduct and the basis on which they face sanctions for breach of the criminal law. As students of criminal law learn, individuals (and corporations) are called to account across a structure of conduct, fault, and defences (*actus reus, mens rea* and justifications and excuses). In Alan Norrie's words, the *mens rea/actus reus* dyad is a 'prevalent and continuing way of doing criminal responsibility.'[4] Here, criminal responsibility is concerned with the kind of person imagined by the law, where this is measured in terms such as agency, autonomy, rationality and moral capacity, and the emphasis is on the respect for persons thought to be entailed in the standard application of criminal law and criminal process, or on the appropriate kind of relationship between such individuals and the state.[5] As Dana Rabin argues in an historical context, this person of criminal law is someone always already

[4] See A. Norrie, 'Legal Form and Moral Judgement: Euthanasia and Assisted Suicide', in R. A. Duff et al. (eds.), *The Structures of Criminal Law* (Oxford: Oxford University Press, 2011), p. 139.

[5] See, e.g., R. A. Duff, *Answering for Crime: Responsibility and Liability in the Criminal Law* (London: Hart Publishing, 2007).

responsible,[6] and the scholarly enquiry centres on the criteria or basis or criminal responsibility – character, capacity, risk or perhaps a combination of these.[7]

In its second dimension, criminal responsibility relates to the form or structure of the law – the arrangement of doctrines and principles that may be understood as the skeleton of the corpus of the criminal law, ensuring the body of the law holds together. Since the mid-twentieth century, this second dimension of criminal responsibility is sometimes referred to as 'the general part' of criminal law,[8] the part of the law that is 'generalisable', comprising the variety of doctrines that underscore more than one offence, or more than one 'family' of offences, and which may be found in more than one system of law.[9] As this suggests, 'the general part' is grounded 'in the nature of the criminal law and the ends it serves'.[10] As the form or structure of the criminal law, criminal responsibility represents the hidden logic of 'the special part' of criminal law – the particular offences and defences that make up any one positive system of law.[11] Here, the focus is on the collection of doctrines and principles, such as the idea that an individual should not be convicted unless he or she is to be blamed (at fault) for an offence (*actus non facit reum nisi mens sit rea*), and the burden and standard of proof, that are thought to define the criminal law – both as law (as opposed to some other form of governance or regulation), and as a particular legal subspecies (compared with tort law, for example).[12]

The two dimensions of criminal responsibility – responsibility ascription and responsibility as the form or structure of the law – represent the particular and the general: responsibility ascription is particular in that it is the application of the criminal law in a singular moment in time to an individual alleged to have committed an offence, and responsibility as form or structure is general in that it denotes the sustained or extended existence of a corpus of legal rules comprising the criminal law as a whole. These two dimensions

6 See D. Rabin, *Identity, Crime, and Legal Responsibility in Eighteenth-Century England* (London: Palgrave MacMillan, 2004).

7 See further N. Lacey, *In Search of Criminal Responsibility: Ideas, Interests, and Institutions* (Oxford: Oxford University Press, 2016), and discussion in Chapter 2.

8 Lacey, *In Search of Criminal Responsibility*, p. 1. As Lacey writes, 'the general part' encompasses 'technical normative and conceptual doctrines and broad procedural values' (such as the principle of legality).

9 See further J. Gardner, 'On the General Part of Criminal Law', in R. A. Duff (ed.), *Philosophy and the Criminal Law: Principle and Critique* (Cambridge: Cambridge University Press, 1998), p. 205; see also G. Fletcher, *The Grammar of Criminal Law: American, Comparative, and International: Volume 1: Foundations* (Oxford: Oxford University Press, 2007), ch. 1.

10 See A. P. Simester and S. Shute, 'On the General Part in Criminal Law', in S. Shute and A. P. Simester (eds.), *Criminal Law Theory: Doctrines of the General Part* (Oxford: Oxford University Press, 2002), p. 12.

11 On the 'special part' – the particular offences and defences that comprise a system of criminal law – and the 'general part' more generally, see G. Williams, *Textbook of Criminal Law* (London: Stevens, 1978).

12 See Farmer, *Making the Modern Criminal Law*, p. 170 (on the way in which criminal responsibility is thought to contra-distinguish criminal law from tort law).

of criminal responsibility are connected. As Farmer argues, there has been a tendency to collapse the latter into the former, such that the work of criminal responsibility to realise justice in an individual case (for instance, by requiring an offence to include a mental or fault element) is taken to mean that the construction of the whole of the criminal law around criminal responsibility is just (for instance, by limiting the ability of the state to rely on the sanctioning power of the criminal law).[13] As this implies, criminal responsibility has become a means of approaching the criminal law *as a whole* that retains sight of the specific coalescence of principles and practices entailed in each instance of the adjudication of responsibility. As I have suggested elsewhere, in part as a result of this synthetic quality of criminal responsibility – according to which it is possible to think and talk about the criminal law in the aggregate and in discrete instances, at the same time – it is not just an object of study, but also a *way* of studying the criminal law.[14]

Reflecting the fact that it is not so much an object of study as a means of studying the criminal law, there is enormous scholarly interest in criminal responsibility. Alongside criminalisation, and state punishment, criminal responsibility now forms one of the main planks of criminal law theory. As I discuss in Chapter 2, criminal responsibility is most often studied by scholars working in the legal-philosophical tradition, broadly, the tradition of criminal law theory inspired by normative philosophical thinking. In this tradition, criminal responsibility is thought about in terms of adherence to or departure from principles, as either principled or non- or unprincipled.[15] As Ngaire Naffine writes, this scholarly tradition is marked by the pursuit of correspondence between the criminal law and moral notions of harm and wrong.[16] In this tradition, there is a 'proper' or ideal criminal law, delimited in scope and depth. The legal-philosophical treatment of criminal responsibility occludes some of the most interesting aspects of responsibility in criminal law: as Nicola Lacey argues, this treatment of criminal responsibility has the effect of bracketing off a set of questions related to the institutional, social and other conditions of existence of concepts of responsibility,[17] and is based on a thin or minimal appreciation of the development of responsibility principles and practices over time.

In response to the limits of legal-philosophical studies of criminal responsibility, in recent years, a growing body of what has been called critical criminal

[13] See Farmer, *Making the Modern Criminal Law*, ch. 6.

[14] See A. Loughnan, 'The Meta-Significance of Criminal Responsibility' (2017) 4(1) *Critical Analysis of Law* 31–41, 36–8.

[15] See, e.g., Simester and Shute, 'On the General Part in Criminal Law' (discussing 'derogation' from the doctrines comprising 'the general part' of criminal law).

[16] See N. Naffine, 'Criminal Conversations: Farmer, Lacey and the New Social Scholarship' (2016) 38(4) *Sydney Law Review* 505–17.

[17] N. Lacey, 'Institutionalising Responsibility: Implications for Jurisprudence' (2013) 4(1) *Jurisprudence* 1–19, 2.

responsibility scholarship has developed.[18] As I discuss in Chapter 2, this body of work has been developed by a number of scholars working within sociological, historical and socio-theoretical disciplinary traditions, including Farmer and Lacey, whose work features in the discussion in that chapter. Critical criminal law theory assesses legal principles and practices within a social, political and institutional context, acknowledging and taking account of contingencies, inconsistencies and change over time. Critical scholars have developed fascinating and provocative accounts of responsibility in criminal law. These scholars chart the dynamic relationship between ideas about criminal responsibility and the development of the modern state,[19] the changing coordination and legitimation requirements of criminal law into the current era,[20] the role of the police power,[21] and the influence of Enlightenment liberalism on the structures and operation of the criminal law.[22] These accounts reveal the complex processes by which individual responsibility for crime has come to act as a lynchpin in criminal law in the late modern era, and are closely attentive to change in responsibility principles and practices over time. Work in the critical criminal responsibility tradition is vibrant and exciting, and this book emerges out of this tradition, and seeks to contribute to it.

In this critical spirit, I approach criminal responsibility as a social practice or a 'thick' legal 'thing', the product of a network of laws, processes, institutions and actors – rather than as a 'thin' product of certain rules.[23] This approach to criminal responsibility generates different responsibility questions – rather than 'who is responsible under criminal law?', the question impliedly guiding legal-philosophical studies, the question becomes something like 'in what ways are individuals held responsible under criminal law?' – and this opens the way for multiple responses, or responses which vary from one part of the law to the other and over time. Approaching

[18] This term was coined by Nicola Lacey: see Lacey, *In Search of Criminal Responsibility*, p. 176. There are a number of types of scholarship that may be (loosely) described as 'critical' and each of these adopts different methods and approaches: see further D. Nelken, 'Critical Criminal Law' (1987) 14(1) *Journal of Law and Society* 105–17, 109–11.

[19] See L. Farmer, *Criminal Law, Tradition and Legal Order: Crime and the Genius of Scots Law, 1747 to the Present* (Cambridge: Cambridge University Press, 1997).

[20] See N. Lacey, 'Responsibility and Modernity in Criminal Law' (2001) 9(3) *Journal of Political Philosophy* 249–76; N. Lacey, 'In Search of the Responsible Subject: History, Philosophy and Social Sciences in Criminal Law Theory' (2001) 64(3) *Modern Law Review* 350–71; N. Lacey, 'Character, Capacity, Outcome: Towards a Framework for Assessing the Shifting Pattern of Criminal Responsibility in Modern English Law', in M. D. Dubber and L. Farmer (eds.), *Modern Histories of Crime and Punishment* (Stanford: Stanford University Press, 2007).

[21] See M. D. Dubber, *The Police Power: Patriarchy and the Foundations of American Government* (New York: Columbia University Press, 2005).

[22] See A. Norrie, *Crime, Reason and History: A Critical Introduction to Criminal Law*, 3rd ed. (Cambridge: Cambridge University Press, 2014).

[23] See also P. Cane, *Responsibility in Law and Morality* (Oxford: Hart Publishing, 2002), pp. 4, 25; S. Veitch, *Law and Irresponsibility: On the Legitimation of Human Suffering* (London: Routledge, 2007), pp. 36–7. I discuss the approach taken to criminal responsibility by Cane and Veitch in Chapter 1.

criminal responsibility this way extends the scholarly lens beyond conceptions of criminal responsibility – the 'nature' of criminal responsibility – to include responsibility principles and practices and the wider processes relating to the organisation of the criminal law around criminal responsibility. As a result of this approach, my study of criminal responsibility is less concerned with 'the traditional chestnuts of the topic' – 'the problem of psychological determinism, the legitimacy of strict liability, or the distinction between tort and criminal responsibility'[24] – and more concerned with the development of responsibility principles and practices in a particular space and time, within the social, political and institutional context in which such principles and practices are given life.

This critical approach to criminal responsibility leads me to adopt a socio-historical method for my study of criminal responsibility and to pay careful attention to space and time in this book. Socio-historical approaches to legal topics take legal principles and concepts as objects of study, and examine them in light of the substantive conditions under which intellectual ideas operate.[25] The book takes as its frame the development of criminal responsibility principles and practices in Australian criminal laws over the twentieth century, a delimited spatial and temporal frame that allows me to offer a study pitched 'close to the ground'.[26] I make a detailed case for the spatial and temporal frame of my study of criminal responsibility in Chapter 1. There, I explain the value of a study set in the context of Australian criminal laws, and prepare the ground for the historical analysis comprising Part II of the book, in which I assess the part played by criminal responsibility in the organisation of Australian criminal laws at three decisive junctures in the period since the turn of the twentieth century. This gives more texture and nuance to the story of the rise to prominence of criminal responsibility as a means of structuring and understanding the criminal law into the current era.

This critical approach to criminal responsibility also leads me to develop a new account of the role and hence the significance of criminal responsibility in criminal law. On my account, criminal responsibility organises keys sets of relations – between self, others and the state – as relations of responsibility, and this is what makes it significant. As I discuss in Chapter 2, recognising this role for criminal responsibility reveals that it is the means

[24] C. Kutz, 'Responsibility', in J. Coleman and S. Shapiro (eds.), *The Oxford Handbook of Jurisprudence and the Philosophy of Law* (Oxford: Oxford University Press, 2004), p. 551.

[25] See further M. D. Dubber and L. Farmer, 'Introduction: Regarding Criminal Law Historically', in M. D. Dubber and L. Farmer (eds.), *Modern Histories of Crime and Punishment* (Stanford: Stanford University Press, 2007), p. 1; see also M. D. Dubber, 'Historical Analysis of Law' (1998) 16(1) *Law and History Review* 159–62.

[26] There are 9 jurisdictions in Australia of which NSW, Victoria and Queensland are by far the most populous (containing over 75 percent of the Australian population between them). Australia has a Federal criminal jurisdiction (and a Commonwealth Criminal Code, which I discuss in Chapter 5), but most criminal law is state-based.

by which matters of subjectivity, relationality and power make themselves felt in the criminal law in particular ways. This account exposes the complexity and dynamism of the relations of responsibility that subtend responsibility principles and practices – substituting the still-dominant account of criminal responsibility as singular, general and universal, for an account of criminal responsibility characterised by multiplicity, specificity and variation across time and across the criminal law field. My account offers both a way of understanding and a basis of critique of criminal responsibility, opening the way for the theoretical examination of relations of responsibility that is offered in Part III of this book.

The Contribution of This Book

This book aims to make a fresh contribution to critical criminal responsibility scholarship. Despite its overall vibrancy, the existing critical scholarship on criminal responsibility has two limitations. First, it has tended to focus on developments up to and including the end of the nineteenth century, viewing the twentieth century (and the early years of the twenty-first century) as the post-script in a drama that had played out much earlier. Second, the existing critical work on criminal responsibility is limited in that it is built around the legal systems of England and Wales and the United States, and, to a lesser extent, Scotland and Canada, raising a question about the explanatory value of existing accounts for the experience in other parts of the common law world, beyond the bounds of the northern geographical context.

This book pushes the boundaries of the critical criminal responsibility scholarship on each of these fronts. On the first front, the book is expressly focused on the development of the law since around the turn of the twentieth century to the first decades of the twenty-first century, a delimited timeframe that permits a close and careful study of the period. The twentieth century is sometimes neglected in critical studies of criminal responsibility. This period is assumed to be one in which the major changes of the earlier periods have been bedded down or consolidated. When the socio-historical narrative given about criminal responsibility is structured in broad chapters – with major changes occurring during the seventeenth and eighteenth centuries, and again over the nineteenth century – the history of criminal responsibility is depicted as the product of developments playing out over large periods of time.[27] The major developments that tend to govern the way we think about criminal principles and practices in the current era – including the appearance of the adversarial criminal trial, and the extension of standards encoded in specific rules to the

[27] See, e.g., K. J. M. Smith, 'General Principles of Criminal Law', in W. Cornish et al. (eds.), *The Oxford History of the Laws of England Volume XIII: 1820–1914 Fields of Development* (Oxford: Oxford University Press, 2010).

criminal law as a whole[28] – had largely played out by about the beginning of the 1900s, rendering the twentieth century a sort of codicil to the main responsibility narrative. As Markus Dubber writes, even if the twentieth century is sometimes recognised as the arrival of modernity, this is 'of a lesser kind', 'merely an adjustment along the path' that began at least a hundred years earlier.[29]

But as mentioned above, the twentieth century is a crucial focus because it is only in this period that criminal responsibility emerged as a principal means of structuring and understanding the criminal law.[30] The mid-century moment is generally assumed to mark the end of the history of criminal responsibility and the beginning of the present era – which is marked by the centrality of criminal responsibility to the understanding and conceptualisation of the criminal law – and this tends to generate a somewhat presentist approach, extending out the current era – for example, to start with the major theoretical developments of the mid-century, when legal-philosophical approaches first rose to prominence with the work of H. L. A. Hart at Oxford – without sufficient attention to change over time.[31] My close examination of the twentieth century resists the neat bifurcation of the first and second halves of the period, and seeks to historicise recent as well as older developments across the timeframe. My approach sensitises us to the nuances and inflections in responsibility in criminal law across this period.

In addition, it is in the twentieth century that responsibility has attained high status as an organising frame for social and political life. Dynamics of responsibility have come to form a central axis along which interpersonal relations are understood and the social order is structured. These dynamics are informed by each of the major themes through which we make sense of the world – including gender relations, the structure of interpersonal relations, and the ambitions and constraints of the nation state. The significance of these dynamics is such that an array of social knowledges, including sociology and criminology, claim them as their core terrain. On this terrain, responsibility is a distinctly powerful and complex notion, neither singular nor a-contextual nor fixed, but multiple, thoroughly contextual, and subject to negotiation and contestation. While the way in which the seismic social, economic and political changes in the period since 1900 bear on criminal law and criminal justice has been the subject of some interest,

[28] See N. Lacey, 'Contingency, Coherence and Conceptualism: Reflections on the Encounter between "Critique" and "Philosophy of the Criminal Law"', in A. Duff (ed.), *Philosophy and the Criminal Law* (Cambridge: Cambridge University Press, 1998); see also L. Farmer, 'The Modest Ambition of Glanville Williams', in M. D. Dubber (ed.), *Foundational Texts in Modern Criminal Law* (Oxford: Oxford University Press, 2014).

[29] See M. D. Dubber, 'Colonial Criminal Law and Other Modernities: European Criminal Law in the Nineteenth and Twentieth Century', in H. Pihlajamäki, M. D. Dubber and M. Godfrey (eds.), *The Oxford Handbook of European Legal History* (Oxford: Oxford University Press, 2018).

[30] See Farmer, *Making the Modern Criminal Law*, ch. 6.

[31] See H. L. A. Hart, *Punishment and Responsibility* (Oxford: Oxford University Press, 1968); on the dangers of collapsing different historical and jurisprudence periods, see Farmer, *Making the Modern Criminal Law*, pp. 2–3, 102–3.

changes in responsibility practices have not been accorded sufficient attention to date. My focus on the twentieth century extends the critical scholarly lens on criminal responsibility to provide a close and detailed examination of this period.

On the second front, this book introduces a new set of jurisdictions to the criminal responsibility field by presenting the analysis in relation to Australian criminal laws. This new focus helps address the inattentiveness to jurisdiction that marks some work on criminal responsibility, and which has been remarked on by others.[32] Australia provides an apposite setting for this fresh study of criminal responsibility principles and practices. As I discuss in this book, the Australian developments are intriguing: the enthusiasm with which 'modern' developments elsewhere were embraced was tempered by an awareness of the specificity of the local context, and a sense – growing over the course of the century – that Australia might be in a position to offer its own contributions to debates about criminal responsibility. Further, the Australian setting implicates what I call interstitial spaces and moments (including spaces of the British Empire and its aftermath), revealing the importance of the circulation of ideas about criminal responsibility, and its practices, across space and time. As such, this book is an attempt to take up Farmer's exhortation to think 'in more complex ways' about wrongdoing and responsibility, and to think across boundaries – such as those between one jurisdiction and another – that have attained a taken-for-granted role in studies of criminal responsibility.[33] This book seeks to make a contribution to such 'more complex' thinking about responsibility.

In relation to criminal responsibility in particular, the view from Australia and Australian criminal laws differently illuminates oft-studied scholarly subject matter. This is because, in comparison to England and America, Australian laws were at a distinctive starting point around the turn of the twentieth century, and principles and practices of criminal responsibility developed in distinct social, political and institutional contexts. In advance of the full discussion in substantive chapters of this book, three illustrations help to make this point. First, the colonial legacy, and the specific situation of Aboriginal peoples,[34] set up a distinctive relation between criminal law and state governance that continues to impact ideas about state responsibility.[35] Second, the existence of a small legal and judicial professional elite into the current era has enhanced receptivity to the synthetisation of criminal responsibility from the 'top down'.[36] Third, the

[32] See Farmer, *Making the Modern Criminal Law*, p. 194; N. Lacey, 'Legal Constructions of Crime', in M. Maguire, R. Morgan and R. Reiner (eds.), *The Oxford Handbook of Criminology*, 4th ed. (Oxford: Oxford University Press, 2007), pp. 179, 190.

[33] L. Farmer, 'Time and Space in Criminal Law' (2010) 13(2) *New Criminal Law Review* 333–56, 354.

[34] In keeping with the approach adopted by other legal historical studies (see, e.g., H. Douglas and M. Finnane, *Indigenous Crime and Settler Law: White Sovereignty after Empire* [Basingstoke: Palgrave Macmillan, 2012]), throughout this book, I use the term 'Aboriginal' to refer to the Indigenous peoples of the Australian continent and Tasmania.

[35] See Chapter 8.

[36] See Chapter 5.

extent of scholar-activism around women's responsibility for crime in recent decades (in particular regarding women's violence in response to domestic violence) has produced distinctive set of responsibility forms in laws of homicide.[37] For these reasons, among others, a study of criminal responsibility set in Australia will be of interest to scholars around the common law world.

Structure of the Book

In Part I of this book, I make the case for the setting of my study of criminal responsibility in the Australian context in the twentieth century and present a new account of the role and significance of criminal responsibility. The chapters comprising this part each address foundational questions – relating to how one might examine criminal responsibility anew, and why one would do so – and set up the discussion that follows in other parts of the book.

Chapter 1 makes the methodological case for my study of criminal responsibility, which proceeds from the conviction that space and time are crucial to a deep understanding of responsibility in criminal law. This chapter commences with the observation that criminal responsibility scholarship has a northern orientation, with most studies 'set' in England and Wales, or in North America. The default northern orientation carries with it the implication that it is possible to fully grasp the development of criminal responsibility within this circumscribed frame (typically centred on English law), on the basis that other legal systems have a lesser or merely derivative place. In this chapter, I subvert the default northern orientation of existing scholarship by pitching my critical account of criminal responsibility 'close to the ground' in Australia criminal laws in the twentieth century. As I discuss in this chapter, this spatial and temporal frame requires that I take into account spaces and moments that are 'in between' or interstitial – spaces existing within or between, or in advance of, standard or orthodox legal spaces. These interstitial spaces and moments form a crucial but neglected dimension of critical criminal responsibility scholarship. My approach sensitises us to the nuances and inflections in responsibility for crime as it develops over the twentieth century, and suggests that responsibility in Australian criminal laws cannot be understood without awareness of these spaces and moments, and, further, that the story of criminal responsibility in English law would be enhanced by reference to this broader context.

Chapter 2 presents a new theoretical account of the role, and hence, significance, of criminal responsibility in criminal law. Criminal responsibility now forms the subject matter of a rich and deep vein of criminal law theory. My assessment of the criminal responsibility scholarly field reveals that it is regarded as having three main roles in criminal law: as constituting the normative heart of the criminal law; as serving the coordination and legitimation needs of the criminal law; and as providing a platform for the development of the modern

[37] See Chapter 6.

criminal law. Notwithstanding the value of existing scholarship, a crucial role of criminal responsibility has been overlooked, and it is this hitherto overlooked role that demands a new account of criminal responsibility. In my account, criminal responsibility organises keys sets of relations – between self, others and the state – as relations of responsibility, and this is what makes it significant. As I discuss in this chapter, on my account, criminal responsibility is revealed as the means by which matters of subjectivity, relationality and power make themselves felt in the criminal law in particular ways. This approach exposes the complexity and dynamism of the relations of responsibility that subtend responsibility principles and practices and provides an insight into what we can think of as the social life of responsibility in criminal law.

Building on the case for the socio-historical methods advanced in Chapter 1, Part II consists of three chapters in which I assess the part played by criminal responsibility in the organisation of Australian criminal laws at decisive junctures: at around the turn of the twentieth century, in the mid-century, and in the final decades of the twentieth century. Taking depth measures at these three points over the period under examination in this book reveals the gradual and distinctive way in which criminal law came to be organised around principles of criminal responsibility.

Chapter 3 provides an assessment of the state of play regarding criminal responsibility around the turn of the twentieth century. Providing a contrast with the more commonly studied English codification debates,[38] the chapter focuses on the *Criminal Law Amendment Act 1883* (NSW), and the *Criminal Code 1899* (Qld), each of which were part of a broad law reform tradition that encompassed consolidation and the distinctive practice of codification. In the Australian context, the practices of codification and consolidation were connected, as each was a response to common concerns with the need to modernise criminal law and criminal justice institutions. Against a background of the early development of institutions of democratic governance, and amid concerns with the exercise of government power, the 1883 Act and the 1899 Code each represent a commitment to modernisation founded on form – comprehensive legislation or a code – and process – the operation of criminal justice – as much as on principles of criminal responsibility. The significance of form and process accounts for the prominence of provisions relating to the administration of criminal justice, and criminal procedure and punishment, in both the Act and the Code. Across these two criminal law reforms, criminal responsibility was only one plank of the modernisation of the criminal law, sharing its weight with the form of the criminal law and the operation of criminal justice.

Chapter 4 takes up the historical story in the mid-century. While the 'birth' of Australian criminal law is sometimes assumed to date either to the turn of the twentieth century, or almost to the turn of the twenty-first century, in this chapter,

[38] See, e.g., L. Farmer, 'Reconstructing the English Codification Debate: The Criminal Law Commissioners, 1833–45' (2000) 18(2) *Law and History Review* 397–426.

I argue that it was in the middle decades of the twentieth century that Australian criminal law came into its own – measured in terms of an orientation around national coordinates, and in the self-confidence of its practitioners and academics. Principles of criminal responsibility played a key role in this 'birth': it was through the elucidation and application of these principles that a sense of a criminal law system with a meaningfully national quality emerged. I support my case for the role of criminal responsibility in the 'birth' of Australian criminal law by tracking mid-century developments across four fronts – the interpretation of the criminal responsibility provisions in the criminal codes of Queensland, Western Australia and Tasmania, the creation of an Australian law of insanity, the emergence of a doctrine of honest and reasonable mistake of fact, and the recognition of a novel partial defence to murder, excessive self-defence – and through an examination of Australia's first criminal law textbooks, which appeared in this period.

Chapter 5 assesses the part played by criminal responsibility in the (re-)construction of Australian criminal laws at the end of the twentieth century. This chapter focuses on the *Commonwealth Criminal Code*, which was developed in the last decade of the twentieth century. Based on a *Model Criminal Code*, which was intended to be a Code for all Australian jurisdictions, the Commonwealth *Criminal Code* represents an attempt to compensate for Australia's federal structure – in which criminal law is a state and territory responsibility – and reconstruct criminal law as national rather than subnational law. The Code came into being at a time when major changes in crime and criminal justice were occurring, and the Code promised to equip Australia for a new century. As 'the very foundations of any system of criminal justice',[39] criminal responsibility was central to this attempt at reconstruction. The *Commonwealth Criminal Code* is a legal systematisation: the emphasis on the (re-)organisation of the laws themselves, rather than on reform of aspects of criminal justice such as criminal process or systems of criminal punishment which animated other codification projects. In this systematisation, the principles of criminal responsibility are fixed at the heart of Australian criminal laws, providing integrity to the Commonwealth Code, meaning that it makes sense on its own terms, and ensuring that it can stand on its own and act as model for adoption in other jurisdictions.

Building on the theoretical argument advanced in Chapter 2, Part III of this book consists of three chapters in which I examine criminal responsibility via the key sets of relations – between self, others and the state – that subtend responsibility principles and practices. Each of these chapters explores one of the three nodes of my tripartite schema of relations of responsibility. By contrast with the chapters contained in Part II, each of the chapters in this part looks across the period under discussion in this book, to explore changes in relations of responsibility as they unfold over time.

[39] Criminal Law Officers' Committee (CLOC), Standing Committee of Attorneys-General, *Model Criminal Code Chapters 1 and 2: General Principles of Criminal Responsibility, Final Report* (1992), ii.

In Chapter 6, I examine the self in relations of responsibility through a focus on women's responsibility for crime. A close examination of criminal responsibility principles and practices pertaining to women reveals a distinctive configuration of relations of responsibility around women as subjects of the law. With reference to the laws of homicide, I argue that, on the level of legal form, women's responsibility for crime is marked by particularity and specificity – as opposed to the generality and universalism claimed for criminal responsibility. This particularity and specificity is evident in the two sets of atypical responsibility forms – those forms that are restricted to particular individuals committing particular offences in particular contexts, and in which elements, such as offence and defence, conduct and fault, that are usually separate, are mixed together – that determine the contours of women's responsibility for crime. These two sets of atypical responsibility forms denote different relations of responsibility between self, others and the state. In the first set of atypical responsibility forms, which was created over the first half of the twentieth century to accommodate violence *by* women, relations of responsibility centred on the relation of the accused woman with herself, where this relation was oriented around a personalised and psychologised notion of individual integrity. In recent decades, a second set of atypical responsibility forms was created in response to the need to accommodate violence *against* women, and, here, relations of responsibility are oriented around the self in relation to others, encompassing an extended sense of women's autonomy, and implicating other actors, including state actors such as the police, in fulfilling that autonomy.

Chapter 7 examines the second of the three nodes of relations of responsibility – others – through a focus on the laws criminalising consorting. Consorting – broadly, the offence of association with criminals – is a prominent way in which the criminal law governs otherwise ordinary relations between individuals. Based on an examination of consorting offences enacted in Australian jurisdictions since their introduction in the early twentieth century, I argue that the laws fall into two generations, each of which has a distinctive orientation, mode (denoting the way in which criminal responsibility is expressed) and form. These generations of laws encode different relations of responsibility. The first generation of laws, which appeared in the first decades of the twentieth century, proscribed 'companionship with thieves', with relations of responsibility reinforcing existing, highly stratified social relations, and the laws operating to keep individuals falling within different categories of 'undesirables' apart from each other. By contrast, the second generation of laws, which appeared on the legal landscape at the end of the twentieth century and turn of the twenty-first century, inculcate 'friendship with the state', with relations of responsibility assuming a standardised structure, according to which the state is brought into the relationship between individuals in a distinct way – as a 'friend'. This shows that *to* whom or what, and *for* what, individuals are responsible in their relations with others has changed over time, with a more extensive conception of responsibility – encompassing personal attitudes and self-regulation – now sustaining relations of responsibility.

In Chapter 8, I turn to the state in relations of responsibility, which I examine through government responses to (allegations of) crimes against children in institutions. As a result of recent and current public inquiries, such as the *Royal Commission into Institutional Responses to Child Sexual Abuse*,[40] this issue is attracting high levels of public and political attention and unprecedented public discussion around both individual responsibility and state responsibility. I argue that there are four historic positions of the state in relations of responsibility. As per the first position, prominent in the first decades of the twentieth century, children and children's institutions were linked to the development of the Australian nation, but in the context of limited capacity, the role of governments was restricted to advocating the modernisation of institutions and child welfare practices to deal with perceived problems. The second position of the state, prominent in the middle decades of the century, involves governments in the development of social welfare and criminal justice institutions, with crimes against children in families, and to a lesser extent in institutions, coming to receive greater attention. The third position of the state is prominent in the last decades of the century and early years of the twenty-first century, and is characterised by a complex mix of assuming and denying responsibility, as Australian governments negotiated their responsibility for crimes against children in institutions across the boundary between past and present, and Empire and nation. As per the fourth position of the state, which has been prominent in recent years, governments are (re-)negotiating responsibility in a global context, and embracing responsibility for crimes against children in a more wholesale way, with the civil law as well as the criminal law harnessed to the task of addressing what is now perceived as a serious injustice. Each of these positions of the state in relations of responsibility correlates with a division of responsibility *between* the state and individuals, where such a division is a dynamic outcome of changing norms about the state and individuals.

The final chapter of the book concludes the discussion by exploring some of the implications of the arguments made in this book for scholarly understanding of criminal responsibility. Here, I consider the implications of both the historical axis of my analysis, relating to the development of criminal responsibility since the turn of the twentieth century, as well as the implications of the theoretical axis of the work, relating to the significance of criminal responsibility in criminal law. In addition, I briefly consider some potential future trajectories of scholarly work on criminal responsibility that are opened up by the re-examination provided in this book.

40 Commonwealth, Royal Commission into Institutional Responses to Child Sexual Abuse, *Final Report* (2017).

Part I
Rethinking Criminal Responsibility

1

Space and Time in Criminal Responsibility

This chapter makes the methodological case for my study of criminal responsibility. It proceeds from the conviction that space and time are crucial to a deep understanding of criminal responsibility principles and practices. This chapter introduces the socio-historical methodological approach I adopt in this book and accounts for my time frame, the spatial and temporal scope of my study. My focus is on the development of criminal responsibility over the twentieth century in the context of Australian criminal laws, a delimited frame centred on a new set of jurisdictions which enables me to develop a located or grounded analysis of criminal responsibility.

Space and time have received somewhat uneven treatment in existing studies of criminal responsibility, despite exhortations to take both seriously.[1] As I discuss in Chapter 2, in the dominant legal-philosophical scholarly tradition, the spatial and temporal setting of criminal responsibility is outlined only in the faintest brush strokes, if at all, with some of this scholarship having, in effect, an a-jurisdictional and a-temporal character. In this tradition, because the emphasis is on the conception of responsibility, rather than its contextual or purposive aspects, accounts are not genuinely 'set' in any particular space or time.[2] In critical accounts of criminal responsibility, these brush strokes are stronger, reflecting the influence of disciplines such as history, criminology and sociology on this body of work. Two of the most sophisticated of these critical studies – by Lindsay Farmer and Nicola Lacey – are examined in detail in Chapter 2 as part of my analysis of

[1] See N. Lacey, 'Space, Time and Function: Intersecting Principles of Responsibility Across the Terrain of Criminal Justice' (2007) 1(3) *Criminal Law and Philosophy* 233–50; L. Farmer, 'Time and Space in Criminal Law' (2010) 13(2) *New Criminal Law Review* 333–56. The enhanced profile of space and time in criminal law theory in recent decades was generated in part by a widely read article by Mark Kelman: see M. Kelman, 'Interpretive Construction in the Substantive Criminal Law' (1981) 33 *Stanford Law Review* 591–673 (referring to the 'time-framing' that is embedded in criminal processes).

[2] N. Lacey, 'Jurisprudence, History and the Institutional Quality of Law' (2015) 101 *Virginia Law Review* 919–45, 939; N. Lacey, 'Legal Constructions of Crime', in M. Maguire, R. Morgan and R. Reiner (eds.), *The Oxford Handbook of Criminology*, 4th ed. (Oxford: Oxford University Press, 2007), p. 190.

the role, and, hence, significance, of criminal responsibility. As discussed there, these scholars offer close and careful analyses of responsibility for crime that take into account the social, political and institutional context in which responsibility principles and practices operate, as well as change over time.[3]

Even within the body of work self-consciously responding to scholarship in the legal-philosophical tradition, however, space and time may not be accorded sufficient attention. Here, the spatial units of analysis adopted by scholars may be supra- or transnational, and consideration of the temporal dimension of criminal responsibility may be minimal or absent. For instance, one popular spatial unit of analysis in such scholarship is 'liberal democracies', which, as Claes Lernestedt comments, brings jurisdictions as diverse as the United States, Scotland and Sweden 'under the same theoretical umbrella' – something Lernestedt describes as 'downright wrong'.[4] Another collective term is in use Peter Cane's careful examination of moral and legal responsibility. Cane refers to 'Anglian' legal systems as those systems that derive their conceptual structure from English law.[5] For Cane, it is appropriate to frame his analysis in this transnational way because his concern is with concepts, and 'differences from one jurisdiction to another in the detailed application and outworking of those concepts are not relevant to the analysis'.[6] This is the case although Cane is concerned to foreground the law and legal systems in his work, contra-distinguishing his approach from legal-philosophical accounts on that basis.[7]

Looking across jurisdictions and time frames in such a way means accounts are not as much a departure from the dominant legal-philosophical approach as might be assumed at first. Looking across jurisdictions tends to reinforce what I call the 'default northern orientation' in critical studies of criminal responsibility. By default northern orientation, I mean that where a system of positive law is considered in the critical study of criminal responsibility, it tends to be the systems of England and Wales, or those of North America, and, because of this relatively restricted jurisdictional range, the specificities of these jurisdictions disappear from view. Of course, the profile of these legal systems in criminal law scholarship partly reflects the impact of English common law on the development of criminal laws (and laws more generally) around

[3] See L. Farmer, *Making the Modern Criminal Law: Criminalization and Civil Order*. Series: Criminalization (Oxford: Oxford University Press, 2016), ch. 6; N. Lacey, *In Search of Criminal Responsibility: Ideas, Interests and Institutions* (Oxford: Oxford University Press, 2016).

[4] See C. Lernestedt, 'Vertical, Horizontal, Backwards, Forwards' (2017) 4(1) *Critical Analysis of Law* 22–30, 22.

[5] P. Cane, *Responsibility in Law and Morality* (Oxford: Hart Publishing, 2002), p. 7.

[6] Cane, *Responsibility in Law and Morality*, p. 10. Cane states that, to the extent that his book has a particular jurisdictional focus, it is the English jurisdiction.

[7] Cane, *Responsibility in Law and Morality*, pp. 2–3.

the world, and, as I discuss in the following chapter, the influence of the intellectual traditions – most notably, the legal-philosophical tradition – that have grown up in those parts of the world.[8] In addition, this default northern orientation reflects the size of these jurisdictions, and their respective legal academies, as well as, in some instances, the assumed significance, in the modern era, of criminal laws that are coextensive with nation-state boundaries.

While the reasons for the default northern orientation of critical criminal responsibility studies are understandable, it has some negative effects. It operates to homogenise aspects of the different legal systems falling within these supra- and transnational categories, and obscure the differences in the social and political contexts where those legal systems are embedded. In addition, where critical accounts are without express time frames, they may be somewhat presentist, extending the current era, for example, to begin in the mid-century when legal-philosophical approaches first rose to prominence, without sufficient attention to change over time.[9] And, crucially, the default northern orientation carries with it the implication that it is possible to fully grasp the development of criminal responsibility within this circumscribed frame (typically centred on English law), on the basis that other legal systems have a lesser or merely derivative place. As I show in this chapter, subverting the default northern orientation of existing scholarship and pitching a critical account of criminal responsibility 'closes the ground' in Australia criminal laws: it sheds a different light on the topic of responsibility in criminal law, preparing the ground for the new story of criminal responsibility presented in this book.

In this chapter, I make a case for a socio-historical account of criminal responsibility that focuses on responsibility principles and practices in Australian criminal laws in the twentieth century. With this delimited approach, I seek to keep space and time in the frame at the same time. My approach introduces a relatively neglected set of jurisdictions to critical criminal responsibility studies and trains critical attention on the twentieth century, which has been subject to less attention than other periods. In addition, and as I discuss in this chapter, my focus on Australia in the twentieth century reveals the importance of spaces and moments that I label 'in between' or interstitial – existing within or between, or 'in advance of', standard or

[8] Some Australian criminal law scholars have sought to demarcate an Australian scholarly tradition of critical and criminologically informed criminal law scholarship that is defined in opposition to this legal-philosophical criminal law theory. See, e.g., D. Brown, 'Criminalisation and Normative Theory' (2013) 25(2) *Current Issues in Criminal Justice* 605–25; L. McNamara, 'Criminalisation Research in Australia: Building a Foundation for Normative Theorising and Principled Law Reform', in T. Crofts and A. Loughnan (eds.), *Criminalisation and Criminal Responsibility in Australia* (Melbourne: Oxford University Press, 2015).

[9] See H. L. A. Hart, *The Concept of Law*, 3rd ed. (Oxford: Oxford University Press, 2012 [first published 1961]); on the dangers of collapsing different historical and jurisprudential periods, see Farmer, *Making the Modern Criminal Law*, pp. 2–3, 102–3.

orthodox legal spaces or moments, such as 'nation' – that typically frame scholarly understanding of criminal responsibility. On the one side, these interstitial spaces are imperial, colonial and post-colonial, constructed through the British Empire and its aftermath. On the other side, interstitial moments are generated by the growth of comparative jurisprudence – broadly, the comparison of two or more legal systems – which took on new vitality and, for the first time, durable institutional form from the mid-nineteenth century. These interstitial spaces and moments form a crucial but hitherto neglected dimension of critical criminal responsibility scholarship. They expose the dynamic ways in which ideas about responsibility in criminal law circulate across space and time, suggesting that Australian criminal responsibility cannot be understood without awareness of these spaces and moments, and, further, that the story of criminal responsibility in English law would be enhanced by reference to this broader context.

This chapter begins with an assessment of the methodological approaches of two studies of the development of criminal responsibility – an intellectual history study and a sociological/socio-theoretic study. This assessment sets the scene for the next section, in which I introduce the socio-historical analysis I adopt in this book. In that section, I explain the value of an account that focuses on developments in Australian criminal laws over the twentieth century, demonstrating the importance of interstitial spaces and moments for scholarly understanding of criminal responsibility principles and practices.

Existing Accounts of the Development of Criminal Responsibility

While there is now a sizable and growing body of scholarship applying socio-historical research methods to the study of responsibility in criminal law – such that it is possible to speak of a body of critical criminal responsibility studies – the topic of criminal responsibility is yet to attract many scholars from the humanities and social theory.[10] In this section, I assess the methodological approaches of two prominent and contrasting studies of the development of criminal responsibility advanced by scholars working in these fields. These studies point to the range of options – around scale, time frame, sources and disciplinary resources – that are open to critical criminal responsibility scholars, and point the way to the socio-historical study of criminal responsibility, which I then go on to introduce.

[10] But see S. L. Blumenthal, *Law and the Modern Mind: Consciousness and Responsibility in American Legal Culture* (Cambridge, MA: Harvard University Press, 2016) (examining responsibility in civil law in the nineteenth century); C. L. Evans, 'Persons Dwelling in the Borderland: Responsibility and Criminal Law in the Late-Nineteenth-Century British Empire', PhD thesis, Princeton University (2016), and L. Rodensky, *The Crime in Mind: Criminal Responsibility and the Victorian Novel* (Oxford: Oxford University Press, 2003).

An Intellectual History Account

The first of the two accounts of the development of criminal responsibility considered here is an intellectual history account, focusing on *ideas* about responsibility for crime. Here, the storyteller is Thomas Green, whose book, *Freedom and Criminal Responsibility in American Legal Thought*, provides a granular treatment of changing legal academic analyses of criminal responsibility over the course of the twentieth century.[11] As an intellectual history, Green's account is of interest for my purposes because of its focus on the twentieth century and its historicised treatment of the legal-philosophical scholarly tradition that continues to dominate studies of criminal responsibility.

In *Freedom and Criminal Responsibility in American Legal Thought*, Green approaches responsibility for crime as a 'critical' expression of 'the underlying concept of free will', holding that the history of the criminal law is 'in part the history of the free will problem'.[12] For Green, the problem of free will – whether individuals can be said to be truly the authors of their own actions and thus can be justly punished for them – is *the* moral issue of the twentieth century, and the writings of criminal jurisprudence scholars – 'the intellectual activity *itself*' – is the most appropriate means by which this issue may be explored.[13] As this suggests, Green understands criminal responsibility in a particular way – as a concrete working out of larger issues related to our understanding of what it is to be human and what blame, guilt and punishment require of individuals. Green's history of criminal responsibility is intended to serve a larger end: it is an exploration of changing ideas about individual freedom and political liberty in American legal thought.

Green offers a tripartite periodisation of twentieth-century criminal jurisprudence in America. In the first period, the Progressive Era, which encompasses the turn of the twentieth century and its first decades, American scholarly thinking about criminal responsibility was influenced by the rise of behavioural science, according to which individual behaviour was understood as caused or determined ('determinism'). Green argues that, in general terms, this period saw scholars engage somewhat with scientific developments – particularly in relation to the work of psychologists and penologists, who identified large numbers of 'insane' and 'feeble-minded' individuals in prisons[14] – but retain a conviction about the uniqueness of the law and the importance and basic truthfulness of individual culpability for crime in the face of the spectre of determinism. The second of Green's three

[11] T. A. Green, *Freedom and Criminal Responsibility in American Legal Thought* (Cambridge: Cambridge University Press, 2014).

[12] Ibid., pp. 2–3.

[13] Ibid., p. 4 (emphasis in original).

[14] Ibid., p. 60.

periods covers the mid-1940s to 1960, a period that represented the maturation of the American legal academy and witnessed the proliferation of legal scholarly work on criminal responsibility. In broader terms, in this period Green argued that political liberty – 'the other aspect of freedom' – received more scholarly attention than individuals' free will.[15] In focusing more on the political and social limits of the criminal law than on its scientific credentials, legal scholars in this period approached free will in a pragmatic way and paid 'new attention to the individual', setting up a close relationship between 'the individual's internalization of freedom and his external freedom-based relationship to the state'.[16] The last of Green's three periods of criminal jurisprudence is given over to the last decades of the century, and the triumph of retributivism – broadly, the idea that responsibility is a moral property of individuals and that punishment should be based on notions of desert – that is its hallmark.[17] Green argues that this convergence around retributivism – as the only way of ensuring punishment is consistent with respect for persons – generated 'a certain confidence' on the part of legal scholars, on the basis that 'the hundred-years' war over the freedom question had (apparently) been won.'[18]

As this brief summary suggests, Green's history is a close treatment of the development of ideas about criminal responsibility in American jurisprudence. While Green gestures to related intellectual developments, such as that of American criminology in the mid-century, his focus is squarely on legal scholarship. His sources are primarily the scholarly writings of academic lawyers working in universities across the period. Green is consistent in his determination not to impose artificial unity on the intellectual debates he chronicles so closely, and he gives full play to the many ways in which those debates circled around each other both within each of his three time periods and across the twentieth century. Green also emphasises the limits of his own study as he acknowledges another history of criminal responsibility might draw on philosophical scholarship in addition to legal scholarship, or include non-American as well as American scholars.[19] Indeed, despite the

[15] Ibid., p. 469.

[16] Ibid., p. 265.

[17] Green refers to the retributivism of this age as 'neo-retributivism' or 'the new retributivism' as its adherents sought to distinguish it from 'an older, revenge-based version of retributivism' (pp. 277–8).

[18] Green, *Freedom and Criminal Responsibility*, p. 475. Again, Green makes clear that some scholars held other beliefs (such as a belief in 'compatibilism', which holds that free will is compatible with a belief in determinism) (p. 12).

[19] Green does include some non-Americans, such as H. L. A. Hart, whose ideas about responsibility as a normal capacity and fair opportunity act are described as the 'dominant rhetorical guideline' of the last of his three periods of twentieth century criminal jurisprudence (p. 474). Green also mentions the Australian scholar, Norval Morris (pp. 460–1), who made the US his home from the mid-1960s, and, as one of the authors of Australia's first criminal law textbooks, features in the mid-century Australian criminal responsibility story: see Chapter 4.

weightiness of the book, Green positions his history as a necessary preliminary step towards a further project in which he seeks to bring the history of criminal responsibility into relation with a history of the criminal trial jury.[20]

While Green pays most attention to ideas about criminal responsibility, and to academic discourse on the topic, he is also interested in the operation of the law and includes among his sources some high-profile court decisions. For Green, the institution of the criminal trial, and more particularly, the criminal trial jury, is the setting in which legal scholarly ideas about criminal responsibility cash out. According to Green, the jury 'exemplifies the relationship between theories of responsibility and conventional ideas about freedom', acting as a 'bridge' between philosophical ideas and conventional morality which, Green suggests, has retained a commitment to free will.[21] Green argues that the jury has been a bulwark against an 'overreaching state', and commitment to jury evaluation of responsibility for crime is one pillar of American 'historical national commitments' to individualism and political liberty.[22] But, in the end, Green sounds a somewhat depressing note, observing (or perhaps admitting) that 'academic concern with the mysteries of human free will' is indeed 'academic', as 'judgment upon persons who society has agreed must be held responsible' continues even in the face of lack of proof beyond reasonable doubt that any person is a free agent.[23]

The depth and reach of *Freedom and Criminal Responsibility in American Legal Thought* is a testament to the richness of criminal jurisprudence in America and, more specifically, to the intellectual significance of scholarship on criminal responsibility. But for my purposes, Green's approach to criminal responsibility occludes important aspects of the topic. His approach tends to present developments in criminal responsibility in an abstract way, as if such developments takes place on a purely intellectual plane, rather than as thoroughly embedded in particular social and political contexts. While Green's conviction that criminal responsibility is the outworking of ideas about freedom, and liberty seems to reflect distinctively American concerns,[24] important features of space – both specific (including the growth of independent American universities with full-time academic staff, and the professionalisation of academic life over the period[25]), and more general (such as the

[20] This places *Freedom and Criminal Responsibility* between Green's earlier monograph on the criminal trial jury, T. A. Green, *Verdict According to Conscience: Perspectives on the English Criminal Trial Jury* (Chicago, IL: University of Chicago Press, 1985), and a planned future monograph: see for discussion T. A. Green, 'The Jury and Criminal Responsibility in Anglo-American History' (2015) 9(3) *Criminal Law and Philosophy* 423–42.

[21] Green, *Freedom and Criminal Responsibility*, pp. 13, 17–18. As Green argues, the 'bifurcated' trial process – in which conviction is separated from sentencing – preserves this role for the jury and limits the inroads that could be made by ideas of determinism (pp. 35, 37).

[22] Green, *Freedom and Criminal Responsibility*, p. 477.

[23] Ibid., pp. 478, 483; on this point, see also Cane, *Responsibility in Law and Morality*, p. 4.

[24] See for discussion Blumenthal, *Law and the Modern Mind*.

[25] See generally R. B. Stevens, *Law School: Legal Education in America from the 1850s to the 1980s* (Union, NJ: The Lawbook Exchange, Ltd., 2001).

politicisation of criminal law and justice in the United States and profound changes in the social and political meanings around responsibility for crime in recent decades[26]) – recede into the background. Even the institutional context for the evaluation of criminal responsibility – the criminal trial – moves in and out of the analysis in an 'uneven' way.[27] In the terms I am adopting in this chapter, in Green's account, space seems somewhat attenuated – the institutional context in which criminal responsibility develops is not explored, meaning that the book's American focus reproduces the universalism of the theoretical concept of responsibility which is at its core – and time acts as a background frame, but does not infuse the analysis Green offers.

More generally, flowing from his primary focus on jurisprudence and reliance on legal scholarly sources, Green's conviction that the historical story of criminal responsibility is 'a hundred years of debunking and reframing' of free will[28] is informed by a particular metaphysical understanding of human action, and taken for granted rather than defended. In this respect, Green shares a commitment to the view of the significance of criminal responsibility held by scholars working in the legal-philosophical mode. As I discuss in detail in Chapter 2, in legal-philosophical accounts of criminal responsibility, the primary significance of responsibility is normative: it connects criminal law rules to moral norms about responsibility and accountability, and connects criminal law to liberal political precepts (which are oriented around individual autonomy, freedom and privacy, and the duties owed by the individual to the polity).[29] But it is this commitment to a particular understanding of the significance of criminal responsibility – and the particular relations between state and self that it posits – that invites historical inquiry. Without this, there seems to be a risk that, in Green's own words, we are left in a state in which 'we know relatively little about the past and too much about the present'.[30]

A Sociological and Socio-theoretic Account

A contrasting account of legal responsibility broadly is offered by Scott Veitch in his book, *Law and Irresponsibility: On the Legitimation of Human Suffering*.[31] In comparison with Green's account, with its focus on the history

[26] See generally D. Garland, *Punishment and Welfare: A History of Penal Strategies* (Aldershot: Gower, 1985) and D. Garland, *The Culture of Control: Crime and Social Order in Contemporary Society* (Chicago: University of Chicago Press, 2001).

[27] See N. Lacey, 'Thomas Andrew Green: Freedom and Criminal Responsibility in American Legal Thought' (2016) 79(6) *Modern Law Review* 1137–41, 1141.

[28] Green, *Freedom and Criminal Responsibility*, p. 477.

[29] See, e.g., R. A. Duff, 'Responsibility, Citizenship and Criminal Law', in R. A. Duff and S. Green (eds.), *Philosophical Foundations of Criminal Law* (Oxford: Oxford University Press, 2011).

[30] Green, *Freedom and Criminal Responsibility*, p. 482.

[31] S. Veitch, *Law and Irresponsibility: On the Legitimation of Human Suffering* (London: Routledge, 2007).

of ideas about responsibility as developed by legal scholars, Veitch engages with socio-theoretical and sociological analyses of modernity, and examines the sociological effects of 'responsibility practices'[32] and the politics of legal arrangements that support them. While Veitch's focus is on legal responsibility in general rather than criminal responsibility in particular – he touches on responsibility in criminal law, tort, international law and public law – his account is of interest for my purposes because of its interdisciplinary coverage and its critical assessment of the social and political effects of legal responsibility.

Veitch's main argument is that, contrary to the standard view of law as a mode of 'asserting and defining the scope and content of responsibilities', law and legal institutions produce and legitimise irresponsibility.[33] Veitch's analysis of legal responsibility is prompted by the magnitude of human suffering that has been the result of large-scale harms in the modern era, and the apparent failure of law in restraining such outrages and attributing responsibility in their aftermath. In advancing this argument about the symbiotic relationship between law and irresponsibility, Veitch draws on a wide array of instances of human suffering and the legal practices that surround such suffering, including colonialism, human rights violations and international sanctions regimes. For Veitch, these are instances of '*organised* irresponsibility'.[34] Grounded in a 'sociological understanding' of responsibility practices, Veitch argues that it is not the case that such suffering represents an excess – that such suffering *exceeds* law and legal arrangements or represents its failure – but rather that, in organising responsibilities, law and legal institutions '*simultaneously* allow for and legitimise the proliferation of their clandestine counterpart: irresponsibility'.[35] On this basis, Veitch concludes that modern law, operating under modern social and political conditions, mean that law is complicit in human suffering.

The temporal setting for the account offered in *Law and Irresponsibility* is the wide arc of 'modern' law – broadly, the form of law dating from the seventeenth century and oriented around reason and will, in which responsibility is a central rationality. For Veitch, responsibility, 'focally conceived of as individual responsibility', rests on the idea of the autonomous individual, who 'emerges fully only post-Enlightenment'.[36] As a result, Veitch rejects the idea

[32] Veitch's emphasis on the 'range of different techniques and purposes' that go under the label 'responsibility' leads him to write of 'responsibility practices' rather than responsibility in the singular (Veitch, *Law and Irresponsibility*, pp. 2–3, 37), following Cane, *Responsibility in Law and Morality*, p. 4.

[33] Veitch, *Law and Irresponsibility*, p. 1.

[34] Ibid., p. 22 (emphasis in original). Indeed, Veitch points to the 'asymmetry' between suffering and legal responsibility for it: 'the greater the suffering caused, the less responsibility can be established for it' (pp. 2, 6). For an analysis of this aspect of Veitch's argument in the context of responsibility for institutional child sexual abuse, see P. Crofts, 'Legal Irresponsibility and Institutional Responses to Child Sex Abuse' (2016) 34(2) *Law in Context: A Socio-Legal Journal* 79–99.

[35] Veitch, *Law and Irresponsibility*, pp. 2–3 (emphasis in original).

[36] Ibid., p. 35.

that there can be any notion of responsibility that exists prior to, or independently from, the social contexts in which it is found.[37] Rather, Veitch examines responsibility as it is connected to dynamics of power, taking into account the 'unprecedented institutional power shifts' that have seen 'the individual increasingly subject to forces over which it had no control' in the modern era.[38] It is these modern social conditions and structures, such as bureaucracy and particular forms of socialisation, which separate 'responsibility for role from responsibility for consequences' and, in so doing, legitimise irresponsibility.[39] As this suggests, Veitch points to the processes that create the agentic subject of the law – individuation – and the ideological dimension of the autonomous individual who can be called to account through law and legal institutions.

Law and Irresponsibility is pitched above any one jurisdiction, but Veitch's analysis is applied to different instances of large-scale human suffering, and he pays close attention to the legal arrangements sustaining such suffering. An application of his argument that is particularly germane to my own interests in this book concerns the British colonisation of Australia and the dispossession of and violence directed against Aboriginal peoples. As Veitch writes, in the 1990s, the Australian High Court decisions of *Mabo No. 1* and *Mabo No. 2* revisited the consequences of the British acquisition of sovereignty for Aboriginal peoples – in order to remove the legal fiction of *terra nullius* (discussed below) and to allow for the ongoing existence of native title – but determined the act of acquisition itself to be non-justiciable.[40] As Veitch argues, this approach 'transferred responsibility for the deeds and consequences of colonialism away from [law] itself to acts of government, and deems them untouchable according to the law of the land'.[41] A similar combination of responsibility and irresponsibility is to be found in relation to legal redress for the Stolen Generations, the Aboriginal children subject to forced removal from their families throughout most of the twentieth century, as part of a government policy of 'protection'.[42] As Veitch notes, despite the manifold harms this policy produced, when the High Court adjudicated claims by members of the Stolen Generations, the lack of intention to do harm meant the policy did not fall under the United Nations *Genocide Convention 1948*.[43]

37 Ibid., p. 39.
38 Ibid., p. 53.
39 Ibid., pp. 41, 48.
40 *Mabo* v. *State of Queensland* (No. 1) (1988) 166 CLR 186 (*Mabo No. 1*) and *Mabo* v. *State of Queensland* (No. 2) (1992) 175 CLR 1 (*Mabo No. 2*).
41 Veitch, *Law and Irresponsibility*, p. 107.
42 See for discussion R. van Krieken, 'The "Stolen Generations" and Cultural Genocide: The Forced Removal of Australian Indigenous Children from Their Families and Its Implications for the Sociology of Childhood' (1999) 6(3) *Childhood* 297–311; R. van Krieken, 'Rethinking Cultural Genocide: Aboriginal Child Removal and Settler-Colonial State Formation' (2004) 75(2) *Oceania* 125–51. I discuss the Stolen Generations in the context of state responsibility: see Chapter 8.
43 *Kruger* v. *Commonwealth* (1997) 190 CLR 1; *Cubillo* v. *Commonwealth* (No. 2) (2000) 103 FCR 1.

Veitch's account of legal responsibility is interdisciplinary and he draws on the work of scholars such as Zygmunt Bauman, Ulrich Beck, Stanley Cohen, and Michel Foucault among others, to mount a strong critique of the tacit assumptions underlining claims that law has developed over time to more fully address suffering or harms. Veitch emphasises that law's complicity in human suffering is the norm, not the exception, and that the production of irresponsibility alongside responsibility is evidence that the legal system is working, not that it is broken. For Veitch, legal legitimation – 'law's claim to correctness, force and social priority' – means that it is the 'normal' operation of law that gives cause for concern, not what might be labelled 'exceptional'.[44] Thus, according to Veitch, the fact that the twentieth century has seen the 'increasing democratisation of death in political violence', and in the same period, the sovereign right of states to engage in destructive warfare has been upheld, is a testament to the role of law in the 'commission and production of suffering'.[45] Further, citizens of modern states are complicit in such conduct in the way in which their personal ethical identity is subsumed into the 'general will'.[46]

The account of legal responsibility offered in *Law and Irresponsibility* represents something of a challenge for legal scholars.[47] As Andrew Goldsmith writes, in focusing on the limits of legal responsibility, Veitch assumes the position of a '*disappointed idealist*', offering a critique from a fictional position of ideal law.[48] In relation to criminal responsibility in particular, and as Ngaire Naffine points out, while Veitch usefully highlights the dangers of 'undercriminalisation and the legal disavowal of responsibility', he does not acknowledge the 'ennobling' effect of treating individuals as rational and agentic in systems such as that of criminal law.[49] More generally, with the broad time frame of modernity, and a multijurisdictional scope, modern space is constructed as a kind of universal space, with the local is treated only as an instance of the universal, and time within or under modernity is left undifferentiated. Veitch's powerful analysis raises further questions for a more circumscribed study. What conditions and structures bear on criminal responsibility in particular? What are the social and political effects of criminal responsibility principles and practices? And what if anything is significant about the time frame of the twentieth century? I take up these questions in the analysis offered in this book.

44 Veitch, *Law and Irresponsibility*, p. 97.

45 Ibid., pp. 131, 143.

46 Ibid., p. 140.

47 Some scholars suggest that Veitch's account tends to over-emphasise the structural effects of law, and under-emphasise the role played by the individuals who deploy the law from powerful positions in domestic and international politics (see M. Kryger, 'Compared to What?' (2009) 34 *Australian Journal of Legal Philosophy* 241–7), or to render the critique of particular laws or particular legal decisions redundant (N. Lacey, 'Scott Veitch: Law and Irresponsibility: On the Legitimation of Human Suffering' (2009) 18(2) *Social & Legal Studies* 270–2.

48 See A. Goldsmith, 'Seeing Red: Legal Indifference on a Field of Pain and Death' (2009) 34 *Australian Journal of Legal Philosophy* 228–33, 232 (emphasis in original).

49 See N. Naffine, 'In Defence of the Responsible Subject' (2009) 34 *Australian Journal of Legal Philosophy* 222–7, 225, 227.

This assessment of the approaches adopted in these accounts of criminal responsibility reveals the importance of space and time for each of the analyses presented, and exposes the methodological choices entailed in a socio-historical study of criminal responsibility. I suggest that there is an opening for a socio-historical approach to the study of criminal responsibility that employs a delimited spatial and temporal frame, permitting equal attention to be given to space and time. This approach places my study *between* these two accounts: I seek to pay attention to *both* ideas about criminal responsibility, and the wider social and political context around responsibility principles and practices as they develop over time. I turn now to introduce my approach to the study of criminal responsibility.

Keeping Space and Time in the Frame: Australia in the Twentieth Century

In this section, I make the case for an account of responsibility principles and practices in Australian criminal laws over the twentieth century, a grounded study of one set of jurisdictions over a delimited period. As I discuss in this section, with its spatial and temporal frame, my study reveals the importance for our understanding of criminal responsibility in Australian criminal laws of spaces and moments that are 'in between' or interstitial. The spatial and temporal dimensions of my frame are closely connected, but I separate them here for analytical purposes.

Accounting for Space

Australian criminal laws provide the spatial frame for my study of criminal responsibility. Australian criminal laws have not featured prominently in criminal responsibility studies to date. As I aim to show here, such a setting is likely to be of interest, not just in itself or to Australian lawyers, as might be assumed, but, in addition, I argue that Australian criminal laws reveal the ways in which 'in between' spaces – imperial, colonial and post-colonial, those created by the British Empire and its aftermath – bear on responsibility in criminal law. Put differently, and by contrast with Green's account discussed above, the context of Australia and Australian criminal laws is a central aspect of the approach taken in this book.

Before 1788, Australia was not *terra nullius* ('empty land' or 'land belonging to no one'), as would later be claimed, but home to diverse communities of Aboriginal peoples with elaborate and distinctive cosmologies involving land, art and law, among other domains.[50] While the doctrine of *terra nullius* meant that, on a formal level, debates about legal pluralism – broadly, the idea of more

[50] See A. Curthoys, 'Indigenous Subjects', in D. M. Schreuder and S. Ward (eds.), *Australia's Empire* (Oxford: Oxford University Press, 2008), pp. 79–80. The intricacies and sophistication of these cosmologies has been recognised only in recent decades, aided by the development of anthropological knowledge of Aboriginal peoples from the nineteenth century, and the formation of land rights and other human rights claims in the second half of the twentieth century.

than one set of laws prevailing in a given space – did not have the same resonance in Australia as in other colonised spaces: there has never been general recognition of Aboriginal laws as a separate system of laws in Australia.[51] Aboriginal laws interacted with colonial and post-colonial legal regimes in numerous ways. In what Heather Douglas and Mark Finnane refer to as a 'prolonged colonization', these interactions extended well into the twentieth century when some Aboriginal peoples encountered colonisers and colonial regimes for the first time.[52] In the current era, discussions revolve around matters such as appropriate ways of accommodating traditional or customary punishments (such as spearing) in sentencing Aboriginal peoples.[53] There is evidence that in places such as the Northern Territory – the last part of Australia to be settled by Europeans, and with the highest Aboriginal population of any state or territory – judges working 'on the ground' have developed a 'soft' or 'weak' legal pluralism, accommodating customary punishments in sentencing Aboriginal defendants and adjusting requirements for witness testimony, among other adaptations.[54] In recent years, this practice of accommodation has been specifically prohibited, but with limited effect, meaning accommodation of custom continues.[55]

In 1788, according to the prevailing modes of thought, Captain James Cook's arrival at Botany Bay, south of Sydney, brought law to the continent at the moment in which Australia was claimed by the British. Under the British Empire, law was regarded as one of the gifts of civilisation that colonisers carried with them as they travelled across the world.[56] What would turn out to be a long-lasting belief that Australia was (peacefully) 'settled' meant that English common law and statute – to the extent that the law and statutes were applicable to the local circumstances – arrived with the British.[57] As Bruce Kercher

[51] Australian Law Reform Commission (ALRC), *Recognition of Aboriginal Customary Laws*, Report No. 31, (1986). This report recommended the Aboriginal customary laws should be recognised, in appropriate ways, by the Australian legal system ([194]).

[52] H. Douglas and M. Finnane, *Indigenous Crime and Settler Law: White Sovereignty after Empire* (Basingstoke: Palgrave Macmillan, 2012), p. 2, and more generally, see Introduction.

[53] See ALRC, *Recognition of Aboriginal Customary Laws*, [491]–[497].

[54] See H. Douglas, 'Customary Law, Sentencing and the Limits of the State' (2005) 20(1) *Canadian Journal of Law and Society/Revue canadienne Droit et Société* 141–56. There are also specific common law protections for police interrogation of Aboriginal people (*R* v. *Anunga* (1976) 11 ALR 412); see for discussion, H. Douglas, 'The Cultural Specificity of Evidence: The Current Scope and Relevance of the Anunga Guidelines' (1998) 21 *University of New South Wales Law Journal* 27–54.

[55] Douglas and Finnane, *Indigenous Crime and Settler Law*, pp. 210–13 (discussing the *Northern Territory National Emergency Response Act 2007* (Cth)).

[56] See for critical discussion I. Hunter and S. Dorsett, 'Introduction', in S. Dorsett and I. Hunter (eds.), *Law and Politics in British Colonial Thought* (London: Palgrave MacMillan, 2010).

[57] P. G. McHugh, *Aboriginal Societies and the Common Law: A History of Sovereignty, Status, and Self-determination* (Oxford: Oxford University Press, 2004), p. 35. This idea that settlers carried the applicable law with them as their birthright is traced to William Blackstone: see W. Blackstone, *Commentaries on the Laws of England in Four Books*, Book 1 (Philadelphia: J.B. Lippincott Co., 1893 [first published in 1768]), p. 107. A copy of *Commentaries* was carried on the First Fleet, serving as an authoritative source of law: see B. Kercher, *An Unruly Child: A History of Law in Australia* (Sydney: Allen & Unwin, 1995), xii.

writes, in Australia, received 'legal tradition' interacted with the distinctive 'local social and economic conditions' that pertained in the colonies.[58] As elsewhere, in Australia, law laid the foundation of new communities and polities, including the creation of new types of spaces ('civilised' and 'uncivilised') and subjectivities (citizen and 'native' or 'savage').[59] Together with Canada and New Zealand, Australia was thought to be a 'settler colony', and regarded as a civilised or semi-civilised outpost of the 'mother country'.[60] This encouraged immigration, and the first convicts (sentenced to transportation for crimes committed 'at home') and marines of 1788 were followed by waves of free settlers as well as more convicts, as European settlements were established across the Australian continent, first as penal colonies and later as colonies.[61]

For a long period after 1788, the space of English law, jurisdiction – the relation of sovereignty and law[62] – was marked by both uncertainty and tight circumscription. As Farmer argues, the key feature of modern criminal law is the idea that it is a 'body of norms which applies consistently and seamlessly within a given legal space', an idea which was cemented in the nineteenth century when territorial jurisdiction came to be a paradigm case of legal space.[63] In the colonial context, criminal law and other laws operated in the absence of detailed knowledge of, or control over, territory, and, in the context of settler societies like Australia, across a bifurcation between white British subjects and Aboriginal peoples, whose status was questioned: as a result, jurisdiction was more of an aspiration than a fact,[64] and territory was a delocalised

[58] See Kercher, *An Unruly Child*, xx–xxi. Kercher argues that nineteenth century judges were willing to depart from English law where it was considered appropriate: see B. Kercher, 'Alex Castles on the Reception of English Law' (2003) 7 *Australian Journal of Legal History* 37–45.

[59] See generally McHugh, *Aboriginal Societies and the Common Law*; on the violence of imperialism, see P. Fitzpatrick, 'Terminal Legality: Imperialism and the (De)composition of Law', in D. Kirkby and C. Coleborne (eds.), *Law, History, Colonialism: The Reach of Empire* (Manchester: Manchester University Press, 2001), pp. 9, 20–2.

[60] D. Bell, 'Empire and Imperialism', in G. S. Jones and G. Claeys (eds.), *Cambridge History of Nineteenth Century Political Thought* (Cambridge: Cambridge University Press, 2011), p. 872.

[61] European penal settlements were established at Hobart in 1803 (but Van Diemen's Land [Tasmania] was part of NSW until 1825), at Brisbane in 1825 (but what is now Queensland was part of NSW until 1859), at Melbourne in 1835 (but Victoria was part of NSW until 1851), and in what would become Western Australia in 1827. The colony of South Australia was established by free settlers in 1836 (South Australia was responsible for the Northern Territory until 1911 when it became a Commonwealth responsibility). The Australian Capital Territory was established in 1913.

[62] S Dorsett and S. McVeigh, 'Just So: "The Law Which Governs Australia Is Australian Law"' (2002) 13 *Law and Critique* 289–309, 289.

[63] L. Farmer, 'Territorial Jurisdiction and Criminalization' (2013) 63 *University of Toronto Law Journal* 225–46, 230. Farmer argues that the cementing of territorial jurisdiction in the nineteenth century was tied up with the 'spread of the administration of the British Empire' (244).

[64] See Dorsett and McVeigh, 'Just So: "The Law Which Governs Australia Is Australian Law"', pp. 294–5.

space. In Australia, the limits of jurisdiction played out in different ways. For example, at different points over the course of the nineteenth century, uncertainty about the status of the court testimony of Aboriginal people generated legal and political concern.[65] Another example of the jurisdiction limits was colonial authority over violence between Aboriginal people (*inter se* violence), which posed a particular challenge to the process of fulfilling English sovereignty over territory as opposed to protection of English subjects.[66] Doubts about authority over *inter se* violence persisted over the 1800s, generating different answers at different times.[67]

The multiple points of intersection of the lives of Aboriginal peoples and white settlers – including around access to land and violence on the frontier – generated sites of domination and resistance that played out over the colonial and post-colonial periods. It is now well known that the dispossession of Aboriginal peoples was violent and that violence extended into the twentieth century.[68] Concerns about the treatment of Aboriginal peoples were raised by governors, missionaries and the Colonial Office from the early 1800s,[69] but, in the face of demands by pastoralists for unimpeded access to land, it proved difficult to translate more humanitarian policy into practice, and reforms were limited to highly circumscribed land grants and provision of supplies to groups of Aboriginal peoples.[70] The legal position of Aboriginal peoples was

[65] Prior to Acts such as the *Evidence Further Amendment Act 1876* (NSW) the testimony of Aboriginal people who had not converted to Christianity was routinely held to be inadmissible (on the basis that belief in God and an afterlife was essential to deter perjury): see N. E. Wright, 'The Problem of Aboriginal Evidence in Early Colonial New South Wales', in D. Kirkby and C. Coleborne (eds.), *Law, History, Colonialism: The Reach of Empire* (Manchester: Manchester University Press, 2001); see also D. Ward, 'Imperial Policy, Colonial Government, and Indigenous Testimony in South Australia and New Zealand in the 1840s', in S. Dorsett and I. Hunter (eds.), *Law and Politics in British Colonial Thought* (London: Palgrave Macmillan, 2010).

[66] See generally L. Ford, *Settler Sovereignty: Jurisdiction and Indigenous People in America and Australia 1788–1836* (Cambridge, MA: Harvard University Press, 2010).

[67] See B. Kercher, '*R* v. *Ballard, R* v. *Murrell* and *R* v. *Bonjon*' (1998) 3(3) *Australian Indigenous Law Report* 410–25. *R* v. *Murrell and Bummaree* (1836) 1 Legge 72 (holding that Aboriginal people are amenable to the law of England for offences committed against one another) is regarded as the decisive decision on this issue.

[68] The pathbreaking work on this aspect of Australian history has been undertaken by Henry Reynolds: see H. Reynolds, *The Other Side of the Frontier: Aboriginal Resistance to the European Invasion of Australia* (London: Penguin Books, 1982).

[69] This concern peaked in the 1830s, at around the same time as the British abolition of slavery in the Empire, with the creation of a House of Commons Select Committee on Aborigines in 1836 (covering various Australian colonies, New Zealand, southern Africa and British North America). The Committee recognised the right of native peoples to their own land, but recommended only protection for Aboriginal peoples and modest compensation for its loss: see A. G. L. Shaw, 'British Policy Towards the Australian Aborigines, 1830–1850' (1992) 25(99) *Australian Historical Studies* 265–85.

[70] Curthoys, 'Indigenous Subjects', p. 91.

'ambiguous': while, formally, Aboriginal peoples were British subjects, this only translated into a right to be protected, and even the racist and paternalistic care associated with the policy of protection did not prevent official and unofficial massacres or the criminalisation of Aboriginal resistance to colonisation.[71] As Kercher writes, while colonial authorities assumed that Aboriginal peoples were British subjects, the primary effect of this was to 'thrust them before the courts as defendants'.[72] By the end of the nineteenth century, Aboriginal peoples had been enclosed in a dense network of colonial laws and processes – including criminal law, church run missions, administrative governance through reserves, status distinctions and population controls.[73]

Although the personnel of the law – governors, judges, magistrates, local police and others – did not enjoy extensive geographic reach, these individuals wielded significant powers. As Finnane argues, with policing one of the earliest functions of the colonial state, the police assumed an 'enormous variety of administrative functions' in the colonial period.[74] The convict system meant that administrators and magistrates had extensive control over individuals, including control over movement.[75] The violence of the convict system and the harshness of colonial life – which included draconian physical punishments, and a penal settlement within penal settlements, Norfolk Island, for those who had committed crimes after transportation – are now notorious.[76] In addition, the responsibility governors had for convicts meant that they took on a multitude of governance tasks, establishing 'the tradition of omni-competence in colonial government'.[77] In John Hirst's words, because the role of the colonies was to generate economic benefit for Britain, rather than functioning 'primarily to keep order within and defeat enemies without', the governmental function was 'to develop the country'.[78] Following self-government in the mid-nineteenth century and with the early development of democratic institutions, these extensive state powers generated concern, and as I show in my discussion of developments around the turn of the twentieth

[71] See Kercher, *An Unruly Child*, p. 6 and more generally, ch. 1.

[72] Kercher, *An Unruly Child*, p. 12.

[73] M. Finnane, 'The Limits of Jurisdiction: Law, Governance and Indigenous Peoples in Colonized Australia', in S. Dorsett and I. Hunter (eds.), *Law and Politics in British Colonial Thought* (London: Palgrave Macmillan, 2010), p. 151. Finnane argues that all these laws and processes were aiming to render Aboriginal peoples modern self-governing citizens.

[74] See M. Finnane, *Police and Government: Histories of Policing in Australia* (Oxford: Oxford University Press, 1994), p. 21 and more generally, ch. 1.

[75] See P. J. Byrne, *Criminal Law and Colonial Subject, New South Wales, 1810–1830* (Cambridge: Cambridge University Press, 1993), ch. 6.

[76] On the penal settlement at Norfolk Island, see J. V. Barry, *Alexander Maconochie of Norfolk Island: A Study of a Pioneer in Penal Reform* (Melbourne: Oxford University Press, 1958). I discuss J. V. Barry's work on criminal justice in Chapter 4.

[77] J. Hirst, 'Empire, State, Nation', in D. M. Schreuder and S. Ward (eds.), *Australia's Empire* (Oxford: Oxford University Press, 2008), p. 145.

[78] Hirst, 'Empire, State, Nation', pp. 146, 150.

century, the modernisation of the criminal law was tied up with issues of legal form – comprehensive legislation or a code – and process – the operation of criminal justice – as much as with principles of criminal responsibility.[79]

Beyond the bounds of the continent, Empire was itself a multitude of geographical and legal spaces. While Empire – the idea of territorially extended rule[80] – has traditionally been contra-distinguished from 'home', the relationship between these spaces was dialectical not dichotomous, meaning that colonies and metropole were mutually constitutive.[81] Backed by economic and military might, Empire provided an organisational structure for the movement (and, in the process, the translation) of European ideas around the world.[82] As a number of scholars point out, discourses around matters such as civilisation, culture and universality provided ideological resources for imperialism and colonialism.[83] In Lauren Benton's words, there was a 'repertoire of available formulae' that could be deployed to meet 'local pressures and constraints'.[84] The common law – which was infused with British national identity, cultural leadership and Empire – was one of these formulae.[85] Empire also generated 'imperial counter-flows', the materials and ideas that travelled from the 'imperial peripheries' to influence the terms and content of political and moral debates in the metropole, and to new found knowledges like anthropology and ethnography.[86]

There was a remarkable cross-fertilisation of ideas about criminal law and reform initiatives across the spaces of the British Empire. The story of the circulation of ideas about criminal law across Empire has been most thoroughly charted in relation to codification movements of the nineteenth century. The movements for the reformation of the common law of crime – as

[79] See Chapter 3.

[80] See J. Mayall, 'Nationalism and Imperialism', in T. Bell and R. Bellamy (eds.), *Cambridge History of Twentieth Century Political Thought* (Cambridge: Cambridge University Press, 2003), p. 105.

[81] See, e.g., B. Ibawoh, *Imperial Justice: Africans in Empire's Court* (Oxford: Oxford University Press, 2013), p. 20; M. D. Dubber, 'Colonial Criminal Law and Other Modernities: European Criminal Law in the Nineteenth and Twentieth Century', in H. Pihlajamäki, M. D. Dubber and M. Godfrey (eds.), *Oxford Handbook of European Legal History* (Oxford: Oxford University Press, 2018).

[82] For a critical discussion of the reception of these ideas, see C. A. Bayly, 'European Political Thought and the Wider World During the Nineteenth Century', in G. S. Jones and G. Claeys (eds.), *Cambridge History of Nineteenth Century Political Thought* (Cambridge: Cambridge University Press, 2011).

[83] For critical discussion see, e.g., I. Hunter, 'Global Justice and Regional Metaphysics: On the Critical History of the Law of Nature and Nations', in S. Dorsett and I. Hunter (eds.), *Law and Politics in British Colonial Thought* (London: Palgrave MacMillan, 2010), p. 13.

[84] See L. A. Benton, *Law and Colonial Cultures: Legal Regimes in World History, 1400–1900* (Cambridge: Cambridge University Press, 2002), p. 170, and more generally, ch. 5.

[85] See D. Sugarman, '"A Hatred of Disorder": Legal Science, Liberalism and Imperialism', in P. Fitzpatrick (ed.), *Dangerous Supplements: Resistance and Renewal in Jurisprudence* (London: Pluto Press, 1991), p. 37.

[86] See Ibawoh, *Imperial Justice*, p. 13; see also Bell, 'Empire and Imperialism', p. 866.

a criminal code – stretched across metropolitan and colonial spaces, law in England and law across Empire. While, famously, codification was less successful 'at home' than abroad, the development of criminal codes in the colonies was closely connected with the (unsuccessful) codification movement in England.[87] For example, coinciding with the work of the English Criminal Law Commissioners, the drafting of the Indian Penal Code in the 1830s was believed by its drafter, Thomas Macaulay, to have 'practical relevance for home consumption'.[88] This indicates that, and as Karuna Mantena argues, India was seen as a 'political blank slate', which could be used as a 'testing ground for a whole series of institutional reforms' that might then be re-exported to England.[89] This state of affairs leads David Skuy to conclude that the Indian Penal Code was 'really a code for England'.[90] As this suggests, codification movements across Empire reflected attempts at reform 'at home' and wider frustration and dissatisfaction with the English criminal law. This kind of cross-jurisdictional interaction informed the development of criminal codes in Australia at the end of the nineteenth century, and again at the end of the twentieth century. I pick up on this point in my discussions of codification in this book.[91]

The development of criminal responsibility principles and practices across the spaces of Empire has not been subject to the same attention as codification, but there is reason to think that this story also stretches across the spaces of metropole and colony, implicating the interstitial spaces created by the Empire and its aftermath. Over and above the coordinating work of the Colonial Office and the Judicial Committee of the Privy Council, which knitted legal policies and practices together across Empire,[92] the main institutions

[87] See, e.g., E. Kolsky, 'Codification and the Rule of Colonial Difference: Criminal Procedure in British India' (2005) 23(3) *Law and History Review* 631–83, 631–4.

[88] See K. J. M. Smith, 'Macaulay's "Utilitarian" Indian Penal Code: An Illustration of the Accidental Function of Time, Place and Personalities in Law Making', in W. M. Gordon and T. D. Fergus (eds.), *Legal History in the Making: Proceedings from the Ninth British Legal History Conference* (London: The Hambledon Press, 1991), p. 163. For discussion of the English developments, see L. Farmer, 'Reconstructing the English Codification Debate: The Criminal Law Commissioners, 1833–45' (2000) 18(2) *Law and History Review* 397–426.

[89] K. Mantena, *Alibis of Empire: Henry Maine and the Ends of Liberal Imperialism* (Princeton, NJ: Princeton University Press, 2010), p. 95.

[90] D. Skuy, 'Macaulay and the Indian Penal Code of 1862: The Myth of the Inherent Superiority and Modernity of the English Legal System Compared to India's Legal System in the Nineteenth Century' (1998) 32(3) *Modern Asian Studies* 513–57, 552.

[91] See Chapter 3 (examining the formation of the *Criminal Code Act 1899* [Qld]) and Chapter 5 (examining the development of the Commonwealth Criminal Code in the 1990s).

[92] The Colonial Office coordinated attempts to develop a criminal code that was initially intended to apply to all British colonies. The idea of a criminal code for the colonies was advanced by Sir Henry Taylor, a powerful figure in the Colonial Office in the second half of the nineteenth century. Taylor had hoped to realise change in England, but when his proposals failed to gain traction, he turned his attention to the colonies, 'a captive audience': see M. L. Friedland, 'R. S. Wright's Model Criminal Code: A Forgotten Chapter in the History of the Criminal Law' (1981) 1 *Oxford Journal of Legal Studies* 307–46, 308.

in the criminal responsibility story – including the House of Lords – and some of its main characters, including James Fitzjames Stephen, the towering figure of criminal law reform in England in this period – exercised influence both 'at home' and abroad.[93] Thus, in the major consolidation of criminal laws in NSW at the end of the nineteenth century (as well as in the codification of criminal laws of Queensland), practitioners and legislators drew on the work of James Fitzjames Stephen.[94] On the level of ideas about criminal responsibility, the moment was not all one way. For example, in the middle of the twentieth century, in the midst of widespread concern that the fault requirement in criminal offences was under threat, developments in criminal responsibility by the High Court of Australia – to preserve the requirement of *mens rea* via the use of a novel defence of honest and reasonable mistake of fact – were considered (albeit ultimately rejected) in England.[95] Along with ideas, individuals also moved across the spaces of the Empire. For example, James Fitzjames Stephen was Legal member of the Viceroy's Council in India from 1869 to 1872.[96] Neither was the movement of individuals across the spaces of the British Empire unidirectional: throughout the period under discussion in this book, Australian lawyers and academics travelled to England both as students and as professionals.[97]

This suggests that the story of criminal responsibility in Australia cannot be told without an awareness of these interstitial spaces and the circulation of ideas permeating them, and further, that the story of criminal responsibility in English law would be enhanced by reference to this broader context. Rather, the circulations of ideas about criminal responsibility across the interstitial spaces and through the institutions of Empire is part of the development of responsibility into the current era. In their movement across dialectical spaces, these ideas were refracted in ways that meant the articulation of ideas 'at home' was also impacted. As a result, a study examining criminal responsibility in Australian criminal laws sheds new light on developments in English law, offering an 'outside-in view of the subject', to borrow Markus Dubber's

93 Fitzjames Stephen served as Legal Member of the Viceroy's Council in India (1868–72): see Skuy, 'Macaulay and the Indian Penal Code of 1862'. The individuals featuring in criminal law reform in England and Wales – and their descendants – also feature in reform efforts in Australia: James Fitzjames Stephen's nephew had a role in the development of the *Criminal Law Amendment Act 1883* (NSW), as I discuss in Chapter 3.

94 See Chapter 3.

95 See further Chapter 4.

96 In this role, Fitzjames Stephen pursued his interest in codification: see for discussion Mantena, *Alibis of Empire*, pp. 40–4.

97 E.g., Sir C. K. Allen (1887–1966), an Australian who travelled to the University of Oxford and became a noted jurisprudence scholar. Allen's lectures at the University of Calcutta in 1926 became *Law in the Making* (London: Clarendon Press, 1927), a seminal text which went through seven editions (the last of which was published in 1964): see K. C. Wheare, 'Allen, Sir Carleton Kemp (1887–1966)', in B. Nairn (ed.), *Australian Dictionary of Biography Volume 7: 1891–1939* (Melbourne: Melbourne University Press, 1979).

words.[98] In addition, recognition of this movement generates an imperative to take the circulation of ideas about criminal responsibility into account in examining responsibility in criminal law. This involves thinking across the jurisdictional boundaries that now mark out the scope of positive legal system studies. As Farmer writes, scholars need to think 'in more complex ways' about responsibility (and wrongdoing), and think across boundaries, such as those between one jurisdiction and another.[99] The study of criminal responsibility in the space of Australian criminal laws invites such 'complex' thinking.

The twentieth century – the 'twilight century' – saw the demise of the British Empire,[100] but it also saw the rise of the British Commonwealth and through it, imperialism remained an important influence on Australian law, as well as politics and culture. Although Australian self-governing colonies became states of the Commonwealth of Australia in 1901, this did not correspond with attainment of sovereignty, and there is genuine debate about when Australia became an independent sovereign country.[101] Various dates are given including the passage of the *Statute of Westminster 1931*, when Australia was recognised as a British Dominion, an independent legal community within the British Empire,[102] and 1942, when the Australian parliament passed the *Statute of Westminster Adoption Act 1942*.[103] In Kercher's words, all that can be said is that, 'sometime between 1931 and 1950', Australia came to be regarded as an independent nation in international law, with the capacity to make treaties on its own behalf.[104] In a further stretch of Empire and colonialism, although the High Court of Australia was established in 1903, until the 1980s, Australian state supreme courts retained rights of appeal to the Privy Council, and civil litigants could bypass the High Court and elect to take appeals directly to London.[105] Overlaying all this was the durable idea of the unity of

98 Dubber, 'Colonial Criminal Law and Other Modernities', pp. 1062–3 (referring to the connection between European criminal law and colonial criminal law, and advocating the study of 'European colonial criminal law').

99 Farmer, 'Time and Space in Criminal Law', p. 354.

100 McHugh, *Aboriginal Societies and the Common Law*, p. 4.

101 Hirst, 'Empire, State, Nation', p. 160.

102 From this date, the Imperial parliament passed no Acts covering the Dominions (such as Australia, Canada and New Zealand) and Dominion parliaments could repeal Imperial legislation: see Kercher, *An Unruly Child*, pp. 175–6.

103 The *Statute of Westminster Adoption Act 1942* (Cth) was prompted by the threat that the British would take control of the Australian armed forces, and was passed with retrospective application to the beginning of World War II: see Kercher, *An Unruly Child*, p. 176.

104 Kercher, *An Unruly Child*, p. 176.

105 The *Australia Act 1986* (England) and *Australia Act 1986* (Cth) ended appeals from state courts, establishing the High Court as Australia's apex court (appeals from the High Court to the Privy Council were abolished in two stages in 1968 and 1975). Like Australia, New Zealand also retained appeals to the Privy Council after they had been abolished in other former colonies (appeals ended in New Zealand with the creation of the Supreme Court in 2003: *Supreme Court Act 2003* [NZ]): see further K. J. Keith, 'The Unity of the Common Law and the Ending of Appeals to the Privy Council' (2005) 54 *International & Comparative Law Quarterly* 197–210.

the common law, which meant that, until the mid-century, Australian judges and courts showed deference to English precedent.[106]

The long shadow of influence of English law on Australian criminal laws suggests that my study covers an interstitial or 'in between' legal space, raising a question as to what is *Australian* about the criminal laws studied here. This sort of question has been raised by scholars who have focused on issues of legal authority. For instance, Cane argues that Australian law was 'in a significant sense, dependent on rather than independent of English law' for most of the twentieth century,[107] meaning it was not possible to speak of Australian laws proper – civil or criminal – until the end of the period. But in Kercher's words, the issue of the role of English law and legal institutions in Australian legal history 'should be the commencing point of historical analysis', not its conclusion.[108] My own approach to the issue is to look beyond questions of form to substance, and focus on the specifics of the criminal law and criminal responsibility story. As I discuss in this book, this approach reveals a distinct picture: while the codification of the criminal law in some states from the end of the nineteenth century entailed an innovative engagement with criminal responsibility, it is the mid-century that is a formative period in the development of a meaningfully Australian criminal law. A close study of case law, textbooks and commentary of this period indicates that the principles of criminal responsibility played a central role in the 'birth' of Australian criminal law.[109]

Accounting for Time

The time frame for this study of criminal responsibility is broadly the twentieth century. As mentioned above, this period has been subject to less attention than other periods. As I discuss in this section, the twentieth century saw the revitalisation of comparative jurisprudence – the study of more than one set of laws or legal system – which, I suggest, created its own set of interstitial moments bearing on criminal responsibility principles and practices. Thus, by contrast with Veitch's account discussed above, I break the time frame of modernity down further to investigate the distinctiveness of the twentieth century.

At the outset of the twentieth century, Federation transformed Australian colonies into states, brought together under a written Constitution that represented a combination of English law and local legal principles, and also borrowed from the United States Constitution (in relation to the balance between the upper and lower houses of Parliament, for example).[110] Reflecting the

[106] I discuss the idea of the unity of the common law across Empire in Chapter 4.

[107] See P. Cane, *Controlling Administrative Power: An Historical Comparison* (Cambridge: Cambridge University Press, 2016), p. 511. Cane states that an historical comparison of Australian and English was not truly possible until after the passage of the *Australia Acts*.

[108] Kercher, *An Unruly Child*, p. 171.

[109] See Chapters 3 and 4 respectively.

[110] Kercher, *An Unruly Child*, pp. 157–8, 171.

influence of labour unions and social reform movements, including feminist activism and church-based groups, the first years of the century saw major developments in labour laws, social welfare and population control.[111] In criminal justice, which had remained a state responsibility at Federation, the early century was marked by heightened social concern and the passage of legislation around vice crimes such as alcohol and drug consumption, gambling and prostitution.[112] Legal developments at this time included innovations in vagrancy laws, which were used to govern public order.[113] These developments reflected the enhanced capacity of the state to regulate social life and the police, who were now employed in state-wide organisations, were harnessed more effectively in the service of state regulation.[114]

At this time, key institutions of criminal law were still in a nascent stage. By contrast with jurisdictions such as England and the United States, at the beginning of the twentieth century, Australia institutions such as summary justice were still developing. In the absence of established systems of local government, magistrates performed a variety of legal and governance activities.[115] Access to legal sources was severely limited, and there was no regular law reporting in Australian jurisdictions until the last decades of the nineteenth century.[116] Australian jurisdictions had had power to pass their own laws since the advent of responsible government in the middle of the nineteenth century, but, as discussed above, until the first decades of the twentieth century, both state and Federal parliaments remained subordinate to the Imperial Parliament at Westminster.[117] The High Court of Australia was created in 1903, and gradually expanded its jurisdiction beyond its core focus on constitutional matters. As I discuss in this book, the High Court's first years were marked by political determination to preserve the independence of the Australian states, and this extended to the criminal law, with the imperative of unity in Australian criminal laws coming to override this independence only in the mid-century.[118]

111 These developments were tied up together: see, e.g., T. Carney and P. Hanks, *Social Security in Australia* (Melbourne: Oxford University Press, 1994), p. 30.

112 See, e.g., M. Finnane, 'The Politics of Police Powers: The Making of the Police Offences Acts', in M. Finnane (ed.), *Policing in Australia: Historical Perspectives* (Sydney: New South Wales University Press, 1987).

113 I discuss vagrancy laws in the context of relations between self and others: see Chapter 7.

114 Finnane, 'The Politics of Police Powers', pp. 103–4.

115 In relation to NSW, see T Mitchell, 'Understanding the Summary Jurisdiction in NSW', PhD thesis, University of Sydney (2017).

116 See B. Kercher, 'Recovering and Reporting Australia's Early Colonial Case Law: The Macquarie Project' (2000) 18(3) *Law and History Review* 659–65.

117 This subordination was the effect of the *Colonial Laws Validity Act 1865* (England); see for discussion Kercher, *An Unruly Child*, pp. 160–1.

118 See Chapter 4.

The growth of these legal institutions over the decades from 1900 was informed by the then recent revitalisation of comparative jurisprudence, which dated from the second half of the nineteenth century. As part of a wider and wide-ranging tradition of comparative analysis, comparative jurisprudence has a long history, sometimes traced back to Ancient Greece and Rome.[119] Comparative approaches to the study of politics, law and society figured prominently in Enlightenment discourses[120] and, along with historical methods, lay at the heart of the development of the social sciences from the eighteenth century.[121] Empire inspired what has been called a 'second renaissance' of comparative legal studies.[122] Up until this point, 'comparative law rested with a few individuals of great learning', but since the mid-nineteenth century, 'the diverse laws and customs and a vast international trade' across Empire stimulated wider interest in and study of comparative jurisprudence.[123] From this point onwards, the experience of commentators and reformers in the colonies was coming to inform understanding of English law and its critique and reform, and 'English law was perforce thrown into juxtaposition with many other legal systems'.[124] Similarly, 'other legal systems' were compared with that of England. For example, the English attempts at codification from the 1830s, including the English draft criminal code prepared by Fitzjames Stephen, influenced the development and content of the *Criminal Code of Canada 1893*.[125]

Just as Empire was a division of time as well as space – the division between civilisation and barbarity, or modernity and tradition, was mapped in terms of differences in developmental states, with 'primitive' societies contrasted with the

[119] See G. Winterton, 'Comparative Law Teaching' (1975) 23(1) *The American Journal of Comparative Law* 69–118, 87–8.

[120] See M. Richter, 'The Comparative Study of Regimes and Societies', in M. Goldie and R. Wokler (eds.), *Cambridge History of Eighteenth Century Political Thought* (Cambridge: Cambridge University Press, 2006) (noting that at this time, the study of law, society and polities were not yet set off from one another) (p. 152).

[121] Because of its connection to civil and political liberty and state power and security, criminal law featured in these comparisons, and debates ranged over the nature of crime (and its relation to sin), punishment (including the death penalty) and proportionality: see F. Rosen, 'Utilitarianism and the Reform of the Criminal Law', in M. Goldie and R. Wokler (eds.), *Cambridge History of Eighteenth Century Political Thought* (Cambridge: Cambridge University Press, 2011).

[122] L. Neville Brown uses this term to describe the period from 1869 (the year in which the French Society for Comparative Legislation was founded), noting that the study of Roman Law – already entrenched in universities – was a species of comparative law: see L. Neville Brown, 'A Century of Comparative Law in England: 1869–1969' (1971) 19(2) *The American Journal of Comparative Law* 232–52, 233.

[123] Winterton, 'Comparative Law Teaching', pp. 90–1.

[124] Neville Brown, 'A Century of Comparative Law in England', p. 236.

[125] D. H. Brown, *The Genesis of the Canadian Criminal Code of 1892* (Toronto: University of Toronto Press, 1989), p. 132; see also G. Parker, 'The Origins of the Canadian Criminal Code', in D. H. Flaherty (ed.), *Essays in the History of Canadian Law Volume 1* (Toronto: University of Toronto Press, 1981), p. 251.

modernity of Europe[126] – so comparative jurisprudence involved looking back in time as well as across in time. An illustration is provided by the use of the legal reform writings and initiatives of Jeremy Bentham, who had commenced work on theories of crime and punishment and organisation of prisons that would come to be known as utilitarianism in the second half of the eighteenth century.[127] As is well known, Bentham applied the language of political economy to the relations between crimes and punishments, advocating 'economic punishment: one that produced its desired effect with the least possible cost of suffering'.[128] Famously, Bentham's ideas about codification of the law heavily influenced nineteenth-century criminal law reformers.[129] Another illustration concerns the closely related development of historical jurisprudence in the second half of the nineteenth century. Sir Henry Maine spear-headed the English-language development of historical jurisprudence, according to which 'a proper explanation of a legal system' required not the elucidation of general legal concepts, but 'an examination of the history of the society living under that system'.[130] As is well known, Maine's major treatise, *Ancient Law*, began as a set of lectures given in India, where he was employed as a Law Member of the Viceroy's Council (1862–1869). Reflecting a strong commitment to progress that characterised the Victorian era,[131] Maine's book presented an account of legal modernity, arguing that, as they developed, societies advanced along a path 'from Status to Contract', with primitive native societies like India 'held together by stable bonds of custom and structures of kinship', and marked out by the dominance of culture as opposed to politics.[132]

From the end of the nineteenth century, the burgeoning scholarly field of comparative jurisprudence took on durable institutional form in learned societies that focused on the exchange of knowledge and ideas about law across jurisdictional boundaries. This period was marked by several major international congresses on comparative law which attracted participants

[126] Mantena, *Alibis of Empire*, p. 82 and more generally, Chapter 2. Mantena argues that Henry Maine's interest in India was premised on the idea of India as an example of 'primitive' law and society, 'the "living past" of Europe' (p. 75).

[127] On Bentham's system of thought, see G. J. Postema, *Bentham and the Common Law Tradition* (Oxford: Clarendon Press, 1986).

[128] Rosen, 'Utilitarianism', p. 558.

[129] On Bentham's influence on the *Criminal Code Act 1899* (Qld), see Chapter 3.

[130] See N. Duxbury, 'English Jurisprudence Between Austin and Hart' (2005) 91(1) *Virginia Law Review* 1–91, 22.

[131] C. Kirkby, 'Review Article: Henry Maine and the Re-Constitution of the British Empire' (2012) 75(4) *Modern Law Review* 655–73.

[132] See Mantena, *Alibis of Empire*, pp. 3, 75–6 and more generally, Chapter 2. While Maine's historical jurisprudence had an 'undistinguished' history in English jurisprudence, his work was taken up in sociology and anthropology: see Duxbury, 'English Jurisprudence Between Austin and Hart', 27, and more generally, pp. 25–9.

from all over the world.[133] At around the same time, the growth of the new science of penology enhanced interest in criminal justice in other legal systems and generated new societies for the study of criminology.[134] Following the establishment of such societies in France and Germany, in 1894 the Society for Comparative Legislation was founded in London, and the Society's journal, the *Journal of the Society of Comparative Legislation* was published from 1896.[135] This journal published summaries of case law and statute developments in jurisdictions such as Australia, and also scholarly articles of comparative law. It provided 'reliable information concerning legislation in the different parts of the Empire and, as far as possible, in foreign countries' to 'persons interested in legal, economic and social questions'.[136] From the 1950s, as the *International & Comparative Law Quarterly*, the journal continued to foreground the British Commonwealth in its ethos and content, reflecting the special place of the countries of the British Empire in English language comparative jurisprudence. In his Foreword to the first issue of the journal under the new title, Lord Denning stated that the journal aimed to be 'a focus for Commonwealth legal studies'.[137] The journal no longer published surveys of Commonwealth legislation, but a separate *Annual Survey of Commonwealth Law* was published between 1965 and 1977.[138] By this time, the number of journals and institutes devoted to comparative jurisprudence had burgeoned, and it had become an established legal subdiscipline.[139]

The institutions of comparative jurisprudence generated a set of intellectual resources for use by lawyers, judges and scholars in legal development and reform in countries such as Australia. Australians contributed to these institutions. For example, a number of practitioners, judges and others wrote articles on Australian laws that were published in the *Journal of the Society of Comparative Legislation*. These articles covered topics such as the 'mode of legislation' in the Australian colonies, developments in criminal procedure

[133] See D. S. Clark, 'Nothing New in 2000? Comparative Law in 1900 and Today' (2000) 75 *Tulsa Law Review* 871–912.

[134] See generally M. Pifferi, *Reinventing Punishment: A Comparative History of Criminology and Penology in the Nineteenth and Twentieth Centuries* (Oxford: Oxford University Press, 2016).

[135] The journal was published as the *Journal of the Society of Comparative Legislation* until 1916, and from 1918, as the *Journal of the Society of Comparative Legislation and International Law*. From 1952, the journal became the *International & Comparative Law Quarterly*, and was published by the British Institute of International and Comparative Law in London from 1958.

[136] Columbia Law Review Association, 'Journal of the Society of Comparative Legislation' (Book Review) (1916) 16(4) *Columbia Law Review* 365–6, 365.

[137] A. T. Denning, 'Foreword' (1952) 1(1) *International & Comparative Law Quarterly* 1–2, 2.

[138] R. Munday, 'Annual Survey of Commonwealth Law 1977' (1980) 39(2) *Cambridge Law Journal* 398–9. Perhaps reflecting the maturity of the field at this point, this survey was organised thematically rather than by jurisdiction. According to Munday, by this time, the citation of Commonwealth authorities was a 'standard feature' in English courts and textbooks.

[139] J. W. Cairns, 'Development of Comparative Law in Great Britain' in M. Reimann and R. Zimmermann (eds.), *The Oxford Handbook of Comparative Law* (Oxford: Oxford University Press 2006).

and punishment, and the Australian constitution.[140] The authors of these articles were notable for their high profile in legal and political circles, and the way in which their biographies and careers reflected the porous boundaries between spaces of the Empire.[141] After the *Criminal Law Review* commenced publication in England in 1954, Australian scholars and practitioners (including the authors of Australia's first criminal law textbooks, written between the 1940s and 1960s) contributed several 'Australian Letters' detailing contemporary developments in case law and legislation for the readership of the *Review*.[142]

As this suggests, the rise of comparative jurisprudence – with cross-Commonwealth comparison at its core for a significant part of the century – informed the development of criminal responsibility in Australian criminal laws. For example, homicide law reform in the first half of the twentieth century – when a new terrain of partial criminal responsibility, applying to women who had killed their children, was carved out on the face of criminal law – tracks reforms in England and Wales.[143] By the last decades of the century, Australia was looking beyond England and Wales for guidance in legal development and law reform. This is evident in the codification of Federal criminal laws in the 1990s. The central chapter of the Commonwealth Criminal Code – on criminal responsibility – was modelled on the corresponding article of the US *Model Penal Code*.[144] Again, as with the interstitial spaces of Empire,

[140] See J. C. H. James, 'Modes of Legislation in the British colonies: Western Australia' (1899) 1(1) *Journal of the Society of Comparative Legislation* 70–4; WF Craies, 'Criminal Law in New South Wales' (1901) 3(1) *Journal of the Society of Comparative Legislation* 95–7; W. H. Moore, 'The Australian Commonwealth Constitution' (1903) 5(1) *Journal of the Society of Comparative Legislation* 115–31, respectively.

[141] See, e.g., Robert Randolph Garran CMG (1867–1957) (who was appointed as Chair of the Indian Defence Expenditure Tribunal by the British government in 1932): see further R. S. Parker, 'Garran, Sir Robert Randolph (1867–1957)', in B. Nairn (ed.), *Australian Dictionary of Biography Volume 8: 1891–1939* (Melbourne: Melbourne University Press, 1981); see also William Harrison Moore KBE CMG (1867–1935) (who was involved in the constitutional conventions in the 1890s, held the Chair of Law at the University of Melbourne from 1892 to 1927, and acted as Australia's delegate to the League of Nations from 1928 to 1930): see further, L. Re, 'Moore, Sir William Harrison (1867–1935)', in B. Nairn (ed.), *Australian Dictionary of Biography Volume 10: 1891–1939* (Melbourne: Melbourne University Press, 1986).

[142] See further Chapter 4.

[143] See further Chapter 6.

[144] I. Leader-Elliott, 'Elements of Liability in the Commonwealth Criminal Code' (2002) 26 *Criminal Law Journal* 28–42, 34; I. Leader-Elliott, 'Benthamite Reflections on Codification of the General Principles of Criminal Liability: Towards the Panopticon' (2006) 9(2) *Buffalo Criminal Law Review* 391–452. On the *Model Penal Code*, see M. D. Dubber, 'The Model Penal Code, Legal Process and the Alegitimacy of American Penality', in M. D. Dubber (ed.), *Foundational Texts in Modern Criminal Law* (Oxford: Oxford University Press, 2014). I discuss the Commonwealth Criminal Code in Chapter 5.

the influence of comparative jurisprudence was multidirectional. After the Queensland Criminal Code was enacted in 1899, it was exported across Empire to influence the criminal codes in Africa, the Middle East and the Pacific.[145]

In addition, and beyond comparative jurisprudence, the twentieth century also saw a number of seismic developments that impacted across jurisdictional boundaries. The massive social and political changes that have taken place over the century – including democratisation, moral pluralism and the rise of human rights discourses – each impacted on the law and society of Western liberal political systems like that of Australia. These changes transcend national boundaries – and indeed seem to render them less significant – but their effects play out on a local level. As a result, it is necessary to pay careful attention to the 'on the ground' impact of large-scale phenomena such as globalisation. In the context of criminal responsibility in Australian criminal laws, social and political changes were particularly crucial in the codification of criminal law at a national level in the 1990s. As I discuss, the increasing complexity of both domestic and international law generated a demand to 'fix' criminal responsibility at the heart of criminal law and reconstruct criminal law as national rather than subnational law.[146]

As this discussion indicates, and echoing the point made above about the relevance of the interstitial spaces of Empire, the story of criminal responsibility cannot be understood by reference to the English law alone. As I show in this book, the development of criminal responsibility principles and practices over the twentieth century involves the movement of individuals and ideas across and between legal spaces and moments as well as within them. While comparative jurisprudence now forms a taken-for-granted aspect of the intellectual landscape of criminal legal inquiry, recognising that it was a distinctive feature of the intellectual environment of the twentieth century usefully exposes the conditions of possibility for the development of responsibility in Australian criminal laws. The study presented in this book is not a comparative study as such[147] – my focus is squarely on Australia and the

[145] The Griffith Criminal Code formed 'the basis of, or was a very strong influence on' the criminal codes of Nigeria (which influenced other African countries), Israel, Fiji, the Solomon Islands and the Seychelles: see G. Mackenzie, 'An Enduring Influence: Sir Samuel Griffith and His Contribution to Criminal Justice in Queensland' (2002) 2(1) *Queensland University of Technology Law and Justice Journal* 53–63, 60.

[146] See Chapter 5.

[147] Criminal responsibility is now coming to the attention of comparative legal scholars: see M. Pifferi, 'Criminal Responsibility and Its Histories: New Perspectives for Comparative Legal History' (2017) 4(2) *Critical Analysis of Law* 222–32.

transference of ideas about responsibility, and principles and practices, to and from Australian criminal laws – but my analysis shows the importance of comparative jurisprudence for criminal responsibility in Australian criminal laws. As such, the book is a criminal responsibility response to Kercher's call for 'a new model of the circulation of legal ideas' that takes into account 'multi-directional influences' on Australian legal thought.[148]

> Historical analysis of law, in other words, is a mode of legal scholarship, not a subspecies of law (nor of history). It is a comprehensive view of law from a particular critical vantage point: a way of doing law, rather than of doing things with law.[149]

In this chapter, I sought to account for the setting of this criminal responsibility study in the context of Australian laws over the twentieth century. With this frame, I introduced a relatively neglected jurisdiction into criminal responsibility scholarship, and focused on a period that has been subject to less attention than other periods. In addition, with my focus on Australia in the twentieth century, my study exposes the importance of spaces and moments that are 'in between' or interstitial – spaces existing within or between, or 'in advance of', standard or orthodox legal spaces. The broad and multifaceted changes in identities, social and legal arrangements and politics that are gathered together under the labels of Empire and colonialism, and the intellectual resources provided by the revitalisation of the field of comparative jurisprudence, form a neglected dimension of the analyses of criminal responsibility offered by critical scholars. As I seek to show throughout this book, in relation to Australia, these spaces and moments are vital ingredients in appreciation of responsibility principles and practices. This, in turn, suggests that the Australian story of criminal responsibility has broad interest and, further, that the story of criminal responsibility in English law would be enhanced by reference to this broader context.

As this chapter indicates, my account of criminal responsibility principles and practices sits 'close to the ground' in Australian criminal laws over the twentieth century. The scholarly decision to pursue a study with these spatial and temporal parameters permits me to examine principles and practices of criminal responsibility in their social, political and institutional context. As Lacey notes, in relation to any theoretical question, a judgment must be made about the appropriate level of generality at which to pitch the analysis – and this is a question of methodology.[150] My delimited frame ensures space and time are taken seriously, and that, as far as possible, the full relevance of jurisdictional and historical specificity informs my critical examination.

[148] Kercher, *An Unruly Child*, p. 205.

[149] M. D. Dubber, 'New Historical Jurisprudence: Legal History as Critical Analysis of Law' (2015) 2(1) *Critical Analysis of Law* 1–18, 2.

[150] See Lacey, 'Jurisprudence, History and the Institutional Quality of Law', p. 933.

2

The Significance of Criminal Responsibility

Criminal responsibility is in need of rethinking. As discussed in the Introduction to this book, criminal responsibility – denoting both the basis on which individuals are called to account for criminal conduct and the form or structure of the law – is now central to the criminal law. Reflecting its high profile, criminal responsibility forms the subject matter of a rich and deep vein of criminal law scholarship. Across this body of scholarship, criminal responsibility is recognised as performing different roles, and hence, as significant in different ways. There is much value in existing scholarship, yet, a crucial aspect of the role of criminal responsibility in criminal law has been overlooked. What makes criminal responsibility significant, I argue, is that it organises key sets of relations as relations of responsibility. These sets of relations are those between self, others and the state. It is this hitherto overlooked aspect of criminal responsibility that demands a new account of its significance.

In developing a new account of the significance of criminal responsibility, I proceed in two steps. In the first step, I assess the existing criminal responsibility scholarship. Looking across the scholarly field reveals that there are three main ways in which criminal responsibility is regarded as significant, relating to its normative, symbolic and functional role in criminal law. These three ways are criminal responsibility as the normative heart of the criminal law; criminal responsibility as serving the coordination and legitimation needs of the criminal law; and criminal responsibility as a platform for the development of the modern criminal law. These three accounts correspond with the work of a group of scholars, or, in the case of the second and third accounts, single scholars – Nicola Lacey and Lindsay Farmer – who have developed *sui generis* analyses.[1] While the first account represents the dominant legal-philosophical tradition of criminal responsibility scholarship, the accounts offered by Lacey and Farmer represent the critical criminal responsibility camp, which, as

[1] There are several points of connection between the accounts of the significance of criminal responsibility offered by Lacey and Farmer, but I separate them here for analytical purposes.

mentioned in the Introduction, assesses responsibility principles and practices within their social, political and institutional context. These three accounts of the role and significance of criminal responsibility in criminal law speak to each other, as critical criminal responsibility scholarship has developed in dialogue with the dominant legal-philosophical scholarship. As I discuss in this chapter, the three accounts vary in their attentiveness to, and appreciation of, the development of the principles and practices of criminal responsibility over time, and in their connections to the institutions and traditions of systems of criminal law.

In the second step of my analysis, I develop a new account of the role of criminal responsibility. I argue that criminal responsibility organises key sets of relations as relations of responsibility that subtend criminal responsibility principles and practices. While criminal law is generally thought to concern relations between subjects (archetypally, individuals) and objects (harms, wrongs or crimes), I argue that criminal responsibility – something that is primarily an 'artefact' of the criminal law, as I discuss below – concerns relations between subjects (and the state). As the basis on which individuals are called to account under criminal law, and the form or structure of the law, criminal responsibility delineates relations between subjects, and plots these relations as relations of responsibility. As such, criminal responsibility concerns the 'people' of criminal law and provides access to the 'social life' of criminal law. This account of the role of criminal responsibility exposes its complexity and dynamism, substituting the still-dominant understanding of criminal responsibility as singular, general and universal, for an understanding characterised by multiplicity, specificity and variation across time and across the criminal law field. Recognising that criminal responsibility organises relations of responsibility reveals that it is the way in which subjectivity, relationality and power make themselves felt in particular ways in criminal law.

Relations of responsibility encompass the individual in relation to him- or herself, to other individuals and to the state, the state in relation to the self and individuals and various permutations of these relations. In my explication of this account, I set out these relations of responsibility via a tripartite schema of self, others and the state. This schema is a heuristic device that permits me to examine the different sets of relations organised under criminal responsibility. As I show, relations of responsibility change over space and time, taking shape in the context of particular systems of criminal law and at particular times. My new account of the role and significance of criminal responsibility emerges out of, and contributes to, the critical criminal responsibility scholarship: it offers both a way of understanding and a basis for critique of criminal responsibility, opening the way for the theoretical analysis of relations of responsibility that is offered in Part III of this book.

This chapter has two main parts. In the first part, I assess existing criminal responsibility scholarship. In the second part of the chapter, I develop my new account of the role of criminal responsibility, focusing on each of the nodes of my tripartite schema of relations of responsibility. Each node of my schema is closely connected to the others, but, as I discuss below, at different points in this book, I foreground either self, others or the state in my analysis.

Three Accounts of Criminal Responsibility

In the scholarly field, criminal responsibility is regarded as significant in three main ways, arising from its normative, symbolic and functional role in the criminal law.

Criminal Responsibility as the Normative Heart of the Criminal Law

The first account of the role of criminal responsibility centres on the idea that it is the normative heart of the criminal law. As such, criminal responsibility connects the criminal law to moral norms about responsibility, and provides the basis of the moral condemnation that comes along with criminal sanction. This is the dominant account of criminal responsibility in the current era, and a number of scholars subscribe to it.

The idea that criminal responsibility is the normative heart of the criminal law is sustained by a perceived connection between criminal law and morality. Specifically, this idea connects legal responsibility and moral responsibility, legal wrongs and moral wrongs, and legal blaming practices and moral blaming practices, with criminal law understood as a system of official censure and sanction or punishment for certain types of conduct.[2] Here, morality is conceived of as independent of both legal and social practices.[3] On this account, the structure of moral wrongdoing – requiring both harm and fault – is carried over to the criminal law.[4] Indeed, on this view, criminal responsibility is derivative of moral practices of calling individuals to account for their conduct. Thus, on this basis, the application of the ordinary principles of liability and punishment – the standard criminal law practices of evaluation, attribution and blame – is taken to be an acknowledgement or affirmation of an individual's ('normal') status as a moral subject. For instance, for John Gardner, criminal responsibility is being able to offer an account of oneself as a rational being, where such account-giving is instantiated in the legal process.[5] As this suggests, the main focus is the 'nature' or conception of criminal responsibility, which brackets off its contextual or

[2] See A. Ashworth and J. Horder, *Principles of Criminal Law*, 7th ed. (Oxford: Oxford University Press, 2013), p. 1.

[3] P. Cane, *Responsibility in Law and Morality* (Oxford: Hart Publishing, 2002), p. 2.

[4] L. Farmer, *Making the Modern Criminal Law: Criminalization and Civil Order. Series: Criminalization* (Oxford: Oxford University Press, 2016), pp. 108–9 (in relation to Andrew Ashworth's work on criminal law, which Farmer analyses as 'neo-classical criminal law').

[5] See J. Gardner, 'The Mark of Responsibility' (2003) 23(2) *Oxford Journal of Legal Studies* 157–71, 166–8.

purposive aspects.[6] And, although understood as embedded in particular legal practices, on this account, criminal responsibility gains meaning from outside the legal realm, in the moral realm, as an aspect of the moral or ethical dimension of individual human and collective life.

This account of criminal responsibility brings along with it a particular perspective on the legal subject. The individual is the archetypal legal subject: he or she occupies a pre-eminent place in criminal law and scholarly thinking about criminal law,[7] and is regarded as a 'basic unit of legal analysis and blame attribution',[8] assumed to exist prior to law. As the archetypal legal subject, the individual is a particular kind of self – an autonomous rational agent – an idea that has a long philosophical pedigree.[9] Grounded in the belief that reason and responsibility are essential aspects of being human, and reflecting the wider liberal-philosophical tradition valorising the individual, it is this agent focus that accounts for the construction of criminal responsibility as comprising an accused's conduct (*actus reus*) and his or her mental state (*mens rea*).[10] As Alan Norrie argues, the construction of criminal responsibility across *actus reus* and *mens rea* is treated as mapping onto a distinction between categories of individual responsibility which are both universal and abstract, and, at the same time, which constitute substantive moral categories.[11] This construction trains the scholarly lens on the 'fundamental aspects of *human agency*' – moral, cognitive and volitional – that an individual must have to be held responsible via criminal processes.[12] Thus, in the terms Victor Tadros uses in his analysis of criminal responsibility, the ascription of criminal responsibility should be dependent on the accused's status as an agent – agent *qua* agent – such that conduct should only be attributed to him or her when it is connected in a proper way to his or her character.[13]

In addition to connecting criminal law to moral norms, this account of the role of criminal responsibility also connects criminal law to liberal political precepts. That is, this account links criminal responsibility to a liberal-political subjectivity that, as Farmer argues, is conceived of as prior to law.[14] This account

[6] N. Lacey, 'Jurisprudence, History and the Institutional Quality of Law' (2015) 101 *Virginia Law Review* 919–45, 939.

[7] N. Lacey, 'Philosophical Foundations of the Common Law: Social Not Metaphysical', in J. Horder (ed.), *Oxford Essays in Jurisprudence* (Oxford: Oxford University Press, 2000), pp. 17, 25.

[8] N. Naffine, 'Human Agents in Criminal Law and Its Scholarship' (2011) 35 *Criminal Law Journal* 51–6, 53.

[9] See N. Naffine, *Law's Meaning of Life: Philosophy, Religion, Darwin and the Legal Person* (London: Hart Publishing, 2009), pp. 64–5 (identifying Immanuel Kant as exercising a powerful influence on legal thinking about the person).

[10] Cane, *Responsibility in Law and Morality*, pp. 4, 49.

[11] See A. Norrie, *Punishment, Responsibility and Justice: A Relational Critique* (Oxford: Oxford University Press, 2000), ch. 2.

[12] N. Lacey, 'Responsibility and Modernity in Criminal Law' (2001) 9(3) *Journal of Political Philosophy* 249–76, 255 (emphasis in original).

[13] See generally V. Tadros, *Criminal Responsibility* (Oxford: Oxford University Press, 2005).

[14] Farmer, *Making the Modern Criminal Law*, pp. 163, 170.

is thought to foster the kind of minimalist criminal law that is most appropriate for liberal-political economic and social systems. Thus, as Antony Duff explains in his analysis of responsibility as answerability, the 'common life' of the polity of citizens for whom the criminal law exists is structured by 'core liberal values such as autonomy, freedom, privacy and pluralism'.[15] This commitment to liberal political precepts puts the individual in a particular kind of relationship with the state: as Thomas Green argues, in contemporary criminal jurisprudence, there is a close relationship between 'the individual's internalization of freedom and his external freedom-based relationship to the state'.[16] This means that criminal responsibility is taken to assume a relation with individuals which seeks to maximise their freedom from interference by the state, and in which the individual experiences himself or herself as free. As a result, criminal responsibility operates as a limit on the criminal law and the power of the state: it creates a space beyond which criminal law is inappropriate or illegitimate, on the basis that it exceeds the boundaries of a liberal legal system and impermissibly impinges on the sovereign self.

Drawing a connection between both moral conceptions of responsibility and individual responsibility for crime, and liberal political precepts and criminal responsibility, this account of the role of criminal responsibility has two main effects. First, in order to respect freedom of action and treat individuals as agents, subjective fault – the idea that 'harmful wrongs or wrongful harms consist centrally in culpable conduct' (such as intention or subjective recklessness) – becomes the cardinal mode of responsibility attribution.[17] By contrast, for some scholars who subscribe to this account of the role of criminal responsibility, objective forms of fault such as negligence liability (which is referenced to the standard of the reasonable person), and strict liability (with only a limited or non-existent fault requirement[18]), are criticised as anomalous as they do not centre on individual will, and are said to be justifiable only in relation to less serious offences, on policy grounds, if at all.[19] Second, in functioning to connect criminal law to liberal political precepts, this account of the role of criminal responsibility reduces the question of responsibility for

[15] R. A. Duff, *Answering for Crime: Responsibility and Liability in the Criminal Law* (London: Hart Publishing, 2007), p. 11.

[16] T. A. Green, *Freedom and Criminal Responsibility in American Legal Thought* (Cambridge: Cambridge University Press, 2014), p. 265. Green's analysis is oriented around American criminal jurisprudence. I discuss Green's work in detail in Chapter 1.

[17] Farmer, *Making the Modern Criminal Law*, p. 164; see also Naffine, 'Human Agents in Criminal Law', 53–4.

[18] In Australian criminal law, strict liability has a distinctive meaning, and what is referred to by English and North American scholars as strict liability is known as absolute liability (offences with no *mens rea* element): see *He Kaw Teh* v. *The Queen* (1985) 157 CLR 523 and discussion in Chapter 5.

[19] Objective forms of fault are not marginalised in all scholarly work falling into this camp: see, e.g., Ashworth and Horder, *Principles of Criminal Law*, ch. 1; H. L. A. Hart, *Punishment and Responsibility: Essays in the Philosophy of Law*, 2nd ed. (Oxford: Oxford University Press, 2008).

crime to the issue of the justification of punishment: justifying state punishment via the idea of the responsible subject of law. On this account, criminal responsibility is able to be constraining on the general level and enabling on the particular level, acting both as a constraint on the scope of the criminal law as a whole *and* as justifying state punishment of an individual. As Farmer writes, the conviction that the concept of *mens rea* may be used to limit the reach of the criminal law focuses on 'fairness of attribution and punishment' in particular instances, displacing 'political questions of state power or criminal *justice*, onto individual fairness'.[20] I return to this point below.

The correspondence between both moral conceptions of responsibility and liberal political precepts, and criminal responsibility, is weaker or stronger in the work of different scholars subscribing to this account of the role of criminal responsibility. Michael Moore's scholarship represents something of the epitome of the account of the role of criminal responsibility as the normative heart of the criminal law. For Moore, legal liability must track moral responsibility and moral responsibility consists of culpability or blameworthiness.[21] It is on this basis that Moore rejects liability without fault.[22] As Lacey points out, approaching criminal responsibility as mapped onto moral responsibility means that such constructions of criminal liability can be dismissed as fundamentally mistaken.[23] Indeed, this is necessary because, reflecting the Kantian moral philosophical tradition, responsibility is regarded as 'a fundamental human characteristic', and so we are only responsible for 'conduct which is a "free" expression of our will'.[24] In Moore's words, 'our desert is determined by what we can control'.[25] Moore's approach to criminal responsibility is intimately connected to his approach to state punishment. As a retributivist – adhering to the idea that responsibility is a moral property of individuals and that punishment should be based on desert – Moore holds that punishment for wrongdoing is deserved, and imposing punishment for crime represents a way of respecting individuals.[26] Moore argues that culpability is necessary for desert, while wrongdoing influences how much punishment is deserved.[27]

20 Farmer, *Making the Modern Criminal Law*, p. 195 (emphasis in original). As Farmer points out, this approach to responsibility is an instance of a wider issue in criminal law theory, in which justification of the scope of the criminal law (criminalisation) is understood in terms of the justification of punishment (p. 170).

21 See, e.g., M. S. Moore, *Placing Blame: A General Theory of the Criminal Law* (Oxford: Clarendon Press, 1997), p. 192.

22 Moore, *Placing Blame*, ch. 5.

23 N. Lacey, *In Search of Criminal Responsibility: Ideas, Interests, and Institutions* (Oxford: Oxford University Press, 2016), p. 5 (discussing Michael Moore).

24 See Cane, *Responsibility in Law and Morality*, p. 23.

25 Moore, *Placing Blame*, p. 196.

26 On retributivism, see D. Dolinko, 'Punishment', in J. Deigh and D. Dolinko (eds.), *The Oxford Handbook of Philosophy of Criminal Law* (Oxford: Oxford University Press, 2011), pp. 412–17; R. A. Duff, *Punishment, Communication, and Community* (Oxford: Oxford University Press, 2001), ch. 1.

27 Moore, *Placing Blame*, p. 193.

As this indicates, Moore's account of responsibility in criminal law is the corollary of his belief in retributivism as the basis for state punishment.

The idea that criminal responsibility is significant because it forms the normative heart of the criminal law is the dominant account of criminal responsibility in the current era. This dominance reflects the profound influence of the legal-philosophical scholarly tradition on the study of criminal responsibility.[28] Here, I use the term legal-philosophical in a broad way to denote the type of criminal law scholarship inspired by normative philosophical thinking. In this tradition, criminal responsibility is understood in terms of fidelity and non-fidelity to principles, as either principled or non- or unprincipled.[29] As Ngaire Naffine writes, this scholarly tradition is marked by 'the search for enduring universal principles', and the pursuit of correspondence between the criminal law and moral notions of harm and wrong.[30] It is on this basis that scholars working in this tradition critique certain features of modern systems of criminal law such as their expansive scope.[31] As this indicates, in this tradition there is a 'proper' or ideal criminal law, delimited in scope and depth. This raises genuine questions about precisely what these theoretical accounts are accounts *of*.[32] It is clear that a number of parts of positive criminal laws are excluded from these accounts, as, faced with undesirable aspects of systems of criminal law, scholars have retreated to the security of 'an ideal account of the law'.[33] This ideal account has generated a particular gloss on criminal responsibility, which is more connected to abstract moral and political norms rather than to institutions and traditions of criminal law.[34]

Although it is now dominant, the legal-philosophical approach to criminal law scholarship developed relatively recently. Legal-philosophical approaches to the study of criminal law have risen to prominence only in the second half of the twentieth century. In England, there was comparatively little new criminal

[28] For critical discussion of this influence, see N. Lacey, 'Institutionalising Responsibility: Implications for Jurisprudence' (2013) 4(1) *Jurisprudence* 1–19; see also A. Loughnan, 'Historicizing Criminal Responsibility', in C. Flanders and Z. Hoskins (eds.), *The New Philosophy of Criminal Law* (Lanham, MD: Rowman & Littlefield, 2015).

[29] See, e.g., A. P. Simester and S. Shute, 'On the General Part in Criminal Law', in S. Shute and A. P. Simester (eds.), *Criminal Law Theory: Doctrines of the General Part* (Oxford: Oxford University Press, 2002) (discussing 'derogation' from the doctrines comprising 'the general part' of criminal law).

[30] See N. Naffine, 'Criminal Conversations: Farmer, Lacey and the New Social Scholarship' (2016) 38(4) *Sydney Law Review* 505–17, 506.

[31] See, e.g., Ashworth and Horder, *Principles of Criminal Law*, ch. 2; D. Husak, *Overcriminalization: The Limits of the Criminal Law* (Oxford: Oxford University Press, 2008); for critique, see N. Lacey, 'Historicising Criminalisation: Conceptual and Empirical Issues' (2009) 72(6) *Modern Law Review* 936–60.

[32] See Lacey, 'Institutionalising Responsibility', 10–11.

[33] Farmer, *Making the Modern Criminal Law*, p. 302.

[34] Claes Lernestedt comments that, as a result of the tendency in criminal law scholarship towards abstract theorising, it is possible to see 'greater resemblance' between 'criminal law systems' produced by legal scholars in different jurisdictions than between the work of each of the scholars and the national systems that he or she is writing about: C. Lernestedt, 'Vertical, Horizontal, Backwards, Forwards' (2017) 4(1) *Critical Analysis of Law* 22–30, 30.

law scholarship in the first half of the twentieth century.[35] In the decades prior to the mid-twentieth century, law was yet to acquire robust academic credibility within the English university system: this circumscribed the possibilities for jurisprudence or theorising about law, more tightly than in the United States, for instance, where the legal realism movement was developing at this time, and law had had a firm place in the university system since the end of the nineteenth century.[36] In England, in the second half of the twentieth century, jurisprudence experienced a heyday, with, prominently, the scholarly work of H. L. A. Hart at Oxford, revitalising the tradition of analytical jurisprudence that continues to dominate in English language legal theory in the current era.[37] As Hart's high profile suggests, the profound influence of the legal-philosophical tradition on the study of criminal responsibility also reflects the part played by particular institutions (most notably, the University of Oxford) in the development of criminal law scholarship.[38] In Chapter 1, I suggested that the rise of the legal-philosophical approach to criminal law theory from the middle of the twentieth century is treated as something of a caesura – the end of the history of criminal responsibility and the beginning of its present – and effectively extends out the current era without sufficient attention to change within this time period.

The account of the role of criminal responsibility as the normative heart of the criminal law rests on a thin or minimal appreciation of the development of responsibility principles and practices over time. In keeping with the philosophical tenor of legal-philosophical scholarly work, the development over time of the relevant responsibility principles and practices is not the subject of express consideration.[39] To the extent that change over time is recognised, criminal responsibility is assumed to have been subject to gradual refinement towards an ever more perfect realisation, an account of criminal responsibility that is framed by a 'very particular, teleological model of historical development'.[40] As Lacey argues, this sort of account assumes

[35] See further L. Farmer, 'The Modest Ambition of Glanville Williams', in M. D. Dubber (ed.), *Foundational Texts in Modern Criminal Law* (Oxford: Oxford University Press, 2014).

[36] See N. Duxbury, 'English Jurisprudence Between Austin and Hart' (2005) 91(1) *Virginia Law Review* 1–91. As Duxbury notes, law faculties only emerged in England from the 1950s, and until this point, English jurisprudence was written with the legal practitioner in mind.

[37] On H. L. A. Hart, see H. L. A. Hart, *The Concept of Law*, 3rd ed. (Oxford: Oxford University Press, 2012 [first published 1961]); Hart, *Punishment and Responsibility: Essays in the Philosophy of Law*; see also N. Lacey, *A Life of H. L. A. Hart: The Nightmare and the Noble Dream* (Oxford: Oxford University Press, 2006). On the history of English jurisprudence, see Duxbury, 'English Jurisprudence Between Austin and Hart'.

[38] See D. Sugarman, '"A Hatred of Disorder": Legal Science, Liberalism and Imperialism', in P. Fitzpatrick (ed.), *Dangerous Supplements: Resistance and Renewal in Jurisprudence* (London: Pluto Press, 1991), pp. 52–5.

[39] Tadros goes so far as to argue that holding individuals to account for their conduct is a universal principle, in effect, an ahistorical constant: see Tadros, *Criminal Responsibility*, pp. 5–8; for critique, Farmer, *Making the Modern Criminal Law*, pp. 164–5.

[40] Lacey, *In Search of Criminal Responsibility*, p. 8.

that a core idea of responsibility exists through time and space, transcending major changes in criminal law, and social and other discourses about responsibility.[41] At the same time as being largely ahistorical, this account of criminal responsibility is a-contextual: philosophical accounts are not really 'located' in time and space, in a set of institutions and a body of law as they exist at a particular juncture and in a particular jurisdiction. As I discussed in Chapter 1, this sort of approach fails to take the influence of space and time on criminal responsibility sufficiently seriously, obscuring the differences in the social and political contexts of criminal responsibility practices, and discounting the importance of change over time.

For my purposes in assessing the criminal responsibility scholarly field, what is crucial is the overall impact of this account of the role of criminal responsibility: it generates a unitary story of responsibility in criminal law in which it underpins the coherence and rationality of criminal law. This story is marked by both generality and universalism: criminal responsibility is thought to be general in that it underpins the corpus of the law as a whole, and universal in that it applies to all individuals charged with criminal offences. Evidence given in support of this story includes the firm imprint of the distinction between offence and defence, and conduct and fault, on the structure of criminal law, and widespread acceptance of the idea that, as a matter of principle, crime is any act that can be committed by any actor. Overall, on this account, criminal responsibility allows the criminal law to be measured against itself. In Farmer's words, criminal responsibility has become central to 'the law's reflexive account of itself', that is, to the criminal legal story about the criminal law.[42] I return to this point below.

Criminal Responsibility as Serving the Coordination and Legitimation Needs of Criminal Law

The second account of the role of criminal responsibility revolves around its coordinating and legitimating function in criminal law. This account has been developed by Nicola Lacey in a body of work undertaken over several years.[43] Proceeding in a more critical vein than the legal-philosophical scholarship referred to above, Lacey's analysis starts on the basis that criminal legal scholars must ask not just what criminal responsibility 'is', but what it is 'for' – a question that exposes its centrality to criminal law as a system of regulation – a system

[41] Ibid., pp. 8–9.

[42] L. Farmer, 'The Obsession with Definition: The Nature of Crime and Critical Legal Theory' (1996) 5 *Social & Legal Studies* 57–73, 68.

[43] See, e.g., N. Lacey, 'In Search of the Responsible Subject: History, Philosophy and Social Sciences in Criminal Law Theory' (2001) 64(3) *Modern Law Review* 350–71; Lacey, 'Responsibility and Modernity in Criminal Law'; Lacey, *In Search of Criminal Responsibility*.

governing individual and group behaviour, and structuring the interaction of people and systems.[44] This leads Lacey to argue that criminal responsibility serves a coordinating and legitimating function, providing a symbolic resource for the criminal legal system, enabling it to be regarded as a system of justice, rather than one of sheer force.[45]

Lacey argues that the significance of criminal responsibility arises from its 'distinctive structural roles in legitimating and coordinating patterns and practices of criminalization understood as a form of social regulation'.[46] In Lacey's account, legitimation concerns the justification of calling individuals and others to account via criminal process, while coordination concerns what information must be marshalled in the service of that legitimated practice of calling to account.[47] For Lacey, criminal responsibility, which is usually thought of solely as a legitimating concept, must be understood in its context, that is, in the context of criminalisation, which is usually thought of as a positive concept shaped by power and interests.[48] As this suggests, Lacey's analysis is based on the idea that normative concepts are shaped by their given institutional and political context, and the practical or regulatory role of the criminal law.[49] In her words, 'criminal responsibility ... is an idea which is located within a social practice of criminalization, which itself is necessarily located within an institutional framework and structured by the imperatives of legitimation and coordination'.[50]

In her analysis, Lacey assesses the coordinating and legitimating functions of criminal responsibility under a tripartite frame – ideas, interests and institutions – which are aspects of the environment that have shaped the changing 'conceptual contours' and roles of criminal responsibility over time.[51] First, in relation to ideas, Lacey argues that there are four main concepts or principles of responsibility attribution operative across criminal law, which are the basis on which individuals are held to account for crimes via the criminal law. The four concepts are: capacity (which stands for concern with agency, choice and individual autonomy), outcome (which concerns the social harms produced by crime), character (which entails an 'evaluation or estimation of the quality of the defendant's [manifested or assumed] disposition as distinct from his or her conduct'), and risk (where risk is

[44] See Lacey, *In Search of Criminal Responsibility*, pp. 178–9, and pp. 178–85 more generally.
[45] Lacey, *In Search of Criminal Responsibility*, pp. 19–20, 137.
[46] Ibid., p. 13.
[47] Ibid., p. 25.
[48] Ibid., p. 15.
[49] Ibid., pp. 15–16.
[50] Ibid., p. 190.
[51] Ibid., pp. 2–3, and, more generally, ch. 1. For Lacey, each of these intersect with each other and must be considered together.

calculated in clinical or actuarial terms).[52] Second, in relation to interests – 'the prevailing structures of power and their dynamics' – Lacey argues that changes in patterns of interests and power have had 'decisive' consequences for doctrines and practices of criminal law.[53] According to Lacey, the distribution of economic and political power (and legislation's domination over common law), cultural and symbolic power and the growth of professions (in particular the legal profession) and the media have all impacted on the attribution of responsibility in criminal law. And third, in relation to institutions, which include the political system, economic institutions and the legal system, Lacey argues that they also have a crucial influence on legal principles and practices because they are the means through which the legitimation and coordination roles of criminal responsibility are realised.[54]

Taking into account the influence of interests and institutions, Lacey tracks changes in ideas about criminal responsibility (responsibility attribution) over time, examining the ascendance and descendance of the different bases on which individuals may be held responsible. She identifies four 'configurations of responsibility' in play over the period from the early eighteenth century to the early twenty-first century: the dominance of responsibility attribution based on character in the eighteenth century; the partial eclipse of character and the gradual realisation of capacity responsibility in the nineteenth century; criminal law divided between capacity and outcome responsibility from the early twentieth century; and a 'further pluralisation' of patterns of responsibility attribution in the late twentieth century and the early twenty-first century.[55] As this indicates, notwithstanding the 'ideological salience' it currently enjoys, subjective or capacity responsibility developed as an institutionalised practice later than criminal law scholars typically assume, and it shares the field with other bases for responsibility attribution.[56]

As this overview shows, Lacey's account of the role and significance of criminal responsibility rests on a broader and more historicised understanding of responsibility in criminal law than that underpinning the accounts of it as the normative heart of the criminal law. In her account, the scholarly lens extends beyond conceptions of criminal responsibility (the 'nature' of criminal responsibility), to include responsibility ascription practices and the wider

52 See Lacey, *In Search of Criminal Responsibility*, ch. 1; see also N. Lacey, 'Space, Time and Function: Intersecting Principles of Responsibility Across the Terrain of Criminal Justice' (2007) 1(3) *Criminal Law and Philosophy* 233–50; N. Lacey, 'The Resurgence of Character: Responsibility in the Context of Criminalization', in R. A. Duff and S. Green (eds.), *Philosophical Foundations of Criminal Law* (Oxford: Oxford University Press, 2011), pp. 153–5.

53 Lacey, *In Search of Criminal Responsibility*, pp. 2, 79.

54 Ibid., p. 107.

55 See Lacey, *In Search of Criminal Responsibility*, ch. 5.

56 N. Lacey, 'Character, Capacity, Outcome: Towards a Framework for Assessing the Shifting Pattern of Criminal Responsibility in Modern English Law', in M. D. Dubber and L. Farmer (eds.), *Modern Histories of Crime and Punishment* (Stanford: Stanford University Press, 2007), p. 17.

processes of evaluation and adjudication of individuals under criminal process. As a result, criminal responsibility encompasses the 'set of institutional arrangements' by which rules, doctrines and practices are put into operation.[57] This leads Lacey to take into account practices not typically included in studies of criminal responsibility – notably, pre-trial practices such as policing and prosecution, and post-trial practice such as sentencing – where she detects subtle changes over time in ideas about responsibility attribution.[58] Rather than reducing to the question of who is or who should be responsible, this broader understanding invites different kinds of responsibility questions, such as 'in what ways are individuals held responsible under criminal law?'; this opens the way for multiple responses, or responses which vary from one part of the law to the other, as well as over time.[59] Lacey is attentive to the development of criminal responsibility over time and her analysis of the role of criminal responsibility operates on two levels – as legal history and legal theory.[60]

Lacey's account of the role and significance of criminal responsibility represents a decisive break from the dominant legal-philosophical account of criminal responsibility, leading the field of critical criminal responsibility scholarship, referred to above. Lacey's analysis points to the importance of given social, political and institutional structures as conditions of possibility for the development of ideas about criminal responsibility. And this, in turn, indicates that criminal responsibility is marked by variability and change, as opposed to singularity, generality and universalism. This opens the possibility of exploring such variability and change beyond the scope of ascriptions of responsibility, Lacey's central focus, in relation to other aspects of criminal responsibility. I pick up on this, and other parts of Lacey's account, below.

Criminal Responsibility as a Platform for the Development of the Modern Criminal Law

The third account of the role of criminal responsibility is also mounted in a critical mode. In this account, developed by Lindsay Farmer, the significance of criminal responsibility flows from the role it has played in the development of the modern criminal law, and, by extension, the role of the modern criminal law in modern governance practices.[61] Farmer's account of criminal responsibility is part of a larger analysis of 'making the modern criminal law', which is

[57] Lacey, *In Search of Criminal Responsibility*, p. 1.
[58] Ibid., pp. 14–15.
[59] Ibid., p. 26.
[60] Lacey's account of the development of criminal responsibility principles and practices is connected to a wider methodological project, addressing the role that history and social science play in theorising law: see Lacey, 'Jurisprudence, History and the Institutional Quality of Law'; Lacey, 'Institutionalising Responsibility'.
[61] Farmer, *Making the Modern Criminal Law*, p. 165.

constructed around criminalisation, broadly, the scope of the law measured in terms of the conduct it proscribes. On his analysis, criminal responsibility is significant because, along with jurisdiction and codification, it has come to be 'central' to 'the modality or form of criminal law' – which is, for Farmer, 'facilitating relative peace and mutual trust between strangers' in complex modern societies, under 'the broad aim of securing civil order'.[62]

Rather than proceed in a legal-philosophical mode, by asking which principles should guide the determination of the appropriate reach and limits of the criminal law, Farmer engages with the prior question: 'how is it that the question of criminalization has come to be framed in these terms?'[63] As he writes, conventional criminal law theory presents a two-dimensional picture of the law – the problem of the attribution of responsibility (criminal responsibility) and the problem of the limits of the law (criminalisation) – and treats both problems as primarily ones of moral philosophy.[64] Like Lacey, Farmer seeks to connect these two problems and to rethink the *a priori* position of legal philosophy as the means by which to address them.[65] Farmer suggests that criminal responsibility should not be thought of as external, or prior, to the criminal law: rather, he argues that criminal responsibility is 'primarily a legal artefact', that is, a creature of the criminal law that is linked to 'the particular nature of civil order in modernity'.[66] This approach renders criminal responsibility less timeless (because it is connected to unchanging moral norms), and more time-sensitive, varying over time and space according to the particular emphases of civil order.

In Farmer's account, in the current era, criminal responsibility plays two different roles, each of which relates to the 'modality or form of the criminal law', and is connected to the other.[67] The first of these coalesces around legal subjectivity. For Farmer, criminal responsibility is the means of defining legal personhood, the issue of who is the proper subject of the law. As he argues, because the subject of the law is (constructed as) an autonomous rational individual, who is deemed to possess certain capacities and be capable of being guided by norms, he or she can be held accountable for his or her conduct in breaching those norms.[68] And, while the focus of most scholarly analysis of responsibility is on 'retrospective responsibility' – being responsible for past

[62] Ibid., pp. 165, 299. Following Neil MacCormick, Farmer understands the law as an institution, in a purposive way, conceptualising law not as 'a system of moral or social norms endowed with institutional existence' but as 'institutions that constitute legal norms' (p. 22).

[63] Farmer, *Making the Modern Criminal Law*, p. 1.

[64] Farmer, 'The Obsession with Definition', 59.

[65] Thus, like Lacey's, Farmer's analysis of criminal responsibility may be read as both a substantive and a methodological contribution to scholarly debates.

[66] Farmer, *Making the Modern Criminal Law*, p. 165.

[67] Ibid.

[68] Ibid., p. 168.

conduct (answerability or accountability) – 'prospective responsibility' is just as important (imposing obligations and duties on a person who can adapt their conduct to norms and plan over time).[69] For this reason, Farmer argues that an account of criminal responsibility must be just as concerned with 'the specification of roles and responsibilities in modern society' and with changing conceptions of personhood, as with attribution for past conduct.[70] When this forward-looking aspect of responsibility is taken into account, it becomes clear that criminal responsibility, 'a juridical model of the responsible person' – the individual, reasoning subject – corresponds to the modern conception of personhood, broadly, the idea of persons as proprietors of their own capacities.[71]

The second dimension of the role of criminal responsibility in Farmer's account coalesces around citizenship, or the relationship between the individual and the state. For Farmer, because, along with civil law, criminal law 'routinely articulates responsibilities and duties',[72] it is intimately linked to both the definition of modes of political organisation and to the legitimacy of the criminal law – which together encompass matters such as the criminalisation of certain conduct and the permission given for other types of conduct, and fairness in the definition of rules, the attribution of liability, at trial, and in punishment.[73] With reference to key criminal law authors of the second half of the twentieth century, Hart and Glanville Williams, and the development of the welfare state, Farmer argues that criminal responsibility has come to be linked to 'political liberty' in a 'complex way': 'social responsibilities specified by the state' have been recognised in law, but the individual is also thought to require protection against state power.[74] For Farmer, this more nuanced connection between criminal responsibility and 'political liberty' explains crucial twentieth-century developments, namely, the shift in the burden of proof to the state, and the critique of objective forms of liability.[75]

Bringing these two dimensions of the role of criminal responsibility together, Farmer argues that, while responsibility is 'primarily a legal artefact', it has shaped the substantive content of the criminal law – criminalisation – in a way that goes 'far beyond the idea of constraint' (which, as discussed above, is its role at the general level according to legal-philosophical accounts of responsibility).[76] With criminal responsibility representing a conceptual structure unique to the

[69] Ibid., p. 169.
[70] Ibid., pp. 169, 172.
[71] See J. F. Collier, B. Maurer and L. Suarez-Navaz, 'Sanctioned Identities: Legal Constructions of Modern Personhood' (1995) 2(1–2) *Identities: Global Studies in Culture and Power* 1–27 (in relation to what the authors call 'bourgeois law').
[72] Farmer, *Making the Modern Criminal Law*, p. 170.
[73] Ibid.
[74] Ibid., p. 187.
[75] Ibid.
[76] Ibid., pp. 165 and 164 respectively.

criminal law, it has been central to the growth of the criminal law in the modern period, performing a systematising function.[77] The role of criminal responsibility in the systematisation of the criminal law has been obscured in scholarship which has a 'narrow focus on form rather than function', and where responsibility is understood as primarily concerned with subjective fault and liability for punishment, rather than with the content of the law.[78] The emphasis on fault or blame means that the different types of conduct proscribed by the criminal law – the *actus reus* or external element of criminal offences – effectively disappear from view, ensuring that this account of criminal responsibility has the potential to underpin a wide range of criminal prohibitions (that is, a wide-ranging criminal law).[79] According to Farmer, 'responsibility must be understood [as] establishing rules and standards of conduct', and the development of the modern law must be understood as a process 'in which the specification of liability has tracked the growth of prospective responsibilities in the criminal law'.[80] That is, criminal responsibility has been a platform for the development of the modern criminal law.

Like Lacey, Farmer is attentive to the impact of change over time on criminal responsibility. Within his broad story about the centrality of criminal responsibility in the modern criminal law, Farmer identifies changes in ideas about responsibility. He traces the way in which responsibility developed from an idea that explained incapacity or exemptions from punishment in the eighteenth century, to a more inculpatory model, which encoded states of behaviour and different degrees of fault over the course of the nineteenth century, and then to an increasingly refined notion that 'closed the gap' between 'the presumed capacities of the legal subject and their actual psychological capacities' in the twentieth century.[81] In the current period, the subjective approach to criminal liability – according to which fault depends on what the accused intended or foresaw – has been consolidated.[82] At the same time, the capacity of the law to enforce 'social responsibilities' – in which individuals are held responsible for creating risk, and for the future consequences of conduct – has been extended, making 'individuals more responsible (or responsible for more)'.[83] Farmer notes that these recent developments are not inconsistent with each other, although there is a tension between them.[84] For Farmer, the

[77] Ibid., pp. 164, 170.

[78] Ibid., pp. 194, 196.

[79] See P. Ramsay, *The Insecurity State: Vulnerable Autonomy and the Right to Security in the Criminal Law* (Oxford: Oxford University Press, 2012), ch. 7.

[80] Farmer, *Making the Modern Criminal Law*, p. 196.

[81] Ibid., p. 182 and, more generally, pp. 171–85. As Farmer argues, this last step linked criminal responsibility to criminal procedure on the basis that guilt is the central condition of criminal liability (p. 183), and paved the way for consensus to build around the idea that strict liability was 'distinct and abnormal' while subjective liability was 'normal' (p. 185).

[82] Farmer, *Making the Modern Criminal Law*, pp. 189–90.

[83] Ibid., pp. 191–2.

[84] Ibid.

significance of these developments 'lies in the interaction between moral and social responsibilities, the extension of social responsibilities and moralized forms of criminal liability'.[85] I pick up on this point again below.

Farmer's account commands a broad approach to the study of criminal responsibility, and, like Lacey's account, presents a stimulus for further analysis. In particular, his account opens up the possibility that responsibility might look different in different corners of the criminal law, 'in relation to different areas or objects'.[86] This leads Farmer to suggest that criminal legal scholars think in terms of *responsibilities* rather than responsibility. In addition, Farmer's suggestion that the criminal law is properly 'a form of public law and a governmental project' helpfully shifts the focus from morality, desert and justification of punishment, to politics, power and the dynamics of social cooperation.[87] His account also opens up the issue of 'how the criminal law has interacted with other areas of law or forms of regulation'.[88] I return to these points below.

In different ways, these three accounts of the role of criminal responsibility help to explain the high profile of criminal responsibility in criminal law scholarship: criminal responsibility is not merely an object of scholarly attention, but a means of studying the criminal law.[89] These three accounts speak to each other, in that both Lacey's and Farmer's accounts incorporate some aspects of the dominant legal-philosophical approach to the role of criminal responsibility, but reinterpret it in various ways, as symbolic and functional as much as normative. This is not all there is to say on this topic. I argue that there is an additional aspect to the role of criminal responsibility to criminal law, and it is to this that I now turn.

A New Account of Criminal Responsibility: Relations of Responsibility

There is an aspect of the role of criminal responsibility that has been overlooked in existing scholarship. Criminal responsibility organises key sets of relations – between self, others and the state – as relations of responsibility.

[85] Ibid., p. 192.

[86] Ibid., p. 197.

[87] Ibid., p. 303 and L. Farmer, 'Making the Modern Criminal Law: A Response' (2017) 4(1) *Critical Analysis of Law* 53–60; see for discussion C. Kennedy, 'Lindsay Farmer: Making the Modern Criminal Law: Criminalization and Civil Order' (2017) 11 *Criminal Law and Philosophy* 637–44 (published online); V. Chiao, 'Making Modern Criminal Law Theory: Reflections on Farmer' (2017) 4(1) *Critical Analysis of Law* 1–10, 6–7; L. Kerr, 'The Legitimate Scope of the Criminal Law: A Question for Legal History?' (2017) 4(1) *Critical Analysis of Law* 11–21, 20–1.

[88] Farmer, *Making the Modern Criminal Law*, p. 29.

[89] See further A. Loughnan, 'The Meta-Significance of Criminal Responsibility' (2017) 4(1) *Critical Analysis of Law* 31–41.

As such, criminal responsibility is the means by which subjectivity, relationality and power make themselves felt in criminal law in particular ways. I argue that it is this aspect of criminal responsibility that makes it significant.

The Self in Relations of Responsibility

The self is at the centre of criminal responsibility, yet, in the dominant strain of responsibility scholarship, he or she is conceptualised in a limited or partial way. In the legal-philosophical tradition of criminal responsibility scholarship, and as discussed above, the self is an autonomous individual, understood in an abstract way, as a rational agent. This conceptualisation of the individual is both factual and normative: individuals are regarded as by nature rational subjects and it is thought they should be treated as if this is the case.[90] Based on this conception, responsibility for crime has been constructed in psychological terms, centred on this abstract entity that is abstracted from his or her social and political context.[91] This approach to criminal responsibility ensures that the individual, who is deemed to possess certain capacities and be capable of being guided by norms, can be held to account for his or her conduct in breaching those norms.[92] It also means that all individuals are able to be treated in the same way, with their situation varying only according to their own voluntary acts.[93] This kind of self is integral to the account of criminal responsibility as the normative heart of the criminal law, because it permits the moral condemnation of the individual convicted of crime, and it forms the basis of the unitary story of criminal responsibility – in which it underpins the coherence and rationality of the criminal law.

But there is more to the self: the self exists in context, and he or she has an embodied and material life, and is situated in relations with him or herself, others and the state. Taking my cue from the critical criminal responsibility scholarship, I approach the self or legal subject in this more fulsome way. This approach requires taking seriously various aspects of the contexts in which subjects are located, and acknowledging the relevance of social norms, institutions and practices for subjectivity. As Lacey's writes, a 'proper recognition of the social location of the individual' requires recognition of 'social context, social institutions, communities and cultures'.[94] On this view, subjects reflect (or, more strongly, are constituted by) the social practices, traditions and other markers of identity, such as gender, class, race, and ethnicity, that arise from

[90] Naffine, *Law's Meaning of Life*, p. 71.

[91] See Lacey, 'Character, Capacity, Outcome', p. 27.

[92] Farmer, *Making the Modern Criminal Law*, p. 168.

[93] See R. Cotterrell, *Sociological Jurisprudence: Juristic Thought and Social Inquiry* (London: Routledge, 2018), p. 160.

[94] N. Lacey, *Unspeakable Subjects: Feminist Essays in Legal and Social Theory* (Oxford: Hart Publishing, 1998), p. 67.

their position in the material world.[95] Locating the legal subject in his or her relations with others and the state acknowledges that, in Norrie's words, the legal subject is 'intrinsically connected to a social context'.[96] In what he labels a 'relational' critique of criminal responsibility, and grounded in the insights of social psychology, Norrie argues that responsibility 'exists both in and beyond individual moral agents at the same moment'.[97] As this suggests, recognising the individual as having an embodied and material existence, and locating him or her in his or her relations with others and the state, puts a more elaborate or 'fleshier' idea of the self at the centre of criminal responsibility.

This idea of the self or legal subject could be examined in different ways. In my exploration of the self as one node of a schema of relations of responsibility, I choose to explore the gendered self. In Chapter 6, with women's criminal responsibility as a focus, I analyse the relations of responsibility that structure women's responsibility for crime in distinct ways. I argue that, on the level of legal form, women's responsibility for crime is marked by particularity and specificity, as opposed to the generality and universalism claimed for criminal responsibility under the dominant legal-philosophical account, discussed above. This particularity and specificity is evident in the two sets of atypical responsibility forms – those forms that are restricted to particular individuals committing particular offences in particular contexts, and in which elements, such as offence and defence, conduct and fault, that are usually separate, are mixed together – that determine the contours of women's responsibility for crime. These two sets of atypical responsibility forms denote different relations of responsibility between self, others and the state. As I discuss in Chapter 6, over the twentieth century, changing ideas about violence by women and against women have given rise to different relations of responsibility, according to which the individual is positioned differently in relation to herself, others and the state.

Viewing the self in relations of responsibility exposes hitherto occluded dimensions of criminal responsibility. This focus reveals the particular ways in which legal subjectivity impacts criminal law. In advance of the full discussion of women's responsibility for crime provided in Chapter 6, it is possible to point to two illustrations from my analysis. First, as I show, the atypical responsibility

[95] See for discussion G. Lloyd, 'Individuals, Responsibility and the Philosophical Imagination', in C. Mackenzie and N. Stoljar (eds.), *Relational Autonomy: Feminist Perspectives on Autonomy, Agency, and the Social Self* (Oxford: Oxford University Press, 2000), p. 112.

[96] Norrie, *Punishment, Responsibility and Justice*, p. 80.

[97] Norrie, *Punishment, Responsibility and Justice*, p. 14. According to Norrie, because there is a dialectical relation between the personal and the social, both the legal subject and the process of blaming must be conceived of in relational terms (p. 202). This in turn means that moral judgments are 'ambivalent', as they involve recognition that social and structural factors, as well as individual agency, cause crime (pp. 220–1); for critical discussion, see M. D. Dubber, 'Alan W. Norrie Punishment Responsibility and Justice: A Relational Critique' (2002) 65(2) *Modern Law Review* 309–11.

forms of infanticide and diminished responsibility construct women as having a distinctive type of criminal responsibility: as partially exculpatory (and partially inculpatory), these provisions have been sustained by the notion that the homicidal woman herself is a victim – of her mental distress and her circumstances – and a less than fully rational subject of the law. As such, my focus reveals how criminal responsibility is connected to 'the formation and re-formation of social subjectivity' over time.[98] Second, my analysis reveals the influence of public and political debates on legal subjectivity. In part as a result of the public and political discourses relating to women's responsibility for crime – particularly what has become a strong societal and moral condemnation of violence against women – women's responsibility for crime concerns a distinctive conjunction of 'the specification of roles and responsibilities in modern society' to which Farmer refers.[99] As such, my focus opens up a way of exploring what Farmer calls 'the interaction between moral and social responsibilities', which, as he argues, is just as significant as 'retrospective responsibility', although it has received far less attention.[100]

Others in Relations of Responsibility

Just as the self at the centre of criminal responsibility principles and practices is an abstract and abstracted individual, so he or she is typically treated in isolation from others, and as acting alone in committing criminal conduct. Where the subject is an individual moral agent, the harm or wrong in question is ascribed to him or her alone, and 'the grounds for holding the subject accountable, consists primarily in facts about that subject'.[101] This approach reflects the pre-eminent status of the individual (and individual agency) in liberal-political philosophy, as discussed above. Thus, for Duff, the focus of the legal-philosophical scholarly work on criminal responsibility is on 'the individual responsibility of individual agents' because 'the responsibilities of individual agents in relation to what they do as individuals' 'must be, for liberal theorists, central to an understanding of criminal responsibility'.[102] As this suggests, and in Alice Ristroph's words, 'responsibility is a matter of agency, but the only agent visible to most theories of criminal responsibility is the wrongdoer herself'.[103]

[98] See M. Valverde, 'As If Subjects Existed: Analyzing Social Discourses' (1991) 28(2) *Canadian Review of Sociology and Anthropology* 173–87, 173.

[99] Farmer, *Making the Modern Criminal Law*, pp. 169, 172.

[100] Ibid., p. 192.

[101] C. Kutz, *Complicity: Ethics and Law for a Collective Age* (Cambridge: Cambridge University Press, 2007), p. 4.

[102] Duff, *Answering for Crime*, p. 18.

[103] See A. Ristroph, 'Responsibility for the Criminal Law', in A. Duff and P. Green (eds.), *Philosophical Foundations of Criminal Law* (Oxford: Oxford University Press, 2011), p. 109; see also L. Farmer, *Criminal Law, Tradition and Legal Order: Crime and the Genius of Scots Law, 1747 to the Present* (Cambridge: Cambridge University Press, 1997), p. 181; Naffine, 'Human Agents in Criminal Law'.

Where relations between individuals, or selves and others, are taken into account in the context of criminal responsibility, it tends to be within a circumscribed subspace of criminal responsibility scholarship – that concerned with complicity or participation in crime. Complicity involves more than one individual in the commission of an offence (through joint perpetration or some form of assistance), and, because it brings with it the potential to significantly expand the scope of the criminal law, it generates significant scholarly criticism.[104] Responsibility scholars examining complicity analyse the extent and nature of participation required for liability, the mental state required by participants, and what justifies or excuses participation.[105] But, even here, shared responsibility tends to be understood in individualistic terms, with the focus on an individual's will rather than the relations between a perpetrator and others.[106] As part of a sophisticated legal-philosophical analysis of responsibility for collective action, Christopher Kutz develops what he calls a 'relational and positional' account of responsibility: for Kutz, although they have been elided in moral philosophy, relationships between agents and respondents (those who are being called to account and those to whom they account) give meaning and value to responsibility, and responsibility structures those relationships and the individuals within them.[107] This leads Kutz to develop a participatory conception of collective action, centred on the individual's intention to play a part in a collective act.[108]

Individuals' relations with others impact criminal responsibility beyond the bounds of complicity, however, even if this is not apparent or taken into account by scholars.[109] Working on the basis that law routinely structures relations, in my analysis of others as one node of my schema of relations of responsibility, I choose to focus on individuals in otherwise ordinary relations with each other. This leads me to focus on the offence of consorting – broadly, the offence of association with criminals – which implicates individuals in their relations with each other. I suggest that, under consorting, the individual becomes meaningful to the criminal law in his or her relations with others, whereby that individual's conduct with, and knowledge of, the other are the basis for the offence. As I discuss in Chapter 7, in my analysis, consorting laws fall into two generations, and relations of responsibility – between self, others

104 See, e.g., M. Dyson, 'Shorn-Off Complicity' (2016) 75(2) *The Cambridge Law Journal* 196–9.

105 See, e.g., J. G. Stewart, 'Complicity', in M. D. Dubber and T. Hörnle (eds.), *The Oxford Handbook of Criminal Law* (New York: Oxford University Press, 2014).

106 Kutz, *Complicity*, p. 4 and more generally ch. 1.

107 Kutz, *Complicity*, pp. 10, 64. Kutz uses the term 'accountability' to distinguish the normative, external affiliations and duties of an agent to other agents from the psychological competencies a person must have to be answerable for harm ('responsibility'), arguing that the former is 'fundamentally relational' and the latter 'nonrelational' (pp. 17–18).

108 Kutz, *Complicity*, ch. 3.

109 See J. Nedelsky, 'Reconceiving Rights as Relationship' (1993) 1(1) *Review of Constitutional Studies* 1–26, 14.

and the state – fall into two corresponding archetypal patterns. While under the first generation of laws, relations of responsibility reinforced existing, highly stratified social relations, in the second generation of laws, relations of responsibility assume a standardised structure, in which all individuals are brought into the same relation with each other and the state. As I suggest, this relation now looks like 'friendship' – with the responsibility individuals bear to the state equated with their responsibility to each other.

My analysis of others in relations of responsibility focuses on the proscription of the conduct of those others, and, as such, it might be thought to be more concerned with criminalisation than with criminal responsibility. As mentioned above, criminal responsibility is typically set apart from criminalisation, with conventional criminal law theory presenting a two-dimensional picture of the law – the problem of the attribution of responsibility (criminal responsibility) and the problem of the limits of the law (criminalisation).[110] But this neat juxtaposition belies a messy reality, and criminal responsibility is closely connected to criminalisation. On one level, as Peter Cane argues, 'without a catalogue of crimes, the concept of *criminal* responsibility has no meaning or content'.[111] On another level, in relation to the development of the law, reliance on strict liability – as a form of liability in which individual fault has an extremely limited role – has been a chief ingredient in the massive expansion of the criminal law since the post-World War II period.[112] And, on my analysis of the two generations of consorting laws, examining others in relation reveals the connections between criminal responsibility and criminalisation, as the proscription of conduct affects relations of responsibility.

Viewing others in relations of responsibility reveals previously obscured aspects of criminal responsibility. It exposes the particular ways relationality – broadly, the interconnectedness of individuals and others – impacts criminal law. This approach opens criminal responsibility up to the different significance of others, and to the idea that humans take their being in part through relations with others.[113] Like the analysis of the self in relation, it exposes the relevance of criminal responsibility for sociality or social relations, the realm of

[110] Farmer, 'The Obsession with Definition', 59.

[111] Cane, *Responsibility in Law and Morality*, p. 54 (emphasis in original). As Cane points out, the distinction between criminal responsibility and what counts as a crime underlies the distinction between the 'general' and the 'special' parts of criminal law (p. 188).

[112] Lacey, *In Search of Criminal Responsibility*, p. 149; see also Law Commission for England and Wales, *Criminal Liability in Regulatory Contexts*, Consultation Paper No. 195 (2010) (noting the rise in formal criminalisation in England and Wales over time and the striking increase in offences since 1997); and J. Chalmers, F. Leverick and A. Shaw, 'Is Formal Criminalisation Really on the Rise? Evidence from the 1950s' [2015] *Criminal Law Review* 177–99.

[113] See J. Nedelsky, 'Reconceiving Autonomy: Sources, Thoughts and Possibilities' (1989) 1 *Yale Journal of Law and Feminism* 7–36, 9.

collective or shared life.[114] Again, in advance of the full discussion contained in Chapter 7, I mention just two points that arise from my analysis. First, my analysis reveals that, over time, institutions of criminal justice and criminal procedure have come to play an important role in criminal responsibility, even as the component parts of individual responsibility for crime – *actus reus*, *mens rea* and defences – in offences such as consorting echo an earlier era. This connects to the point Lacey makes about the need for scholars to take into account the 'set of institutional arrangements' by which rules, doctrines and practices of criminal responsibility are put into operation.[115] Second, my analysis shows that *to* whom or what, and *for* what, individuals are responsible in their relations with others has changed over time, with a more extensive conception of responsibility – going beyond public order and encompassing self-regulation – now sustaining relations of responsibility, and responsibility now owed to the state. This connects to Farmer's argument that 'responsibility must be understood in the much broader sense of establishing rules and standards of conduct', beyond responsibility for past conduct, which has received the most attention from criminal responsibility scholars.[116]

The State in Relations of Responsibility

The state is foundational to criminal responsibility. Reflecting modern democratic beliefs about the authority of legal institutions, through principles and practices of criminal responsibility, a person is prosecuted for criminal conduct in the name of the state or community.[117] In accordance with the dominant mode of criminal process – in which an individual accounts for his or her alleged offence via a criminal trial – the state is understood as the organ which acts and speaks 'on behalf of the polity as a whole'.[118] On this understanding, the state is taken as a unitary polity that is sovereign in a given space, and it is acknowledged that the state is in a 'special responsive position' as 'the expressive and enforcement agency' in criminal responsibility.[119] This understanding of the state as an enforcement agency reflects liberal political

[114] Sociality is a key concern of critical legal scholars and sociologists of law: see S. Lavi and G. Schneebaum, 'Criminal Law and Sociology', in M. D. Dubber and T. Hörnle (eds.), *The Oxford Handbook of Criminal Law* (New York: Oxford University Press, 2014), pp. 155–6.

[115] Lacey, *In Search of Criminal Responsibility*, p. 1.

[116] Farmer, *Making the Modern Criminal Law*, p. 196.

[117] Ibid., p. 195.

[118] Duff, *Answering for Crime*, p. 53. As part of his 'liberal-communitarian' conception of a polity of citizens, for Duff, this idea is connected to the idea that criminal wrongs are public wrongs (pp. 11, 53), and to his triadic structure of responsibility 'as a matter of being responsible (i.e. answerable) *for* something, *to* someone or body, within a responsibility ascribing practice' (pp. 15–16).

[119] C. Kutz, 'Responsibility', in J. Coleman and S. Shapiro (eds.), *The Oxford Handbook of Jurisprudence and the Philosophy of Law* (Oxford: Oxford University Press, 2004), p. 565. On the history of the concept of the state, see Q. Skinner, 'A Genealogy of the Modern State' (2009) 162 *Proceedings of the British Academy* 325–70.

precepts about the distinctiveness of the criminal law, as a system of official censure and sanction or punishment for certain types of conduct. Here, the state is understood in a minimal or 'thin' way – in terms of democratic norms, political legitimacy and as an authority for punishment.

The ways in which the state impacts criminal responsibility goes far beyond these boundaries, however. The state is empirically and theoretically complex and the criminal law is linked to the state in different ways at different points in time.[120] Taking up ideas about the state from sociology and related fields – in which modernity is defined as the era in which the state provides the framework for individual and collective human life[121] – I approach the state as a set of institutions coordinating a large set of regulatory and governance practices relating to all aspects of social, political and economic life. A number of critical criminal responsibility scholars have adopted this approach to the state. For instance, both Lacey and Farmer note that, over the nineteenth and early twentieth centuries the growing ambition of the nation state to govern its populations – evident in the development of criminal laws, criminal justice institutions, poor laws and, later, education and health systems – altered relations between the state and the individual.[122] In my analysis, I look behind the doctrinal arrangements of criminal responsibility and the procedural context in which these arrangements play out – the criminal trial – to open up a prior issue of the state's position and function in relations of responsibility, revealing that responsibility is something that is distributed between individuals and the state.

A study of the state in relations of responsibility could be undertaken in different ways. In Chapter 8, I examine the state in relations of responsibility through government responses to (allegations of) crimes against children in institutions.[123] This focus leads me to examine a reflective aspect of state

[120] See for discussion M. D. Dubber, 'Paradigms of Penal Law', in M. D. Dubber and T. Hörnle (eds.), *The Oxford Handbook of Criminal Law* (New York: Oxford University Press, 2014); J. Q. Whitman, 'The Transition to Modernity', in M. D. Dubber and T. Hörnle (eds.), *The Oxford Handbook of Criminal Law* (New York: Oxford University Press, 2014).

[121] See A. Giddens, *The Consequences of Modernity* (Stanford: Stanford University Press, 1990), p. 4; see also A. Giddens, *Modernity and Self-Identity: Self and Society in the Late Modern Age* (Stanford: Stanford University Press, 1991). For an intellectual history, see J. Getzler, 'Law, History and the Social Sciences: Intellectual Traditions of the Late Nineteenth- and Early Twentieth-Century Europe', in A. Lewis and M. Lobban (eds.), *Law and History: Current Legal Issues Volume 6* (London: University College of London, 2003), p. 215.

[122] See Lacey, *In Search of Criminal Responsibility*, pp. 53–4; Farmer, *Making the Modern Criminal Law*, pp. 78–82.

[123] This focus may be contrasted with the role of the state as the perpetrator of crime, which refers to 'the violence and corruption perpetrated or instigated by governments': see P. Green, T. Ward, and K. Lasslett, 'The Advance of State Crime Scholarship' (2012) 1(1) *State Crime Journal* 1–7. The role of the state as the perpetrator of crime is traditionally a matter of international criminal law, rather than domestic criminal law: see, e.g., N. Jain, *Perpetrators and Accessories in International Criminal Law: Individual Modes of Responsibility for Collective Crimes* (London: Bloomsbury Publishing, 2014), but, among criminal law theorists, see A. Norrie, 'Justice on the Slaughter-Bench: The Problem of War Guilt in Arendt and Jaspers' (2008) 2 *New Criminal Law Review* 187–231.

governance – public inquiries – because it opens up, rather than closes off, questions about the state in relations of responsibility. I argue that there are four historic positions of the state in relations of responsibility, which are prominent at particular times across the twentieth century and in the first years of the twenty-first century. I suggest that, under these four historic positions, state responsibility is negotiated across dynamics of the modernisation of children's institutions and child welfare practices; the development of institutions associated with the welfare state and the professionalisation of welfare; and across the boundary between past and present, and Empire and nation; and now in a global context. Each of these positions of the state in relations of responsibility correlates with a division of responsibility *between* the state and individuals, where such a division is a dynamic outcome of changing norms about the state and individuals.

Adopting this approach to the state in my account of relations of responsibility reveals new dimensions of criminal responsibility; in particular, it exposes the role of power in responsibility in criminal law. The state is a structure of power and structures power relations,[124] and, as such, power is central to the analysis of criminal responsibility. As Lacey writes, 'the prevailing structures of power and their dynamics' have had 'decisive' consequences for doctrines and practices of criminal law.[125] In addition, as feminist moral philosophers and other theorists have argued in relation to responsibility generally, the attribution of responsibility in a particular context reflects the power relations that pertain in that context.[126] My account of the relations of responsibility that subtend criminal responsibility principles and practices opens up another front in the way in which power and power relations in responsibility in criminal law may be examined. Going beyond the legal-philosophical concern with the role of criminal responsibility as a limit on state power, I explore the productiveness of state power, and the ways in which it gives rise to changing relations of responsibility in criminal law.

Again, in advance of the full discussion contained in Chapter 8, here, I mention just two points that arise from my analysis. First, the changing scope of state responsibility in relation to crimes in children's institutions shows the temporal aspect of responsibility, as the Australian state now takes retrospective responsibility for past crimes or historical abuses, at the same time as it supports procedures – such as mandatory reporting – which are designed to

124 See for discussion R. W. Connell, 'The State, Gender and Sexual Politics: Theory and Appraisal' (1990) 19 *Theory and Society* 507–44, 520.

125 Lacey, *In Search of Criminal Responsibility*, pp. 2, 79.

126 See, e.g., P. Benson, 'Feeling Crazy: Self-Worth and the Social Character of Responsibility', in C. Mackenzie and N. Stoljar (eds.), *Relational Autonomy: Feminist Perspectives on Autonomy, Agency, and the Social Self* (Oxford: Oxford University Press, 2000). Benson argues that the 'systematic distortion' of responsibility is a feature of social oppression and that responsibility is central to liberation ethics (pp. 72, 86).

prevent crime going forward. Second, approaching state responsibility as I do points up the connection between criminal law and public law. This relates to a point made by Farmer, discussed above, that the criminal law is properly 'a form of public law and a governmental project', according to which it is connected to issues of politics, power and the dynamics of social cooperation.[127] As I show in my examination of state responsibility in relation to crimes committed against children in institutions, the division of responsibility *between* the state and individuals is a product of changing social and political norms, even as this division is hidden in studies that focus on doctrinal arrangements of criminal responsibility.

The purpose of this chapter was to examine accounts of the role and significance of criminal responsibility in criminal law scholarship and present a new account of its role in criminal law. My assessment of the literature revealed that criminal responsibility is regarded as significant in three main ways: as the normative heart of the criminal law; as serving the coordination and legitimation needs of the criminal law; and as a platform for development of the modern criminal law. As discussed above, these accounts are more or less attentive to the development of criminal responsibility principles and practices, and more or less connected to institutions, traditions and practices of systems of criminal law. I argued that there is a role of criminal responsibility that has been overlooked: criminal responsibility as organising relations of responsibility between self, others and the state. Recognising this role of criminal responsibility reveals that it is the means by which subjectivity, relationality and power make themselves felt in the criminal law in particular ways. And it is this aspect of criminal responsibility that makes it significant.

As with other critical criminal responsibility scholarship, I approach criminal responsibility as a social practice or a 'thick' legal 'thing', the product of a network of laws, processes, institutions and actors.[128] As Lacey argues, and as discussed above, 'criminal responsibility ... is an idea which is located within a social practice of criminalization',[129] and this social practice sits in the broader frame of the social and legal order. This means that the development of conceptual frameworks – for instance, of responsibility – are themselves social practices which form one of the objects of scholarly analysis.[130] Critical scholars have argued convincingly that responsibility practices are marked by both variability and change over time, and that responsibility in criminal

[127] Farmer, *Making the Modern Criminal Law*, p. 303.
[128] For accounts that adopt this 'thick' approach, see, e.g., Cane, *Responsibility in Law and Morality*; Veitch, *Law and Irresponsibility*. I discuss Veitch's work in detail in Chapter 2.
[129] Lacey, *In Search of Criminal Responsibility*, p. 190.
[130] N. Lacey, 'Philosophy, History and Criminal Law Theory' (1998) 1 *Buffalo Criminal Law Review* 295–328, 311.

law is intimately connected to larger issues about the nature of the legal and social order. My account builds on these studies with a close and contextualised explication of criminal responsibility, pushing scholarly understanding of this central aspect of criminal law forward.

My account offers both a way of understanding and a basis of critique of criminal responsibility. Criminal responsibility is now accorded strong symbolic value in the legal order and the wider social order of which it is part. Approaching criminal responsibility as organising relations of responsibility in criminal law helps to analyse this value. This is the inverse of Farmer's point that criminal responsibility is 'primarily a legal artefact' (albeit one that 'tracks' conceptions of moral responsibility).[131] To me, the significance of criminal responsibility is that 'primarily a legal artefact' carries with it wide relational resonance. Even acknowledging that responsibility does not exist outside distinct disciplinary frames – of criminal law or moral philosophy[132] – scholars must recognise what we can think of as the social life of criminal responsibility, and appreciating this social life enhances our understanding of responsibility in criminal law.

131 Farmer, *Making the Modern Criminal Law*, pp. 165, 170.

132 See for discussion N. MacCormick, 'Taking Responsibility Seriously' (2005) 9(1) *Edinburgh Law Review* 168–75. MacCormick disagrees with Peter Cane's claim (in *Responsibility in Law and Morality*) that responsibility is a 'fundamental' concept, like right, duty and property (174–5).

Part II
Responsibility in Criminal Law

3

Modernisation through Form and Process

Criminal Responsibility at the Turn of the Twentieth Century

This chapter provides the first of my point-in-time analyses of criminal responsibility. Each of the three chapters in this Part of the book takes a depth measure of criminal responsibility at a crucial juncture, and, together, they reveal the gradual and distinctive way in which criminal law came to be organised around criminal responsibility. This chapter is focused on the turn of the twentieth century, which was a decisive moment in Australian criminal law. In order to understand twentieth-century developments, it is necessary to start at the end of the colonial period, in the last decades of the nineteenth century. Against the background of the political transformation of Australian colonies into self-governing entities, major criminal law reforms in several jurisdictions – including the first codification of Australian criminal laws and large-scale consolidations – modernised criminal law, criminal justice institutions and criminal procedure, and set the scene for the development of criminal responsibility principles and practices over the course of the twentieth century.

In order to provide a detailed picture of the state of play in criminal responsibility at the turn of the twentieth century, in this chapter, I focus on two major reforms from the period: the *Criminal Law Amendment Act 1883* (NSW) and the Queensland Criminal Code enacted in 1899. The *Criminal Law Amendment Act 1883* (NSW) was the first significant reform of criminal law in NSW following the achievement of self-government in the mid-century. Despite the reference to criminal law in its title, the 1883 Act extended beyond the law to provide comprehensive coverage of criminal justice in the colony. It contained 472 clauses covering offences, rules of evidence and procedure, punishment and police powers. The Act formed the foundation of the *Crimes Act 1900* (NSW), which continues to provide the basis of the criminal law in NSW. North of the border, in Queensland, reform of the criminal law produced the Queensland *Criminal Code*, the first codification of Australian criminal laws, in 1899.[1]

[1] The Queensland Criminal Code was enacted as a schedule to the *Criminal Code Act 1899* (Qld).

As enacted, the Code contained 707 clauses covering criminal responsibility, offences and defences, the administration of criminal justice, and procedure and punishment, and was said to be 'as complete and as satisfactory as any Code could possibly be'.[2] The Queensland *Criminal Code* provided the template for the subsequent codification of criminal laws in several other Australian states in the first decades of the twentieth century,[3] and also influenced the development of criminal codes in Africa, the Middle East and the Pacific.[4] As amended, it continues to constitute the criminal law of Queensland.[5]

In focusing on the 1883 Act and 1899 Code, I explore both the common law and code modes of criminal laws in Australia. The code track of Australian criminal laws was established by the Queensland Code, and advanced when criminal codes were enacted in other states. In Australian criminal law scholarship and legal thinking, the common law and code modes are often set up in opposition to each other.[6] These two modes of Australian criminal laws are rarely considered side by side – historically, the code jurisdictions have been treated as 'islands in Australian criminal law'[7] – and, where the genesis of the code mode of criminal laws is examined, it tends to be connected to codification movements elsewhere, rather than contemporaneous Australian developments.[8] This has impoverished critical analysis of Australian criminal laws. I suggest that, in a study of principles and practices of criminal responsibility set in the Australian context, the comparison of two significant developments in the common law and code modes of the law, the 1883 Act and the 1899 Code, is instructive. As I discuss in this chapter, the 1883 Act

[2] Hansard, Queensland Legislative Council, col. 818, 7 November 1899.

[3] See *Criminal Code Act 1902* (WA) (and *Criminal Code Act Compilation Act 1913* [WA]) and *Criminal Code Act 1924* (Tas), enacting the Criminal Codes of Western Australia and Tasmania respectively. Each of these was modelled on the Queensland Code. The Queensland Code also exercised some influence on the criminal code of the Northern Territory: *Criminal Code 1983* (NT).

[4] Reflecting the reach of the British Empire, and Australia's own imperial role in Papua New Guinea, the Queensland Code was exported to Papua New Guinea, and influenced the penal codes of Nigeria, Kenya, Cyprus, Israel, Fiji and the Solomon Islands: see for discussion R. S. O'Regan, *New Essays on the Australian Criminal Codes* (Sydney: Law Book Co., 1988), ch. VIII.

[5] A new criminal code was developed in the early 1990s by a government commission chaired by R. S. O'Regan, but following a change of government, it was not proclaimed: see for discussion R. S. O'Regan, 'Law Reform and Politics' (1996) 14 *Australian Bar Review* 1–5.

[6] See for critical discussion S. Tarrant, 'Building Bridges in Australian Criminal Law: Codification and the Common Law' (2012) 39(3) *Monash University Law Review* 838–63; T. Crofts and S. Tarrant, 'Criminal Law Pedagogy and the Australian State Codes', in K. Gledhill and B. Livings (eds.), *The Teaching of Criminal Law: The Pedagogical Imperatives* (Abingdon: Palgrave MacMillan, 2016).

[7] See S. Tarrant and M. Blake, 'Introduction to the UWA Law Review Special Issue' (2019) 45(2) *University of Western Australia Law Review* 1–7.

[8] See, e.g., B. Wright, 'Self-Governing Codifications of English Criminal Law and Empire: The Queensland and Canadian Examples' (2007) 26(1) *University of Queensland Law Journal* 39–65.

and the 1899 Code adopted different approaches to criminal responsibility – on the one hand, oriented around common law concepts of *mens rea* or fault articulated in relation to specific offences, and, on the other hand, oriented around a general statement of criminal responsibility mounted on objective liability – but the significance of responsibility in each of these major reforms was broadly similar.

In this chapter, I make two main arguments. First, while there has been a tendency to associate the modernisation of the criminal law with codification,[9] I argue that, in the Australian context, the practices of codification and consolidation were each a response to common concerns with the need to modernise criminal law and criminal justice institutions, and, as such, the practices are connected. The 1883 Act and the 1899 Code were each a product of broad systematising and rationalising law reform efforts in which consolidation and the distinctive practice of codification were understood as different options for reform of the criminal law, distinguished in part by pragmatic concerns, and the ambition and scale of the reform. Second, I argue that, against a background of the early development of institutions of democratic governance, and amid concerns with the exercise of government power, the 1883 Act and the 1899 Code represent a commitment to modernisation founded on form – comprehensive legislation or a code – and process – the operation of criminal justice – as much as on principles of criminal responsibility. The significance of form and process accounts for the inclusion of detailed and numerous provisions relating to the administration of criminal justice, and criminal procedure and punishment, in both the Act and the Code. Across these two criminal law reforms, criminal responsibility was only one plank of the modernisation of the criminal law, sharing its weight with the form of the criminal law and the operation of criminal justice. Thus, although the Act and the Code adopted different approaches to criminal responsibility, the significance of criminal responsibility in the two reforms – placing criminal responsibility onto a legislative platform and making clearer what was considered opaque – was common to each reform.

In my analysis, I draw on the parliamentary debates regarding the 1883 Act and the 1899 Code. The provisions of both the Act and the Code were subject to extensive parliamentary discussion over a number of years. By the time the 1883 Act was passed into law, it had been debated for many years.[10]

[9] See, e.g., K. J. M. Smith, 'Macaulay's "Utilitarian" Indian Penal Code: An Illustration of the Accidental Function of Time, Place and Personalities in Law Making', in W. M. Gordon and T. D. Fergus (eds.), *Legal History in the Making: Proceedings from the Ninth British Legal History Conference* (London: The Hambledon Press, 1991), pp. 158–60.

[10] Hansard, NSW Legislative Council, col. 124, 24 January 1883. In the period leading up to 1883, the bill that became the Act was 'on the eve of becoming law' on several occasions, but 'political difficulties' got in the way: Hansard, NSW Legislative Council, col. 131, 25 January 1883.

As a result, it was possible to say that 'every line of the measure was considered most earnestly, most anxiously, and most laboriously many years ago by men who were among the most highly competent in the country to perform that work'.[11] The Queensland Code, which was first drafted in 1897, was also subject to extensive discussion in parliament, as well as among legal professionals both within and beyond Queensland. It was said that the judges of the colony had spared 'neither their time nor their ability' in their work on the Code, and that 'as a legal production', it could not be 'improved upon'.[12] As the NSW and Queensland parliamentary debates reveal, concerns about the clarity and simplicity of the criminal law, ease of access to it, and procedure and punishment, as well as the appropriate and efficient administration of criminal justice institutions, occupied each legislature.

This chapter consists of three main parts. First, I connect the 1883 Act and 1899 Code in the context of broad systematising and rationalising criminal law reform efforts. I then compare the principles of criminal responsibility in the two reforms. In the final section, I consider the significance of the provisions relating to the administration of criminal justice and procedure and punishment in the Act and the Code.

Connecting Consolidation and Codification

In the Australian context, both codification and consolidation were responses to common concerns with the need to modernise criminal law and criminal justice institutions. The 1883 Act and the 1899 Code were each a product of broad systematising and rationalising law reform efforts in which consolidation and the distinctive practice of codification were understood as different options for reform of the criminal law.

Against the background of rapid social change, from the early nineteenth century, English criminal law was subject to a number of systematisation and rationalisation efforts. At this time, the work of Jeremy Bentham, who had begun writing in the late 1700s, was picked up by reformers. As part of a wider reform agenda aiming to base law on universal principles that applied across time and place, and driven by the foundational principle of utility, Bentham attempted a wholesale revision and codification of penal laws along 'scientific' lines.[13] At around the same time, as part of larger changes in constitutional

[11] Hansard, NSW Legislative Council, col. 132, 25 January 1883.

[12] Hansard, Queensland Legislative Council, col. 1139, 15 November 1898, and Hansard, Queensland Legislative Assembly, col. 113, 21 September 1899, respectively.

[13] See G. J. Postema, *Bentham and the Common Law Tradition* (Oxford: Clarendon Press, 1986); M. Lobban, *The Common Law and English Jurisprudence 1760–1850* (Oxford: Clarendon Press, 1991), ch. 5; see also K. J. M. Smith, 'The Sources and Form of the Criminal Law: The Medium of Change and Development: Consolidation or Codification?', in W. Cornish et al. (eds.), *The Oxford History of the Laws of England Volume XIII: 1820–1914 Fields of Development* (Oxford: Oxford University Press, 2010), pp. 187–93.

order and the modernisation of state power, from the 1830s, successive sets of Criminal Law Commissioners sort to address the 'haphazard structure of the criminal law', and to advance its development, by collecting and arranging the widely dispersed materials that comprised the criminal law.[14] These efforts did not result in codification of the law but generated seven consolidation acts, including the *Offences Against the Person Act 1861* (England), that were passed in the mid-century.[15] In the latter part of the century, acting in a private capacity, Sir James Fitzjames Stephen took up the mantle to codify the English criminal law. Following the publication of his Digest, *A Digest of Criminal Law* (1877), Fitzjames Stephen drafted a criminal code in 1878.[16] This draft included all offences but left defences to the common law, and it articulated principles of criminal responsibility only in relation to specific offences: as this suggests, Fitzjames Stephen's draft code was conservative in that it did not exclude the common law, and offered only a minimal general part that did not attempt to define criminal responsibility.[17] Fitzjames Stephens' 1878 code was examined by a Royal Commission which produced an amended code and a draft bill in 1880, but, following a change of government, the code was not enacted. However, Fitzjames Stephen's draft of the English criminal law had a significant influence on reform efforts in NSW and Queensland, as I discuss below.

Famously, codification of the criminal law was more successful across Empire than 'at home'. The formation of criminal codes in the British colonies intersected with the unsuccessful codification movement in England.[18] As I discussed in Chapter 1, the movements for codification of the criminal law stretched across metropolitan and colonial spaces, law in England and law across Empire. The colonial context – complexity arising from the combination of English and local laws, a less developed bar and bench, practical challenges of accessing sources, and concerns about excessive executive power – 'enhanced receptivity' to a 'simplified and more accessible criminal law', and 'favoured the

[14] See L. Farmer, 'Reconstructing the English Codification Debate: The Criminal Law Commissioners, 1833–45' (2000) 18(2) *Law and History Review* 397–426, and J. Hostettler, *The Politics of Criminal Law Reform in the Nineteenth Century* (Southampton, UK: Barry Rose Law Publishers, 1992), p. 41, and, generally, ch. 3.

[15] On the connection between the consolidation acts and codification, see J. Rowbotham and K. Stevenson, 'Societal Dystopias and Legal Utopias? Reflections on Visions Past and the Enduring Ideal of Criminal Codification' (2000) 9(25) *Nottingham Law Journal* 25–38, 30–1.

[16] This code adopted a novel structure, with Fitzjames Stephen describing it as 'expressing the leading idea in a particular definition', followed by 'explanations of certain expressions used in the definition', and 'exceptions with their own explanations if they are needed': see R. Cross, 'The Making of the English Criminal Law (5) Macaulay' [1978] *Criminal Law Review* 519–28, 524.

[17] See generally R. Cross, 'The Making of the English Criminal Law (6) Sir James Fitzjames Stephen' [1978] *Criminal Law Review* 652–61.

[18] See, e.g., E. Kolsky, 'Codification and the Rule of Colonial Difference: Criminal Procedure in British India' (2005) 23(3) *Law and History Review* 631–83, pp. 631–4.

prospects of codification'.[19] Other factors, such as strong leadership and parliaments open to significant change, also played a role.[20] Thus, in the nineteenth century, a number of codes were enacted across the spaces of Empire, as well as in post-imperial contexts. Several of these codes were Benthamite Codes, in that they followed Bentham's 'scientific' model and were intended to provide a complete statement of the law.[21] For instance, Thomas Macaulay, the author of the *Indian Penal Code 1860* (which was the earliest penal code in a common law country), followed Bentham in seeking to draft a code that would be simple, complete, accessible and efficient.[22] The *Indian Penal Code* was seen as 'practical proof of the possibility of scientific jurisprudence, or building effective codes of substantive law built upon rational, deductive principles'.[23] In 1870, in a move directed by the Colonial Office to promote legal unity across Empire, a code was developed that was intended to serve as a model penal code for all the colonies, but this code was only adopted in a couple of jurisdictions.[24] In the last decade of the century, a criminal code was enacted in New Zealand, and, after discussion and debate taking place over decades, the *Criminal Code of Canada*, covering both criminal law and criminal procedure, came into force in 1893.[25] The New Zealand and Canadian codes each closely followed Fitzjames Stephens' draft criminal code.[26]

19 See B. Wright, 'Criminal Law Codification and Imperial Projects: The Self-Governing Jurisdiction Codes of the 1890s' (2008) 12 *Legal History* 19–49, p. 20, and, more generally, pp. 27–30.

20 See J. Finn, 'Codification of the Criminal Law: The Australasian Parliamentary Experience', in B. Godfrey and G. Dunstall (eds.), *Crime and Empire, 1840–1940: Criminal Justice in Local and Global Context* (Cullompton, Devon: Willan Publishing, 2005), p. 235.

21 See S. H. Kadish, 'Codifiers of the Criminal Law: Wechsler's Predecessors' (1978) 78 *Columbia Law Review* 1098–144 (discussing the Indian Penal Code, the New York Penal Code and the Louisiana Criminal Code).

22 In an innovative move, Macaulay included 'Illustrations' with each provision included in the Code, which were hypothetical applications of the provision intended to limit the scope of the power of judges to interpret the law: see Smith, 'Macaulay's "Utilitarian" Indian Penal Code'; see also D. Skuy, 'Macaulay and the Indian Penal Code of 1862: The Myth of the Inherent Superiority and Modernity of the English Legal System Compared to India's Legal System in the Nineteenth Century' (1998) 32(3) *Modern Asian Studies* 513–57.

23 K. Mantena, *Alibis of Empire: Henry Maine and the Ends of Liberal Imperialism* (Princeton, NJ: Princeton University Press, 2010), p. 91.

24 The Colonial Office engaged R. S. Wright, an English barrister, to draft this code: see M. L. Friedland, 'R S Wright's Model Criminal Code: A Forgotten Chapter in the History of the Criminal Law' (1981) 1 *Oxford Journal of Legal Studies* 307–46. Wright's code was developed for Jamaica and adopted in other colonies including British Honduras, Tobago and British Guiana, but not Jamaica (337).

25 *Criminal Code Act 1893* (NZ) and *Criminal Code of Canada 1893*, respectively.

26 Thus, the Canadian Code made only a few changes to the law, including clarifying the offence of murder (removing reference to 'malice aforethought'), replacing larceny with a new offence of theft, and placing the partial defence of provocation on a statutory basis: see further A. W. Mewett, 'The Canadian Criminal Code, 1892–1992' (1993) 72(1) *The Canadian Bar Review* 1–27, 3–5. On the New Zealand Code, see S. White, 'The Making of the New Zealand Criminal Code Act of 1893: A Sketch' (1986) 16 *Victoria University of Wellington Law Review* 353–76.

It was in this fertile criminal law reform context that the 1883 Act and 1899 Code emerged. By this time, there was widespread recognition of the need for the modernisation of Australian criminal laws and criminal justice institutions. At this time, local institutions of government did not yet match the strong central power of each of the colonies, and key institutions of the criminal law and criminal justice were still in a nascent stage. Trial by jury had been introduced in Australian jurisdictions from the mid-nineteenth century,[27] and there were established courts of Petty Sessions (where lay justices of the piece or police or stipendiary magistrates presided), courts of Quarter Sessions (where judges sat with a jury of twelve men) and Supreme Courts as superior courts of record.[28] But, prosecutions were not yet regularised and rights of appeal from convictions for serious offences were limited.[29] In addition, other than the standard offences of assault, theft, robbery, rape and homicide, it was difficult to identify all the crimes in force in the jurisdiction due to the myriad sources of the law.[30] Limited resources meant it was hard to access the law, with lawyers and judges dependent on small numbers of holdings of English treatises and reports.[31] Difficulties also arose from perceived inconsistencies between statutes and confusion about the relevant law.[32] The sense that 'the sources of the criminal law are altogether bewildering in their extent' and the idea that the law was full of 'the most conspicuous and glaring inconsistencies and incongruities'[33] reinforced a sense in which it was not fit for purpose. At the same time, population growth and social change put pressure on criminal law and justice. Over the second half of the century, cities like Sydney, Melbourne and Brisbane grew substantially, leading to increases in crime.[34] A middle class developed at this time, and this raised the political profile of crime.[35] The orientation of the urban middle class towards criminal behaviour

27 On the introduction of jury trials in NSW, see D. Neal, *The Rule of Law in a Penal Colony: Law and Power in Early New South Wales* (Cambridge: Cambridge University Press, 1991).

28 See generally A. Castles, *An Australian Legal History* (Sydney: Law Book Co., 1982), ch. 13.

29 See Castles, *An Australian Legal History*, pp. 337–40.

30 G. D. Woods, *A History of Criminal Law in New South Wales Volume 2: The New State: 1901–1955* (Sydney: The Federation Press, 2018), p. 40.

31 S. Bronitt, 'Australia', in K. J. Heller and M. D. Dubber (eds.), *Handbook of Comparative Criminal Law* (Stanford, CA: Stanford Law Books, 2011), p. 50; J. McKenna, *Supreme Court of Queensland: A Concise History* (Brisbane: University of Queensland Press, 2012), p. 95. Authorised law reporting of Australian cases began in 1865 but remained limited and piecemeal for a long time thereafter: see M. Byran, 'The Modern History of Law Reporting' (2012) 11 *University of Melbourne Collections* 32–6.

32 Hansard, NSW Legislative Assembly, col. 615, 22 February 1883.

33 Hansard, Queensland Legislative Council, col. 1139, 15 November 1898, and Hansard, Queensland Legislative Assembly, col. 106, 21 September 1899, respectively.

34 Woods, *A History of Criminal Law in New South Wales Volume 2*, p. 6.

35 On class relations in the Australian colonies, see further G. Cross, 'Labour in Settler-State Democracies: Comparative Perspectives on Australia and US, 1860–1920' (1996) 70 *Labour History* 1–24.

was 'strongly grounded in the dominant climate of Victorian morality',[36] and this period was marked by high levels of social concern about sexual deviancy and sexual offences,[37] and ongoing concerns with public order and vice crimes likes drunkenness and gambling.[38]

It was in recognition of the need to modernise Australian criminal laws and criminal justice institutions that criminal law and justice reform came onto the legislative agenda in NSW and Queensland (and elsewhere in Australia). In NSW, replicating the pattern in other jurisdictions, including England, the bill that became the *Criminal Law Amendment Act 1883* (NSW) was the product of the work of the Law Reform Commission, which had been established in 1870 to direct reform of the law. The chairman of the Commission from 1870 to 1872 was Sir Alfred Stephen, who had been the Chief Justice of the NSW Supreme Court since 1942, and was a 'dominating force' in the colony's legal realm.[39] Alfred Stephen, a cousin of Fitzjames Stephen, was the main author of the 1883 Act (and, later, as a member of the Legislative Council, helped pass the Act into law). Alfred Stephen was aware of the work of reformers in England, including Fitzjames Stephen's draft code, and he and the Commission consulted key individuals involved in criminal justice in the development of the Act.[40] In parliamentary debates, Alfred Stephen's 'zealous and indefatigable exertions' in bringing the bill to a state of 'perfection' were praised.[41] While, during debates about the bill, a few parliamentarians expressed concern that the colony was parting company with England, suggesting that reform work 'would be done much better' by gentlemen in England, and that NSW should wait to see the outcome of proposed reforms 'at home',[42] Alfred Stephen and others advocated moving ahead. Alfred Stephen pointed out to other members of parliament that Fitzjames Stephen's code had been amended and suggested that it might take many years to become law in England, and, in the end, might not be adopted in any case.[43] Those in favour of reform carried the day, and the *Criminal Law Amendment Act 1883* (NSW) became law on 26 April 1883.

36 P. Grabosky, *Sydney in Ferment: Crime, Dissent and Official Reaction, 1788 to 1973* (Canberra: ANU Press, 1977), p. 91.

37 E.g., the 'Mount Rennie Outrage', a gang rape of a 16 year old servant girl, in 1886: for discussion, see J. Ramsland, *With Just but Relentless Discipline: A Social History of Corrective Services in New South Wales* (Sydney: Kangaroo Press, 1996), pp. 58–67.

38 These problems were met with state attempts to enforce moral norms – for example, in NSW, through the Intoxicating Drink Inquiry Commission established in 1887, and the Royal Commission into gambling, opium smoking and slave trading by members of Sydney's Chinese community in 1891: see Grabosky, *Sydney in Ferment*, pp. 94–5.

39 G. D. Woods, *A History of Criminal Law in New South Wales Volume 1: The Colonial Period: 1788–1900* (Sydney: Federation Press, 2002), p. 429.

40 See Hansard, NSW Legislative Council, col. 178–9, 31 January 1883, and C. H. Currey, 'The Influence of the English Law Reformers of the Early Nineteenth Century on the Law of New South Wales' (1937) XXIII *Royal Australian Historical Society* 227–41, respectively.

41 Hansard, NSW Legislative Assembly, col. 623, 22 February 1883.

42 See, e.g., Hansard, NSW Legislative Assembly, col. 1008, 15 March 1883; Hansard, NSW Legislative Assembly, col. 1079, 1 November 1882.

43 Hansard, NSW Legislative Council, col. 1533, 17 April 1883.

Given the concerns about the 'almost insuperable difficulties' that had 'surrounded the administration of the criminal law' in NSW,[44] the 1883 Act was intended to 'simplify' and modernise the criminal law, and facilitate its operation.[45] While the Act largely reproduced the existing law, its value lay in bringing it together in one statute. The Act was a consolidation act: it repealed 64 Acts and numerous other parts of Acts. As parliamentary discussion indicates, the bill that became the 1883 Act was viewed as a 'handbook' of the criminal law, which might be read by the general public as well as 'professional men'.[46] It was said to promise that judges would no longer need to 'appeal from act to act, some apparently conflicting, and others actually conflicting, in order to find out what is the law'.[47] As part of these efforts to simplify and modernise the law, the Act presented the law in a straightforward way. Thus, the Act was organised into families of offences: following the 'Interpretation and General Clauses', the Act was divided into eleven Parts (including 'Offences against the Person', 'Larceny and Similar Offences' and 'Procedure Evidence and Verdict'). Under each Part, a section provided for some offences to be tried summarily (as I discuss below). While, within each family of offences, several offences testify to the particular needs of the developing colony,[48] the method of presenting the criminal law in families of offences was borrowed from English law: because the 1883 Act would have to be applied by magistrates – some of whom were 'gentlemen unlearned in the law' – it was self-consciously structured to replicate the consolidation acts like the *Offences Against the Person Act 1861* (England), with which it was assumed everyone would be familiar.[49]

North of the border, in Queensland, reform of the criminal law was also on the legislative agenda due to the felt need to modernise the law and its institutions. Here, another towering figure significantly influenced the direction reform was to take. This figure was Sir Samuel Griffith, a Queensland lawyer and politician who had been Attorney-General and Premier of Queensland, and was the Chief Justice of the Queensland Supreme Court from 1893.[50] Griffith was a dominant force in the colony, and his 'master hand' could be found on the statute law of Queensland 'to an extent unsurpassed by that of

44 Hansard, NSW Legislative Assembly, col. 615, 22 February 1883.

45 Ibid., col. 615-6, 22 February 1883.

46 Ibid., col. 615, 22 February 1883.

47 Ibid.

48 For example, the offence of stealing cattle or killing them with intent to steal (Clause 73), which attracted a sentence of ten years, was intended to prevent the 'wholesale stealing of cattle and sheep': Hansard, NSW Legislative Council, col. 136, 25 January 1883. This was said to be 'a very common offence' among settlers: Hansard, NSW Legislative Assembly, col. 1011, 15 March 1883.

49 Hansard, NSW Legislative Council, col. 137, 25 January 1883; Hansard, NSW Legislative Council, col. 1533, 17 April 1883.

50 See R. B. Joyce, 'Griffith, Sir Samuel Walker (1845–1920)', in B. Nairn and G. Serle (eds.), *Australian Dictionary of Biography Volume 9: 1891–1939* (Melbourne: Melbourne University Press, 1983).

any other legislator'.[51] As a result, it was Griffith who was asked to draft a criminal code for the colony. In 1896, Griffith compiled a digest of all statutes in force in Queensland,[52] noting with concern that the written criminal law of Queensland was 'scattered through nearly two hundred and fifty Statutes, while the unwritten portion of the criminal law, which forms a very large part of it, is only to be found in the books of writers on the subject of the criminal law in England or in the decisions of course of criminal jurisdiction'.[53] Based on his digest, Griffith prepared a draft code in 1897. After some debate in parliament, in 1898, the draft code was referred to a Royal Commission, with Griffith appointed as chair.[54] The Royal Commission was tasked with examining the expediency of enacting a Code, the completeness of the draft Code, and the changes to the existing law that were proposed.[55] While the Commission proposed some amendments to Griffith's draft, its members were unanimous in concluding that it was expedient to enact a Code and positive about its completeness.[56] In parliamentary debates, the Code was considered to be 'a work displaying the greatest ability on the part of the Chief Justice',[57] and, appropriately, the Queensland Code, and the Western Australian and Tasmanian criminal codes, modelled on it, are known as 'Griffith Codes'. The Queensland Code came into force on 1 January 1901.

Like the 1883 Act, the 1899 Code drew on the unsuccessful efforts to codify the English criminal law, in particular, the work of the English Law Commissioners and Fitzjames Stephen's draft criminal code.[58] But, in addition, Griffith drew what he acknowledged as 'very valuable assistance' from the *New York Penal Code 1881* and the *Italian Penal Code 1889* (known as the Zanardelli Code).[59] Indeed, Griffith regarded the Italian Penal Code 'as the most complete and perfect Penal Code in existence'.[60] Conceptualising his

[51] Hansard, Queensland Legislative Council, col. 1046, 8 November 1898; for discussion of Griffith's influence, see G. Mackenzie, 'An Enduring Influence: Sir Samuel Griffith and his Contribution to Criminal Justice in Queensland' (2002) 2(1) *Queensland University of Technology Law and Justice Journal* 53–63.

[52] Griffith, Sir Samuel Walker, *Digest of the Statutory Criminal Law in Force in Queensland on the first day of January, 1896 (which it is within the competence of the Parliament of Queensland to Repeal or Amend)* (Brisbane: Government Printer, 1896).

[53] Letter from Sir Samuel Griffith to the Queensland Attorney-General, 29 October 1897 (Brisbane: Government Printer, 1897), iii–xiv, iv ('Explanatory Letter').

[54] Other members of the Royal Commission included all Justices of the Supreme Court, the District Court Judges and Crown Prosecutors.

[55] Hansard, Queensland Legislative Council, col. 818, 7 November 1899.

[56] Ibid.

[57] Ibid, col. 1903, 8 December 1897.

[58] See Hansard, Queensland Legislative Council, col. 1046, 8 November 1898, and Griffith, 'Explanatory Letter', iv.

[59] Hansard, Queensland Legislative Assembly, col. 106, 21 September 1899. Griffith spoke Italian and his italophilia was well known: see K. Cullinane, 'Preface: The Zanardelli Code and Codification in the Countries of the Common Law' (2000) 7 *James Cook University Law Review* 116–18, 116.

[60] Griffith, 'Explanatory Letter', vii.

draft as following in the tradition of Bentham, in the process of codification, Griffith sought to modernise and simplify the common law.[61] He also sought to improve the accessibility of criminal laws, as codification promised that 'any man, turning to [the laws], can find what he wants and understand it when found'.[62] The Code was said to be 'as free from technicality as it was possible to be', substituting 'complication and prolixity' for condensed and simplified provisions.[63] Griffith received praise from the Chief Justice of England, Lord Cockburn, for replacing the 'cumbrous and inartistic phraseology of the statutes' with the 'language of everyday use'.[64] The Code largely reproduced the criminal offences in English common law and statute, and it was Fitzjames Stephens' draft criminal code that was 'the most persuasive influence' on Griffith's Code,[65] although some of its provisions, including those relating to criminal responsibility, broke away from common law reform models, as I discuss below.

The structure of the Queensland *Criminal Code* differed from that of the 1883 Act. The Code contained a general part, Part I, as well as a special part, which contained offences and several chapters on procedure. The general part included chapters on matters of jurisdiction, and some general provisions on punishments, as well as criminal responsibility.[66] The offences contained in the special part of the Code were divided into five substantive sections: offences against public order, offences against the administration of law and justice, acts injurious to the public in general, offences relating to the person and marriage (including sexual offences), and offences relating to property and contract.[67] The Code also provided definitions of offences, to enable 'every intelligent person to understand what are the ingredients... necessary to constitute certain classes of offences punishable by law'.[68] The Code abolished felonies

[61] See I. Leader-Elliott, 'Benthamite Reflections on Codification of the General Principles of Criminal Liability: Towards the Panopticon' (2006) 9(2) *Buffalo Criminal Law Review* 391–452. For critical discussion of the place of the Griffith Codes in the Benthamite codification tradition, see Wright, 'Self-Governing Codifications' (drawing a distinction between 'imposed' imperial codes and the codes of the 'self-governing' colonies, like Queensland, New Zealand and Canada).

[62] Hansard, Queensland Legislative Council, col. 1048, 8 November 1898; see also Hansard, Queensland Legislative Assembly, col. 85, 20 September 1899.

[63] See Hansard, Queensland Legislative Assembly, col. 105, 21 September 1899, and Hansard, Queensland Legislative Council, col. 1046, 8 November 1898, respectively.

[64] Letter from Lord Chief Justice Cockburn to the Attorney General on the Criminal Code, 7 February 1880 (1880) 22 *Law Journal* 184–8, 202–8, 186.

[65] R. S. O'Regan, 'Sir Samuel Griffith's Criminal Code' (1991) XIV(8) *Royal Historical Society of Queensland Journal* 305–17, 307.

[66] The provisions governing jurisdiction (sections 12–14) covered offences commenced or completed outside Queensland, a 'modest extra-territorial jurisdiction' that went 'a little further' than was orthodox for colonial legislatures: see O'Regan, *New Essays on the Australian Criminal Codes*, p. 9.

[67] This structure reflects nineteenth century views about the interests requiring the protection of the criminal law: see Bronitt, 'Australia', p. 77.

[68] Hansard, Queensland Legislative Assembly, col. 105, 21 September 1899.

as a category of offences (in favour of 'crimes') – on the basis that the term felony had ceased to have 'definite meaning' – and introduced a distinction between misdemeanours and simple offences.[69] The comprehensive inclusion of offences in the Code meant that it excluded common law offences (with the exception of the offence of contempt of court), rendering all criminal offences in Queensland statutory offences. Part VIII, covering procedure, included chapters on arrest, pleas, trial process and verdicts, among other matters.

Those involved in the drafting and enactment of the 1899 Code recognised the distinctiveness of the practice of codification, regarding it as one (albeit the preferable) option for law reform, with different options distinguished in part by pragmatic concerns, and in the ambition and scale of reform. In Queensland parliamentary debates, codification was said to offer 'all the advantages of the existing law with the additional benefits of, first, supplying a complete and intelligible statement of the law, and, second, amending it in such points as are obviously desirable', and there was a belief that codification was 'not only practicable but advisable'.[70] The choice between codification and consolidation was partly a pragmatic one: Alfred Stephen thought that, as a practical matter, the NSW legislature would not enact a criminal code, and so he focused his efforts on consolidation,[71] while Griffith believed generally that 'the desirability, indeed, of a collected and explicit statement of the Criminal Law' required no argument, that either codification or consolidation was 'very necessary', and that the task of codifying the criminal law was 'no more impossible in Queensland than in other civilized countries'.[72] Thus, although codification was recognised as 'a very different thing' from consolidation,[73] the difference was also partly in the ambition and scale of reform of the law: consolidation was thought to 'comparatively easy', while codification was more difficult.[74] Queensland parliamentary debates convey the sense of pride of a colony realising the goal of codification of the criminal law, something that 'a nation boasting the civilisation of England should still be without'.[75] Crucially, there was also a general expectation that the codification of English criminal

[69] Griffith, 'Explanatory Letter', xx. Conceptualised as administrative wrongs, simple offences were not included in the Code.

[70] Hansard, Queensland Legislative Council, col. 1047, 8 November 1898, and Hansard, Queensland Legislative Council, col. 818, 7 November 1899, respectively.

[71] Woods, *A History of Criminal Law in New South Wales Volume 1*, pp. 260–1.

[72] Griffith, 'Explanatory Letter', iv, and Letter from Sir Samuel Griffith to the Queensland Attorney-General, 1 June 1896 (Brisbane: Government Printer, 1896), iii–viii, viii, respectively.

[73] Hansard, Queensland Legislative Council, col. 1046, 8 November 1898.

[74] S. Griffith, 'Criminal Responsibility: A Chapter from a Criminal Code', in *Report of the Seventh Meeting of the Australasian Association for the Advancement of Science* (Sydney: Australasian Association for the Advancement of Science, 1898), p. 896.

[75] Hansard, Queensland Legislative Council, col. 1139, 15 November 1898; see also Hansard, Queensland Legislative Assembly, col. 105–6, 21 September 1899.

law was likely at some point,[76] which meant that Queensland was ahead of, but not out of step with, 'the mother country'.

Reflecting the connections between consolidation and codification as criminal law reform practices, the *Criminal Law Amendment Act 1883* (NSW) and the Queensland *Criminal Code* were not positioned as far apart from each other as is sometimes assumed. Although it did not attempt to exclude the common law, the 1883 Act provided an extensive coverage of the criminal law in NSW, including 'all those crimes which were of the commonest occurrence'.[77] As Jeremy Finn writes, while the 1883 Act was 'not a true code in that it did not define many of the offences, it was more than a mere consolidation in that it made significant changes to a number of areas'.[78] As this suggests, the 1883 Act may be thought of as an 'attenuated' codification.[79] Equally, even in codification, the Queensland law retained a close connection to the common law of the time: because the substantive provisions of the Queensland Code were largely made up of English statutory provisions supplemented by the common law, the Code remained 'a common law product', 'comprehensive legislation derived from a common law system'.[80] The connection between the Queensland Code and the common law were reinforced in the decades after it entered into force as its provisions fell to be interpreted by the High Court of Australia in the broader context of the common law of crime, and against the backdrop of a growing sense of the value of consistency across Australian criminal laws.[81]

Comparing Criminal Responsibility

The 1883 Act and the 1899 Code diverged in their approaches to criminal responsibility. The *Criminal Law Amendment Act 1883* (NSW) largely reinscribed the existing common law on criminal responsibility in individual offence and defence provisions, while the Queensland Criminal Code contained a general part which pertained to the Code (and the criminal law) as a

[76] In his communication with Griffith, the Lord Chief Justice of England stated that he was 'a firm believer in, not only the expediency and possibility, but also in the coming necessity, of codification': Letter from Lord Chief Justice Cockburn containing Comments and Suggestions in relation to the Criminal Code (Indictable Offences) Bill, 12 June 1879, H. C. Papers, 1878–79, vol. 59, p. 233.

[77] Hansard, NSW Legislative Council, col. 1533, 17 April 1883.

[78] Finn, 'Codification of the Criminal Law', p. 233.

[79] Kadish, 'Codifiers of the Criminal Law'. On consolidation acts generally, see Rowbotham and Stevenson, 'Societal Dystopias and Legal Utopias?', pp. 30–1.

[80] Wright, 'Self-Governing Codifications', p. 60. Wright concludes that the civil law influences on the Griffith Code did not determine its 'fundamental character'. See also Finn, 'Codification of the Criminal Law' (contrasting the Australasian criminal codes with the Code Napoleon, a 'relatively brief single statute', setting out 'all the relevant principles of an area of law') (p. 224).

[81] See Chapter 4.

whole, and adopted objective fault as the standard for criminal responsibility. But, crucially, the significance of these principles was broadly similar in the Act and the Code: to put criminal responsibility onto a legislative platform and to make clearer a part of the criminal law that was considered opaque.

At around the turn of the nineteenth century, criminal responsibility had not yet been subject to any significant conceptual elaboration, and was not completely separated from liability. While references to concepts such as wickedness had long been present in criminal law texts, these were moral rather than legal notions.[82] Even after the outlines of particular exculpatory doctrines like insanity had become apparent, individual responsibility-cum-liability remained largely unimportant. As Nicola Lacey points out, William Blackstone, writing his *Commentaries* in the second half of the 1700s, was relatively unconcerned with criminal responsibility, placing greater emphasis on the special part of criminal law, individual offences and defences.[83] In the nineteenth century, treatise writers were focused on doctrines which applied to specific areas, and which, 'at most', could be understood as shaping the definitions of particular offences.[84] Similarly, the English Code Commissioners discussion of intention was largely confined to the law of homicide.[85] General positive doctrines of *mens rea* or fault emerged as inculpating principles only gradually.[86] Over the course of the century, the emergence of the institutional conditions for the elaboration of criminal responsibility – such as legal representation, and systems of appeals – facilitated the development of a set of general, technical principles of criminal responsibility.[87] 'The recognisably modern' division of criminal fault – intention, recklessness and negligence – in which mental states are distinguished on

[82] As Farmer writes in relation to the criminal law in Scotland, 'the primary concern was with the action and its wrongfulness', and, because 'legal guilt was equivalent to a moral wrong', a particular degree of intention did not have to be proved as a condition of liability: see L. Farmer, *Criminal Law, Tradition and Legal Order: Crime and the Genius of Scots Law, 1747 to the Present* (Cambridge: Cambridge University Press, 1997), p. 133.

[83] N. Lacey, 'In Search of the Responsible Subject: History, Philosophy and Social Sciences in Criminal Law Theory' (2001) 64(3) *Modern Law Review* 350–71, p. 359. According to Lacey, this reflects the 'relative weakness of liberal, democratic and humanist sentiments' at the end of the eighteenth century, meaning it was not yet necessary to appeal to individual responsibility to legitimise criminal law: see N Lacey, 'Character, Capacity, Outcome: Towards a Framework for Assessing the Shifting Pattern of Criminal Responsibility in Modern English Law', in M. D. Dubber and L. Farmer (eds.), *Modern Histories of Crime and Punishment* (Stanford: Stanford University Press, 2007), p. 21.

[84] See L. Farmer, 'Of Treatises and Textbooks: The Literature of Criminal Law in Nineteenth Century Britain', in M. Dubber and A. Fernandez (eds.), *Law Books in Action: Essays on the Anglo-American Legal Treatise* (Oxford: Hart Publishing, 2012), pp. 158, 160. Farmer argues that the major achievements of these treatise writers were the formalisation of criminal law doctrine and the consolidation of the role of lawyers in criminal justice.

[85] Farmer, 'Reconstructing the English Codification Debate', p. 413.

[86] N. Lacey, *In Search of Criminal Responsibility: Ideas, Interests and Institutions* (Oxford: Oxford University Press, 2016), p. 33.

[87] See, generally, Lacey, *In Search of Criminal Responsibility*, ch. 4.

the basis of 'the relation between possible consequences and the attitude of the accused towards these consequences',[88] and the familiar common law construction of criminal responsibility – across *actus reus*, *mens rea* and defences – took firm hold in the criminal law in the twentieth century.

Coming at the end of the nineteenth century, the 1883 Act and 1899 Code capture the emergence of these general, technical conceptions of criminal responsibility at the same time as older moralised notions remained present in the law. The 1883 largely reflects the persistence of older common law notions of fault and constructions of criminal responsibility. The persistence of older notions of fault is evidenced in the Act's heavy use of the undifferentiated and moralised concept of malice. The meaning of 'malice' and 'maliciously' had changed over time, from something like wilfulness, to intention and recklessness.[89] This changed meaning is reflected in the Act's interpretation section, which provided that 'every act done of malice' or 'done without malice but with indifference to human life or suffering or with intent to injure', without lawful excuse or done 'recklessly or wantonly', shall be taken to have been done maliciously within the meaning of this Act (clause 7).[90] 'Malice' was included in numerous offences, such as the offence of 'maliciously' impeding a person escaping a shipwreck (clause 21) and 'maliciously' setting fire to a building 'with intent to injure or defraud' (clause 178). Evidence of reliance on older constructions of criminal responsibility is provided by the conceptualisation of what would now be recognised as defences but were included in the Act as provisos on criminal prohibition, or as provisions relating to procedure. An example is provided by the partial defence of provocation (clause 370), which was included in the 1883 Act not as part of the law of homicide but in Part VIII, on trial procedure, evidence and verdict. Clause 370 provides that, in a murder trial, where it appears that the act or omission causing death does not amount to murder but to manslaughter, the jury may acquit the accused of murder and convict him or her of manslaughter. The same clause then provides the elements of the defence (including that provocation could not be self-induced), and extends provocation to include 'grossly insulting words or gestures'.[91]

[88] L. Farmer, 'Criminal Responsibility and the Proof of Guilt', in M. D. Dubber and L. Farmer (eds.), *Modern Histories of Crime and Punishment* (Stanford: Stanford University Press, 2007), pp. 42–3.

[89] See Hostettler, *The Politics of Criminal Law Reform in the Nineteenth Century*, p. 99.

[90] It was a defence to an allegation of malice that the act was done by the accused 'under a reasonable suspicion that he had a right to do such an act' (clause 229).

[91] When discussed in parliament, this was labelled a 'very important' amendment to the 1882 version of the bill, continuing to protect the public, but 'reasonably' extending the law in favour of the accused: see Hansard, NSW Legislative Assembly, col. 618, 22 February 1883. A provision extending provocation to encompass insults was included in Fitzjames Stephens' unsuccessful Bill in England.

The 1883 Act embraced modern notions of fault, however, in its formulation of the offence of murder: it provided a positive definition of murder without the old fault concept, 'malice aforethought'.[92] As it moved from an exculpatory factor into a positive element of murder, 'malice aforethought' had acquired multiple meanings:[93] by the end of the nineteenth century, the phrase became confused and confusing, as it did not necessarily imply 'either ill-will or premeditation', or even an intention to cause death, as might be assumed.[94] In parliamentary debates, Alfred Stephen acknowledged that '[g]reat confusion and difficulty' had arisen over the phrase 'malice aforethought'.[95] As a result, in the 1883 Act, murder was defined to require that the act or omission causing death be done with 'reckless indifference to human life' or 'intent to kill or inflict grievous bodily harm' or in an attempt to commit or the commission of an act 'obviously dangerous to life' and or punishable by death or penal servitude for life (clause 9).[96] The inclusion of 'reckless indifference to life' in the definition of murder was controversial, as it departed from the definition proposed by Fitzjames Stephen in his draft code.[97] In parliament, questions were raised about why the definition of murder differed from that which applied in England, and debate turned on the scope of the offence (encompassing acts and omissions) as well as the novel phraseology.[98] In defence of the formulation, Alfred Stephen stated that the definition of murder was 'very much more simple' than that proposed by Fitzjames Stephen, and that '[a]ll the judges were opposed to the use' of the words 'malice aforethought', and preferred to direct juries in the 'very language' he used in the clause.[99]

[92] It has been argued that the origins of 'malice aforethought' lie in the medieval practice of issuing royal pardons for certain killings (those in which a 'jury' appointed by the King found that the killing had taken place *without* malice aforethought on the part of the accused): see Editor, 'Malice Aforethought' (1924) 33(5) *Yale Law Journal* 528–36. See also R. M. Perkins, 'A Re-examination of Malice Aforethought' (1934) 43(4) *Yale Law Review* 537–70.

[93] See A. J. Ashworth, 'The Making of the English Criminal Law (4) Blackstone, Foster and East' [1978] *Criminal Law Review* 389–99.

[94] Griffith, 'Explanatory letter', xi (giving his reasons for omitting the term from the Queensland Code).

[95] Hansard, NSW Legislative Council, col. 133, 25 January 1883.

[96] The elements of the current offence of murder (including the NSW-specific clause, 'reckless indifference to life'), and felony murder, can be detected in this provision: see *Crimes Act 1900* (NSW) s 18.

[97] The definition of murder contained in Fitzjames Stephen's draft Code of 1878 included a reference to 'indifference' to causing death or grievous bodily harm, as part of the limb of the offence regarding knowledge of the probability of death or grievous bodily harm: see for discussion Cross, 'The Making of the English Criminal Law (6) Sir James Fitzjames Stephen', pp. 659–60.

[98] See Hansard, NSW Legislative Assembly, col. 1099, 21 March 1883; Hansard, NSW Legislative Assembly, col. 1096–102, 21 March 1883.

[99] Hansard, NSW Legislative Council, col. 133, 25 January 1883.

By contrast with the 1883 Act, in relation to criminal responsibility, the *Criminal Code* broke away from common law models. Griffith regarded this area of the criminal law as the 'most important and difficult branch of the law'.[100] Revealing its debt to the *Italian Penal Code 1889*, the Queensland Code included criminal responsibility principles in the general part of the code. The Code's chapter on criminal responsibility, Chapter V, comprised a number of sections covering matters such as insanity and intoxication (sections 27 and 28) and immaturity or non-age (section 29).[101] Unlike Fitzjames Stephen's draft code, the Queensland Code included a provision on justifications and excuses that related to compulsion (section 31). Griffith opted to use the term 'wilfully' to connote the intention to cause injury,[102] so that, unlike the *Criminal Law Amendment Act 1883* (NSW), the Queensland Code did not rely on 'malice' or 'maliciously', with Griffith stating that these terms had acquired a 'technical meaning quite different from that which they bear in ordinary language'.[103] Chapter V of the Queensland Code offered a 'systematic approach to liability', and represented its 'particular contribution' to nineteenth century codification efforts.[104] In parliamentary debates, this part of the Code was hailed as reducing a 'difficult' area of law to 'the clearest and most concise language'.[105] The provisions contained in Chapter V applied to all persons charged with any offence under the Queensland law (section 36), meaning that that chapter had to be read alongside every criminal offence.

The central criminal responsibility provisions in Chapter V of the Code are those relating to ignorance of the law (section 22), intention and motive (section 23), and mistake of fact (section 24). Section 22 provides that ignorance of the law is no excuse, replicating the position at common law. Section 23 covers intention and motive, and, at the time of enactment, provided that, subject to the express provisions of the Code, 'a person is not criminally responsible for an act or omission which occurs independently of the exercise of his will, or an event which occurs by accident'.[106] The section also provides that, unless

[100] Griffith, 'Explanatory letter', x.

[101] In an innovative move that reflected then recent developments in expert psychological and psychiatric knowledge, the provision on insanity extended the common law governing non-responsibility due to mental incapacity with the incorporation of 'irresistible impulse' (incapacity to control actions) as a basis for a plea of insanity: see *Criminal Code 1899* (Qld) s 27. I discuss the Griffith Code innovations in insanity in Chapter 4.

[102] Griffith, 'Explanatory letter', viii. The term 'willfully' was later interpreted to encompass recklessness: see *R* v. *Lockwood; ex parte Attorney-General* [1981] Qd R 209.

[103] Griffith, 'Explanatory Letter', viii.

[104] Wright, 'Self-Governing Codifications', pp. 59 and 57, respectively. See also Mackenzie, 'An Enduring Influence'.

[105] Hansard, Queensland Legislative Assembly, col. 108, 21 September 1899.

[106] Section 23 has been amended remove reference to 'accident' in favour of 'reasonably foreseeable consequence': see *Criminal Code and Other Legislation Amendment Act 2011* (Qld), and, for discussion, see A. Hemming 'Why the Queensland, Western Australian and Tasmanian Criminal Codes are Anachronisms' (2012) 31(2) *University of Tasmania Law Review* 1–31.

intention to cause a particular result is an express element of an offence, the result intended is immaterial. Griffith formulated this section, and, because it was 'so admirably done', it was 'very little interfered with' by the Royal Commission.[107] Griffith regarded this section as having the effect that it was 'unnecessary' to express the elements of criminal responsibility in the definition of offences,[108] and as a result, it has been labelled 'perhaps the most obvious sign' of the influence of Bentham and the 'more evolved continental codes' on the 1899 Code.[109] Section 24 provides the mistake of fact defence. This section states that 'a person who does or omits to do an act under an honest and reasonable, but mistaken, belief in the existence of any state of things is not criminally responsible for the act or omission to any greater extent than if the real state of things had been such as he believed to exist'. The effect of this section is that only reasonable mistakes will provide a defence. Taken together, these provisions mean that an accused is held responsible not because his or her state of mind is blameworthy in itself, but because of a 'blameworthy failure to live up to an objective standard of thought and behaviour'.[110] In other words, the threshold or baseline for criminal responsibility under the Queensland Code is negligence.[111]

With the inclusion in the Queensland Code of a chapter on criminal responsibility, pertaining to the Code as a whole, and all criminal offences, the individual offences and defences contained in the special part of the Code generally comprised only what would be considered conduct or *actus reus* elements under the common law. Thus, several offences against the person (such as causing grievous bodily harm) (section 320) state only the conduct elements of the offence. The special part of the Code contains some exceptions to the general principles of criminal responsibility, however, with mental or *mens rea* elements included in the offence provisions. For example, the Code includes subjective fault elements for offences against property (stealing in section 391). Murder was also one of the exceptional instances in the Queensland Code in which subjective fault is required. The Code redefined murder, creating a distinction between 'murder' and 'wilful murder', with the latter corresponding to intentional killing (section 301).[112] Murder was formulated to correspond to

107 Hansard, Queensland Legislative Assembly, col. 108, 21 September 1899.

108 Griffith, 'Explanatory Letter', viii.

109 Section 23 of the Code corresponded with Article 45 of the Zanardelli Code: see A. Cadoppi and K. Cullinane, 'Translation: The Zanardelli Code and Codification in the Countries of the Common Law' (2000) 7 *James Cook University Law Review* 119–90, 149.

110 E. Colvin, 'Criminal Responsibility under the South Pacific Codes' (2002) 26 *Criminal Law Journal* 98–113, 104.

111 See *R* v. *Taiters; ex parte Attorney-General* [1996] 1 Qd R 333 at 338.

112 The creation of an offence of 'wilful murder' appears to have been an original innovation of Griffith's, as, by contrast with other material in his draft code, he did not indicate a source for the distinction from murder: see G. Taylor, 'Dr Pennefather's Criminal Code for South Australia' (2002) 31(1) *Common Law World Review* 62–102, 92; see also T. Crofts 'Two Degrees of Murder: Homicide Law Reform in England and Western Australia' (2008) 8(2) *Oxford University Commonwealth Law Journal* 187–210, 191–2.

an intention to endanger human life, or reckless endangerment of human life (section 302). Only those convicted of 'wilful murder' were liable for the death penalty, and after capital punishment was abolished in Queensland, the distinction was redundant, and later abolished, leaving the homicide offences of murder and manslaughter.[113] Like the 1883 Act, the Code provided that provocation was a defence to murder (section 304), but, as Griffith was convinced that it was 'of at least equal importance as applied to other cases of personal violence', the Code also provided for provocation to be a defence for assault (section 268).[114]

As this discussion indicates, under the 1899 Code, criminal responsibility was (and continues to be) based on objective liability, according to which criminal responsibility is negated by accident (and now automatism), or honest and reasonable mistake. At the time the Queensland Code was drafted, objective liability was thought to represent the common law position.[115] But in the decades since the 1899, subjective fault – the idea that responsibility rests on the accused' appreciation of the risk he or she takes or the circumstances in which he or she acts – has become more important in common law jurisdictions such as NSW. The rising profile of subjective fault reflects its role in the legitimation of criminal conviction and punishment in a wider social and political context in which human agency is taken seriously.[116] This has meant that, since the turn of the twentieth century, the Australian common law and code jurisdictions have moved apart from each other, and, further, as Stella Tarrant argues, that the code jurisdictions have come to be associated with 'a certain obtuseness and conservatism'.[117] When, in the 1990s, the Criminal Law Officers' Committee came to formulate the criminal responsibility provisions of the Commonwealth Criminal Code, it was required to decide between a subjective and objective approach to criminal responsibility – in effect, an evaluation of the relative value of the two approaches to criminal responsibility – it opted for a subjective approach.[118]

Although adopting contrasting approaches to criminal responsibility, the significance of these principles in the 1883 Act and the 1899 Code was broadly similar: criminal responsibility was placed onto a legislative platform, making clearer a part of the criminal law that was considered opaque. Backed by the authority of a democratically elected parliament, and in the comprehensible form of a statute or a code, clarity about criminal responsibility was a plank of

[113] *Criminal Code and the Offenders Probation and Parole Act Amendment Act* 1971 (Qld).

[114] See Griffith, 'Explanatory letter', xi. On the basis that provocation is a technical term, it is interpreted by reference to the common law rather than to ordinary language: see *R* v. *Johnson* [1964] Qd R 1.

[115] S. Yeo, 'Revitalising the Penal Code with A General Part' [2004] *Singapore Journal of Legal Studies* 1–19, 9.

[116] For critical discussion, see Lacey, *In Search of Criminal Responsibility*, ch. 4.

[117] Tarrant and Blake, 'Introduction to the UWA Law Review Special Issue'.

[118] See further Chapter 5.

the modernisation of criminal law. This was more thoroughly pursued in the Queensland Code, with its statement of general principles of criminal responsibility standing apart from individual offences and defences. For Griffith, the value of a clear statement on the 'rules' of criminal responsibility exemplified the value of codification more generally: for him, the 'rules' of criminal responsibility provided an 'excellent illustration of the old saying that the common law is the embodiment of common sense'.[119] As criminal responsibility 'often figures so very largely as an element in criminal offences', it made sense to express the part of the criminal law that had 'the widest application' in clear terms.[120] In the context of the 1883 Act, the significance of placing criminal responsibility onto legislative platform and making clearer what was considered opaque was less developed but still evident. In the case of the 1883 Act, as a consolidation statute, this idea was bound up with the improvement that the comprehensive coverage and simplification of the criminal law ('getting our criminal law expressed in one act'[121]) would provide. While the English common law of crime – 'framed by the eminent judges in England' – was valuable, 'with all the complications of the present time not even lawyers could understand it'.[122] The consolidation would 'simplify' the criminal law, and 'make the principles involved in it more in accordance with modern notions of justice'.[123]

While the relevance of the differences between the basis of criminal responsibility – in either subjective or objective fault – in the 1833 Act and the 1899 Code has amplified over time, in neither the Act nor the Code did criminal responsibility bear the central weight of the modernisation of the criminal law. Rather, this weight was shared with the operation of criminal justice, as I now turn to discuss.

Recognising the Significance of the Administration of Criminal Justice, Procedure and Punishment

The *Criminal Law Amendment Act 1883* (NSW) and the *Criminal Code 1899* (Qld) each extend beyond the criminal law and contain sets of provisions relating to the administration of criminal justice, and procedure and punishment. The inclusion of detailed and numerous provisions on the administration of justice and criminal process in both the Act and the Code reveals their significance – as a plank of the modernisation of criminal law and criminal justice institutions in Australia.

[119] Griffith, 'Criminal Responsibility', p. 903.

[120] Hansard, Queensland Legislative Assembly, col. 108, 21 September 1899, and Griffith, 'Criminal Responsibility', p. 903, respectively.

[121] Hansard, NSW Legislative Council, col. 1264, 16 November 1882.

[122] See Hansard, Queensland Legislative Assembly, col. 285, 5 October 1899, and Hansard, NSW Legislative Council, col. 177, 31 January 1883.

[123] Hansard, NSW Legislative Assembly, col. 615–6, 22 February 1883.

By the 1880s and 1890s, NSW and Queensland had changed radically since the early days of penal settlement,[124] and institutions of democratic governance were developing. Transportation of convicts to Australia had ended in 1840, and from the mid-century, there was a serious attempt to move away from the convict past and attract free settlers and develop the population.[125] Adopting Westminster principles (in which the executive is responsible to parliament), NSW achieved self-government in 1855, and Queensland separated from NSW and became self-governing in 1859. In 1856, NSW established an elected Legislative Assembly and an appointed Legislative Council, taking over most of the legislative powers of the governor of the colony. A bicameral parliament was established in Queensland in 1860. These parliaments passed their own laws, although the laws required the assent of local governors and the queen, and certain areas, such as divorce, continued to be controlled by Britain.[126] At the end of the nineteenth century, when 'the rapid spread of liberal and progressive thought caused innovation to replace imitation', the standard practice of adopting laws that were passed in England began to change.[127] In the context of the extended federation debates, through which the six colonies prepared to join together as the Commonwealth of Australia, lawyers, political figures, and the public more generally, reflected on the nature of Australian government and society, with discussion revolving around the political and legal institutions that would serve the new states and the new nation in the new century.[128]

Against this background of the early development of institutions of democratic governance, in the last decades of the nineteenth century, the administration of criminal justice and criminal process assumed a high profile. Criminal justice was central to the way state power was imagined in the now independent democratic colonies, and the proper working and efficient operation of criminal justice institutions was linked to the extension of the freedoms of the common law to all people in the new societies.[129] As evident in parliamentary debates on the 1883 Act and 1899 Code, in NSW and Queensland, there was deep

[124] On the early colonial period in NSW, see P. J. Byrne, *Criminal Law and Colonial Subject, New South Wales, 1810–1830* (Cambridge: Cambridge University Press, 1993); re Queensland, see T. Banivanua-Mar, 'Consolidating violence and colonial rule: Discipline and protection in colonial Queensland' (2005) 8(3) *Postcolonial Studies* 303–19.

[125] At this point, buoyed by growth of agriculture, and together with Canada, the Australian colonies were wealthy parts of the British Empire: see B. Palmer, 'Nineteenth-Century Canada and Australia: The Paradoxes of Class Formation' (1996) 71 *Labour History* 16–36.

[126] See B. Kercher, *An Unruly Child: A History of Law in Australia* (Sydney: Allen & Unwin, 1995), p. 124.

[127] Kercher, *An Unruly Child*, p. 125. As Kercher discusses, areas of innovation included labour law and land law (ch. 7).

[128] See, generally, H. Irving, 'New South Wales', in H. Irving (ed.), *The Centenary Companion to Australian Federation* (Cambridge: Cambridge University Press, 1999).

[129] Woods, *A History of Criminal Law in New South Wales Volume 1*, p. 429.

recognition of the importance of criminal justice – which 'so largely affected the interests and liberty of the people' – and a felt commitment to the idea that the law should be administered in a way that would serve 'the well-being of the community'.[130] Parliamentary debates are replete with references to the Magna Carta, 'the charter of 1215', the inheritance of the Norman Conquest and the 'wonderful constitutional liberties which had been handed down to us by our ancestors'.[131] In this context, the 'right administration of justice'[132] was a matter of equity and fairness, as well as the maturity of the colonies, and the distance they had travelled since the days of penal settlement.

As they were on the ground, the institutions of criminal justice fell short of their democratic significance. Concerns about the administration of criminal justice were oriented around the personnel who staffed the institutions, and, at the time of the 1883 Act and 1899 Code, the most important people in the administration of criminal justice were police, and police and stipendiary magistrates. There were concerns that each of these actors might be abusing their power. In relation to police, by this time, police were focused on enforcing changing norms around the use of public space, displacing practices that had been public, such as drunkenness.[133] In debates on the Queensland Code, police were criticised for distinguishing between 'the parties who carried on the gambling whether Europeans, Chinese, or any other alien' in their targeting of 'gambling houses',[134] and there were also concerns about abuse of police powers.[135] In relation to magistrates, while they had carried significant administrative responsibilities in earlier decades, by the last decades of the century, the work of magistrates in the full-time paid employment of the government (stipendiary magistrates) had become more legal and less administrative, and magistrates were coming to form the 'backbone' of the administration of criminal justice.[136] But the standard of the magistracy was of significant concern, with one parliamentarian describing some magistrates as 'incapable nincompoops'.[137] There were also concerns about both the standard and the shortage of lawyers in more remote parts of the colonies. In NSW, concerns

[130] See Hansard, NSW Legislative Assembly, col. 1137, 28 March 1883, and Hansard, Queensland Legislative Council, col. 818, 7 November 1899, respectively.

[131] See, e.g., Hansard, NSW Legislative Council, col. 1075, 1 November 1882; Hansard, NSW Legislative Assembly, col. 1282, 4 April 1883; and Hansard, NSW Legislative Council, col. 1077, 1 November 1882, respectively.

[132] Hansard, NSW Legislative Council, col. 132, 25 January 1883.

[133] See, generally, R. Hogg and H. Golder, 'Policing Sydney in the Late Nineteenth Century', in M. Finnane (ed.), *Policing in Australia: Historical Perspectives* (Sydney: New South Wales University Press, 1987).

[134] See Hansard, Queensland Legislative Assembly, col. 281, 5 October 1899.

[135] See, e.g., Hansard, Queensland Legislative Assembly, col. 282–3, 5 October 1899.

[136] See P. Finn, *Law and Government in Colonial Australia* (Melbourne: Oxford University Press, 1987), p. 118 (re Queensland) and Woods, *A History of Criminal Law in New South Wales Volume 1*, p. 326, respectively; see also Castles, *An Australian Legal History*, pp. 326–7.

[137] Hansard, NSW Legislative Assembly, col. 1181, 30 March 1883.

were expressed that 'bush lawyers', 'who know everything except the law', would be engaged as defence counsel if an amendment to the bill was passed to allow representation by an 'agent', in recognition of the limited number of lawyers in country areas,[138] This proposed amendment was defeated in the face of concerns about 'persons of doubtful competency' attempting to defend a prisoner.[139]

In light of these concerns, both the 1883 Act and the 1899 Code contained a number of provisions seeking to improve the administration of criminal justice in the colonies. In NSW, the 1883 Act provided that, like witnesses for the Crown, material witnesses for the defence would have their expenses covered (clause 346). The 1883 Act also contained a number of provisions on appeals (clauses 440–45) (although it did not expand rights to appeal). In Queensland, the 1899 Code included provisions covering perjury and corrupting witnesses (sections 123–25 and 127). The Queensland Code also provided for the establishment of a Court of Criminal Appeal (sections 669–70). Overall, the Code was said to 'enable judges, crown prosecutors, and everybody engaged in the administration of the law to see at a glance what it is, and to administer it with convenience and intelligence'.[140]

Unlike the 1883 Act, the Queensland Code also reached beyond the administration of justice to encompass the regulation of government power and the relationship between state and citizen more generally. In this respect, the Code reveals its Benthamite or utilitarian tenor, as it aimed to promote the rule of law and reduce reliance on discretionary power.[141] Alongside familiar common law offences against the state, such as treason and sedition, the Code included several sections that provided for liability on the part of state actors, in matters such as political, judicial and electoral corruption. Borrowing from the *Italian Penal Code 1889*, the 1899 Code also included an offence of interference with political liberty (section 78), an offence relating to the disclosure of state secrets (section 84), and an offence of abuse of office (section 92).[142] In addition, the Code included sections providing for the protection of elections (sections 98–117). With these provisions, the Criminal Code has been described as having a 'quasi-constitutional character', attempting to 'articulate and structure state powers in a manner that reflects a modern conception of the role of criminal law as a form of public intervention'.[143] Pointing

[138] See Hansard, NSW Legislative Council, col. 175, 31 January 1883, and Hansard, NSW Legislative Assembly, col. 1171–3, 29 March 1883, respectively.

[139] See Hansard, NSW Legislative Council, col. 175, 31 January 1883. There was also some discussion about amalgamation of the two branches of the legal profession, e.g., Hansard, NSW Legislative Assembly, col. 1082–6, 21 March 1883.

[140] Hansard, Queensland Legislative Council, col. 819, 7 November 1899.

[141] Wright, 'Self-Governing Codifications', p. 64.

[142] See for discussion Cadoppi and Cullinane, 'Translation: The Zanardelli Code and Codification in the Countries of the Common Law', pp. 157–9.

[143] Wright, 'Self-Governing Codifications', p. 49.

to provisions criminalising abuse of public office, Barry Wright argues that Griffith's work on criminal law codification was in some respects an 'extension' of his constitutional work, with the Code revealing 'more than a concern about the efficient management of crime'.[144]

Both the 1883 Act and 1899 Code included numerous provisions relating to criminal process. The 1883 Act contained 'significant' reform of criminal procedure, including raising the age of consent to 14 years (clause 42) and providing for challenges to jurors (clause 336).[145] Part VIII of the Queensland Code included provisions covering arrests, trials, evidence, and appeals, which, according to Griffith, and was intended to be a 'complete statement of the existing written and unwritten rules respecting procedure after committal', including 'some rules which dispose of difficulties that not infrequently arise and have not been authoritatively settled'.[146] The Act and the Code reflected attempts to improve and streamline criminal procedure for indictable offences. For instance, in light of concerns about 'indictments of inconceivable length', 'overladen with verbiage',[147] the 1883 Act attempted to provide a cure-all provision to correct any defects in the formulation of indictments: the Act provided that 'no indictment shall be held bad or insufficient' for, for instance, designating any person by a name other than his proper name, or for 'stating the time wrongly' where time was not of the essence (clause 308). The Queensland Code provided for the amendment of indictments by courts if there was no prejudice to the accused, allowing trials to proceed without delay (section 572). Some parliamentarians called for the procedural provisions of the Code to be further extended, to cover matters such as wrongful convictions and the role of the judge and jury.[148] The Code did not contain an express general provision on the burden of proof, a matter that would leave the issue of what was intended under the Code to the interpretation of the Australian High Court in the mid-century.[149]

At the time of the enactment of the 1883 Act and 1899 Code, summary procedure – trials before magistrates sitting without a jury – was still controversial, and each reform attempted to put it on a firmer footing. The *Jervis Acts 1848* (England) and the *Criminal Justice Act 1855* (England) had regularised and expanded summary procedure in England,[150] and summary process was

144 Ibid., p. 57, and, more generally, pp. 56–8. Griffith was one of the drafters of the Australian constitution: see J. Hirst, 'Empire, State, Nation', in D. M. Schreuder and S. Ward (eds.), *Australia's Empire* (Oxford: Oxford University Press, 2008), pp. 156–61.

145 Finn, 'Codification of the criminal law', pp. 233–4.

146 Griffith, 'Explanatory letter', xiv.

147 Hansard, NSW Legislative Assembly, col. 615, 22 February 1883.

148 See, e.g., Hansard, Queensland Legislative Assembly, col. 159 and col. 162, 27 September 1899, respectively.

149 See Chapter 4.

150 See C. Emsley, *Crime and Society in England 1750–1900*, 3rd ed. (Harlow, UK: Pearson, 2005), pp. 208–10. The *Jervis Acts 1848* (England) had been adopted in NSW by the *Justices Act 1850* (NSW).

becoming a more prominent part of criminal justice in the colonies. While the Queensland Code was limited to indictable offences – provisions on summary procedure had been included in the *Police Acts of mid-century,* and provisions governing summary offences and committals had been brought together in the *Justices Act 1886* (Qld)[151] – it provided for children to be charged summarily (section 678). In NSW, in addition to those offences that were only triable summarily, the 1883 Act included a number of the procedural provisions that stipulated that some offences within each family could be dealt with summarily as misdemeanours, with the accused's consent. Offences punishable in this way represented 'petty cases', such as simple larceny, and conviction attracted shorter terms of imprisonment.[152] According to the parliamentary debates, the availability of summary process was considered desirable in part because it removed a 'gross reflection' on the then current law – which seems to mean that petty offences could be dealt with in an appropriate way, by magistrates, rather than having to be heard by a judge in court[153] – but, also because the development of the summary jurisdiction would be more efficient and would relieve the courts of quarter sessions and the Supreme Court.[154] While there were concerns that trial by jury would better safeguard the rights of accused,[155] this sort of argument was met by countervailing concerns about undesirability of the delay entailed in bringing individuals before the Court of Quarter Sessions, and the greater notoriety of appearing before a judge.[156]

Reflecting the place of the criminal trial at the centre of the criminal justice process at the end of the nineteenth century,[157] the 1883 Act and 1899 Code each also attempted to modernise the law of evidence. For example, echoing the *Prisoners Counsel Act 1836* (England), the 1883 Act provided that every accused person, in all courts, was able to make a 'full answer and defence by counsel', and all witnesses could be examined and cross-examined by counsel or an attorney (clause 342). The Queensland Code included a similar provision (section 616). Formalising existing practice, and on the basis that it was of 'great importance to the interests of justice' and 'at least a provision in the

[151] These exclusions from the Code attracted criticism from the English Lord Chief Justice, who stated that it was 'in the highest degree illogical' to omit such offences. According to the Lord Chief Justice, what was wanted was 'a consolidation or code of the law relating to crimes, not matter what may be the method of proceeding applicable to them': see Letter from Lord Chief Justice Cockburn containing Comments and Suggestions in relation to the Criminal Code (Indictable Offences) Bill, pp. 241–2.

[152] This represented the beginning of the 'hybrid' process in NSW, in which indictable offences may be tried summarily: see for discussion T. Mitchell, 'Understanding the Summary Jurisdiction in NSW', PhD thesis, University of Sydney (2017).

[153] Hansard, NSW Legislative Assembly, col. 615, 22 February 1883.

[154] Hansard, NSW Legislative Council, col. 1533–4, 17 April 1883.

[155] See, e.g., Hansard, NSW Legislative Assembly, col. 1179, 1181, 30 March 1883; Hansard, NSW Legislative Assembly, col. 1421, 11 April 1883.

[156] See Hansard, NSW Legislative Assembly, col. 1184 and 1187, 30 March 1883, respectively.

[157] See Farmer, 'Criminal Responsibility and the Proof of Guilt', pp. 57–8.

interest of the prisoner', the 1883 Act also included a provision for the accused to make a statement of facts, but not be cross-examined on it (clause 470).[158] In addition, the 1883 Act provided that, in those circumstances in which the accused was in a unique position to provide facts for the court, an accused could testify on oath (clause 351). This fell short of the then still controversial issue of permitting the accused to give sworn testimony, which was being debated in several common law jurisdictions around this time, and had been included in Fitzjames Stephens' draft criminal code.[159]

In relation to punishment, both the 1883 Act and the 1899 Code continued to rely on existing punishments for criminal offences – a mix of capital punishment, imprisonment and corporal punishment – but there were attempts to modernise punishment practices. Capital punishment had been used intensely in the period up to 1850, but, by the last decades of the century, opposition to the death penalty was gaining ground.[160] The retention of capital punishment under the Act and the Code was strongly opposed by several parliamentary representatives in each jurisdiction – on the basis of its inhumanity, its failure to deter crime and its irrevocability (if an innocent person were hanged, 'no reparation could be made').[161] In the drafting and passage of the new laws, there were attempts to restrict the use of the death penalty and modernise other punishment practices. For instance, in Queensland, Griffith's draft code provided for the death penalty on conviction for rape (which was, by that time, no longer a capital offence in England), but, in the face of opposition from the majority of members of the Royal Commission and parliamentarians, as enacted, rape was not made a capital offence under the Code (leaving only murder, treason and piracy punishable by hanging).[162] As an additional safeguard on capital punishment, the 1899 Code provided that a sentence of death could be recorded rather than pronounced, allowing for the exercise of clemency (section 652). In NSW, the 1883 Act retained the death penalty for rape: the colonial context, and specifically, the 'sparsely-populated territory', where women and girls were left alone, was said to make 'the most terrible of punishments' a necessity (as a deterrent) and to justify maintaining a different penalty from that which applied under English law.[163] As an additional

[158] Hansard, NSW Legislative Council, col. 1534, 17 April 1883.

[159] See Finn, 'Codification of the Criminal Law', p. 235. The right of the accused to give evidence on oath in indictable matters was enshrined in the *Criminal Law and Evidence Act 1891* (NSW): see for discussion Woods, *A History of Criminal Law in New South Wales Volume 1*, pp. 367–8.

[160] See M. Finnane, *Punishment in Australian Society* (Melbourne: Oxford University Press, 1997), pp. 128–9.

[161] See, e.g., Hansard, NSW Legislative Assembly, col. 1094–5, 1103, 21 March 1883; Hansard, NSW Legislative Assembly, col. 1137, 28 March 1883; Hansard, NSW Legislative Assembly, col. 1095, 21 March 1883; and Hansard, Queensland Legislative Assembly, col. 149–60, 7 September 1899.

[162] See O'Regan, 'Sir Samuel Griffith's Criminal Code', pp. 309–10.

[163] Hansard, NSW Legislative Assembly, col. 1139, 28 March 1883. See also Hansard, NSW Legislative Assembly, col. 1094–5, 21 March 1883.

safeguard, the 1883 Act included a provision that established a special procedure to deal with doubts or mitigating circumstances that were raised after an individual had been convicted of a capital offence (clause 383).[164] This seems to have reflected a need to accommodate public opposition to the death penalty and concerns around private prosecutions, which, in NSW, persisted in the absence of a formalised system of public prosecutions, but were coming to be seen as partisan. These post-conviction procedures provided 'solid ground' on which the Executive could act to mitigate sentence,[165] representing a move towards the regularisation of executive clemency.

The Act and the Code also reinscribed corporal punishment, but, as with capital punishment, there were also moves to restrict reliance on physical punishments. In the context of changing social attitudes to punishment of the body, and as a rejection of the brutality of the convict period, punishments such as flogging had been declining since the 1850s, but sentences including corporal punishment continued to be passed infrequently.[166] Under the 1883 Act, whipping was available as an alternative to prison for young people (clause 401) – something that was considered necessary to respond to 'larrikinism', a loose term connoting the public violence of working class men that plagued cities like Sydney at this time[167] – and for adults charged with certain offences (including sodomy, carnal knowledge and indecent assaults) (clause 402). Under the Queensland Code, punishments included whipping (which could only be inflicted on men) (section 18) and punishment with hard labour (for 'unnatural offences') (section 208). As this list of offences reveals, corporal punishment was connected with a moralised attitude to certain crimes. Like capital punishment, corporal punishments occasioned much debate in NSW and Queensland parliaments. One NSW parliamentarian was concerned about whipping boys convicted of minor offences, suggesting that the law would be abused by certain police magistrates ('whose intellect is impaired by age' or 'whose facilities are dulled by intemperance'), and would, in reality, be imposed only on 'the poor and indigent of the interior'.[168] In Queensland, one parliamentarian referred to the inequity of the application of physical punishments such as the lash, stating that such punishment was 'entirely reserved for those in the lower ranks of life'.[169] There were calls for

164 According to this procedure, any Judge of the Supreme Court, or any Justice acting by direction of the Governor, could summon and examine all persons with information, and reporting the evidence to the Governor for the exercise of his discretion.

165 Hansard, NSW Legislative Assembly, col. 618, 22 February 1883; see, for discussion, Woods, *A History of Criminal Law in New South Wales Volume 1*, p. 430.

166 See for discussion Finnane, *Punishment in Australian Society*, p. 115 and more generally, ch. 4.

167 See for discussion A. Loughnan, 'In Accordance with Modern Notions: Criminal Responsibility at the Turn of the Twentieth Century', in T. Crofts and A. Loughnan (eds.), *Criminalisation and Criminal Responsibility in Australia* (Melbourne: Oxford University Press, 2015).

168 Hansard, NSW Legislative Assembly, col. 628, 22 February 1883.

169 Hansard, Queensland Legislative Assembly, col. 202, 28 September 1899.

corporal punishments to attract 'greater safeguards', such as requiring such punishments to be imposed by a jury rather than a magistrate.[170] While this particular proposal was not accepted, in their passage through the parliaments, physical punishments for a number of the offences contained in the Act and the Code were restricted or removed.[171]

Although they retained capital and corporal punishment, reflecting wider trans-jurisdictional changes in rationales for punishment, both the Act and the Code moved away from what was labelled as 'the old practice of inflicting severe penalties',[172] in favour of moderate and moderated punishment, and reform and rehabilitation.[173] In light of emerging theories advanced by Cesare Lombroso concerning the hereditary nature of criminality, crime was starting to be thought about as a disease which demanded reform rather than punishment.[174] In parliamentary debates, some representatives referenced the 'new science of criminology' which advocated dealing with criminals in a 'scientific manner', and focusing on prevention rather than punishment.[175] Reflecting the changing rationale of punishment, the Queensland Code provided for the suspension of punishment for first time offenders (section 656), carrying forward one of Griffith's earlier criminal justice initiatives which represented the first probation scheme in Australia.[176] In NSW, at around the same time as the 1883 Act was passed, and amidst concerns about overcrowded prisons, parliament enacted the *First Offenders Probation Act 1894* (NSW), permitting judges to impose probation rather than imprisonment on first time offenders.[177] These initiatives reflected the idea, voiced by one parliamentarian, that the 'new civilisation' being developed in the 'new land' should ensure that punishment is based on 'humanitarian principles'.[178]

170 Hansard, NSW Legislative Assembly, col. 1184–5, 30 March 1883.

171 See e.g. Hansard, NSW Legislative Assembly, col. 1404–5, 10 April 1883 (amending the Bill to provide that two magistrates must agree before a sentence of whipping could be imposed on boys and youths), and Hansard, Queensland Legislative Assembly, col. 325–6, 10 October 1899 (amending the draft Code to remove whipping as a possible punishment for stealing and robbery).

172 Hansard, NSW Legislative Council, col. 136, 25 January 1883.

173 See, e.g., Hansard, NSW Legislative Council, col. 1535, 17 April 1883.

174 See for discussion P. Pasquino, 'Criminology: The Birth of a Special Saviour', in P. Beirne (ed.), *The Origins and Growth of Criminology: Essays on Intellectual History, 1760–1945* (Aldershot, UK: Dartmouth Publishing, 1994).

175 Hansard, Queensland Legislative Assembly, col. 155–6, 27 September 1899.

176 *The Offenders Probation Act 1886* (Qld): see for discussion O'Regan, 'Sir Samuel Griffith's Criminal Code', p. 310.

177 Grabosky, *Sydney in Ferment*, p. 96. Grabosky suggests that this Act virtually halved the prison population per thousand between 1895 and 1907. The *Justice Fines Act 1899* (NSW) permitted imprisoned debtors to have their sentences remitted where they could pay a portion of the fine.

178 Hansard, Queensland Legislative Assembly, col. 160, 27 September 1899; see also Hansard, Queensland Legislative Assembly, col. 222, 3 October 1899.

As this discussion indicates, the administration of justice and criminal procedure and punishment were prominent inclusions in the 1883 Act and the 1899 Code. The inclusion of detailed and numerous provisions on the administration of justice and criminal process in both the Act and the Code reveals the high profile of criminal process – the operation of the criminal law – in the broad systematising and rationalising law reform efforts of the turn of the twentieth century. While Fitzjames Stephen had been tasked with drafting a code of criminal procedure following his draft penal code,[179] against a backdrop of the early development of institutions of democratic governance in each colony, the improvement of criminal process and the proper working of systems of criminal justice assumed outsized significance in modernising efforts in NSW and Queensland when compared with England.

The *Criminal Law Amendment Act 1883* (NSW) and the *Criminal Code 1899* (Qld) were products of a broad systematising and rationalising law reform practice, which encompassed consolidation and the distinctive practice of codification. In the Australian context, codification and consolidation were connected rather than separate, as each was a response to felt need for the modernisation of criminal law and criminal justice. The 1883 Act and the 1899 Code represent a commitment to modernisation founded on form – comprehensive legislation or a code – and process – the operation of criminal justice – as much as on principles of criminal responsibility. This accounts for the prominence of provisions on the administration of criminal justice, and criminal procedure and punishment, in both the Act and the Code. While the principles of criminal responsibility were largely restated rather than developed in the 1883 Act, criminal responsibility was substantially amended in the 1899 Code; but, in each reform, the significance of the principles of criminal responsibility was broadly similar – to put criminal responsibility onto a legislative platform and make clearer a part of the criminal law that was considered opaque. In neither case, however, did the principles of criminal responsibility bear the weight of the modernisation of the criminal law alone, as they shared this weight with the form of the criminal law and the governance of the operation of criminal justice.

[179] See Smith, 'The Sources and Form of the Criminal Law', p. 210.

4

The 'Birth' of Australian Criminal Law

The Role of Criminal Responsibility in the Mid-Century

This chapter picks up the historical story in the middle of the twentieth century. This period was a formative one for the development of principles and practices of criminal responsibility, and, through them, for Australian criminal laws. Against a background of an enhanced sense of independence and confidence of people and institutions that developed following World War I and World War II, I argue that it was in the middle of the twentieth century, from the 1930s to 1960s, that Australian criminal law came into its own – measured in terms of an orientation around national coordinates, and in the self-confidence of its practitioners and academics. I demonstrate that, with close reference to the decisions of English courts, and commentaries such as that of Glanville Williams – and, increasingly over the period, to US developments like the *Model Penal Code* – Australian lawyers and commentators came to forge an independent path for the criminal law in the mid-century. Working over and above developments that occurred within state jurisdictions, and across code and common law modes of criminal law, practitioners and scholars were thoroughly engaged in a global debate about the development and improvement of the law of crime, and in a complex and subtle negotiation between what Australia shared with others, and what might mark it out. In the mid-century, it became possible to think about Australian criminal law as such, that is, to conceptualise Australian criminal law as a meaningful idea.

Principles of criminal responsibility played a key role in the 'birth' of Australian criminal law in the mid-century. As elsewhere, the idea that the criminal law is comprised of a set of general principles of criminal responsibility took firm hold in Australia in this period, enjoying widespread acceptance among both practitioners and scholars. The Australian story has a distinct inflection, however. Although such principles are typically understood as the bedrock of the criminal law that is shared by common law systems across the world – in George Fletcher's words, the 'grammar' of the criminal law, present despite differences in systems of positive law[1] – it

[1] See G. Fletcher, *The Grammar of Criminal Law: American, Comparative and International* (Oxford: Oxford University Press, 2007), ch. 1.

was through the elucidation and application of these principles – by judges, lawyers and academics – that a sense of a criminal law system with a meaningful national quality emerged. I argue that it was with an abiding ethos of fidelity to principle that Australian courts and Australian academics came to elaborate a criminal law of Australia, and, as part of that process, to distinguish that law from that of England and Wales. In judicial interpretation and application of the law, and in scholarly argument for its reform, Australian practitioners and scholars saw themselves as making both principled *and* progressive decisions and arguments.

The story told in this chapter about the 'birth' of Australian criminal law in the mid-century is a new story, and it departs from the standard account of the development of Australian criminal law. In the standard account – often assumed rather than argued or defended – Australian criminal law emerged either around the turn of the twentieth century, or at its end. That is, it emerged either with the enactment of the criminal codes in the state jurisdictions of Queensland, Western Australia and Tasmania at the end of the nineteenth century and in the first decades of the twentieth century,[2] or, by contrast, not until the 1980s following the passage of the *Australia Acts* and the end of appeals from the High Court and state Supreme Courts to the Privy Council in England.[3] This standard story is largely dependent on form rather than substance – the form of the criminal law in the Code jurisdictions, as a code – or on constitutional rather than criminal law developments – the formal independence of Australian courts and Australian law. As I show in this chapter, looking beyond questions of form to substance, and focusing on the specifics of the criminal law and criminal responsibility story, reveals a distinct picture about the development of Australian criminal law.

This new story about the 'birth' of Australian criminal law emerges in part through an examination of the first Australian criminal law textbooks, which were published from the late 1940s to the 1960s.[4] As elsewhere in the common law

[2] See, e.g., R. F. B. Philip, 'Criminal Responsibility at Common Law and Under the Criminal Code – Some Comparisons' (1948–51) 1(2) *University of Queensland Law Journal* 1–13.

[3] See, e.g., P. Cane, *Controlling Administrative Power: An Historical Comparison* (Cambridge: Cambridge University Press, 2016), p. 511 (arguing that Australian law was 'dependent on rather than independent of' English law until the Australian High Court became the final court of appeal for all matters in the 1980s). Appeals from the High Court to the Privy Council were abolished in two stages in 1968 and 1975, but the *Australia Acts* ended appeals from state courts, establishing the High Court as Australia's apex court: see *Australia Act 1986* (England) and *Australia Act 1986* (Cth).

[4] A couple of these textbooks covered all Australian jurisdictions, but a textbook devoted exclusively to the Code jurisdictions did not appear until the 1970s: J. M. Herlihy and R. G. Kenny, *An Introduction to Criminal Law in Queensland* (Melbourne: Butterworths, 1978). Collections of cases and materials pertaining to the Code jurisdictions were published in 1958 (R. Carter, *Criminal Law of Queensland,* Melbourne: Butterworths,

world, in the early decades of the twentieth century; the most significant criminal law texts were legal treatises and practitioner manuals such as those produced for magistrates.[5] These sorts of publications, which compiled criminal legislation and reproduced some significant decisions for easy access by legal practitioners, were published in Australia during that period.[6] Australia's first criminal law textbooks both reflected and advanced the sense of an Australian criminal law. Textbooks presented a novel legal form, playing a central role in the systematisation of the criminal law, law teaching and legal practice.[7] As Lindsay Farmer argues, criminal law textbooks are implicated in the rise to prominence of the idea that the criminal law is constituted by general principles,[8] and, as I discuss, this role of textbooks is a significant part of the Australian story. The authors of Australia's first textbooks formed a cohort of academics-cum-practitioners that was deeply engaged with criminal law in Australia in the mid-century, and in conveying information about Australian developments to academics and practitioners overseas,[9] presenting Australian criminal law to the world.

This chapter comprises four parts, corresponding to the four significant fronts across which the 'birth' of Australian criminal law proceeded: the interpretation of the criminal responsibility provisions in the criminal codes of Queensland, Western Australia and Tasmania; the creation of an Australian law of insanity; the emergence of a doctrine of honest and reasonable mistake

1958) and 1969 (E. J. Edwards, R. A. Hayes and R. S. O'Regan, *Cases on the Criminal Code: Being Cases and Material on the Criminal Law in Queensland, Western Australia and Papua and New Guinea*, Sydney: Law Book Co., 1969) (the Queensland code was exported to Papua and New Guinea when it was an Australian protectorate after World War II).

5 See for discussion L. Farmer, 'Of Treatises and Textbooks: The Literature of Criminal Law in Nineteenth Century Britain', in M. Dubber and A. Fernandez (eds.), *Law Books in Action: Essays on the Anglo-American Legal Treatise* (Oxford: Hart Publishing, 2012).

6 In the Australian context, see, e.g., W. F. Wilson and A. D. Graham (eds.), *The Criminal Code of Queensland and the Criminal Practice Rules of 1900* (Brisbane: Government Printer, 1901); H. M. Hamilton, *Hamilton and Addison, Criminal Law and Procedure, N.S.W.* (Sydney: Law Book Co., 1921).

7 See L. Farmer, 'The Modest Ambition of Glanville Williams', in M. D. Dubber (ed.), *Foundational Texts in Modern Criminal Law* (Oxford: Oxford University Press, 2014). On the early Australian criminology texts, see M. Finnane, 'The Origins of Criminology in Australia' (2012) 45(2) *Australia & New Zealand Journal of Criminology* 157–78, 161–9.

8 See L. Farmer, *Making the Modern Criminal Law: Criminalization and Civil Order. Series: Criminalization* (Oxford: Oxford University Press, 2016), ch. 3.

9 Several members of this cohort wrote a series of 'Australian Letters' published in the *Criminal Law Review* from its first year of publication, 1954, to the late 1960s. These letters provided reports on those decisions of Australian courts that were thought to be 'of considerable significance to the formulation of important doctrines of substantive criminal law': see N. Morris, 'An Australian Letter' [1958] *Criminal Law Review* 520–8. Other 'Letters' published in this journal were written by commentators from jurisdictions such as Scotland and New Zealand.

of fact; and the recognition of a novel partial defence to murder, excessive self-defence.[10] Across these fronts, and over the mid-century period, it is possible to detect an emergent and then more fulsome belief in, and understanding of, *Australian* criminal law.

'Interesting Legislative Experiments'[11]: Interpreting the Griffith Codes

It was in the middle decades of the twentieth century that the implications of the earlier enactment of criminal codes in the states of Queensland, Western Australia and Tasmania were realised. The task of interpreting these codes presented significant challenges. While in the 1930s, the High Court accepted that the code provisions should not be interpreted by reference to the common law,[12] in the 1960s, it was still possible for commentators to point to a 'general failure by Australian judges to agree about how to interpret a code'.[13] For my purposes here, the significance of the mid-century engagement with these criminal codes lies in how it pushed Australian jurists and commentators to debate the principles of criminal responsibility, in an attempt to bring the codes and the common law into alignment on those principles, and to forge some national coherence in criminal law.

Australia's first criminal codes were formulated at the end of the nineteenth century and in the first decades of the twentieth century.[14] These codes are generally known as the Griffith Codes, reflecting the influence of Sir Samuel Griffith on their drafting and enactment.[15] As discussed in Chapter 3 of this book, these codes sought to modernise and simplify the common law through codification, and, in relation to criminal responsibility, broke away from common law models.[16] The Griffith Codes each contain a general part that precedes the main body of the Code, and in which provisions relating to criminal responsibility

[10] There were of course other novel developments advanced by Australian practitioners and scholars in this period, including, for example, in relation to the use of issue estoppel in the criminal context: see *Mraz* v. *R* (No. 2) (1956) 96 CLR 62, and, for discussion, A. Kaladelfos, 'The Maliciousness of Rape' (2016) 40 *Criminal Law Journal* 230–2.

[11] J. V. Barry and G. W. Paton (with G. Sawer), *An Introduction to the Criminal Law in Australia* (London: Macmillan, 1948), p. 16.

[12] See *Brennan* v. *The King* (1936) 55 CLR 253 at 263 per Dixon and Evatt JJ, referring to *Criminal Code Act 1913* (WA) s 7 and citing the House of Lords decision *Bank of England* v. *Vagliano Brothers* [1891] AC 107.

[13] N. Morris and C. Howard, *Studies in Criminal Law* (Oxford: Clarendon Press, 1964), p. 100.

[14] These codes are the Queensland Criminal Code, which provided a model for Western Australia's *Criminal Code 1902* (repealed and re-enacted in 1913), and also influenced the Tasmanian *Criminal Code 1924*. These Codes were each enacted as schedules to criminal code Acts.

[15] See, for discussion, G. Fricke, *Judges of the High Court* (Melbourne: Hutchinson, 1986), ch. 1.

[16] See Chapter 3.

are collected together.[17] These provisions apply to the offences contained in the special part of the codes 'without further restatement'.[18] Reflecting the ideas current at the end of the nineteenth century, criminal responsibility principles in the Griffith Codes are based on objective fault.[19] The model provision, section 23 of the Queensland Criminal Code (reproduced in the Western Australian Code) provides that 'a person is not criminally responsible for an act or omission which occurs independently of the exercise of his will, or for an event which occurs by accident'. The effect of the criminal responsibility provisions in the Griffith Codes is that an accused is held responsible not because his or her state of mind is blameworthy in itself, but because of a 'blameworthy failure to live up to an objective standard of thought and behaviour'.[20] Including criminal responsibility provisions in the Codes fixed them at the point in time of codification. This was and continues to be regarded as a virtue by some commentators: one mid-century commentator stated that, under the Codes, criminal responsibility depends not on the 'unruly horse' of the 'moral doctrine' of *mens rea*, but on the 'steadier steed of statutory enactment'.[21]

The Griffith Codes came to be interpreted by the High Court against a backdrop of the ethos of unity with English law that prevailed up until the mid-century. At this time, the legal system in Australia and other former colonies was framed by the political and legal reality of the British Commonwealth, across which English law was thought to apply.[22] Although Australian states had gained authority to pass their own statutes in the mid-nineteenth century, in the mid-twentieth century, what was called 'Imperial unity' constituted political and legal orthodoxy.[23] This ethos of unity with England impacted on understanding of criminal law in Australia. Thus, although the High Court of Australia was only bound by decisions of the Privy Council, 'legal deference' to the House of Lords – then the final authority for declaring English law – was the norm.[24] As the High Court stated in 1943, it is 'a wise general rule of practice' that, where there is a conflict between a decision of the House of Lords and

[17] See Chapter V of both the *Criminal Code Act 1899* (Qld) and *Criminal Code Act Compilation Act 1913* (WA).

[18] C. Howard, *Australian Criminal Law* (Sydney: Law Book Co., 1982), p. 341.

[19] See, e.g., *Criminal Code Act 1899* (Qld) ss 22–25.

[20] E. Colvin, 'Criminal Responsibility Under the South Pacific Codes' (2002) 26 *Criminal Law Journal* 98–113, 104.

[21] See Philip, 'Criminal Responsibility at Common Law and under the Criminal Code', p. 1.

[22] The application of the law to Australia's Indigenous people was not so clear-cut: see for discussion L. Ford, *Settler Sovereignty: Jurisdiction and Indigenous People in America and Australia 1788–1836* (Cambridge, MA: Harvard University Press, 2010); H. Douglas and M. Finnane, *Indigenous Crime and Settler Law: White Sovereignty after Empire* (Basingstoke: Palgrave Macmillan, 2012).

[23] See, for discussion, P. C. Oliver, *The Constitution of Independence: The Development of Constitutional Theory in Australia, Canada and New Zealand* (Oxford: Oxford University Press, 2005), p. 216, and, more generally, chs 9 and 10.

[24] See Morris and Howard, *Studies in Criminal Law*, viii.

the High Court, 'this Court, and other courts in Australia, should follow a decision of the House of Lords upon matters of general legal principle'.[25]

The text that may be regarded as Australia's first criminal law textbook, *An Introduction to the Criminal Law in Australia*, by J. V. Barry and G. W. Paton, published in England in 1948,[26] testifies to this idea of 'Imperial unity'. Although the text appeared in the years after World War II, it seems to have been begun beforehand,[27] indicating it represents a moment at the outset of the mid-century period under discussion in this chapter. As hinted at in the book's title (which refers to the criminal law 'in' Australia, as opposed to the criminal law 'of' Australia), in this book, Australian criminal law does not appear as a distinct entity, nor do the authors suggest that it should be studied (by Australian law students and practitioners) for its own sake. Rather, the aim of the book was to 'delineate broadly the characteristic features of the criminal law in Australia in order to stimulate interest in comparative law'.[28] At this time, referring to both the criminal law of common law states and Code states, the authors stated that 'there is much greater uniformity with modern English law than might be imagined'.[29] As evidence of this 'uniformity', they point to the fact that 'no great inconvenience is caused if a student uses standard English text-books'.[30]

The Griffith Codes undercut this idea of unity with English law, and its corollary, unity in Australian criminal laws, but, in the first decades of the twentieth century, this did not seem to present a problem. The first years after Federation in 1901 were marked by political determination to preserve the independence of the Australian states, and this extended to the criminal law, which had remained a state responsibility. At first aided by the presence of Griffith as the first Chief Justice of the High Court, the task of interpreting the fault provisions of the Codes appeared to be straightforward. It seemed clear that, in Code jurisdictions, it was 'never necessary to have recourse to the old doctrine of *mens rea*', because 'the test now to be applied is whether this

[25] See *Piro* v. *Foster* (1943) 68 CLR 313 at 320 per Latham CJ.

[26] J. V. Barry and G. W. Paton (with G. Sawer), *An Introduction to the Criminal Law in Australia* (London: Macmillan, 1948). The text formed the sixth volume in the series *English Studies in Criminal Science*, edited by University of Cambridge Professors Leon Radzinowicz and J. W. C. Turner, who were said to have commissioned the book because they were 'impressed by recent developments in the criminal law of Australia': Barry and Paton, *An Introduction to the Criminal Law in Australia*, ix.

[27] In the Foreword, the authors indicate that the book was 'somewhat delayed' due to the war and the 'scattering' of both the legal profession and the University staff: Barry and Paton, *An Introduction to the Criminal Law in Australia*, x.

[28] Barry and Paton, *An Introduction to the Criminal Law in Australia*, x. Another early textbook, *Studies in Criminal Law*, by Norval Morris and Colin Howard, was also intended to serve comparative law purposes. The stated aim of the book was to 'acquaint a wider public than hitherto with a number of original and valuable contributions to the criminal law by the courts of Australia', but it was also hoped that the book would encourage English lawyers to cite Commonwealth cases: Morris and Howard, *Studies in Criminal Law*, iii.

[29] Barry and Paton, *An Introduction to the Criminal Law in Australia*, p. 6.

[30] Ibid.

prohibited act was, or was not, done accidentally or independently of the exercise of the will of the accused person'.[31] In 1936, in relation to the Criminal Code of Western Australia, the High Court stated that, as the Code was 'intended to replace the common law', 'its language should be construed according to its natural meaning and without any presumption that it was intended to do no more than restate the existing law'.[32] These statements indicate that Code provisions were to be interpreted on their own terms, without reference to common law doctrines such as *mens rea*.

In the mid-century, an emergent sense of the value of coherence across Australia put pressure on this state of affairs, and differences *within* criminal laws in Australia became less tolerable. This was particularly the case if the preservation of difference was thought to retard the development of the criminal law. Thus, when, in 1938, the issue of the burden of proof under the Griffith Codes came to the High Court via an appeal from Queensland, the High Court held that the burden of proving the elements of the offence lay with the prosecution.[33] None of the Codes had an express general rule about the burden of proof, but it was 'reasonably clear' that the drafters of the Queensland Code intended to place a legal burden on the defendant to prove the alleged offence was an accident.[34] However, just a few years before the issue came before the High Court, the House of Lords reached the opposite conclusion in *Woolmington*, holding that the burden of proof at common law was on the prosecution to prove the elements of the offence.[35] In his judgment in the High Court, Dixon J held that the preference for a legal burden on the defendant to prove the alleged offence was an accident was not sufficiently clearly expressed in the Code so as to exclude the application of *Woolmington*.[36] This decision is notable not just because the House of Lords' clear statement about the burden of proof in *Woolmington* post-dated the enactment of the Griffith Codes, but also because it exposed the High Courts' rather blatant attempts to avoid 'the emergence of an undesirable difference in the law between the states'.[37] By the mid-century, it was possible for two commentators to refer to a 'natural tendency to interpret the Code, as far as possible, in accordance with the rules of the common law'[38] – a tendency that blunted the distinctiveness of the Code provisions, in favour of national coherence in the criminal law.

31 *Widgee Shire Council* v. *Bonney* (1907) 4 CLR 977 at 981–2 per Griffith CJ (referring to *Criminal Code Act 1899* (Qld) s 23).

32 *Brennan* v. *The King* (1936) 55 CLR 253 at 263 per Dixon and Evatt JJ.

33 *The King* v. *Mullen* (1938) 59 CLR 124. In this decision, the High Court agreed with the Queensland Court of Appeal: see *Mullen* v. *The King* [1938] St R Qd 97.

34 See Howard, *Australian Criminal Law*, p. 4; *The King* v. *Mullen* (1938) 59 CLR 124 at 136. This had been the practice regarding the burden of proof in criminal cases in Queensland until this time.

35 See *Woolmington* v. *Director of Public Prosecutions* [1935] AC 462.

36 *The King* v. *Mullen* (1938) 59 CLR 124 at 136 per Dixon J.

37 See Howard, *Australian Criminal Law*, p. 5.

38 Barry and Paton, *An Introduction to the Criminal Law in Australia*, p. 49.

A decisive test of the Code fault provisions occurred in the early 1960s, when the High Court heard the case of *Vallance* v. *The Queen*.[39] The Tasmanian Court of Criminal Appeal granted the prosecution permission to appeal the acquittal of Kevin Vallance, who had been charged with unlawful wounding under the Tasmanian Criminal Code, having hit a young girl with an airgun pellet, but claiming that he had not intended to hit her.[40] Vallance was then convicted by the Tasmanian Court of Criminal Appeal and appealed to the High Court. At issue was the scope of the provision of the Tasmanian Code providing that 'no person shall be criminally responsible for an act, unless it is voluntary and intentional', nor for 'an event which occurs by chance'.[41] In its refusal to grant special leave to hear the appeal, the High Court provided a detailed consideration of Code fault provisions. Dixon CJ noted that, despite the structure of the Tasmanian Code, with its 'General Part', it had failed to provide for specific offences to be 'finally controlled by Chapter IV (criminal responsibility)', as had been planned.[42] On this basis, the High Court read recklessness into the Tasmanian Code provision, concluding that Vallance could be convicted if he had foreseen the likelihood of wounding the victim and ignored the risk.[43] This conclusion about recklessness meant that, in effect, the Code rules of criminal responsibility were equated with those of the common law.[44] In the words of one early textbook writer, this interpretation of the Code was 'satisfactory', but 'by no means inevitable as a matter of construction'.[45]

This decision in *Vallance* entailed bringing the Griffith Codes into alignment with the common law of crime, with the deeper impetus for the move the more nebulous but increasing value of coherence in criminal law across Australia. The idea of coherence in criminal law rested on an emergent orientation of the criminal law around national coordinates. Even as the formal status of English law in Australia was unchanged, the idea of one Imperial legal system was dissolving, and the law in the Dominions was developing into multiple legal systems.[46] At the same time, experience of World War I and World War II in particular enhanced the sense of independence and confidence of people and institutions in Australia.[47] In large part via the leadership of the

39 *Vallance* v. *The Queen* (1961) 108 CLR 56.

40 Under the Tasmanian Code, it is possible for the Attorney-General to appeal an acquittal after obtaining leave to appeal from the Court of Criminal Appeal or with a certificate from the trial court that it is a fit case for appeal: *Criminal Code Act 1924* (Tas) s 401.

41 See *Criminal Code Act 1924* (Tas) s 13(1).

42 *Vallance* v. *The Queen* (1961) 108 CLR 56 at 58 per Dixon CJ.

43 Ibid.

44 See C. Howard, 'An Australian Letter – The Meaning of Accident' [1965] *Criminal Law Review* 516–22, 517–19.

45 Howard, *Australian Criminal Law*, p. 5. As Howard put it, the concept of recklessness was 'neither mentioned nor envisaged' in the general parts of the Codes.

46 See generally Oliver, *The Constitution of Independence*.

47 See generally S. MacIntyre, *Australia's Boldest Experiment: War and reconstruction in the 1940s* (Sydney: NewSouth Publishing, 2015); R. White, 'War and Australian Society', in M. McKernan and M. Brown (eds.), *Australia: Two Centuries of War and Peace* (Canberra: Allen & Unwin, 1988).

High Court as Australia's highest court,[48] it was becoming possible to think about Australian criminal law as such, to conceptualise *Australian* criminal law as a meaningful idea. This national orientation, which was also displayed in Australia's first criminal law textbooks,[49] meant that relevant coordinates for criminal law were increasingly national, rather than radiating from London.

Non-responsibility: An Australian Law of Insanity

The second front that is significant for the 'birth' of Australian criminal law is the creation of an Australian law of insanity. As is well known, the insanity defence marks out those defendants who are not considered responsible for their conduct, as a result of mental disorder, and is typically regarded as the pre-eminent instance of non-responsibility in criminal law.[50] While Australia had inherited the famous common law test for insanity, the *M'Naghten Rules*, in three stages over the twentieth century, an Australian law of insanity was created, with crucial developments occurring in the mid-century. Questions of legal principle, and questions of justice for mentally disordered defendants, prompted Australian legislators and jurists to formulate a *sui generis* law of insanity that was regarded as both principled *and* progressive, a development that captured the increasing confidence of Australian legal practitioners and commentators.

The first stage of the development of an Australian law of insanity pre-dates the period under discussion in this chapter, and forms the backdrop to the mid-century developments. This stage corresponded to the Griffith Codes, which, as mentioned above, were drafted by Griffith. Together with Owen Dixon, discussed below, Griffith exerted considerable influence on the development of the law on insanity in Australia.[51] As part of the wider project of codification, the Griffith Codes updated the test for insanity, on the basis that such an update

[48] The High Court, which was established in 1903, has limited criminal jurisdiction, but hears civil and criminal appeals from state and federal courts by way of a special leave mechanism: see G. Urbas and S. Bronitt, 'Courts, Criminal Law and Procedure', in A. Graycar and P. Grabosky (eds.), *The Cambridge Handbook of Australian Criminology* (Cambridge: Cambridge University Press, 2002), pp. 73, 78–9.

[49] Two vignettes in Australia's first textbooks symbolise these new national coordinates. The date of the Preface of Morris and Howard's 1964 textbook is given as 'Anzac Day 1963' – a reference to the Australian national holiday that commemorates the World War I battle at Gallipoli, Turkey, in which large numbers of Australian and New Zealander servicemen ('Anzacs') were killed. Similarly, the Preface to Howard's 1965 textbook (Howard, *Australian Criminal Law*) is given only as 'Cup Day, 1965' – a peculiarly Australian reference to the famous horse race, the Melbourne Cup, held on the first Tuesday of November every year since 1875.

[50] See A. Loughnan, 'Asking (Different) Responsibility Questions: Responsibility and Non-Responsibility in Criminal Law' (2016) 4(1) *Bergen Journal of Criminal Law and Criminal Justice* 24–46; on the insanity defence more generally, see A. Loughnan, *Manifest Madness: Mental Incapacity in Criminal Law* (Oxford: Oxford University Press, 2012), chapters 4 and 5.

[51] This was acknowledged by another man who heavily influenced the Australian law of insanity – J. V. Barry: see J. V. Barry, 'Insanity in the criminal law in Australia' (1943) 21 *Canadian Bar Review* 427–39, 429, 430; see also Morris and Howard, *Studies in Criminal Law*, p. 37.

would improve the law. Simplifying the language of, and expanding the reach of, the *M'Naghten Rules*, all three of the Griffith Codes replaced the *M'Naghten* phrase, 'disease of the mind', with 'mental disease'.[52] The Codes also replaced the *M'Naghten Rules* references to the defendant's appreciation of 'the nature and quality of the act' or its 'wrongness' with a reference to his 'capacity to understand what he is doing, or of capacity to control actions, or of capacity to know that he ought not to do the act or make the omission'.[53] With this latter change, the Code provisions brought lack of control (volitional incapacity or 'irresistible impulse') within the scope of the insanity defence.[54] In a further departure from the common law, the Code provisions also provided that 'natural mental infirmity' would be a basis for the defence, expressly extending the reach of the insanity defence to intellectual impairment as well as mental disorder.[55] With no want of modesty, these changes to the law were said by two textbook writers to have reduced 'medico-legal conflict', and to have 'anticipated' the subsequent proposals of the US *Model Penal Code*.[56]

The novel insanity provisions in the Griffith Codes paved the way for the second, and crucial, stage of development of the Australian law of insanity in the mid-century: interpretation of the *M'Naghten Rules* by the High Court. The High Court had its first opportunity to consider the *Rules* in *R* v. *Porter* in 1933. Porter raised the insanity defence when charged with the murder of his baby, having poisoned the baby and attempted to poison himself following separation from his wife. As the offence took place in the Australian Capital Territory (ACT), and the High Court then had original jurisdiction in local criminal matters, the High Court acted as a trial court, issuing a judgment that directly addressed the facts of the case, unmediated by the existence of a prior direction from a trial judge.[57] Building on the earlier innovation in the insanity defence under the codes, in *Porter*, Dixon J offered a fresh direction on *M'Naghten*, interpreting the *M'Naghten Rules* to provide that the insanity defence applied to someone who could not 'reason with a moderate degree of

[52] See *Criminal Code 1899* (Qld) s 27 and *Criminal Code Act Compilation Act 1913* (WA) s 27.

[53] See *Criminal Code 1899* (Qld) s 27, *Criminal Code Act Compilation Act 1913* (WA) s 27 and *Criminal Code Act 1924* (Tas) s 16(1).

[54] These changes to the common law of insanity reflect the influence of the *Italian Penal Code 1889* on Griffith: see A. Cadoppi and K. Cullinane, 'Translation: The Zanardelli Code and Codification in the Countries of the Common Law' (2000) 7 *James Cook University Law Review* 119–90, 151–2. I discuss this influence in Chapter 3.

[55] See *Criminal Code Act 1899* (Qld) s 27 and *Criminal Code Act Compilation Act 1913* (WA) s 27. The Tasmanian Criminal Code provides that 'mental disease' includes 'natural imbecility': *Criminal Code Act 1924* (Tas) s 16.

[56] Morris and Howard, *Studies in Criminal Law*, p. 56.

[57] This was a rare instance of Australia's apex court hearing a criminal case at first instance. The High Court exercised this power under s 76 of the Australian Constitution, but lost this jurisdiction in 1933 when the Supreme Court of the ACT was established by the *Seat of Government Supreme Court Act 1933* (Cth).

sense and composure'.[58] This direction has come to be regarded as a model, and indeed is sometimes treated as a default insanity test.[59]

Only a few years after hearing *Porter*, insanity came to the attention of the High Court again in *Sodeman*.[60] In *Sodeman*, the High Court dealt with an application for leave to appeal a murder conviction that arose after Sodeman confessed to killing four young women over a period of five years. Reflecting Dixon's influence on the court, all justices agreed that 'irresistible impulse' could be evidence of insanity for the purposes of the *M'Naghten Rules*.[61] Dixon, who was now Chief Justice, repeated what he had said in *Porter*, and stated that 'if through disorder of the faculties a prisoner is incapable of controlling his relevant acts, this may afford the strongest reason for supposing that he is incapable of forming a judgment that they are wrong, and in some cases even of understanding their nature'.[62] As this indicates, although not itself a basis for the insanity defence, 'irresistible impulse' was held to provide support for an insanity plea.[63] Soderman was convicted and his application to the Privy Council for special leave to appeal was denied, with the Council appearing to have understood the High Court decision to have been even more radical, having held that 'irresistible impulse' was itself within the scope of the *M'Naghten Rules*.[64] The effect of *Sodeman* is that, in the common law Australian states, proof of an 'irresistible impulse' may assist a defendant to bring him or herself within the *M'Naghten* test for insanity.[65]

In the early 1950s, the High Court had the opportunity to consider the meaning of 'wrongness' in the *M'Naghten Rules*, in the case of *Stapleton*, which was the definitive decision in the establishment of an Australian law of insanity.[66] Just a few months before *Stapleton*, the English Court of Criminal Appeal had decided that the use of the term 'wrongness' in *M'Naghten* denoted legal wrongness, meaning that an individual would not be able to raise insanity if he or she knew the act comprising the offence was against the law.[67] In *Stapleton*,

[58] *R* v. *Porter* (1933) 55 CLR 182 at 189.

[59] See Barry, 'Insanity in the criminal law in Australia', p. 439; see also Howard, *Australian Criminal Law*, p. 289.

[60] *Sodeman* v. *The King* (1936) 55 CLR 192.

[61] *Sodeman* v. *The King* (1936) 55 CLR 192 at 214–15 per Dixon J, at 204 per Latham CJ, at 208 per Starke J, at 227 per Evatt J. As only four High Court justices were available to hear the appeal, and they were evenly divided regarding the grounds of appeal, leave to appeal was refused.

[62] *Sodeman* v. *The King* (1936) 55 CLR 192 at 214–15.

[63] See further M. Finnane, '"Irresistible Impulse": Historicizing a Judicial Innovation in Australian Insanity Jurisprudence' (2012) 23(4) *History of Psychiatry* 454–68.

[64] See *Attorney-General for the State of South Australia* v. *John Whelan Brown* (Australia) (1960) 44 Cr App R 100; see, for discussion, Finnane, 'Irresistible impulse'.

[65] When the Privy Council had the opportunity to consider *Sodeman*, as a result of an appeal from another Australian case concerning insanity, it expressly agreed with the High Court that 'irresistible impulse' might be evidence that the defendant did not know that his or her actions were wrong: see *Attorney-General for the State of South Australia* v. *Brown* (1960) 44 Cr App R 100.

[66] *Stapleton* v. *The Queen* (1952) 86 CLR 358.

[67] See *R* v. *Windle* (1952) 36 Cr App R 85.

the High Court declined to follow England and interpreted the 'wrongness' part of the *M'Naghten Rules* test for insanity to denote moral, not legal, wrongness. In a joint judgment, three justices of the High Court, including Dixon CJ, stated that a defendant's criminal responsibility depends on his ability to reason about the wrongness of his act with a 'moderate degree of sense and composure', not merely on his appreciation of its illegality.[68] This judgment cemented the distinctive approach to the interpretation of *M'Naghten* in Australia: *M'Naghten* has a wider scope in the common law of Australia compared with that of England and Wales. These mid-century developments had the effect of establishing an Australian law of insanity, and, on a more general level, helped mark Australia out as an independent criminal law jurisdiction.

Like the earlier innovations in the Griffith Code provisions on insanity, the mid-century developments in the common law were regarded as progressive. As elsewhere, in Australia, the mid-century was characterised by widespread concerns about crime and social welfare, and by the thorough-going infusion of psychological and psychiatric knowledges in understandings of individual and social lives. These knowledges were harnessed by the state through the development of the institutions and governance practices of the welfare state, which redefined the relationship between the individual and the state. As Nicholas Brown argues, individuals were encouraged to 'make the most of new opportunities for citizenship through a process of guided introspection rather than any more inclusive sense of participating in social processes'.[69] These knowledges influenced contemporaneous thinking about the insanity defence. For instance, in 1965, the Chief Justice's Law Reform Committee of Victoria recommended that, in the interests of fairness, defendants should only bear an evidential (rather than substantive) burden in relation to insanity, and that the scope of the insanity defence be extended.[70] Psychological and psychiatric knowledges also influenced thinking about the criminal law more generally. For example, Barry and Paton's 1948 textbook, *An Introduction to the Criminal Law in Australia*, bears the imprint of the fashionable focus on treatment and reform, rather than retribution, with the authors advocating a 'scientific approach to the criminal problem', encouraging the involvement of psychiatrists and psychologists in criminal justice processes.[71]

As well as being regarded as progressive, the High Court decisions on the law of insanity were considered to be faithful to principles of criminal responsibility. Advocating a parting of ways with England, this fidelity to principle was expressed by reference to older, rather than newer, authorities

[68] *Stapleton* v. *The Queen* (1952) 86 CLR 358 at 367 per Dixon CJ, Webb and Kitto JJ.

[69] See N. Brown, *Governing Prosperity: Social Change and Social Analysis in Australia in the 1950s* (Cambridge: Cambridge University Press, 1995), p. 175.

[70] See discussion in I. Leader-Elliott, 'Australian Letter' [1969] *Criminal Law Review* 511–23, 511, 522–3.

[71] See generally Barry and Paton, *An Introduction to the Criminal Law in Australia*, p. 117 and Part VI.

on the criminal law. For Dixon, who was at the forefront of these developments, the interpretations of *M'Naghten* offered by Australian courts were in keeping with eighteenth and nineteenth century cases and commentaries on insanity, including that of James Fitzjames Stephen, and it was an improvement on *M'Naghten* and its standard interpretation to restore these earlier approaches.[72] Writing extra-judicially in 1957, Dixon was highly critical of the *M'Naghten Rules*, arguing that their result was to 'imprison the common law in a formula', depriving it of its capacity for development and flexibility.[73] According to Dixon, the problem was that words of the *M'Naghten Rules* had been 'weighed like diamonds'.[74] Dixon did not like hearing of the law of insanity referred to as the *M'Naghten Rules*, criticising the way an 'extra-judicial utterance' had taken the place of precedent.[75] This interpretation of the law of insanity was backed up by Australian commentators. According to two commentators, on the basis that it was a more faithful interpretation of the *Rules* at the time of the *M'Naghten* decision, the analysis in *Stapleton* was labelled 'compelling', while the English Court of Appeal's opposing analysis about the meaning of 'wrongness' was said to be 'plainly wrong'.[76] As this stark evaluation indicates, it was in the elucidation of principle that an approach to the law of insanity with distinctively national character emerged.

As this discussion suggests, the law of insanity bears the stamp of a couple of key jurists in the Australian criminal law story: Samuel Griffith and Owen Dixon. As the chief architect of the Queensland Criminal Code, Griffith looked beyond *M'Naghten* to establish what he believed was the proper scope of the insanity defence (in cognitive, moral or volitional incapacity).[77] Dixon, who is regarded as one of Australia's most prominent jurists, sat on the High Court from 1929 to 1964, and profoundly affected many aspects of Australian law, including criminal law. Dixon took a special interest in medico-legal matters and in the insanity defence in particular, becoming a member of the Medico-Legal Society of Victoria in 1933, early in his career as a High Court Justice.[78]

72 For instance, in *Sodeman*, in relation to the scope of responsibility, Dixon J cited *R* v. *Davis* (1881) 14 Cox CC 563 at 215.

73 See O. Dixon, 'A Legacy of Hadfield, McNaghten and Maclean' (1957) 31 *The Australian Law Journal* 255–66, 261; see also P. Brett, *An Inquiry into Criminal Guilt* (Sydney: Lawbook Co., 1963), pp. 160–4.

74 Dixon, 'A Legacy of Hadfield, McNaghten and Maclean', 260: see also O. Dixon, 'Response to Questions' (1957) 31 *Australian Law Journal* 265–6, 66.

75 Dixon, 'Response to Questions', 266. More generally, on the legacy of *M'Naghten*, see A. Loughnan, 'M'Naghten's Case (1843)', in P. Handler, H. Mares and I. Williams (eds.), *Landmark Cases in Criminal Law* (London: Hart Publishing, 2017).

76 Morris and Howard, *Studies in Criminal Law*, p. 46.

77 See S. Griffith, 'Criminal Responsibility: A Chapter from a Criminal Code', in *Report of the Seventh Meeting of the Australasian Association for the Advancement of Science* (Sydney: Australasian Association for the Advancement of Science, 1898), pp. 900–1.

78 See Finnane, '"Irresistible impulse"'; O. Dixon, 'Science and Judicial Proceedings', in J. V. Barry and A. E. Coates (eds.), *The Proceedings of the Medico-Legal Society of Victoria During the Years 1933–1934 and 1935–1936* (Melbourne: Brown, Prior, Anderson Pty. Ltd., 1937).

In addition, J. V. Barry, a barrister and one of the authors of the 1948 text, *Introduction to the Criminal Law in Australia*, mentioned above, was also a member of the Medico-Legal Society, and had a special interest in insanity. Barry played a central role in publicising the Australian developments to an international academic readership, as the author of a high-profile article in the *Canadian Bar Review* which was commissioned by Leon Radzinowicz and J. W. C. Turner for the Cambridge series *English Studies in Criminal Science*.[79]

The wider context for the influence of this small group of men was the then still small legal community in Australia. In the mid-century, a circumscribed bar and bench meant that certain individuals exercised enormous influence on the criminal law and its operation. For instance, J. V. Barry was able to influence the legal developments discussed in this chapter from his position on the Victorian Supreme Court from 1947 to 1969.[80] From this position, Barry promoted the principles of subjective fault that he had earlier defended in *An Introduction to Criminal Law in Australia* (which I discuss below).[81] The influence of this small group extended to Australia law schools. At this time, in Australia, legal education was closely tied to legal practice, although there were also signs of the independence and professionalisation of law schools, such as in the creation of university law reviews.[82] Reflecting the inter-relatedness of the Australian legal academy and the legal profession, the authors of Australia's first criminal law textbooks featuring in this chapter were engaged as teachers of law at the same time as they pursued careers as legal practitioners.[83] This cohort enjoyed strong international standing,[84] and had a significant influence on the development of the criminal law in Australia – in advocacy at the Bar and law reform,[85] but also in the way their textbooks systematised and analysed the law for future practitioners.

[79] See Barry, 'Insanity in the Criminal Law in Australia'; on J. V. Barry more generally, see M. Finnane, *JV Barry: A Life* (Sydney: UNSW Press, 2007).

[80] On insanity, see, e.g., *R* v. *Jeffrey* [1967] VR 467, *R* v. *Weise* [1969] VR 953. J. V. Barry also published 'The Defence of Insanity and the Burden of Proof' (1939) *Res Judicatae* 42–9. Barry's direction on excessive self-defence in the decision of *McKay* was approved by the Victorian Court of Appeal: *R* v. *McKay* [1957] VR 560.

[81] See, e.g., *R* v. *Bonnor* [1957] VR 227, regarding the burden of proof in relation to bigamy.

[82] The mid-century saw the establishment of several university law journals, including the *University of Queensland Law Review* (1948), the *University of Western Australia Law Review* (1948), the *Sydney Law Review* (1953), *Melbourne University Law Review* (1957) and *Adelaide Law Review* (1960). On the history of legal education in Australia, see generally M. Thornton, *Privatising the Public University: The Case of Law* (London: Routledge, 2012).

[83] For example, Morris and Howard were both employed at the University of Adelaide; Brett and Waller taught criminal law at the University of Melbourne.

[84] Norval Morris was at the University of Melbourne until he was recruited to the University of Chicago in 1964. He is perhaps best known as the author, with Gordon Hawkins, of *The Honest Politician's Guide to Crime Control* (Chicago, IL: University of Chicago Press, 1970).

[85] For instance, in relation to law reform, Louis Waller, who was a Professor at Monash University, became the first Law Reform Commissioner of Victoria in 1982, and the inaugural Chair of the Victorian Law Reform Commission in 1984; Colin Howard was a member of the South Australian Mitchell Committee which recommended the criminalisation of rape in marriage after separation: see Criminal Law and Penal Methods Reform Committee of South Australia, *Special Report: Rape and Other Sexual Offences* (1976).

The development of an Australian law of insanity captures the increasing confidence of these individuals and other Australian practitioners and academics to 'go it alone' in this mid-century period. The early criminal law textbooks testify to growing confidence of Australian practitioners and academics at this time. By contrast with the first Australian criminal law textbook, which, as mentioned above, was presented as serving the interests of comparative law, Australia's second textbook, *Cases and Materials in Criminal Law*, published in 1962,[86] is confident and self-assured – there is no sense that criminal law in Australia serves comparative value only, or that an English textbook would be sufficient for Australian students of criminal law. And, rather than be of interest to lawyers overseas, the book is 'essentially a teaching tool', with the intended readership comprised of students at Australian law schools.[87] Just a few years later, in 1965, the author of another Australian textbook could refer to 'Australian criminal law' – indeed, the title of that textbook is *Australian Criminal Law* – and state that the textbook was written 'in response to the manifest need for a narrative account of Australian criminal law'.[88]

The third stage of the development of an Australian insanity law corresponded with the drafting and enactment of the Commonwealth Criminal Code, in the last decades of the century. As I discuss in Chapter 5, the development of the Commonwealth Criminal Code in the 1990s was a major law reform project intended to provide consistency in Australian criminal law, and to act as a centripetal force in a field that was characterised by diverse state criminal law systems. In this stage of the development of an Australian law of insanity, subsequent to the period discussed here, the law of insanity was codified at the Commonwealth level. In relation to what was by then called mental impairment, the drafters of the Commonwealth Criminal Code elected to emulate the Griffith Code provisions. As a result, over and above the expanded scope of the *M'Naghten Rules* in the Australian common law, the test for insanity under the Commonwealth Code provides that the basis for defence may be an inability to control conduct (volitional incapacity).[89] The codification of the insanity defence was a fulfilment of the developments canvassed here, incorporating the

86 P. Brett and P. Waller, *Cases and Materials in Criminal Law* (Oxford: Butterworths, 1962). Reflecting the growth of the law, and belief in its inherent interest, Brett and Waller's *Cases and Materials in Criminal Law* is confined to the common law of crime rather than extending to cover evidence and procedure and sentencing, or the law in the Australian jurisdictions with criminal codes. This book – with changes in authorship – has been through multiple editions in the period since 1962. The most recent edition is the thirteenth; P. Crofts et al., *Waller and Williams Cases and Materials in Criminal Law*, 13th ed. (Sydney: LexisNexis, 2015).

87 Brett and Waller, *Cases and Materials in Criminal Law*, viii.

88 Howard, *Australian Criminal Law*, Preface.

89 See Criminal Code (Cth) s 302. It appears that this decision was reached based on then recent reviews of the criminal law in WA and QLD which recommended retaining this provision, and on feedback received on the draft code materials: Model Criminal Code Officers' Committee, Standing Committee of Attorneys-General, *Discussion Paper* (1998), p. 35. I discuss the Commonwealth Criminal Code in Chapter 5.

Australian approach to insanity into the national face of Australian criminal law, the Commonwealth Criminal Code.

The Emergence of the Australian Doctrine of Honest and Reasonable Mistake of Fact

The third front that is significant for the 'birth' of Australian criminal law is the emergence of the doctrine of honest and reasonable mistake of fact in the common law.[90] The doctrine of honest and reasonable mistake of fact (also known as 'strict liability' in Australia),[91] established a 'halfway house' of statutory offences, located between common law offences with full *mens rea*, on the one hand, and statutory offences of absolute liability, on the other hand, to which an 'honest and reasonable mistake of fact' is a defence. In the mid-century, in the context of wide-ranging debates about the legitimacy of negligence as a basis for criminal responsibility, this doctrine represented a distinctive response to more general perceptions that the fault requirement in criminal offences was under threat.

In broad terms, the background to the development of a doctrine of honest and reasonable mistake of fact in the twentieth century was the growing recognition of the significance of fault for criminal responsibility over the course of the nineteenth century. As discussed in the previous chapter, understanding of criminal responsibility developed over this period to prepare the way for the emergence of general positive, technical doctrines.[92] As both Lindsay Farmer and Nicola Lacey argue, these doctrines were based on a factualised concept of *mens rea* or fault.[93] Against this background, towards the end of the nineteenth century and in the early twentieth century, as rules of evidence and proof, and the division of labour between prosecution and defence formalised, mistake crystallised as a defence.[94] While initially complicated by uncertainty over the issue of the burden of proof in criminal cases,[95] in general terms, mistake operated to indicate that *mens rea* was not made out and the prosecution had

[90] The distinctive fault provisions of the Griffith Codes have ensured that this doctrine does not apply in these jurisdictions: see for discussion Herlihy and Kenny, *An Introduction to Criminal Law in Queensland*, pp. 81–3; see generally K. Burton, T. Crofts and S. Tarrant, *Principles of Criminal Law in Queensland and Western Australia*, 2nd ed. (Sydney: Thomson Reuters, 2016).

[91] Somewhat confusingly, what is known as 'strict liability' in England and Wales is known as 'absolute liability' in Australia: see *He Kaw Teh* v. *The Queen* (1985) 157 CLR 523. In relation to the law in England and Wales, see J. Horder, *Ashworth's Principles of Criminal Law*, 9th ed. (Oxford: Oxford University Press, 2019), pp. 181–9.

[92] See Chapter 3.

[93] See Farmer, *Making the Modern Criminal Law*, pp. 175–81; N. Lacey, *In Search of Criminal Responsibility: Ideas, Interests and Institutions* (Oxford: Oxford University Press, 2016), ch. 2.

[94] See J. W. C. Turner, 'The Mental Element in Crimes at Common Law' (1936) 6(1) *Cambridge Law Journal* 31–66, 36–7.

[95] Before the House of Lords decision in *Woolmington* v. *Director of Public Prosecutions* [1935] AC 462, it was not clear that the prosecution bore the burden of proving the elements of a criminal offence to the beyond reasonable doubt standard.

failed to prove its case. The defence of mistake was thought to be an extension of the maxim *actus non facit reum, nisi mens sit rea* (there is no guilty act without a guilty mind).[96] It was on this basis that mistake was included in the general principles of criminal responsibility set out in the Queensland *Criminal Code 1899*.[97] In this context, the reasonableness of the mistake was an evidentiary matter: it went to proving that the defendant had made a mistake, and was not a requirement of law.

In the early decades of the twentieth century, the development of a distinct doctrine of honest and reasonable mistake of fact was significantly advanced in relation to the crime of bigamy, 'being married' while getting married to another person, which was a statutory offence.[98] The high legal profile of bigamy reflects the fact that, in addition to being more commonly charged in the 1800s and early 1900s than in the current era, it was thought to be one of the few common law offences in relation to which what the defendant knew presented a challenge to prosecution (specifically, whether the defendant knew he or she was married when marrying again).[99] The legal approach to bigamy had been set by the 1889 English decision of *R* v. *Tolson*, in which the English Court for Crown Cases Reserved held that the belief that the defendant's husband was dead, if honest and held on reasonable grounds, was a good defence to a charge of bigamy.[100] A subsequent English Court of Appeal decision, *R* v. *Wheat and Stocks*, reached the opposite conclusion, however. *Wheat and Stocks* distinguished *Tolson*, finding that a belief held in good faith and on reasonable grounds was no defence to a bigamous marriage.[101]

Before this conflict could come before the appellate courts in England, the High Court heard a case that invited resolution of these competing authorities. The case concerned John Thomas, who, following a direction from the trial judge, had been convicted of bigamy, although the jury found that

[96] *Thomas* v. *R* (1937) 59 CLR 279 at 287 per Latham CJ. In its discussion of mistake in relation to the offence of bigamy, the High Court stated that it is a 'truth' of the law that 'mistaken belief in the existence of circumstances cannot be separated from the manifestation of the will which it prompts': *Thomas* v. *R* (1937) 59 CLR 279 at 299 per Dixon J.

[97] Section 24 of the Code provides that a reasonable and mistaken belief means a person is not criminally responsible for the act or omission that forms the basis of an offence: see *Criminal Code 1899* (Qld) and see further Chapter 3.

[98] On the history of the offence of bigamy, see *Thomas* v. *R* (1937) 59 CLR 279 at 302–3 per Dixon J. Bigamy is now an offence under Commonwealth criminal law, which expressly excludes state laws regarding bigamy: *Marriage Act 1961* (Cth) s 94(1) provides that it is an offence for any married person to 'go through a form or ceremony of marriage with any person'.

[99] Writing in the late nineteenth century, Sir James Fitzjames Stephen commented that bigamy was one of the few offences 'upon which any real difficulty as to criminal knowledge can arise': see J. F. Stephen, *A History of the Criminal Law of England Volume 2* (London: Macmillan and Co., 1883), p. 117.

[100] *R* v. *Tolson* (1889) 23 QBD 168.

[101] *R* v. *Wheat and Stocks* [1921] 2 KB 119.

he had an honest and reasonable belief that the marriage was genuine.[102] The Supreme Court of Victoria upheld the conviction and the High Court granted Thomas' application for special leave to appeal. In a majority decision that was well-received around the common law world, the High Court sided with *Tolson*, holding that an honest and reasonable mistake was an answer to the charge of bigamy, on the basis that to decide otherwise would be inconsistent with 'any humane or liberal system of law or with the acknowledged principles of the common law'.[103] Contrary to earlier decisions, in which the High Court concluded that *mens rea* was not an essential element of every criminal offence,[104] the High Court stated that the defence of honest and reasonable mistake of fact applied equally to statutory offences, absent a 'contrary intention' in the 'words, subject matter or nature of the enactment'.[105] In *Thomas*, the High Court criticised the direction issued by the trial judge (as usurping the role of the jury), quashed Thomas' conviction, and observed that there had been a 'strong current' of authority that 'the general rule in the graver class of crimes' is that an honest and reasonable mistake means a defendant is not guilty.[106]

The language of honest and reasonable mistake of fact formalised into a distinct doctrine in the most significant case in this area, *Proudman* v. *Dayman*, which was handed down by the High Court in 1941.[107] As is well known, in *Proudman* v. *Dayman*, the High Court considered an appeal against the conviction of Mrs. Proudman for the statutory offence of permitting an unlicensed driver to drive her car.[108] Mrs. Proudman argued that she had believed, on reasonable grounds, that the driver was licensed. The High Court refused the application for special leave to appeal, holding that a defence of honest and reasonable mistake of fact was available under the statutory offence, but that it had not been made out on the facts; hence Mrs. Proudman was rightly convicted. According to Dixon J, while the presumption of *mens rea* is 'but a weak one' when measured across the breath of legislation, 'it still remains a presumption'.[109] The High Court confirmed that the burden of proof is on the defendant

[102] Thomas was convicted under *Crimes Act 1928* (Vic) s 61. The trial judge asked the jury to answer a specific question about the defendant's beliefs, and, after Thomas was convicted, stated a case for the Full Court under *Crimes Act 1928* (Vic) s 478 regarding a defence to bigamy and the appropriate direction to the jury.

[103] *Thomas* v. *R* (1937) 59 CLR 279 at 302 per Dixon J. On the reception of *Thomas* v. *R*, see *R* v. *Gould* [1968] 1 All ER 849 and J. B. S. Diehl, 'R. v. Wheat and Stocks. R. I. P.' (1968) 31(5) *The Modern Law Review* 576–80.

[104] See *Ferrier* v. *Wilson* (1906) 4 CLR 785 and *Duncan* v. *Ellis* (1916) 21 CLR 379 (in which the High Court followed the Queen's Bench in *Sherras* v. *De Rutzen* [1895] 1 QB 918); see also *Hardgrave* v. *The King* (1906) 4 CLR 232.

[105] *Thomas* v. *R* (1937) 59 CLR 279 at 303 per Dixon J.

[106] *Thomas* v. *R* (1937) 59 CLR 279 at 287 per Latham CJ.

[107] *Proudman* v. *Dayman* (1941) 67 CLR 536.

[108] *Road Traffic Act 1934-39* (SA) s 30.

[109] *Proudman* v. *Dayman* (1941) 67 CLR 536 at 541 per Dixon J.

to raise evidence of honest and reasonable mistake of fact. Now famously, Dixon J stated that the presumption of *mens rea* applied to statutory offences:

> ... unless from the words, context, subject-matter or general nature of the enactment, some reason to the contrary appears, you are to treat honest and reasonable mistake as a ground of exculpation even from a summary offence.[110]

This part of the *Proudman* v. *Dayman* judgment was taken up again by the High Court in *He Kaw Teh* in 1986.[111] In reiterating the presumption of *mens rea*, and formalising a tripartite classification of criminal offences in Australian common law of crime – comprising ordinary offences with a *mens rea* requirement, offences of strict liability, and offences of absolute liability – this decision provided a template for the criminal responsibility provision of the Commonwealth Criminal Code.[112]

The distinctiveness of the High Court's approach to honest and reasonable mistake of fact was not clear initially. At the time, it was understood as one way to defend the fault requirement in criminal offences. Thus, in summarising the state of the law in common law states in the late 1940s, Barry and Paton wrote that, in general, 'at least in the High Court, the eclipse of *mens rea* has not proceeded as far as it has in England with reference to the interpretation of criminal statutes'.[113] Only in hindsight was it possible to see that Dixon J's judgment in *Proudman* v. *Dayman,* reaffirming the presumption of *mens rea* in statutory offences, as a 'turning point' in the law.[114] As Brett and Waller wrote in 1962, Dixon J's judgment provided that the defence of honest and reasonable mistake of fact is 'separate and distinct from that of criminal intent',[115] rather than the flipside of the requirement that the prosecution must prove the mental element of the offence.

In the period following *Proudman* v. *Dayman*, judicial engagement with honest and reasonable mistake of fact, and consideration of its relationship to principles of criminal responsibility, took place in the context of non-fatal offences against the person, and, in particular, the offence of assaulting a police officer in the execution of his duty.[116] Like bigamy, this offence raised a genuine issue about what a defendant knew (in relation to this offence, whether the defendant knew that the victim was a police officer). After some vacillation by Australian courts,[117] in 1961, the High Court handed down

110 See *Proudman* v. *Dayman* (1941) 67 CLR 536 at 540-1 per Dixon J.

111 *He Kaw Teh* v. *The Queen* (1985) 157 CLR 523.

112 See Chapter 5 for discussion.

113 Barry and Paton, *An Introduction to the Criminal Law in Australia*, p. 22.

114 Brett and Waller, *Cases and Materials in Criminal Law*, p. 564.

115 Ibid., pp. 563–4.

116 This is an offence in each Australian state: see, e.g., *Crimes Act 1958* (Vic) s 40. The Australia offences are based on *Offences Against the Person Act 1861* (England) s 38.

117 See, e.g., *R* v. *Galvin* (No. 1) [1961] VR 733 and *R* v. *Galvin* (No. 2) [1961] VR 740, in which differently constituted Victorian Supreme Courts reached different conclusions about this offence. For discussion, see Howard, *Australian Criminal Law*, pp. 115–16.

a definitive decision in *Reynhoudt*.[118] Reynhoudt was charged with three offences arising from an armed robbery: he was convicted of the first two offences, and acquitted of the third, assaulting a police officer, Shaw, in the execution of his duty. In relation to this charge, the trial judge had directed the jury that the prosecution did not have to prove that Reynhoudt knew that Shaw was a police officer in order to convict him of the offence. By majority, the High Court agreed, holding that the prosecution did not have to prove that the defendant knew that the victim was a police officer on duty, but that the defendant could raise evidence, to prove to the balance of probability standard, that he or she believed on reasonable grounds that the victim was not a police officer.[119] As this indicates, the High Court identified the offence of assaulting a police officer in the execution of his duty as one of strict liability (that is, one to which the defence of honest and reasonable mistake of fact was available).

The wider context for the development of the doctrine of honest and reasonable mistake of fact in the mid-century was a growing concern, in Australia and beyond, that the fault requirement in criminal offences was under threat. This concern was based on 'the increasing tendency of legislators … to designate as crimes, acts which interfere with the policy and methods of control of centralised governments, but which are morally indifferent'.[120] At this time, the idea that, properly constituted, '*mens rea* equals intention or recklessness' – an idea that now goes under the label subjectivism – was in ascendance.[121] In the mid-century, Australian courts and commentators expressed concern about the erosion of fault requirements – either through the use of negligence as a basis for liability for statutory offences, or in the removal of fault provisions altogether ('absolute liability') (although some commentators were prepared to defend the use of negligence as a fault element for some offences[122]). For instance, in *Parker* v. *R*, Dixon CJ broke with the House of Lords in holding that a *mens rea* of intent required the defendant to have had the intention, and that it was not sufficient to rely on the presumption that he or she intended the

118 *R* v. *Reynhoudt* (1962) 107 CLR 381.

119 *R* v. *Reynhoudt* (1962) 107 CLR 381 at 408 per Owen J. Dixon CJ was in the minority.

120 See J. V. Barry, 'Criminal Law: The General Part' (1954) 27 *The Australian Law Journal* 736–7, 736.

121 See C. Wells, 'Swatting the Subjectivist Bug' [1982] *Criminal Law Review* 209–20, 215. On subjectivism more generally, see J. Horder, 'Criminal Law', in P. Cane and M. Tushnet (eds.), *Oxford Handbook of Legal Studies* (Oxford: Oxford University Press, 2003).

122 For instance, for Howard, negligence was not just a convenient halfway house between subjective fault and absolute liability, as Glanville Williams had it (G. L. Williams, *Criminal Law: The General Part* (London: Stevens, 1953), p. 262), but also valuable in other ways, including for the discretion it conferred on a trial court, allowing for the development of new legal principles: Howard, *Australian Criminal Law*, pp. 321–2; see also Brett and Waller, *Cases and Materials in Criminal Law*, p. 208.

reasonable consequences of his or her acts.[123] In general, the development of strict liability was seen as the lesser evil when compared with absolute liability. Even commentators who criticised the rule in *Reynhoudt* – as 'productive of serious injustice' because it introduced strict liability for an indictable offence – recognised that it was preferable to absolute liability, and praised the High Court for encouraging the use of honest and reasonable mistake of fact, inhibiting the growth of absolute liability.[124] Commentators also expressed some hope that the Australian defence might be adopted in England, where the law was a 'sorry picture of inconsistency and uncertainty', holding that the English courts would benefit from adopting the 'coherent body of doctrine' the High Court had developed.[125]

The idea that a discrete doctrine of honest and reasonable mistake of fact might protect the integrity of criminal offences exposes the wider significance of principles of criminal responsibility in the organisation of the criminal law in the mid-century. The multifaceted and long-term development of criminal law around criminal responsibility crystallised in the mid-century, when the idea that the criminal law was constituted by a set of general principles of responsibility gained widespread acceptance among both practitioners and scholars. In this period, Glanville Williams published *Criminal Law: The General Part*, which appeared in 1953, and encapsulated faith in the idea of principled criminal law. As J. V. Barry commented in a review of the second edition of Williams' text, the book is 'infused by a philosophic understanding of the social purposes the criminal law should serve, of the principles upon which it should rest, and of the desirable limits within which it should operate'.[126] Williams' text had a seismic impact on understandings of the criminal law.[127] It was consulted and extracted by judges and lawyers, as well as academics, in Australia and around the common law world.[128] As Farmer argues, Williams saw his task as a rationalisation of the criminal law, and he set out a theory of the criminal law for the welfare state.[129]

123 *Parker* v. *R* (1963) 111 CLR 610 at 632 (declining to apply the House of Lords decision of *Director of Public Prosecutions* v. *Smith* [1963] AC 220, on the basis that it was 'misconceived and wrong').

124 Howard, *Australian Criminal Law*, pp. 115, 307, 338.

125 Morris and Howard, *Studies in Criminal Law*, p. 222.

126 See J. V. Barry, 'Criminal Law, The General Part' (1962) 35 *The Australian Law Journal* 352; for a more circumspect engagement with Williams, and the development of general principles of criminal law, see P. Brett, *An Inquiry into Criminal Guilt* (Sydney: Law Book Co., 1963), ch. 3.

127 See Williams, *Criminal Law*, and, for analysis see Farmer, 'The Modest Ambition of Glanville Williams'.

128 For example, in his 1965 textbook, Howard made express his 'intellectual debt' to Williams, stating that it was 'in evidence on every page': see Howard, *Australian Criminal Law*, Preface.

129 See further Farmer, 'The Modest Ambition of Glanville Williams'.

The first Australian criminal law textbooks played a key role in the embrace of principles of criminal responsibility in Australia. Australia's first criminal law textbook included a section on 'general principles of criminal liability',[130] but the significance of such general principles had grown significantly by the time of the publication of the second Australian criminal law textbook, more than a decade later, in 1962.[131] By this time, the idea that criminal law was constituted by a set of principles that were generally applicable across the body of the law had taken firm hold, and it was possible to present what was a new and contingent idea as if it was a timeless truth. In the Preface to the 1962 book, *Cases and Materials in Criminal Law,* by Peter Brett and Peter Waller, the authors' state:

> We believe that the common law consists of principles; and that individual decisions, if inconsistent with these principles (which are to be derived from the whole body of precedent which they permeate, not from isolated instances), must be treated as wrong. This seems to be the attitude of Australian courts; although they do not lightly refuse to follow English decisions, or overrule their own, they regard themselves as free to do so if sound principle so requires.[132]

This creed-like statement that 'the common law consists of principles' reflects confidence in the integrity of the criminal law, assessed by reference to an internal measure ('principles'). It also testifies to the self-ascribed role of textbook authors in the systematisation of the criminal law around such principles. Thus, as J. V. Barry wrote in the Introduction to another Australian textbook, that text offered a 'widening and strengthening of a rational and constructive' approach to the problems dealt with by the criminal law.[133]

While the defence of honest and reasonable mistake of fact was not exported to England – where courts declined to exercise their power to create 'halfway houses' between offences without *mens rea* elements, and those with *mens rea* elements[134] – it is now entrenched in the Australian common law of crime. Since *Thomas* and *Proudman* v. *Dayman*, a number of statutory offences have been recognised as offences of strict liability.[135] As is well known, the doctrine provides for an affirmative defence of reasonable mistake of fact to be available

[130] Under 'general principles of criminal liability', the authors included discussion of *mens rea*, capacity, insanity, drunkenness, conspiracy and attempts, among other issues: Barry and Paton, *An Introduction to the Criminal Law in Australia*, Part III.

[131] Brett and Waller, *Cases and Materials in Criminal Law.*

[132] Ibid., vii–viii.

[133] Morris and Howard, *Studies in Criminal Law*, xxxiv.

[134] See A. Ashworth, 'Towards a Theory of Criminal Legislation' (1989) 1(1) *Criminal Law Forum* 41–63, 60. Ashworth laments this state of affairs, suggesting that legislators need to take the lead in developing 'a theory of criminal legislation'.

[135] See D. Brown et al., *Criminal Laws: Materials and Commentary on Criminal Law and Process of NSW*, 6th ed. (Sydney: The Federation Press, 2015), p. 222, and more broadly see [3.6.1].

in response to a charge of one of a subset of statutory offences. If an offence is one of strict liability, the prosecution is not required to prove *mens rea*, unless the defence raises evidence of an honest and reasonable mistake of fact. Thus, by contrast with absolute liability, strict liability offences contain a *mens rea* element, but there is no requirement to prove it unless the defence discharges its burden.[136] If the defence satisfies the evidentiary burden in relation to this defence, the prosecution must negative it beyond a reasonable doubt.[137] The doctrine of honest and reasonable mistake of fact, available across the corpus of criminal offences, represents a distinctive Australian 'solution' to the challenge to fault requirements posed by statutory offences.

'A Major Development in the Law of Homicide'[138]: A Partial Defence of Excessive Self-defence

> Australian courts have recently made a major contribution to the law of homicide by developing a new qualified defence to murder, which, although applied in some American jurisdictions, does not appear previously to have been recognised by either the courts or the commentators of the British Commonwealth.[139]

The fourth front across which the 'birth' of Australian criminal law took place concerns the law of homicide: in the mid-century, Australian courts made express what was held to be implicit in the common law: that while self-defence is a full defence to any offence, the use of excessive self-defence operates to reduce murder to manslaughter.[140] In the course of elucidating this qualified defence, the Australian courts negotiated the boundary between conviction and mitigation, trial and sentence, and, in sanctioning the defence, the courts forged a new path for the Australian law of homicide.

In the 1950s, a series of cases recognised the existence of a qualified or partial defence of excessive self-defence at common law. These cases concerned the use of excessive force both in the prevention of a felony, and in the defence

[136] The defendant must raise evidence of a positive mistake (mere ignorance is insufficient), in relation to an issue of fact (not law), which was reasonable in the circumstances and which, if true, would render the defendant innocent (which, it is now clear, means innocent of any offence): see for discussion S. Bronitt and B. McSherry, *Principles of Criminal Law*, 4th ed. (Sydney: Lawbook Co., 2017), [3.275]–[3.305].

[137] See *CTM* v. *The Queen* (2008) 236 CLR 440.

[138] Morris and Howard, *Studies in Criminal Law*, p. 114.

[139] Ibid., p. 113.

[140] Excessive self-defence is not a defence under the Griffith Codes, where the use of more force than justified by the circumstances renders the action unlawful: see *Criminal Code Act 1899* (Qld) s 283 and *Criminal Code Act Compilation Act 1913* (WA) s 260. In WA, the rule has been amended: see now *Criminal Code Act Compilation Act 1913* (WA) s 248(3).

of property and persons.[141] In a way that would later prove significant for the development of the law, each of these cases involved male defendants. For example, in *McKay*, the defendant was convicted of the murder of an intruder on his chicken farm: at trial, Justice Barry directed the jury that if he used 'more force than is reasonably necessary' McKay should be convicted of manslaughter, a direction that was accepted by the Victorian Court of Criminal Appeal.[142] In *Howe*, the defendant responded to a non-violent sexual advance by a male friend with lethal force.[143] The South Australian trial judge directed the jury that the only basis on which it could find manslaughter was provocation, but the South Australian Court of Appeal held that manslaughter could be based on excessive force.[144] The prosecution in *Howe* appealed to the High Court. The High Court granted special leave to appeal and confirmed that the use of excessive force in self-defence could be the basis of a manslaughter conviction.[145] Four of the Justices approved the judgment of the South Australia Court of Appeal that if a person uses 'more force than a reasonable man would consider necessary in the circumstances, but no more force than he honestly believes to be necessary in the circumstances', he is guilty of manslaughter, not murder.[146]

As was the case with the development of the law of insanity, recognition of a partial defence of excessive self-defence was regarded as both progressive *and* faithful to criminal law principles. On the one hand, recognition of the defence was thought to be in the social interest: on the basis that excessive self-defence reflected a moral distinction between a defendant with this excuse and one without it, it was thought likely to ensure convictions (for manslaughter) in circumstances that might otherwise result in an acquittal, which in turn may operate to enhance the 'reverence for life which is a fundamental characteristic of a civilized community'.[147] On the other hand, excessive self-defence was also regarded as principled, marking out 'a middle-ground between a conviction of murder and an acquittal', a verdict which is 'neither a jury compromise

141 See *R* v. *McKay* [1957] VR 560, *R* v. *Howe* [1958] SASR 95, *R* v. *Buffalo* [1958] VR 363; *R* v. *Haley* [1959] WN (NSW) 550, *R* v. *Tikos* (No. 1) [1963] VR 285; *R* v. *Tikos* (No. 2) [1963] VR 306; see also *McClelland* v. *Symons* [1951] VLR 157 (concerning a civil case in which the plaintiff argued excessive self-defence). For contemporaneous discussion of *McKay*, see N. Morris, 'The Slain Chicken Thief' (1958) 2(3) *Sydney Law Review* 414–35.

142 See *R* v. *McKay* [1957] VR 560 at 564. An application for special leave to appeal the conviction to the High Court was sought but refused.

143 *R* v. *Howe* [1958] SASR 95. Howe was the first of a series of cases raising what became known as the 'homosexual panic defence', in which male defendants successfully pleaded provocation in relation to lethal violence after a same-sex sexual advance. The highest profile of these cases was *Green* v. *R* (1997) 191 CLR 334. For discussion, see T. Crofts and A. Loughnan, 'Provocation: The Good, the Bad and the Ugly' (2013) 37(1) *Criminal Law Journal* 23–37.

144 Referred to in *R* v. *Howe* (1958) 100 CLR 448 at 470.

145 *R* v. *Howe* (1958) 100 CLR 448.

146 *R* v. *Howe* [1958] SASR 95 at 121. In reaching this conclusion, the High Court bracketed the House of Lords decision of *Mancini* v. *Director of Public Prosecutions* [1942] AC 1 on the basis that it had been decided in relation to provocation, not excessive self-defence, which had not been argued before the Law Lords: see *R* v. *Howe* (1958) 100 CLR 448 at 476 per Menzies J.

147 Morris and Howard, *Studies in Criminal Law*, pp. 144–6.

nor a verdict of manslaughter based on the provocation of the accused by the deceased'.[148] The existence of excessive self-defence was said to be traceable to the seventeenth century and the development of the modern law of homicide, but to have been obscured by factors such as an expansive defence of provocation.[149] As such, excessive self-defence was regarded as implicit in the common law, and Australian commentators found support for it in US criminal law, with its distinction between 'perfect' and 'imperfect' rights to self-defence.[150] Strength of conviction about the rightness of excessive self-defence was apparent in the argument, put forward by some commentators, that the same principles should apply to duress and necessity (with excessive force operating to reduce murder to manslaughter).[151] With a shared understanding that the law of homicide was in a 'constant state of evolution', there was some hope that, when excessive self-defence came before English courts, 'Australian authorities will be followed'.[152] This was not to be the case: in *Clegg*, the House of Lords described excessive self-defence as 'attractive', but held that the creation of a partial defence was a matter for the legislature.[153]

The recognition of excessive self-defence in the common law of crime reflected in part the growing influence of American criminal law on Australia in the mid-century. The influence of American law and American commentaries is illustrated by one of Australia's early criminal law textbooks, Brett and Waller's *Cases and Materials in Criminal Law*, referred to above. This textbook reveals the prominence that American criminal law and American legal academia had on the Australian legal landscape by the 1960s.[154] Reflecting the case method pioneered at Harvard Law School, the book was organised around twenty-one 'problems' which student readers were asked to discuss and solve, with extracts of relevant cases, statutes and commentary provided to assist in this task.[155] The book included

148 N. Morris, 'A New Qualified Defence to Murder' (1960) 1(1) *Adelaide Law Review* 23–52, 23; see also Morris and Howard, *Studies in Criminal Law*, p. 114.

149 Morris, 'A New Qualified Defence to Murder'; Morris and Howard, *Studies in Criminal Law*, pp. 124–7.

150 See for discussion Morris, 'A New Qualified Defence to Murder'; Morris and Howard, *Studies in Criminal Law*, pp. 114–15.

151 Morris and Howard, *Studies in Criminal Law*, pp. 142–4.

152 See C. Howard, 'An Australian Letter' [1962] *Criminal Law Review*, 435–44, 442.

153 *R* v. *Clegg* [1995] 1 AC 482 at 499 per Lord Berwick. Excessive self-defence had found favour with the Law Commission for England and Wales: see Law Commission for England and Wales, *Criminal Law: A Criminal Code for England and Wales*, Report No. 177 (1989), vol. 1, p. 68.

154 One of the authors, Peter Brett, had studied at Harvard Law School, and the significance of this experience on Brett is acknowledged in the book's Preface: see Brett and Waller, *Cases and Materials in Criminal Law*, vii. The influence of the US on Australian individuals and ideas was also evident in the emerging field of criminology: see Finnane, 'The Origins of Criminology in Australia'.

155 It was intended that one problem be considered in each week of the university year (Brett and Waller, *Cases and Materials in Criminal Law*, ix), and, reflecting the model of teaching at Harvard, student readers were instructed to 'advise whether Smith may be successfully prosecuted for murder' (p. 114), on the basis of the relevant chapter in the book. On the take up of the case method in Australia, see R. Cranston, 'Law and Society: A different Approach to Legal Education' (1978–79) 5 *Monash University Law Review* 54–69.

a large amount of material from America, on the basis that it dealt with 'questions which had received no judicial consideration elsewhere', and because some of that material contained 'judicial exposition of a particular matter far superior to that to be found in an authoritative decision'.[156] *Cases and Materials in Criminal Law* also extracted extensively the provisions of the US *Model Penal Code*.[157] The *Model Penal Code* was lauded as setting a 'standard against which existing legislation and common law rules may be measured'.[158] And, like Brett and Waller, in his 1965 text, *Australian Criminal Law*, Colin Howard drew in particular on American criminal cases, commentary, and legislation, including the *Model Penal Code* provisions.[159]

As these international influences indicate, Australian practitioners and scholars regarded themselves as part of a global debate about the principles of criminal responsibility. The Australian contribution to the debate was perspectival: Australia generated a different viewpoint on the criminal law. Perhaps because Australian judges 'feel possibly slightly freer than their English brothers within the helpful bonds of precedent',[160] Australian legal practitioners and scholars were thought to offer new or fresh viewpoints on legal principles, and an independent assessment of the law. Thus, two authors of early textbooks held that, although situated in a 'social context differing significantly from that of the United Kingdom', because the decisions of Australian courts were 'in the main characterized by wide learning, robust common sense, and an acute grip of principle', they might be of use to lawyers and judges elsewhere in the common law world.[161] Less deferentially, and with confidence about 'applicable' legal principles, Justice Dixon wrote of the end of 'an age of pedantic legal scholarship when dusty learning will operate to restrain or retard the process of displacing older and less familiar doctrine by generalizations from principles which appear applicable and are held in high esteem'.[162] Impliedly, these 'generalizations from principles' might emerge from the 'periphery', the jurisdictions like Australia to which the common law had been exported, as well as from the 'centre' (England), where common law had emerged.

[156] Brett and Waller, *Cases and Materials in Criminal Law*, vii. The authors made this statement even as they acknowledged that American case law is 'at most of persuasive authority in Australian courts' (vii).

[157] The *Model Penal Code*, drafted over a period of 10 years by the American Law Institute (without government backing), had been published in 1962. The *Model Penal Code* was intended as a model for future legislators: see L. Farmer, 'Codification', in M. D. Dubber and T. Hörnle (eds.), *Oxford Handbook of Criminal Law* (New York: Oxford University Press, 2014).

[158] Brett and Waller, *Cases and Materials in Criminal Law*, viii.

[159] Howard also rejected the use of the terms *actus reus* and *mens rea*, in favour of 'external element' and 'mental element' of the offence, on the basis that terms were used in the *Model Penal Code*: see Howard, *Australian Criminal Law*, pp. 10–12.

[160] N. Morris, 'An Australian Letter' [1957] *Criminal Law Review*, 389–98, 396 (commenting on issue estoppel).

[161] Morris and Howard, *Studies in Criminal Law*, viii.

[162] O. Dixon, 'The Development of the Law of Homicide' (1935) 9 *Australian Law Journal (Supplement)* 64–72, 68 (in relation to the demise of a duty to retreat in the law of self-defence).

As the Australian contribution was perspectival, the way in which the specificities of the Australian social and historical context fed into the discussion of the criminal law was muted. With the value of Australian context assumed to be that it generated a different vantage point, differences of context did not operate to reflect back on the criminal law itself. There was some (limited) recognition of the distinctiveness of jurisdictions such as the Northern Territory, with a high population of Aboriginal peoples.[163] The first Australian criminal law textbook, *An Introduction to the Criminal Law in Australia,* included an extended discussion of the status of Aboriginal peoples (addressing questions of whether they were protected by the law and whether they were subject to it), something that disappeared from later textbooks published in this period.[164] In general, as Mark Finnane argues in relation to the development of criminology in Australia, the disadvantage of and discrimination against Aboriginal peoples struggled to make a mark on the intellectual shape of the discipline.[165] In relation to the criminal law, difference was regarded as a challenge for the application of the law, not its principles: the Australian context threw up some challenges, but did not disrupt fundamentally the precepts of the criminal law. In the words of one commentator, Australia was a 'laboratory' for the comparative study of the criminal law, and, following through on the metaphor of experimentation, stated that the only 'defect' was that the 'data' generated is ignored.[166]

Despite the confidence of Australian practitioners and scholars, excessive self-defence did not find favour at the 'centre', in England. As part of a broader set of moves toward judicial independence from England, which included rejecting the presumption that a person intends the reasonable consequences of his or her actions, referred to above, the status of excessive self-defence caused a significant rupture between Australian courts and those of Empire after mid-century. When excessive self-defence came before the Privy Council in 1971, in *Palmer*, on appeal from Jamaica, the Council rejected the idea of a halfway

[163] See M. Kriewaldt, 'The Application of the Criminal Law to the Aborigines of the Northern Territory of Australia' (1960–1962) 5(1) *University of Western Australia Law Review* 1–50. Justice Kriewaldt was a judge of the Supreme Court of the Northern Territory from 1951 to 1960: for critical discussion of his views of Aboriginal people, see H. Douglas, 'Justice Kriewaldt, Aboriginal Identity and the Criminal Law' (2002) 26 *Criminal Law Journal* 204–22.

[164] See, e.g., Barry and Paton, *An Introduction to the Criminal Law in Australia*, pp. 12–15, and compare Brett and Waller, *Cases and Materials in Criminal Law*. The discussion of the status of Indigenous peoples by Barry and Paton concludes with a comment that it is 'curious' that Australia has not 'pursued a more liberal policy so far as its own aborigines are concerned' (Barry and Paton, *An Introduction to the Criminal Law in Australia*, p. 15). This textbook has been described as a 'grounded' and historical account of criminal law 'in specific Australian conditions': M. Finnane, 'Law as an Intellectual Vocation' (2015) 38(3) *Melbourne University Law Review* 1060–79, 1069.

[165] See Finnane, 'The Origins of Criminology in Australia'.

[166] Morris, 'An Australian Letter'.

house defence, and stated that proportionality was an essential element of self-defence.[167] By the time excessive self-defence came before the High Court again, the Federal Parliament had legislated to abolish appeals from the High Court to the Privy Council.[168] Then, in what constituted an 'open break' with the Privy Council, in *Viro* v. *The Queen* in 1978, the High Court elected not to follow *Palmer*, and declared itself no longer bound by the Privy Council.[169] In *Viro*, Mason J gave the leading judgment confirming the existence of excessive self-defence, and provided a detailed, six-point statement of the jury's task in evaluating the defence.[170] This strong statement contained the seeds of the demise of the defence, however.[171] In 1987, in light of evidence that the directions on excessive self-defence proved hard for juries to follow, a different High Court bench rejected the defence.[172] In *Zecevic* v. *DPP* a majority of the High Court stated that lack of proportionality could only be taken into account as a circumstance of the case, rather than as a rule of law or a separate requirement.

The demise of the partial defence of excessive self-defence was not the end of the story of this part of Australian criminal law. In the decades after the abrogation of excessive self-defence, it has been revived, and four Australian states have re-introduced a defence of excessive self-defence, operating to reduce murder to manslaughter.[173] By contrast with the first tranche of cases concerning excessive self-defence, all of which involved men, the revival of excessive self-defence in recent decades was a response to violence by women. In particular, the re-introduction of excessive self-defence was one of a set of legislative responses to a specific construction of women accused of murder in the context of domestic violence. As I discuss in an analysis of women's responsibility for crime, in its current form, excessive self-defence

[167] See *Palmer* v. *The Queen* [1971] AC 814.

[168] See *Privy Council (Limitation of Appeals) Act 1968* (Cth) and *Privy Council (Appeals from the High Court) Act 1975* (Cth). A right of appeal to the Privy Council remained from state courts (in matters governed by state law).

[169] *Viro* v. *The Queen* (1978) 141 CLR 88 at 93 per Barwick CJ, at 120 per Gibbs J, at 151 per Jacobs J, at 161 per Murphy J, at 174 per Aickin J; see also M. Gleeson, 'The Privy Council: An Australian Perspective' (Address delivered at the Anglo-Australasian Lawyers Society, The Commercial Bar Association and Chancery Association, 18 June 2008). In *Viro*, Gibbs J (at 121) also stated expressly that the High Court was no longer bound by the House of Lords.

[170] *Viro* v. *The Queen* (1978) 141 CLR 88 at 146–7 per Mason J; see also S. Yeo, 'Revisiting Excessive Self-Defence' (2000) 12 *Current Issues in Criminal Justice* 39–57; see also S. Yeo, 'The New Developments in the Law of Self-Defence in Australia' (1987) 7 *Oxford Journal of Legal Studies* 489–96.

[171] Yeo, 'Revisiting Excessive Self-Defence'.

[172] *Zecevic* v. *Director of Public Prosecutions* (Vic) (1987) 162 CLR 645.

[173] These states are South Australia (*Criminal Law Consolidation Act 1935* s 15), NSW (*Crimes Act 1900* s 421), WA (*Criminal Code Act Compilation Act 1913* s 248(3)), and Victoria (*Crimes Act 1958* s 9AD). Each of these provisions contains both objective and subjective elements. When the Model Criminal Code was drafted in the 1990s, the drafters decided against excessive self-defence on the basis that it was 'inherently vague': see Model Criminal Code Officers' Committee, *Discussion Paper*, ch. 5, p. 113.

now accommodates women's violence, which is understood as responsive – comprehensible only as an answer to what has already happened – with women's responsibility for crime constructed as an amalgam of agency and victimhood/survivorhood.[174]

> Considering Australia's population and her relatively low rate of crime, it is somewhat surprising how much attention her courts have devoted to analysing and developing some of the fundamental principles of the criminal law – an inarticulate awareness of convict origins may partly account for this interest.[175]

This chapter has made the case that Australian criminal law was 'born' in the mid-century. As discussed, in this period, there was a growing sense that 'uniformity [with England] could be bought at too high a price',[176] and the period is marked by an emergent and then more fulsome independence of Australian criminal law. It was in the mid-century that it became possible to talk meaningfully of *Australian* criminal law. As demonstrated by tracking developments across four fronts, and with reference to Australia's first textbooks of criminal law, Australian practitioners and academics of this time regarded themselves as part of a wide legal world, and as participants in a global debate about the development and improvement of the law of crime. Against this backdrop, the developments canvassed here represent a complex and subtle negotiation between what Australia shared with others, and what might be thought mark it out, according to which what Australian lawyers and scholars offered was a fresh perspective. It is possible to detect an orientation of criminal law around a set of national coordinates, and a growing self-confidence of Australian academics and practitioners of criminal law, in this period. Taking seriously the rise of a palpable if nebulous sense of an Australian criminal law revealed in this chapter puts its 'birth' squarely in the mid-twentieth century – neither earlier nor later.

The principles of criminal responsibility played a title role in this national story. It was in the elucidation and application of the principles of criminal responsibility that practitioners and academics produced a meaningful idea of Australian criminal law. In this way, the Australian story offers a distinct inflection on the more general story of the rise to dominance of the idea that the criminal law consists of a set of principles of criminal responsibility. As mentioned above, in this more general story, criminal responsibility principles are regarded as the shared bedrock of common law systems of criminal law. But the Australian case has demonstrated that the elucidation and application of these principles was vital to the development of a sense of *national* criminal law. Negotiating a position for themselves between the jurisprudence of

[174] See further Chapter 6.
[175] Morris, 'An Australian Letter' [1958] 520.
[176] Barry and Paton, *An Introduction to the Criminal Law in Australia*, p. 8.

English courts, and commentaries such as that of Glanville Williams, on the one hand, and American developments such as the *Model Penal Code*, on the other hand, Australian lawyers and commentators came to forge an independent path for the criminal law by reference to these principles. In this context, the principles of criminal responsibility were the 'tools of the trade', and their independent deployment was the means of securing a place for Australia in a global debate about the development and improvement of the law of crime.

5

Peak Responsibility?

Codifying Criminal Responsibility in the Late Twentieth Century

This chapter takes up the story of the development of criminal responsibility in Australian criminal laws in the last decades of the twentieth century. At this point, a number of currents running through the century – including modernisation, codification and the coherence of Australian criminal laws – which are discussed in preceding chapters of this book, come together. This period represents the high watermark of faith in the value and feasibility of organising criminal law around criminal responsibility, as legal and other changes occurring on the national and international levels were met with an attempt to fix criminal responsibility principles at the heart of Australian criminal law. As I show in this chapter, in this period criminal responsibility became key to the self-definition of the criminal law, and the language of criminal responsibility became the language of the criminal law.

By the last decades of the twentieth century, the idea that criminal law was constituted by a set of principles of criminal responsibility had gained widespread acceptance. At around the turn of the twentieth century, criminal responsibility was understood as only one part of the criminal law: at this time, criminal responsibility shared the weight of the modernising reforms of the law then undertaken with both the form of the criminal law – comprehensive legislation or a code – and process – the operation of criminal justice.[1] It was in the mid-century period that the idea that the criminal law is comprised of principles of criminal responsibility took a firm hold in Australia. In the mid-century, both practitioners and scholars shared an interest in the development and improvement of the law of crime, and the elucidation and application of principles of criminal responsibility by judges, lawyers and academics contributed to the development of an idea of *Australian* criminal law.[2] As a result, by the last decades of the century, criminal responsibility had taken on an enhanced prominence. As I suggest in

[1] See further Chapter 3.
[2] See further Chapter 4.

this chapter, the concerns with the criminal law that existed at this point – in particular, its rationality and workability – were each refracted through the lens of criminal responsibility.

These concerns came together, first, in momentum for reform of Commonwealth criminal law, then in the development of the *Model Criminal Code* in the early 1990s, and, subsequently, in the enactment of the Commonwealth *Criminal Code* in 1995.[3] The Commonwealth *Criminal Code* forms the focus of this chapter. The Code was intended to act as a centripetal force in criminal laws in Australia, drawing the laws toward a common central point. Measured in terms of ambition and scope, the Commonwealth *Criminal Code* was the most significant criminal law reform project in Australian history, and it attracted significant levels of professional commentary and media coverage at the time it was formulated. When the Code bill was introduced in Federal Parliament, it was heralded as 'one of the most ambitious legal simplification programs ever attempted in Australia',[4] and the advent of the Code was said to herald a 'new era' not just for Commonwealth law but for the criminal law generally.[5] Criminal responsibility was crucial to this law reform project, with the Code placing criminal responsibility at the centre of the criminal law. The main pivot of the Code is Chapter 2, 'General Principles of Criminal Responsibility', which has as its purpose 'to codify the general principles of criminal responsibility under laws of the Commonwealth' (section 2.1). In addition, the offence and defence provisions comprising the special part of the Code form a significant component of Federal criminal law, and are intended to serve as model provisions for reform in other jurisdictions.

I make two main arguments in this chapter. First, I argue that the Commonwealth *Criminal Code* represents an attempt to compensate for Australia's federal structure – in which criminal law is a state and territory responsibility – and reconstruct criminal law as national rather than subnational law. The Commonwealth *Criminal Code* came into being at a time when major changes in crime and criminal justice were occurring: at this time, first reform and then codification of Commonwealth law came to be seen as the answer to a range of problems and challenges, and the Code promised to equip Australia for a new century. Second, I argue that, as 'the very foundations of any system of criminal justice',[6] criminal responsibility was

[3] The Commonwealth Criminal Code was enacted as a Schedule to the *Criminal Code Act 1995* (Cth). The criminal codes of the Australian federal territories – the ACT, Norfolk Island and the Northern Territory – are modelled on the Commonwealth Code.

[4] Parliament of Australia, Explanatory Memorandum, *Criminal Code Bill 1994* (Cth), p. 1.

[5] Hansard, Commonwealth Senate, col. 2382, 30 June 1994.

[6] Criminal Law Officers' Committee (CLOC), Standing Committee of Attorneys-General, *Model Criminal Code Chapters 1 and 2: General Principles of Criminal Responsibility, Final Report* (1992), ii.

central to this attempt at reconstruction. The Commonwealth *Criminal Code* is a legal systematisation – as such, the emphasis on the (re-)organisation of the *laws*, rather than on reform of aspects of criminal justice such as criminal process or systems of criminal punishment. As a late twentieth century codification, the Criminal Code responds to the massive growth of the criminal law over preceding decades, and reflects the firmer conceptual divisions between criminal law, procedure and punishment that had developed by this time. The emphasis on the (re-)organisation of criminal laws in the codification of Commonwealth criminal law brought with it a particular role for criminal responsibility. As the principles of criminal responsibility are fixed at the heart of Australian criminal laws, they provide the Commonwealth Code with integrity, meaning that it makes sense on its own terms, and ensuring that it can stand on its own and act as a model for adoption in other jurisdictions.

In my analysis of the Commonwealth *Criminal Code* I make reference to the American *Model Penal Code*. The Penal Code, which influenced the Commonwealth Code in both form and substance, was developed from the 1930s by the American Law Institute and published in 1962.[7] It is the twentieth-century criminal law codification project that has garnered the most attention from scholars, and is the main reference point for debates about criminal law codification in the current era. As is well known, the *Model Penal Code* constructed a rational system of criminal law in the service of particular 'purposes' that were included in the Code itself.[8] The general part of the Penal Code includes principles, including those relating to responsibility, that apply to all offences in the special part of the Code.[9] The *Model Penal Code* was formulated as a model for future legislators, rather than as a piece of legislation.[10] The Penal Code has been a successful code project, and has been taken up (in part) by a number of states in the United States. The Code and the official commentaries published on it have exerted a strong influence on the development of criminal law more generally in particular through American criminal law scholarship and teaching.[11] Reference to the *Model Penal Code* enables me to point to key features of the Commonwealth Code and provides valuable perspective on the Code, which, because of its recency, and because

[7] The full title of the *Model Penal Code* is the Model Penal and Correctional Code: see American Law Institute, *Model Penal and Correctional Code: Official Draft and Explanatory Notes* (adopted 24 May 1962) (Philadelphia, PA: The American Law Institute, 1985).

[8] For critical discussion, see M. D. Dubber, 'Penal Panopticon: The Idea of a Modern Model Penal Code' (2000) 4(1) *Buffalo Criminal Law Review* 53–100; J. Q. Whitman, 'The Case for Penal Modernism: Beyond Utility and Desert' (2014) 1(2) *Critical Analysis of Law* 143–81.

[9] Article 2, *Model Penal Code* (covering *actus reus, mens rea*, causation, mistake and complicity).

[10] See L. Farmer, 'Codification', in M. D. Dubber and T. Hörnle (eds.), *The Oxford Handbook of Criminal Law* (New York: Oxford University Press, 2014), p. 387.

[11] The official commentaries were published by the American Law Institute in 1980 (special part) and 1985 (general part): see generally P. H. Robinson and M. D. Dubber, 'The American Model Penal Code: A Brief Overview' (2007) 10(3) *New Criminal Law Review* 319–41.

Commonwealth criminal law is a specialist area within both criminal law scholarship and legal practice, has been subject to limited critical analysis.[12]

This chapter contains two main sections. In the first section, I offer an analysis of the reasons the Code appeared in the last decades of the century and examine the development of the Commonwealth *Criminal Code*. In the second section, I assess the principles of criminal responsibility contained in Chapter 2 of the Code and analyse their role in the Code.

Developing a Code of Australian Criminal Law

In the last decades of the twentieth century, a range of problems and challenges – including the growth of a body of Commonwealth criminal law, frustrations with Australia's Federal political system, and the changing reality of crime – combined to generate momentum for reform of Commonwealth criminal law. Reform represented an attempt to compensate for Australia's Federal structure, and to reconstruct criminal law as national law, holding out the promise of equipping the Australian nation for a new century. Notable levels of state–Federal cooperation, and a wider spirit of reforming zeal on the part of Australian governments, resulted in, first, a review of Commonwealth law, followed by the development of the Model Criminal Code, and then the codification of Commonwealth criminal law.

Momentum for Reform

By the last decades of the twentieth century, Australia's state and territory-based system of criminal laws was under some pressure. Against a backdrop of a number of high-profile public inquiries into police corruption,[13] which exposed systemic problems with state criminal justice, policing practices and the prevention of crime had become prominent political issues.[14] At the same

[12] As Australian law schools generally teach state and territory criminal law, there are only a small number of textbooks on the Commonwealth Criminal Code: see, e.g., J. Gans, *Modern Australian Criminal Law* (Melbourne: Cambridge University Press, 2012) (referring to the 'unfortunate neglect' of the Commonwealth Code in Australian textbooks (p. 7)); S. Odgers, *Principles of Federal Criminal Law*, 4th ed. (Sydney: Thomson Reuters, 2019). A significant part of the limited academic commentary on the Code has been written by individuals who were involved in its development (e.g., Matthew Goode and Ian Leader-Elliott).

[13] See, e.g., Commission of Inquiry into Possible Illegal Activities and Associated Police Misconduct (the Fitzgerald Inquiry) (1987–89) into the Queensland Police Service, and the Royal Commission into the New South Wales Police Service (the Wood Royal Commission) (1995–97); for discussion, see D. Landa and C. Lewis, 'Making the Police Accountable for their Conduct', in D. Chappell and P. Wilson (eds.), *Australian Policing*, 2nd ed. (Sydney: Butterworths, 1996).

[14] In touting the benefits of a series of national law reforms, including the Commonwealth Criminal Code, the then Prime Minister, Paul Keating, called for a 'more sophisticated emphasis on prevention' rather than reactive reposes to crime: see I. Willox, 'Keating strives for national law reform', *The Age*, 22 September 1994, p. 4.

time, public debate about victims' rights had generated a sense that criminal justice systems were 'soft on crime'.[15] In addition, state criminal justice systems had grown significantly, and governments had recognised the high costs of maintaining such systems.[16] There was a sense that multiple criminal legal regimes represented 'difference for difference sake' and were both unnecessary and unjustified.[17] As Paul Fairall wrote in 2000, 'eight sets of criminal laws seem excessive for a country of 19 million people'.[18]

Criminal responsibility was a particular cause for concern. The mixed criminal responsibility framework across common law and Code jurisdictions (in which the Griffith Codes had been in place since around the turn of the twentieth century),[19] meant there was variation in what were recognised as fundamental aspects of criminal law. This variation related to both the structure of criminal responsibility – across conduct, fault and defences, as under common law, or broadly around general principles that apply to all offences, as under the Griffith Codes – and the basis of responsibility – in subjective or objective liability. In the context of this variation, the absence of guidance on issues such as the quantum of proof for criminal offences, and the legitimacy of offences of strict or absolute liability, raised questions about the extent of the burden on the prosecution in proving a criminal charge.[20] In addition, the rising profile of human rights jurisprudence was impacting on domestic criminal justice,[21] and fostering a sense that criminal responsibility was in need of 'refurbishment'.[22] At this time, differences between Australian jurisdictions regarding matters such as the age of criminal responsibility and the age of consent (and in particular, variation between the ages of consent for homosexual and heterosexual sex) took on enhanced importance.[23] Differences on

15 See K. Borick, 'Report on the Brisbane Seminar' (1991) *Criminal Law Forum* 515–25, 515–16.

16 Hansard, Commonwealth Senate, col. 351–2, 25 August 1994. In spruiking the Commonwealth Criminal Code, the Minister for Justice emphasised that it would remove barriers facing law enforcement officers investigating interstate crimes, and cut down the cost of administering justice: M. Easterbrook, 'Moves Begin Toward National Criminal Code', *The Age*, 9 September 1993, p. 9.

17 M. Goode, 'Codification of the Australian Criminal Law' (1992) 16(1) *Criminal Law Journal* 5–19, 6–7.

18 P. Fairall, 'The Reform of the Criminal Law', in D. Chappell and P. Wilson (eds.), *Crime and the Criminal Justice System in Australia: 2000 and Beyond* (Sydney: Butterworths, 2000), p. 35.

19 The Griffith Codes are the Queensland Code, the Western Australian and Tasmanian criminal codes: see *Criminal Code Act 1899* (Qld); *Criminal Code Act 1902* (WA) (and *Criminal Code Act Compilation Act 1913* (WA)) and *Criminal Code Act 1924* (Tas).

20 R. Fox, 'New Crimes or New Responses?: Future Directions in Australian Criminal Law' (2002) 28 *Monash University Law Review* 103–25, 110.

21 See, e.g., *Toonen* v. *Australia* (1994) Communication No. 488/1992 (concerning rights to privacy and non-discrimination that were infringed by Tasmanian laws criminalising sex between men).

22 Fox, 'New Crimes or New Responses?', 109.

23 See, e.g., Editorial, 'Consent Question Should Be Faced', *The Australian*, 17 December 1996, p. 10; Editorial, 'Consent Laws Barriers to Reform', *The Australian*, 21 December 1996, p. 25.

these matters were decried by the Attorney-General for Queensland as 'lunacy or at best illogicality' in a country as 'homogenous as Australia'.[24]

At the same time, the scope of Commonwealth criminal law was expanding, a development which has been labelled the main impetus for its subsequent codification.[25] Under Australia's Constitution, states retained power to pass criminal laws after Federation in 1901, and, throughout the century, most criminal law was state law. But, utilising residual and other constitutional powers, from its establishment, the Commonwealth created criminal offences, relating to matters such as Commonwealth officers and property and customs.[26] The most serious of these offences were located in the *Crimes Act 1914* (Cth), which has gradually expanded over time, reflecting, for example, the demands of national defence and related matters associated with World War I and World War II.[27] As Australian governmental powers became increasingly centralised – a development that is closely associated with the formation of the apparatus of the welfare state in the mid-century[28] – the body of Commonwealth criminal law came to include offences in areas such as taxation. In the 1980s, Federal criminal law grew significantly, following a number of royal commissions and other inquiries into matters such as drug trafficking and tax evasion, which revealed 'criminal activities beyond the capacity of conventional enforcement agencies to suppress'.[29] These inquiries highlighted the new and emerging challenges facing Australian governments, and 'promoted the regulation of crime on a national scale'.[30]

Commonwealth criminal justice institutions also developed in the last decades of the century, providing some of the infrastructure that would prove necessary for enhanced Federal leadership in criminal law. Reflecting cost restraints, at Federation, the Commonwealth government did not establish its own criminal justice institutions to support its criminal laws: Commonwealth offences were (and continue to be) prosecuted in state and territory courts, and offenders were (and continue to be) detained in state and territory

[24] See D. Wills, 'One Nation: Nine Codes', *The Bulletin*, 16 October 1990, p. 111.

[25] See V. Bell, 'Keeping the Criminal Law in "Serviceable Condition": A Task for the Courts or the Parliament?' (2016) 27(3) *Current Issues in Criminal Justice* 335–44, 336.

[26] Under the Constitution, Commonwealth has no general power to legislate with respect to crime: it does so under the express incidental power (s 51[xxxix]), the implied incidental powers (ss 51 and 52), the executive power (s 61), and the external affairs power (s 51[xxix]; *Polyukhovich* v. *Commonwealth* (1991) 172 CLR 501): see P. Gerangelos et al., *Winterton's Australian Federal Constitutional Law: Commentary and Materials*, 4th ed. (Sydney: Thomas Reuters, 2017).

[27] For example, sedition was made a Commonwealth offence by the *War Precautions Act Repeal Act 1920* (Cth).

[28] I discuss the development of the welfare state in Australia as part of my analysis of the state in relations of responsibility in Chapter 8.

[29] See Fox, 'New Crimes or New Responses: Future Directions in Australian Criminal Law', 111–12 (referring for instance to the Royal Commission of Inquiry into Drug Trafficking (the Stewart Royal Commission) (1981–1983)).

[30] M. Kirby, 'Criminal Law Futurology' (2005) 17(1) *Current Issues in Criminal Justice* 122–36, 124. Legislation enacted following these inquiries included the *Proceeds of Crime Act 1987* (Cth).

prisons.[31] In the 1970s, the rising international profile of terrorism took concrete, local form with the bombing of the Hilton Hotel in Sydney while it was hosting a Commonwealth Heads of Government meeting, and, in 1979, the small Commonwealth Police, the police force of the Australian Capital Territory (ACT) and the Narcotics Bureau were brought together to form the Australian Federal Police.[32] Just a few years later, in 1984, Federal Parliament created the Office of the Commonwealth Director of Public Prosecutions to coordinate the prosecution of Commonwealth offences, and the National Crime Authority to analyse criminal intelligence.[33] At about the same time, under the leadership of Chief Justice Barwick and Chief Justice Gibbs, the High Court of Australia came to hear more criminal appeals,[34] and, in the 1990s, it handed down several significant decisions regarding criminal law and criminal process.[35] Through the leadership of the High Court, by this time, practitioners and commentators had come to speak of an Australian (as opposed to state-based) common law.[36]

The expansion of Commonwealth criminal law exacerbated problems with Federalism for criminal justice in Australia. By the 1980s, the growth in the number of Commonwealth offences sitting *outside* the *Crimes Act 1914* (Cth) was burgeoning. Although these offences were regarded as part of Commonwealth law, as a result of sections 79 and 80 of the *Judiciary Act 1903* (Cth), they were subject to the general criminal and procedural

[31] The Australian Constitution provides that federal jurisdiction can be invested in state courts (section 71, Australian Constitution), and requires states to make provision for those convicted of Commonwealth offences (section 120, Australian Constitution; *R* v. *Turnbull; ex parte Taylor* (1968) 123 CLR 28). This has been labelled the 'autochthonous expedient': see *R* v. *Kirby; Ex parte Boilermakers Society of Australia* (1956) 94 CLR 254 at 268 per Dixon J.

[32] On the creation of the Australian Federal Police, and its early operation, see D. Chappell, 'A Review of Federal Law Enforcement Arrangements', in D. Chappell and P. Wilson (eds.), *Australian Policing*, 2nd ed. (Sydney: Butterworths, 1996), pp. 126–31.

[33] See Director of Public Prosecutions Act 1983 (Cth) and National Crime Authority Act 1984 (Cth), respectively.

[34] See M. Kirby, 'Why Has the High Court Become More Involved in Criminal Appeals?' (2002) 23 *Australian Bar Review* 4–23 (identifying ten 'basic reasons' for this change including the development of a specialist criminal bar and provision of legal aid); M. Kirby, 'Editorial' (2001) 25 *Criminal Law Journal* 181–3. The special leave process requires that leave will only be granted for the appeal to be heard by the High Court where the matter involves a point of law of general importance: see *Liberato* v. *The Queen* (1985) 159 CLR 507.

[35] See, e.g., *Jago* v. *District Court of New South Wales* (1989) 168 CLR 23 (regarding a court's jurisdiction to stay proceedings for abuse of process where delay has jeopardised the prospects of a fair trial); *Dietrich* v. *The Queen* (1992) 177 CLR 292 (regarding a defendant's right to legal representation when charged with a serious criminal offence). The development of an implied rights jurisprudence, enhanced the political profile of the High Court: see R. Hall, 'The new politics of the High Court: Breaking with constitutional tradition or securing a political future?', in P. Boreham, G. Stokes and R. Hall (eds.), *The Politics of Australian Society: Political Issues for the New Century* (Sydney: Pearson Longman, 2000), pp. 147–9, 150–1.

[36] See, e.g., A. Mason, 'Changing the Law in a Changing Society' (1992) 18 *Commonwealth Law Bulletin* 1166–72, 1168; see also B. H. K. Donovan, 'The Committee for the Review of the Commonwealth Criminal Law' (1992) 66 *Australian Law Journal* 732–37, 732.

rules – including the principles of criminal responsibility – of the state in which the offence was tried.[37] As a result, and as the High Court stated, 'criminal liability for many Commonwealth offences was susceptible of varying application depending on the jurisdiction in which the offence was prosecuted'.[38] This situation was widely regarded as 'unsatisfactory',[39] with the existence of these extra-mural offences seen as adversely affecting the rule of law and equality before the law. Several commentators pointed to the difficulties of charging individuals with the same (Commonwealth) offence, yet having them subject to different criminal and procedural rules depending on the jurisdiction.[40] When the Commonwealth Criminal Code was enacted, the fact that it ensured that, 'for the first time since Federation those accused of Federal offences will be dealt with under the same principles' was lauded, and the Minister for Justice, Duncan Kerr, stated that the Commonwealth Code advanced 'true equality before the law in Australia'.[41]

At the same time as the criminal law and criminal justice landscape was changing, in the last decades of the century, crime itself was changing. These changes were connected to wider social, political and economic developments which typically go under the umbrella concept of globalisation and which have come to be thought of as defining a new political, social and economic era. Trans-jurisdictional crime, particularly drug crime and organised crime, had risen in profile and was impacting on Australia, and modern information and communications technology was seen to be generating new opportunities for criminal conduct.[42] Drug policy was high on the political agenda, in large part because of the profile of heroin use,[43] and the William Drugs Royal Commission had called for a uniform drug trafficking act in 1980.[44] Lack of uniformity in drug laws was thought to be a serious problem because the health and regulatory goals of these laws would be frustrated by variation between Australia's criminal jurisdictions.[45] Organised crime was regarded as a growing threat to government control over border security and immigration

[37] See *Leeth* v. *The Commonwealth of Australia* (1992) 174 CLR 455 (regarding variation in sentencing laws).

[38] *R* v. *LK*; *R* v. *RK* (2010) 241 CLR 177 at [99] per Gummow, Hayne, Crennan, Kiefel and Bell JJ.

[39] Hansard, Commonwealth House of Representatives, col. 1331, 1 March 1995.

[40] See, e.g., E. Colvin, 'Unity and Diversity in Australian Criminal Law: A Comment on the Draft Commonwealth Code' (1991) 15 *Criminal Law Journal* 82–94; M. Goode, 'The Model Criminal Code Project' (1997) 5(4) *Australian Law Librarian* 265–77.

[41] Hansard, Commonwealth Senate, col. 2379, 30 June 1994; Department of Justice, *Introduction of Criminal Code Bill is Legal History in the Making Says Minister for Justice*, Press Release (1 July 1994).

[42] Fairall, 'The Reform of the Criminal Law', p. 36.

[43] C. Bennett, 'The Emergence of Australia's National Campaign Against Drug Abuse: A Case-Study in the Politics of Drug Control' (2008) 32(3) *Journal of Australian Studies* 309–21.

[44] Commonwealth, Australian Royal Commission of Inquiry into Drugs, *Report* (1980); see also B. Bush, 'A Model Code?' (2009) 7(2) *Of Substance: The National Magazine on Alcohol, Tobacco and Other Drugs* 18–19.

[45] Model Criminal Code Officers' Committee, Standing Committee of Attorneys-General, *Report on Serious Drug Offences* (1998), p. 2.

practices.[46] Developments such as these heightened political awareness that crime does not respect jurisdictional boundaries; in the Minister for Justice words, 'criminal activity does not recognise the boundary lines drawn on the map of Australia'.[47] This awareness placed pressure on sub-national criminal justice systems, making state and territory divisions in criminal laws in Australia seem less relevant.

Outside criminal law and criminal justice, the last decades of the century were marked by several other major, national developments, which reveal that the reforming zeal on the part of Australian governments extended beyond the criminal law. At this time, successive Federal governments enacted a raft of economic and other reforms aimed at market liberalisation to ensure efficiency and growth.[48] The early 1990s saw the enactment of national *Corporations Law* across Australia. Following 'the excesses of the 1980s', these reforms focused on responsibility and accountability, broadening duties of directors, and enhancing shareholders' rights.[49] At about the same time as reform of Commonwealth criminal law was being debated, the *Uniform Evidence Act* – producing standard rules of evidence to be enacted into each jurisdiction – was also being formulated.[50] While the economic case for criminal law reform might seem less self-evident that that for corporations law, debate at the time included a number of references to the economic benefits associated with a uniform criminal law, including the ability of lawyers to work in more than one jurisdiction, and the accommodation of an increasingly mobile populace involved in business and recreation across state and territory boundaries.[51] In general, law reform was depicted as key to social progress and growth: Prime Minister Paul Keating connected it to ensuring Australia could count itself as a 'great social democracy'.[52]

As this discussion indicates, the pressure that state systems were under and the complexity arising from multiple systems of criminal law gave rise to calls for reform: and it was reform of the Commonwealth criminal law that came to be seen as the answer to the range of problems and challenges facing Australian criminal justice. Reform of Commonwealth law represented an attempt to compensate for Australia's Federal structure, shifting the centre of gravity away from the states and towards a common central point, and

[46] See A. Schloenhardt, 'Organised Crime and the Business of Migrant Trafficking: An Economic Analysis' (1999) 32(3) *Crime, Law and Social Change* 203–33.

[47] See Easterbrook, 'Moves Begin Toward National Criminal Code', p. 9, and Hansard, Commonwealth Senate, col. 2379, 30 June 1994, respectively.

[48] See for discussion R. Hogg and D. Brown, *Rethinking Law and Order* (Sydney: Pluto Press, 1998), ch. 6.

[49] A. Rose, 'Developments in Criminal Law and Criminal Justice: 1995 Australian Criminal Code Act: Corporate Criminal Provisions' (1995) 6(1) *Criminal Law Forum* 129–47, 130.

[50] See, e.g., *Evidence Act 1995* (Cth).

[51] Hansard, Commonwealth House of Representatives, col. 1332, 1 March 1995; Explanatory Memorandum, *Criminal Code Bill 1994* (Cth), p. 2.

[52] Willox, 'Keating Strives for National Law Reform', p. 4.

re-inscribing the boundaries of the criminal law at a national rather than sub-national level. Fixing such boundaries at the national level presented a stronger and more relevant front in the face of trans-jurisdictional crime and global change, and the reform of Commonwealth criminal law seemed to include an implicit promise: to equip the Australian nation for a new century. When the Commonwealth Criminal Code was introduced in parliament in 1994, and echoing the ideas of institution-building associated with the Queensland Criminal Code, reference was made to the need for uniform criminal law as 'we become closer together and as we seek to operate as a nation'.[53]

Moving Towards a Code

The first step towards reform of the Commonwealth criminal law was taken with the formation of the Review of Commonwealth Criminal Law Committee in 1987, a committee which had as its brief the overhaul of the law.[54] The Committee was chaired by Sir Harry Gibbs, who had just completed his term as Chief Justice of the High Court of Australia.[55] The Committee consulted widely within the legal profession and government,[56] reviewed the law across Australia and overseas, and produced several discussion papers and a number of reports on discrete topics ('interim reports') each of which contained draft Bills.[57] Topics examined included computer crime, detention before charge, and offences relating to the administration of justice and arrest. The Gibbs Committee's task was framed in terms of 'consolidating' or rationalising (rather than codifying) Commonwealth law, and it's draft materials were presented as being able to be enacted either in parts or in a single consolidating Act that would repeal the *Crimes Act 1914* (Cth).[58]

The Gibbs Committee's interim report on the principles of criminal responsibility, published in 1990, and covering topics including voluntary acts, the mental element of offences, age of criminal responsibility and insanity,

[53] Hansard, Commonwealth House of Representatives, col. 1337, 1 March 1995. I discuss the Queensland Criminal Code in Chapter 3.

[54] A preliminary step had been taken in June 1984, when, on the invitation of the Commonwealth Attorney-General, Justice Watson commenced a review of Commonwealth criminal law but, before the completion of this review, the Review of Commonwealth Criminal Law Committee was established, with Justice Watson as a member: see *R* v. *LK*; *R* v. *RK* (2010) 241 CLR 177 at [99] per Gummow, Hayne, Crennan, Kiefel and Bell JJ.

[55] On Gibbs CJ's tenure, see M. Kirby, 'Recollections of Sir Harry Gibbs' (2005) 49(9) *Quadrant* 54–7.

[56] The *Society for the Reform of the Criminal Law*, an international organisation of judges, practitioners and others, hosted a seminar on the Gibbs Committee's work on reform of Commonwealth criminal law, in 1991: see Borick, 'Report on the Brisbane Seminar', 516.

[57] The Committee's interim reports on computer crime and detention before charge formed the basis of reforms to the *Crimes Act 1914* (Cth) prior to the development of the *Model Criminal Code*.

[58] See Review of Commonwealth Criminal Law (Australia), *Final Report* (1991), [1.6].

marked an important step towards reform.[59] The Committee's assessment of criminal responsibility was largely based on the common law.[60] For example, in relation to insanity, the Committee recommended a simplified version of the *M'Naughten Rules*, avoiding reliance on the term 'disease of the mind', on the basis that it was overly narrow.[61] Making particular reference to different approaches to self-induced intoxication, and the law of mistake, in its report, the Committee criticised the absence of 'any statement of the general principles upon which criminal responsibility depends', stating that this had led to 'obscurity and inconsistency'.[62] Given the significance of these principles, the Gibbs Committee proposed that 'the most convenient course' would be 'to codify all relevant principles relating to criminal responsibility', noting that this would involve a general restatement of existing principles (as opposed to radical reform) that would also 'fill gaps, remove obscurities and correct anomalies'.[63] The Committee concluded that the codification of the principles of criminal responsibility would achieve 'uniformity of principle' in Commonwealth criminal trials across Australia, and make the principles 'more readily accessible' as well as 'more clear and certain'.[64] While the Gibbs Committee's Draft Bill on the principles of criminal responsibility was not introduced into parliament, the reforms it proposed were taken up in the *Model Criminal Code,* as I discuss below.

Although the Gibbs Committee was concerned solely with Commonwealth criminal law, its work inspired efforts to develop a criminal code for all Australian jurisdictions. Reflecting notable state-Federal cooperation, in 1990, the Standing Committee of Attorneys-General of Australian states and territories (SCAG) put the development of a uniform criminal code for Australia on its agenda.[65] At this time, a number of Australian jurisdictions were undertaking, or about to undertake, reviews of their criminal law[66] and, on this basis, it was argued that 'the time was right to consider moves towards

[59] Review of Commonwealth Criminal Law (Australia), *Interim Report [i.e. third]: Principles of Criminal Responsibility and Other Matters* (1990): see also M. Goode, 'Fault Elements' (1991) 15 *Criminal Law Journal* 95–108.

[60] B. Wells, 'Criminal Codes for the Commonwealth and the States?' (1991) 62 *Reform* 108–10, 110.

[61] Review of Commonwealth Criminal Law, *Principles of Criminal Responsibility and Other Matters*, [9.36]–[9.39]. I discuss the insanity defence in Chapter 3.

[62] Review of Commonwealth Criminal Law, *Principles of Criminal Responsibility and Other Matters*, [3.10], [3.2].

[63] Review of Commonwealth Criminal Law, *Principles of Criminal Responsibility and Other Matters*, [3.12]. The recommendation of the Committee was that 'the proposed consolidation law should contain a statement of the principles governing criminal responsibility' ([3.14](a)).

[64] Review of Commonwealth Criminal Law, *Principles of Criminal Responsibility and Other Matters*, [3.12].

[65] Criminal Law Officers' Committee (CLOC), *Model Criminal Code: General Principles of Criminal Responsibility, Final Report*, i.

[66] See, e.g., South Australia: Attorney-General's Department (SA), *First Interim Report to the Attorney-General of South Australia on Reform of the Criminal Law in South Australia, Consistency in Criminal Law Reform at a National Level, and Progress Toward a Model Penal Code for Australia* (1991).

at least consistency, if not uniformity in criminal law'.[67] There was a felt sense that the 'centuries of development, much of it ad hoc', of the criminal law had generated 'loopholes and gaps' that 'in depth and principled' review of the criminal law could address.[68] There seems to have been little discussion of the mode of proposed reform – as a code. Early on in the process, and without much debate, the goal shifted from a uniform code to a model code – that is, from a code that would be *applied* in all jurisdictions, to a code which would be an *example* to all jurisdictions – on the basis that this would provide the best means of 'bridging' the differences between the common law and code jurisdictions in Australia.[69] The lack of debate about the code mode of law reform, and the ready shift from a uniform to a model code, exposed the rather loose approach to the code mode that prevailed at this time. I pick up on this point below.

A committee to prepare a model code, comprising representatives of each Australian state and territory, was formed as a subcommittee of SCAG, operating at first under the leadership of Dean Wells, then Attorney-General of Queensland.[70] Unlike the American Law Institute's advisory committee on the *Model Penal Code,* which was independent of government and included experts in psychiatry and criminology as well as legal academics, judges, lawyers and prison officials,[71] the Code Committee consisted only of lawyers, and did not have any separate institutional identity, existing only to perform the task of drafting the Model Code. The Code Committee was a *sui generis* law reform body that was unusual in its composition and its brief.[72] Committee members were drawn from within the senior ranks of the public service as well as the legal profession, with academics engaged as consultants.[73] The members of the public service appointed to the Committee were those who had special responsibility for advising their state Attorney-General on criminal law issues.[74] The Committee's direct connections to the government of the day – 'it consisted of

[67] CLOC, *Model Criminal Code: General Principles of Criminal Responsibility, Final Report*, ii.

[68] See T. Griffin, 'A Retrospective – Policy and Legislative Reform themes in the Attorney-General's areas of Responsibility, 1991–2001' (2003) 6(2) *Flinders Journal of Law Reform* 263–83, 264.

[69] G. Scott, 'A Model Criminal Code' (1992) 16 *Criminal Law Journal* 350–2, 351. The suggestion of a model rather than uniform criminal code for Australia was made by the then Attorney-General for the Northern Territory, Daryl Manzie: see Rose, 'Developments in Criminal Law and Criminal Justice', 130.

[70] The Committee was initially called the Criminal Law Officers' Committee (CLOC), but, from 1993, it was known as the Model Criminal Code Officers' Committee (MCCOC), and, later, the Model Criminal Law Officers' Committee (MCLOC). In this chapter, I refer to the 'Code Committee' or CLOC for simplicity.

[71] See Robinson and Dubber, 'The American Model Penal Code', 323.

[72] See M. Goode, 'Constructing Criminal Law Reform and the Model Criminal Code' (2002) 26 *Criminal Law Journal* 152–66, 155–6.

[73] Academic consultants included Brent Fisse, from the University of Sydney, and Ian Leader-Elliott, from the University of Adelaide.

[74] CLOC, *Model Criminal Code: General Principles of Criminal Responsibility, Final Report*, ii.

the very people who were in a position to push for change', in the words of one member – were thought to improve the chances its proposals would be acted upon.[75] The Code Committee was also distinctive because it was tasked with drafting new law, rather than merely reviewing existing law and making recommendations for reform. By this time, law reform bodies existed in a number of Australian jurisdictions, including at the national level, but none was enlisted in the task of drafting a model criminal code.[76]

The *Model Criminal Code* was envisaged as an administrative project with a technical legal exercise at its core, and its drafters were devoted to the task of crafting a more perfect criminal law as a public service. While the Code Committee consulted with judges, practitioners and others, as the contemporaneous calls for Australian lawyers to provide more support for the project suggest,[77] the *Model Criminal Code* was drafted and finalised by a small circle of individuals. Guided by adherence to principle over policy, or politics, the drafters approached work on the Model Code as an opportunity to formulate 'best practice basic criminal law provisions',[78] developed free from the restrictions of a particular case, and unsullied by political or policy considerations. Like the *Model Penal Code*, the Model Criminal Code was aimed at the legislature, and the drafters intended the Code to be a model in that it represented 'ideal law', 'devoid as much as possible of local, parochial, political considerations'.[79] At the same time, their aim was to draft a practically useful Code, with one of the drafters proudly stating that it was not 'the child of academics designed to serve the needs of academics', and not 'about neatness and symmetry alone'.[80] As the Code Committee stated confidently, 'the Code will eventually provide model provisions capable of replacing all common law offences and Crimes Act provisions in the common law jurisdictions, and the Criminal Code provisions in the Griffith Code jurisdictions'.[81]

Reflecting the way in which concerns about the rationality and workability of the criminal law were refracted through the lens of criminal responsibility, responsibility principles were central to the reform endeavour encapsulated in the Model Code. When the Code Committee held its first formal meeting, it was decided to give priority to the principles of criminal responsibility, on the basis that these were 'the very foundations

[75] M. Goode, 'Codification of the Criminal Law' (2004) 28 *Criminal Law Journal* 226–36, 232; see also R. S. O'Regan, 'Law Reform and Politics' (1996) 14 *Australian Bar Review* 1–5.

[76] The Australian Law Reform Commission was established in 1975 (as the Law Reform Commission) and, in the 1980s, it was given the task of reviewing the law of evidence with a view to developing a comprehensive code of evidence: see Law Reform Commission, *Evidence Law Reform Stage 2*, Discussion Paper No. 23 (1985).

[77] See, e.g., Borick, 'Report on the Brisbane Seminar', 516; R. Howie, 'Letter to the Editor' (1996) 14 *Australian Bar Review* 87–9.

[78] Goode, 'Constructing Criminal Law Reform and the Model Criminal Code', 163.

[79] Scott, 'A Model Criminal Code', 351; on the *Model Penal Code*, see Farmer, 'Codification', 387.

[80] See Goode, 'Codification of the Australian Criminal Law', 19.

[81] CLOC, *Model Criminal Code: General Principles of Criminal Responsibility, Final Report*, p. 3.

of any system of criminal justice'.[82] This first set of materials, published in 1992, borrowed from the earlier statement on principles of criminal responsibility drafted by the Gibbs Committee,[83] and would become Chapter 2 of the Model Criminal Code, entitled the 'General Principles of Criminal Responsibility'. It was intended that the principles of criminal responsibility would be capable of adoption by all jurisdictions, and be able to be implemented independently of the rest of the Code.[84] The drafters held these principles as sacred, stating that, 'in principle', the 'basic rules of criminal responsibility' should not vary from state to state.[85] Although the drafters held that the principles of criminal responsibility should not bear the stamp of any particular jurisdiction, they bore the stamp of the common law in their embrace of the tripartite structure of criminal responsibility – across conduct, fault and defences – and subjective fault as a basis for liability, as I discuss in the following section of this chapter.

The drafters viewed the development of the *Model Criminal Code* as falling within the well-established tradition of the codification of the common law of crime. One of the drafters of the Code, and a key author of its material on principles of criminal responsibility, Matthew Goode, invoked Jeremy Bentham in advocating for codification on the basis that the criminal law should be 'easy to discover, easy to understand, cheap to buy, and democratically made and amended'.[86] In relation to the qualities of ease of access and understanding, the Model Code was intended to be comprehensible to ordinary people, and not just to lawyers.[87] In relation to its democratic credentials, like other codes, it's objective was democratic and constitutional reform thought to flow from putting the legislature in charge of the criminal law.[88] Famously, for Bentham, the 'unwritten' nature of the English common law, and the lack of transparency of its language usurped the power of the legislature.[89] As Andrew Ashworth

[82] CLOC, *Model Criminal Code: General Principles of Criminal Responsibility, Final Report*, ii.

[83] See for discussion Colvin, 'Unity and Diversity in Australian Criminal Law'; K. Mulqueeny, 'Fault Elements from a Code Perspective' (1991) 15 *Criminal Law Journal* 109–12.

[84] CLOC, Standing Committee of Attorneys-General, *Model Criminal Code: Chapter 2: General Principles of Criminal Responsibility, Discussion Draft*, ii, p. 7.

[85] CLOC, *Model Criminal Code: General Principles of Criminal Responsibility, Final Report*, p. 5.

[86] Goode, 'Codification of the Australian Criminal Law', 8, 10, 15–16. For critical discussion of these features of modern codes, see Farmer, 'Codification', pp. 384–93.

[87] The Code Committee self-consciously avoided drafting a code that could only be interpreted by lawyers, as this would 'fail a basic test of acceptability': CLOC, *Model Criminal Code: General Principles of Criminal Responsibility, Final Report*, ii.

[88] I. Leader-Elliott, 'Benthamite Reflections on Codification of the General Principles of Criminal Liability: Towards the Panopticon' (2006) 9(2) *Buffalo Criminal Law Review* 391–452, 393.

[89] See M. A. Kayman, 'A Memorial for Jeremy Bentham: Memory, Fiction and Writing the Law' (2004) 15 *Law and Critique* 207–29, 214–16. In Bentham's terms, and by contrast with common law ('dog law'), written (statute) law does not invite interpretation and constant re-interpretation (317). I discuss Bentham's influence on codification across Empire in Chapter 1 and the Queensland Criminal Code in Chapter 3.

writes, the enactment of a criminal code makes it clear that 'the creation of offences is for Parliament alone, and that the role of the judiciary is to interpret rather than add or subtract'.[90] In this sense, codification involves what Lindsay Farmer refers to as a 'recodifying of political order', 'framing the relation between state and citizen as a matter of public law'.[91]

But, as a particular mode of law reform, codification does not seem to have been fully explored by the Code Committee, and belief in the Model Code as a code seems to have come down to a somewhat imprecise idea – of ideal law and super legislation. Following their brief to formulate a model code, the drafters of the *Model Criminal Code* left unarticulated the precise concept of codification they utilised.[92] Similarly, when it came to debate in parliament, the mode or form of the reform as a code had been settled,[93] and this choice does not seem to have been thoroughly considered by legislators.[94] This commitment to the code mode seems to have arisen in part as the result of a generalised belief that the process of reform should closely resemble the creation of the *Model Penal Code*, and, as Goode stated at the time, this '*necessarily* involves codification in non-Code states and territories'.[95] In addition, and as the Code Committee members were aware, at the time the work on the *Model Criminal Code* commenced, work on criminal codes had been undertaken in Canada and England as well as other common law countries,[96] which seemed to suggest that codification was the chosen mode of reform across the

90 A. Ashworth, 'Interpreting Criminal Statutes: A Crisis of Legality?' (1991) 107 *Law Quarterly Review* 419–49, 420. This article was cited by the Code Committee: CLOC, *Model Criminal Code: General Principles of Criminal Responsibility, Discussion Draft*, p. 3.

91 Farmer, 'Codification', p. 396.

92 M. Gani, 'Codifying the Criminal Law: Implications for Interpretation' (2005) 29 *Criminal Law Journal* 264–80, 267–8.

93 In the Australian political system, drafting offences is a bureaucratic exercise: legislation only reaches parliament after public servants operating under ministerial guidance have drafted it: see S. Bronitt and M. Gani, 'Criminal Codes in the 21st Century: The Paradox of the Liberal Promise', in B. McSherry, A. Norrie and S. Bronitt (eds.), *Regulating Deviance: The Redirection of Criminalisation and the Futures of Criminal Law* (Oxford: Hart, 2009), pp. 246–7 (arguing that codification shifts power to the executive as well as to the legislature) (p. 247).

94 Parliamentarians made references to Bentham's famous quip about common law as 'dog law', a number of legislators referenced the virtues of codification (Hansard, Commonwealth House of Representatives, col. 1349–52, 1 March 1995; Hansard, Commonwealth House of Representatives, col. 1352–3, 1 March 1995) and Philip Ruddock MP referred to 'almost unanimous' support for 'the *concept* of the model national Criminal Code', (Hansard, Commonwealth House of Representatives, col. 1340, 1 March 1995 (emphasis added)), but the distinctiveness of the mode of reform of the criminal law as a code did not garner much attention.

95 Attorney-General's Department (SA), *First Interim Report*, p. 9 (emphasis in original).

96 See Law Reform Commission of Canada, *Recodifying Criminal Law* (Report No. 31) (1987); Law Commission for England and Wales, *Criminal Law: A Criminal Code for England and Wales Volumes 1 and 2*, Law Com. No. 177 (1989); Law Commission for England and Wales, *Criminal Law: Codification of the Criminal Law*, Law Com. No. 143 (1985). The modern project of codifying English criminal law had begun in 1967 and was only abandoned in 2008: see for discussion Farmer, 'Codification', pp. 387–8.

common law world. It is in part because the mode of reform of the criminal law as a code was not fully explored that the Code does not contain general principles of interpretation, as I discuss below.

The efforts of the drafters and others involved in the *Model Criminal Code* bore fruit in what was initially a short draft criminal code. The Criminal Code Bill 1994 containing a revised version of the Model Code was introduced to the Commonwealth parliament in June 1994. At this point, what is now the Commonwealth Criminal Code contained only Chapter 1 (containing just one clause, providing that offences can only be created under this or any other Act of parliament) and Chapter 2 (on the general principles of criminal responsibility). The other chapters of the Commonwealth Criminal Code, which were drafted progressively throughout the 1990s, covered the 'core' or 'mainstream' of the criminal law, such as sexual offences, and more peripheral parts of the corpus, such as conspiracy to defraud.[97] Around the same time that the Code was introduced in parliament, the Commonwealth, state and territory Premiers' Leaders Forum endorsed the Commonwealth *Criminal* Code as a project of national significance and gave a unanimous commitment to implement it by 2001.[98] At this point, it was confidently anticipated that its model provisions would have a decisive influence on criminal laws in Australia and be implemented progressively by all Australian states.[99]

Against a political and constitutional backdrop sometimes characterised as 'uncooperative federalism', the momentum of exceptional state-Federal collaboration sustained the formation of the Commonwealth Code, which received a largely positive if brief welcome across the political spectrum when it was introduced into Federal Parliament. In Commonwealth parliamentary debates, the Commonwealth *Criminal Code* was considered a 'landmark in cooperative federalism', as well as a demonstration that Federalism works, and a 'fitting project' with which to mark the then forthcoming centenary of Australian Federation, in 2001.[100] In what, with hindsight, seems overly optimistic or perhaps naive, there was even a suggestion that raising crime to the

[97] The Code Committee produced eight reports in total, each of which included draft legislation. After the report on general principles of criminal responsibility, these reports covered: non-fatal offences against the person (1994); blackmail, forgery and bribery and theft, fraud and related offences (1995); sexual offences (which also covered some evidentiary and procedural issues, and age of consent) (1996); conspiracy to defraud (1997); serious drug offences (1998); offences against the administration of justice; and public order offences (1998).

[98] See Hansard, Commonwealth Senate, col. 379–80, 2 February 1995.

[99] Hansard, Commonwealth Senate, col. 2382, 30 June 1994. At the time of writing, some sets of Code provisions, such as those relating to self-defence, have been adopted by some states, such as NSW: see Gani, 'Codifying the Criminal Law'. This approach has been referred to as 'picking the eyes out' of the Code: see Griffin, 'A Retrospective', 265. In relation to criminal responsibility, only the ACT and Northern Territory have adopted Chapter 2 of the Code (in 2002 and 2006 respectively): see for discussion Leader-Elliott, 'Elements of Liability in the Commonwealth Criminal Code', 29.

[100] See Hansard, Commonwealth House of Representatives, col. 1349, 1 March 1995; Hansard, Commonwealth Senate, col. 2380, 30 June 1994, respectively.

national stage and encasing it in the Commonwealth *Criminal Code* would immunise it from media sensationalism and populist concerns, thereby reducing pressure on politicians and permitting 'more rational debate' on criminal justice policy than that allowed at a local level.[101] The Criminal Code Bill 1994 became the *Criminal Code Act 1995* (Cth), with the Commonwealth *Criminal Code* included as a Schedule. The Commonwealth Code commenced on 1 January 1997.

Codified Criminal Responsibility

Codification of the Commonwealth law fixed the principles of criminal responsibility at the heart of Australian criminal laws. Codification constituted a legal systematisation – a (re-)organisation of criminal law – with criminal responsibility constituting the main pivot of the legal systematisation. It is the principles of Chapter 2 that provide the basis on which the Code was said to offer 'consistency, if not uniformity' in the criminal law.[102] These principles provide integrity to the Commonwealth Code, meaning the criminal law makes sense on its own terms, and ensuring that it can stand on its own and act as model for adoption in other jurisdictions.

Criminal Responsibility in the Commonwealth Code

As it contained 'the foundations of the Commonwealth criminal law',[103] Chapter 2 was regarded as the most important chapter of the Commonwealth Code. Chapter 2's central provision, which Ian Leader-Elliott describes as its 'primary analytical achievement',[104] is the provision relating to elements of an offence, Part 2.2. Following the *Model Penal Code* – which introduced an element-based approach as opposed to an offence-based approach to the common law of crime[105] – this Part of the chapter describes all offences as comprising physical elements and fault elements, permitting different fault elements to correspond to the physical elements of an offence. Physical elements are conduct, result and 'a circumstance in which conduct, or a result of conduct, occurs', and the chapter specifies that conduct can only be a physical element if it is voluntary (sections 4.1 and 4.2(1)). Fault elements are intention, knowledge, recklessness and negligence (sections 5.2–5.5).[106] Chapter 2 provides that

[101] Hansard, Commonwealth House of Representatives, col. 1343–4, 1 March 1995.

[102] CLOC, *Model Criminal Code: General Principles of Criminal Responsibility, Final Report*, ii.

[103] Hansard, Commonwealth Senate, col. 2379, 30 June 1994.

[104] I. Leader-Elliott, 'Elements of Liability in the Commonwealth Criminal Code' (2002) 26 *Criminal Law Journal* 28–42, 31.

[105] See Robinson and Dubber, 'The American Model Penal Code', 334–5.

[106] The Code adopts a broad definition of intention in relation to a result that encompasses oblique intention, whereby a person will be held to have intended a result if they are 'aware that it will result in the ordinary course of events': see *Criminal Code* (Cth) s 5.2(3).

the default fault element for a criminal offence is recklessness, which is defined following the *Model Penal Code,* as the advertent taking of a substantial and unjustifiable risk (section 5.4). Definitions of each of these physical and fault elements are included in the chapter. Chapter 2 states that a fault element attaches to each physical element unless the legislature imposes strict or absolute liability for that element (the presumption of fault) (section 3.1), and includes provisions on strict and absolute liability offences (sections 5.1 and 5.2). As this indicates, the Commonwealth Code intended the legislature to consider the type of offence – absolute liability, strict liability or an 'ordinary' criminal offence, as I discuss below – at the time of enactment, rather than waiting for interpretation by courts.[107]

Chapter 2 also sets out the circumstances in which there is no criminal responsibility (children aged under 10, children aged between 10 and 14 and mental impairment), defences and extensions of liability. In relation to mental impairment, the Code Committee recommended an addition to the *M'Naughten Rules* that are relied on in common law jurisdictions: the test for insanity under the Code includes inability to control conduct ('volitional impairment') (section 7.3), which is a limb of mental impairment under the Queensland *Criminal Code* and its progeny.[108] Following the *Model Criminal Code,* discussed above, in relation to defences, the Commonwealth Code did not adopt a distinction between justifications and excuses, opting instead to set out general defences as those relating to lack of capacity (sections 7.1–7.3), intoxication (sections 8.1–8.5), which I discuss below, mistake or ignorance (sections 9.1–9.4) or external factors (such as self-defence or duress) (sections 10.1–10.5).[109] Provisions relating to extensions of liability (including attempt, complicity and conspiracy) (sections 11.1–11.5), corporate criminal responsibility (also discussed below), the burden and standard of proof of criminal responsibility (section 13.1), and geographical jurisdiction (sections 14.1–15.4) make up the rest of Chapter 2. The principles contained in Chapter 2 govern the offence provisions contained in the special part of the Commonwealth *Criminal Code,* and also apply to other Commonwealth offences (section 2.2).

The principles of criminal responsibility that make up Chapter 2 of the Commonwealth Code had several sources. First, Chapter 2 was modelled on the corresponding article of the *Model Penal Code,* which covered physical

[107] Explanatory Memorandum, *Criminal Code Bill 1994* (Cth), p. 17.

[108] It appears that this decision was reached based on recent reviews of the law in Western Australia and Queensland, which recommended retaining this provision, and on feedback received on the draft code materials: CLOC, *Model Criminal Code: General Principles of Criminal Responsibility, Final Report,* p. 35. I discuss the Commonwealth Code provisions on mental impairment in Chapter 4.

[109] The Commonwealth Code incorporated the defence of honest and reasonable mistake of fact in relation to strict liability offences (section 9.2); for discussion of this defence, see Chapter 4.

and fault elements, causation, mistake and complicity.[110] Second, the analysis of offence structure in Chapter 2 also owed a debt to Justice Brennan's influential judgment in *He Kaw Teh*.[111] As is well known, in *He Kaw Teh*, the High Court affirmed the presumption that statutory offences require proof of fault, stating that '*mens rea* is an essential element in every statutory offence unless, having regard to the language of the statute and its subject matter, it is excluded expressly or by necessary implication'.[112] *He Kaw Teh* also provided that strict liability offences – to which honest and reasonable mistake of fact is a defence – represent a 'middle course' between ordinary offences requiring proof of *mens rea* and absolute liability offences that do not require proof of *mens rea*.[113] The third source of principles contained in Chapter 2 was the recommendations of the Gibbs Committee, which, as discussed above, had drafted criminal responsibility provisions that would not involve 'radical reform', but would 'restate existing principles' and 'fill gaps, remove obscurities and correct anomalies'.[114] Fourth, and most significantly, Chapter 2's source was the common law of criminal responsibility, according to which criminal responsibility is structured across conduct, fault and defences, and subjective fault occupies a cardinal position as a basis for criminal liability.[115]

The Commonwealth *Criminal Code*'s organisation of principles of criminal responsibility around conduct, fault and defences, and on subjective liability – the idea that criminal fault should depend on what the accused himself or herself 'knew, believed or intended at the time of the conduct'[116] – was intended as a definitive adjudication between the common law and Griffith Code state approaches to criminal responsibility. The language of physical and fault elements – by contrast with the language of will, accident and chance – and the embrace of subjectivism, entailed a conscious rejection of the principles of criminal responsibility as they applied in the Griffith code jurisdictions.[117] Reflecting then current ideas, the Queensland *Criminal Code* and its progeny include a general set of principles of criminal responsibility that apply to all

[110] Article 2, *Model Penal Code*; Leader-Elliott, 'Elements of Liability in the Commonwealth Criminal Code', 34; Leader-Elliott, 'Benthamite Reflections on Codification', 398. Leader-Elliott suggests that Colin Howard's text, *Australian Criminal Law*, first published in 1965, was another 'precursor' to Chapter 2 (398). I discuss Howard's text in Chapter 4 as part of my analysis of mid-century Australian developments.

[111] *He Kaw Teh* v. *The Queen* (1985) 157 CLR 523.

[112] *He Kaw Teh* v. *The Queen* (1985) 157 CLR 523 at 566 per Brennan J.

[113] *He Kaw Teh* v. *The Queen* (1985) 157 CLR 523 at 533 per Gibbs CJ I discuss the defence of honest and reasonable mistake of fact in Chapter 4.

[114] Review of Commonwealth Criminal Law, *Principles of Criminal Responsibility and Other Matters*, [3.12].

[115] CLOC, *Model Criminal Code: General Principles of Criminal Responsibility, Discussion Draft*, p. 23; CLOC, *Model Criminal Code: General Principles of Criminal Responsibility, Final Report*, ii. It was noted that the *Model Penal Code* had embraced subjective fault: see Explanatory Memorandum, *Criminal Code Bill 1994* (Cth), p. 13.

[116] CLOC, *Model Criminal Code: General Principles of Criminal Responsibility, Final Report*, p. 21.

[117] See Colvin, 'Unity and Diversity in Australian Criminal Law'.

offences and is based on objective liability – where criminal responsibility is negated by accident (and now automatism), or honest and reasonable mistake.[118] Over the twentieth century, as common law evolved, subjective liability became more important, the gap between the approach taken by code and common law states grew, and the codification of general principles of criminal responsibility in the Griffith Codes came to be associated with 'inflexibility'.[119] As a result, and as discussed in the previous chapter, the Griffith Codes were subject to 'judicial surgery' to bring them into line with the contemporary criminal responsibility standards.[120] The decision to opt for subjective liability disappointed lawyers from code states: as one such commentator lamented, the Commonwealth Criminal Code opted for 'systematic subjectivism' which was 'alien' to the Code jurisdictions.[121]

The Commonwealth *Criminal Code* also marked a decisive moment in relation to corporate criminal responsibility. As is well known, corporations are considered legal persons, and corporations can be held liable for criminal offences under the common law.[122] However, because of the limitations of doctrines which rely on andromorphic constructions of the corporation as a human body, such as a 'controlling mind and will', it has proved difficult to prosecute corporations.[123] The Gibbs Committee and the Code Committee considered that the common law had dealt inadequately with the liability of corporations.[124] Drawing on the work of two prominent Australian criminal law and regulation scholars, John Braithwaite and Brent Fisse,[125] the Commonwealth Code departed from the common law in relation to corporate liability. The Code provided different bases on which a corporation can be found to satisfy the fault element of a criminal offence: in addition to intention, knowledge or recklessness on the part of the board of directors, or a 'high managerial agent', fault can be attributed to a corporation by proving that 'a corporate culture existed within the body corporate that directed, encouraged, tolerated or led to noncompliance with the relevant provision' or proving that 'the body corporate failed to create and maintain a corporate culture that required compliance with the relevant

118 See further Chapter 3.

119 Bell, 'Keeping the Criminal Law in "Serviceable Condition"', 337.

120 Ibid., 339; see further Chapter 4.

121 Colvin, 'Unity and Diversity in Australian Criminal Law', 85.

122 See *Tesco* v. *Nattrass* [1972] AC 153; *R* v. *P & O European Ferries* (Dover) Ltd (1990) 93 Cr App R 72.

123 See generally C. Wells, *Corporations and Criminal Responsibility* (Oxford: Oxford University Press, 2001).

124 See Review of Commonwealth Criminal Law, *Principles of Criminal Responsibility and Other Matters*, [26.7]; CLOC, *Model Criminal Code: General Principles of Criminal Responsibility, Discussion Draft*, p. 95–6.

125 See, e.g., B. Fisse and J. Braithwaite, *Corporations, Crime and Accountability* (Cambridge: Cambridge University Press, 1993).

provision' (sections 12.3(2)(c) and (d)).[126] The concept of 'corporate culture' was intended to provide an analogy to 'the key concept of personal responsibility – intent.'[127] As stated in parliament, this inclusion in the Code 'makes companies accountable for their general managerial responsibilities and policy'.[128]

As it was enacted, Chapter 2 departed from the *Model Criminal Code* in relation to the law regarding intoxicated offending. The Model Code provisions on intoxication were based on the High Court's decision of *R* v. *O'Connor* in 1980, according to which voluntary intoxication may be used as evidence to cast doubt on whether the accused had formed the requisite intent in relation to an offence of any kind.[129] In taking this position, the Code Committee, like the majority of the High Court, elected to uphold the principles of criminal responsibility in relation to intoxicated offending, rather than to derogate from them in order to support policy-based concerns condemning intoxicated offending.[130] The Code Committee defended its position on the basis that 'the need to base the Code on a consistent and rational set of principles – especially in the fundamentals of criminal responsibility – was of paramount importance'.[131] When it came to enacting the Code, however, parliament sought a more pragmatic and policy-driven approach and opted for the dominant common law approach to intoxicated offending. As is well known, this approach, which had been set out by the House of Lords in *Majewski* in 1977, restricts the cases in which voluntary intoxication may be raised by the defence to a subset of cases – those in which the accused is charged with an offence of 'specific intent'.[132]

With a main pivot around the principles of criminal responsibility contained in Chapter 2, the remainder of the Code was intended to 'cover the field'. This intention to 'cover the field' was an important dimension of the Commonwealth Criminal Code as a law reform project as it related to the idea that the Code was to function as a model for other jurisdictions, with its provisions able to be introduced in state and territory criminal laws. The special part of the Commonwealth Code organised criminal offences systematically, covering

[126] Corporate culture is defined as 'an attitude, rule, course of conduct or practice existing within a body corporate generally or in the part of the body corporate in which the relevant activities takes place' (s 12.3(6)). See for analysis, J. Clough, 'Bridging the Theoretical Gap: The Search for a Realist Model of Corporate Criminal Liability' (2007) 18(3–4) *Criminal Law Forum* 267–300.

[127] CLOC, *Model Criminal Code: General Principles of Criminal Responsibility, Discussion Draft*, p. 109.

[128] Hansard, Commonwealth House of Representatives, col. 1335, 1 March 1995.

[129] CLOC, *Model Criminal Code: General Principles of Criminal Responsibility, Final Report*, pp. 49–51; *R* v. *O'Connor* (1980) 146 CLR 64 (holding that evidence of voluntary intoxication should be allowed to go to the jury as part of all the evidence on which they may make a finding of fact in relation to any offence).

[130] See for analysis A. Loughnan and S. Gless, 'Understanding the Law on Intoxicated Offending: Principle, Pragmatism and Legal Culture' (2016) 3(2) *Journal of International and Comparative Law* 345–73.

[131] CLOC, *Model Criminal Code: General Principles of Criminal Responsibility, Discussion Draft*, p. 17.

[132] *Director of Public Prosecutions* v. *Majewski* [1977] AC 443; see also A. Loughnan, *Manifest Madness: Mental Incapacity in Criminal Law* (Oxford: Oxford University Press, 2012), ch. 7.

matters such as serious drug offences and computer crime that reflect the interests which, in the current era, the criminal law seeks to protect.[133] Although there were some notable omissions,[134] and while it was recognised that part of the corpus of Commonwealth criminal law would continue to sit *outside* the Commonwealth Criminal Code, the Code aimed to cover a significant part of Commonwealth criminal law, and to provide model offence and defence provisions in the major areas of substantive criminal law.

As this discussion suggests, as a legal systematisation, the emphasis in the *Commonwealth Criminal Code* was on the (re-)organisation of criminal *laws*. As a result, aspects of criminal justice such as criminal process or punishment are left to the side. By contrast with the Commonwealth Code, these aspects of criminal justice animated other codifications and major consolidations, and they provide vital context for the approaches taken to criminal responsibility in these reforms. For example, in the Australian context, around the turn of the twentieth century, criminal responsibility was one plank of the reform of the criminal law in NSW (via consolidation) and Queensland (via codification). Against a background of the early development of institutions of democratic governance in Australia, and amid concerns with the exercise of government power, modernisation of legal form – comprehensive legislation or a code – and process – the operation of criminal justice – was as important as principles of criminal responsibility.[135] The importance of form and process accounts for the inclusion of detailed and extensive provisions relating to the administration of criminal justice, and criminal procedure and punishment, in the codification and major consolidation dating from this time.

Another contrast with the Commonwealth Code in this respect is provided by the *Model Penal Code* in the US context. By the mid-century, when the *Model Penal Code* was in development in the United States, the rise of criminology and other social knowledges had ushered in the era of 'penal modernism', according to which crime was regarded as a social problem that could be addressed via a range of different regulatory responses,[136] and punishment was to be tailored to the individual according to his or her dangerousness.[137]

[133] S. Bronitt, 'Australia', in K. J. Heller and M. D. Dubber (eds.), *Handbook of Comparative Criminal Law* (Stanford, CA: Stanford Law Books, 2011), pp. 77–8.

[134] The Code Committee 'ran out of time and resources' on homicide: Goode, 'Codification of the Criminal Law', 229.

[135] See further Chapter 3.

[136] See D. Garland, 'Penal Modernism and Postmodernism', in T. G. Blomberg and S. Cohen (eds.), *Punishment and Social Control* (New York: Walter de Gruyter, 2003).

[137] See generally M. Pifferi, *Reinventing Punishment: A Comparative History of Criminology and Penology in the Nineteenth and Twentieth Centuries* (Oxford: Oxford University Press, 2016). Pifferi argues that this core idea produced different approaches in Europe (where the dual track system was adopted, allowing for supplementary detention on the basis of dangerousness following ordinary punishment) and the US (where sentencing is a judicial responsibility and the precise length of a sentence is determined via an administrative process controlled by a parole board).

The profile of punishment, and the particular approach taken to it, explains the way in which the *Model Penal Code* dove-tailed with its other half, the *Model Correctional Code*.[138] In its full context, the *Model Penal Code*'s primary goal – the prevention of crime, and, where this failed, the provision of a scientific regime of treatment as opposed to punishment of the criminal – becomes apparent,[139] and the role of criminal responsibility is to assist in evaluating criminal 'disposition'.[140] As Markus Dubber argues, the *Model Penal Code* embraces subjectivism not as a normative principle but to insist on 'scientific accuracy' in grasping the dangerousness of the criminal actor.[141]

The legal systematisation that the *Commonwealth* Criminal Code centres on criminal responsibility, which provides the main pivot of the (re-)organisation of the criminal law. As a late twentieth-century codification, the Criminal Code responds to the massive growth of the criminal law over preceding decades, and reflects the firmer conceptual divisions between criminal law, procedure and punishment that had developed by this time and which worked to prevent the inclusion of these topics in the (re-)organisation of the law. Thus, unlike the *Model Penal Code*, which covered criminal procedures as part of its elucidation of criminal laws,[142] the Commonwealth *Criminal Code* does not encompass criminal procedure. While the Code Committee intended to draft a chapter on procedure (covering matters such as unfitness to plead and double jeopardy),[143] this was not developed. Concerns about aspects of criminal procedure were expressed around the time of the development of the Code,[144] but, because of the perceived messiness of Australian criminal laws, the focus of those involved in the formulation of the Code was closely trained on the law itself. Similarly, the Code does not address criminal punishment beyond specifying maximum penalties for criminal offences. By the late twentieth century, in Australia, debates about punishment were circumscribed around the issue

[138] The Penal Code covers 'general provisions' and specific offences (Parts I and II), and the Correctional Code covers 'treatment and correction' and 'organization of correction' (Parts III and IV): see further Dubber, *An Introduction to the Model Penal Code*, 10–15.

[139] Dubber, 'Penal Panopticon', 69. Dubber argues that the theoretical basis for the *Model Penal Code* was not coherent, and that, in the decades since it appeared, it has been further undermined by the collapse of belief in 'treatmentalism' and the rise of retributivism as a theoretical basis for punishment.

[140] See generally Dubber, 'Penal Panopticon'. Dubber points to the *Model Penal Code's* 'harsh' provisions on inchoate offences like attempts as evidence of the Code's focus on the 'disposition' of the criminal actor (67–8).

[141] See M. D. Dubber, 'The Model Penal Code, Legal Process and the Alegitimacy of American Penality', in M. D. Dubber (ed.) *Foundational Texts in Modern Criminal Law* (Oxford: Oxford University Press, 2014), p. 241.

[142] See M. D. Dubber, *An Introduction to the Model Penal Code* (New York: Oxford University Press, 2015).

[143] CLOC, *Model Criminal Code: General Principles of Criminal Responsibility, Discussion Draft*, p. 7.

[144] See, e.g., Borick, 'Report on the Brisbane Seminar'.

of consistency in sentencing.[145] The emphasis on the (re-)organisation of criminal laws in the codification of Commonwealth criminal law brought with it a particular role for criminal responsibility, as I now turn to discuss.

The Role of Criminal Responsibility in the Commonwealth Code

The principles of criminal responsibility provide the Commonwealth Code with integrity, meaning that it makes sense on its own terms, can stand on its own and act as a model for adoption in other jurisdictions.

This integrity is realised in three main ways. First, the principles of criminal responsibility provide the language in which the Code is to be understood, and control and order meaning within the Code. As discussed above, Chapter 2 sets out the structure of criminal responsibility – across conduct, fault and defences – and provides definitions of core terms like conduct, intention and recklessness, ensuring that the meaning of these terms is the same across the Criminal Code. The chapter also defines key types of offences such as strict liability and absolute liability offences, substituting for common law description of these offence types. In this way, criminal responsibility operates as a common language for the Code and criminal law and criminal lawyers. This common language sets the terms of the debate, permitting the articulation of substantive issues in a way that is comprehensible to all. As Goode writes in relation to the *Model Criminal* Code provisions on criminal responsibility, 'even if the various jurisdictions agree to disagree, at least they should be speaking the same language'.[146] Thus, it is not so much that enshrining the principles of criminal responsibility in Chapter 2 of the Commonwealth *Criminal Code* was 'an expression of confidence in the aim of uniformity' in criminal law, as stated by the Minister for Justice,[147] but rather that these principles make possible a common or uniform way of speaking.

In providing the language in which the Code is to be understood, the principles of criminal responsibility control and order meaning, but do not operate to limit what can be said in this language. As is well known, the principles contained in Chapter 2 are default principles, and, although criminal responsibility was recognised as fundamental to the criminal law, and, as the Code's explanatory memorandum stated, parliament should not make a decision to override them lightly nor do so without 'clear justification',[148] there was nothing in the Code itself to prevent this from occurring. Further, and by contrast with the *Model Penal Code*, which contains a section directing

145 It was in this period that concerted efforts were made to achieve consistency in sentencing, and guideline judgments and mandatory minimum sentences appeared: see R. Edney and M. Bagaric, *Australian Sentencing: Principles and Practice* (Cambridge: Cambridge University Press, 2007), pp. 33–41.

146 Attorney-General's Department (SA), *First Interim Report*, p. 45.

147 Hansard, Commonwealth House of Representatives, col. 1359, 1 March 1995.

148 See Explanatory Memorandum, *Criminal Code Bill 1994* (Cth), pp. 6–7.

judges to interpret ambiguous provisions to further the Code's purposes,[149] there are no principles to ensure consistent decision-making, or to outline the priority between principles.[150] Indeed, the principles of criminal responsibility contained in the Commonwealth Criminal Code apply only in the event that parliament is unclear in its intentions regarding new criminal offences.[151] In addition, although the purpose of Chapter 2 was to 'codify' the principles of criminal responsibility (section 2.1), it does not offer comprehensive coverage of the principles of criminal responsibility. Thus, while the Chapter provides that fault elements shall be intention, knowledge, recklessness and negligence, it also provides that a Commonwealth offence may specify 'other fault elements for a physical element of that offence' (section 5.1(2)). Similarly, the Chapter provides that the standard of proof is the beyond reasonable doubt standard, but also provides that a law creating an offence can specify a different standard of proof (section 13.2(2)).[152] More generally, Chapter 2 as a whole can also be held not to apply to Commonwealth offences.[153] As this suggests, and in Leader-Elliott's words, the designation of Chapter 2 as a 'codification' of principles of criminal responsibility 'masks the ambiguity of its provisions'.[154]

The second way in which the principles of criminal responsibility provide the Commonwealth Code with integrity relates to their role in the interpretation of the Code: the principles of criminal responsibility compose part of the general interpretive framework for the Code. This role is enhanced by the absence of general interpretation provisions in the Code. As mentioned above, the mode of reform of the criminal law as a code was not fully explored by its drafters, and the Code did not contain any general interpretation provisions. Chapter 1 of the Model Code was intended to cover the 'mechanics of implementing a Code',[155] and provide guidance on interpretation of its provisions, but it was never written.[156] As it stands, Chapter 1

[149] Article 1.05, *Model Penal Code*. The Code's purposes include to forbid and prevent harmful conduct, to control persons disposed to commit crimes, to safeguard faultless conduct from being condemned as criminal, to give fair warning about the nature of conduct that is an offence and to differentiate on reasonable grounds between serious and minor offences. For discussion, see Robinson and Dubber, 'The American Model Penal Code', 332–3.

[150] See Bronitt and Gani, 'Criminal Codes in the 21st Century'.

[151] Leader-Elliott, 'The Australian Criminal Code', 206.

[152] See for discussion *Lee* v. *The Queen* (2007) 71 NSWLR 120.

[153] For example, the provisions on corporate criminal responsibility contained in the Code do not apply to offences included in Chapter 7 of the *Corporations Act 2001* (Cth): see *Corporations Act 2001* (Cth) s 769A (referring to section 2.5 of the Commonwealth Code).

[154] Leader-Elliott, 'Benthamite Reflections on Codification', 400.

[155] CLOC, *Model Criminal Code: General Principles of Criminal Responsibility, Final Report*, p. 3.

[156] See Gani, 'Codifying the Criminal Law', 269. Controversy over the interpretation clauses that had been drafted for the criminal code for England and Wales, and uncertainty about whether principles of interpretation were a legislative or judicial responsibility, seems to have dampened the Code Committee's efforts to develop such principles. As it was, the Model Criminal Code drafters relied on an analysis by Andrew Ashworth (Ashworth, 'Interpreting Criminal Statutes') regarding the English criminal code to conclude that such principles of interpretation were not essential.

comprises just one clause, which provides that all criminal offences must be created by statute (section 1.1).[157] In the absence of general interpretation provisions, the principles governing interpretation of the Code have been judicially developed. In broad terms, these principles provide that, while 'the first loyalty is to the Code', in circumstances of ambiguity, or technical or special meaning, courts may take into account pre-existing common law as well as developments in common law jurisdictions.[158] As the drafters of the Model Code acknowledged, the common law would continue to be relevant to the interpretation of the Code.[159] In relation to criminal statutes in particular, principles of statutory interpretation has come to entail interpretation consistent with 'the general part' of criminal law – not just with general principles of statutory interpretation such as strict construction.[160]

Within this general interpretive framework, judicial interpretation of Chapter 2 provisions has pointed in different directions. In 2011, in a matter concerning whether omission to act could be a physical element of the offence of obtaining a financial advantage from a Commonwealth entity, the High Court considered the effect of section 4.3 of Chapter 2 regarding omissions. The court held that the common law principles relating to omissions had not been imported into the Code, and that, in this instance, an omission had not been made a physical element of the alleged offence because it had not been specifically proscribed.[161] In reaching this conclusion, the High Court stated that

> The principles of criminal responsibility stated in the Code proceed from the view that the criminal law should be certain and that its reach should be able to be ascertained by those who are subject to it.[162]

While this statement reflects the intentions of those involved in the formation of the Commonwealth Code, the High Court has not found the Code to be so

[157] The Griffith Codes do not contain statements about principles of interpretation, although judicial statements about interpretation of the Codes from case law have come to be regarded as 'rules of interpretation': see for discussion S. Tarrant, 'Building Bridges in Australian Criminal Law: Codification and the Common Law' (2012) 39(3) *Monash University Law Review* 838–63, 854–7. Tarrant argues that these 'rules' amount to exhortations not to be distracted by the common law (855).

[158] See *R* v. *Barlow* (1997) 188 CLR 1 at 32 per Kirby J; see also *Boughey* v. *The Queen* (1986) 161 CLR 10.

[159] CLOC, *Model Criminal Code: General Principles of Criminal Responsibility, Final Report*, p. 3. In explaining how this would work, the Code Committee drew an analogy to the use of the English common law in the interpretation of the *Theft Act 1968* (England).

[160] Gani, 'Codifying the Criminal Law', 271; see also *He Kaw Teh* v. *The Queen* (1985) 157 CLR 523.

[161] *Director of Public Prosecutions (Cth)* v. *Poniatowska* (2011) 244 CLR 408 at [44] per French CJ, Gummow, Kiefel and Bell JJ (regarding section 135.2(1) on obtaining financial advantage from a Commonwealth entity, and section 4.3 on omissions liability).

[162] *Director of Public Prosecutions (Cth)* v. *Poniatowska* (2011) 244 CLR 408 at [44] per French CJ, Gummow, Kiefel and Bell JJ.

comprehensive in relation to every aspect of criminal responsibility. In *R* v. *LK; R* v. *RK*, which concerned the provision on conspiracy in section 11.5(2) of Chapter 2 of the Commonwealth Code, the High Court held that the common law concept of conspiracy (specifically, agreement as to the *actus reus* and intention to do the unlawful act) had been imported into the Code by use of the term 'conspiracy' and 'conspires' and failure to define those terms, and thus that the section of the Code 'cannot be taken as defining elements of the offence', and may be said to only provide prerequisites to a finding of guilt.[163] Decisions such as these have led one member of the High Court to suggest that the codification of the principles of criminal responsibility in Chapter 2 has not made them 'clearer' or 'easier to apply'.[164]

The third way in which the principles of criminal responsibility provide the Commonwealth Code with integrity relates to their role in offering a normative basis for the coercive power exercised through the criminal law. As mentioned above, the Code embraces subjective liability – the idea that criminal fault should depend on what the accused himself or herself 'knew, believed or intended at the time of the conduct'[165] – as the default basis for criminal responsibility. The inclusion of a default basis of criminal responsibility means that, even if Australian jurisdictions might take different approaches to the basis for criminal fault, legislatures will have to say so.[166] In addition, it places subjective liability at the heart of criminal responsibility. The explanation for the embrace of subjective liability was limited to the fact that it represented modern developments – the 'mainstream of legal development in the late twentieth century'[167] – with the idea that subjectivism provided a 'moral justification for high measures of penal liability' assumed rather than argued by those involved in the development of the Code.[168] While there was some awareness that codification is a political exercise, this was limited to a sense of the pragmatics of drafting and enacting reforms through legislatures,[169] rather than any sense of codification as a democratic activity.

163 See *R* v. *LK; R* v. *RK* (2010) 241 CLR 177 at [57] per French CJ (rejecting the argument that recklessness about the commission of the physical element of the offence was sufficient for conspiracy under Commonwealth law); see also *Ansari* v. *The Queen* (2010) 241 CLR 299; for discussion, see M. Bagaric, 'The High Court on Crime in 2010: Analysis and Jurisprudence' (2011) 35 *Criminal Law Journal* 5–20, 14–15, and S. Odgers, 'Conspiracy to Commit a Commonwealth Offence' (2010) 34 *Criminal Law Journal* 240–9.

164 Bell, 'Keeping the Criminal Law in "Serviceable Condition"', 342.

165 CLOC, *Model Criminal Code: General Principles of Criminal Responsibility, Final Report*, p. 21.

166 Attorney-General's Department (SA), *First Interim Report*, p. 45.

167 CLOC, *Model Criminal Code: General Principles of Criminal Responsibility, Discussion Draft*, p. 23.

168 Colvin, 'Unity and Diversity in Australian Criminal Law', 90.

169 See, e.g., M. Goode, 'An Evaluation of Judicial Interpretations of the Australian Model Criminal Code', in W. C. Chan, B. Wright and S. Yeo (eds.), *Codification, Macaulay and the Indian Penal Code: The Legacies and Modern Challenges of Criminal Law Reform* (Farnham: Ashgate Publishing, 2011), p. 317.

The role of criminal responsibility in offering a normative basis for the coercive power exercised through the criminal law is a thin foundation and has not constrained the legislature in the development of Commonwealth criminal law. Thus, reflecting the absence of any statement of its purposes in the Code, and no principles to ensure consistent decision-making, discussed above, the legislature has departed from presumption of subject liability in multiple instances. Here, anti-terrorism laws offer the most prominent example. In an arena of major legal change, in particular since the terrorist attacks of 9/11, new offences have proliferated in the fields of anti-terrorism and related fields such as cybercrime. On the basis of their exceptionality, these offences tend to honour the principles of criminal responsibility contained in Chapter 2 of the Commonwealth Code in the breach rather than the observance. Federal anti-terrorism laws, like laws in state criminal justice systems, are notable for their reliance on reverse burdens of proof, strict liability and preparatory offences, and for the way in which they are linked to expanded police powers of investigation and surveillance.[170] In addition, some of these laws have had retrospective operation.[171] As Bernadette McSherry writes, the new offences created by these laws were not based on foundational work by the Code Committee, and the offences show a 'careless disregard of the principles enshrined in Chapter 2 of the *Criminal Code*'.[172] Going further, Leader-Elliott suggests that anti-terrorism offences show that the legislature has taken Chapter 2 as 'an effective set of instructions for subverting common law principles' of criminal responsibility.[173]

This chapter has argued that the formation of the Commonwealth *Criminal Code* in the last decades of the twentieth century represented an attempt to compensate for Australia's federal structure, in which criminal law is a state and territory responsibility, and reconstruct criminal law as national rather than subnational law. Driven by a distinctive law reform process, and reflecting a sense of optimism that the Commonwealth could act as a leader in the field of criminal justice, the Commonwealth Criminal Code came into being at a time when major changes in crime and criminal law were occurring. At this time, first reform and then codification of Commonwealth law came to be seen as the answer to a range of problems and challenges, and, in addressing these issues,

170 See generally E. MacDonald and G. Williams, 'Combating Terrorism: Australia's Criminal Code Since September 11, 2001' (2007) 16(1) *Griffith Law Review* 27–54.

171 See *Criminal Code 1995* (Cth) ss 115.1–115.4 (creating a range of extraterritorial offences against the person, including murder, enacted following terrorist attacks in Bali in 2002): see for discussion Bronitt, 'Australia', p. 53. Bronitt notes, strict liability and the reverse burden of proof have become 'the rule rather than the exception' in terrorism offences (p. 82).

172 See B. McSherry, 'Terrorism Offences in the Criminal Code: Broadening the Boundaries of Australian Criminal Laws' (2004) 27(2) *UNSW Law Journal* 354–72, 371.

173 Leader-Elliott, 'Benthamite Reflections on Codification', 401; see also Leader-Elliott, 'The Australian Criminal Code', 206, 232.

the Code promised to position Australia for a new century. As 'the very foundations of any system of criminal justice',[174] criminal responsibility was central to the legal systematisation that the Commonwealth Code represented. With the principles of criminal responsibility fixed at the heart of the Commonwealth law, their role is to provide the Criminal Code with integrity, meaning the criminal law makes sense on its own terms, and ensuring that it can stand on its own and act as model for adoption in other jurisdictions.

[174] Criminal Law Officers' Committee (CLOC), *Model Criminal Code Chapters 1 and 2: General Principles of Criminal Responsibility, Final Report* (Canberra: Parliament of Australia, 1992), ii.

Part III
Criminal Responsibility in Relation

6

Self

In this Part of the book, I return to the role and significance of criminal responsibility, and present three investigations into relations of responsibility. As I argued in Chapter 2, the significance of criminal responsibility arises from the way in which it organises keys sets of relations – between self, others and the state – as relations of responsibility. My analysis reveals that criminal responsibility is the means by which matters of subjectivity, relationality and power make themselves felt in the criminal law in particular ways. The three chapters in this Part of the book traverse each aspect of my tripartite construction of relations of responsibility, but foreground one or other of these three nodes: in this chapter, I focus on the self in relations of responsibility. As I show in this chapter, the way in which criminal responsibility organises relations of responsibility is impacted by the broader understandings of the self, and his or her relations with others and the state, that have occurred over the twentieth century.

My argument about the self in relations of responsibility is developed through an analysis of women's responsibility for crime. This focus allows me to explore the role of gender in relations between self, others and the state.[1] Although women's responsibility for crime has attracted sustained scholarly attention from feminist theorists, in general, this work has not been taken up by criminal responsibility scholars.[2] As discussed in Chapter 2, the self that is at the centre of criminal responsibility and its

[1] The category of women is now a matter of some debate within feminist circles. Reflecting the extensive engagement feminist legal theorists have with the abstract individual of liberal legalism, the category of women is familiar in legal scholarship, and I adopt this category here. For discussion of this issue in relation to criminal law and sociology, see S. Lavi and G. Schneebaum, 'Criminal Law and Sociology', in M. D. Dubber and T. Hörnle (eds.), *The Oxford Handbook of Criminal Law* (New York: Oxford University Press, 2014), p. 159; and, in relation to feminist legal work in international law, see G. Heathcote, *Feminist Dialogues on International Law* (Oxford: Oxford University Press, 2019).

[2] See N. Naffine, 'Criminal Conversations: Farmer, Lacey and the New Social Scholarship' (2016) 38(4) *Sydney Law Review* 505–17.

scholarship is a particular kind of self: in the legal-philosophical tradition of scholarly thinking about criminal responsibility, he or she is an autonomous individual, conceptualised in an abstract way, as a rational agent, abstracted from his or her social and political context. As I discussed, this kind of self is integral to the dominant account of criminal responsibility as the normative heart of the criminal law, because it connects the criminal law to moral norms about responsibility and permits the moral condemnation of the individual convicted of crime. I suggested that this account generates a unitary story of responsibility in criminal law in which its significance is based on the centrality of responsibility as an aspect of the coherence and rationality of criminal law. This story is marked by generality and universalism: criminal responsibility is thought to be general in that it underpins the corpus of the law as a whole, and universal in that it applies to all individuals charged with criminal offences.

Through my analysis of women's responsibility for crime, in this chapter, I engage with this unitary story of criminal responsibility from two perspectives and make two main arguments. First, I argue that, on the level of legal form, women's responsibility for crime is marked by particularity and specificity, rather than generality and universalism, making women's responsibility for crime distinctive. This particularity and specificity has been the product of two dynamics, relating to violence by women, and violence against women. In the first of the dynamics giving rise to the distinctiveness of women's responsibility for crime, which was dominant up to the mid-century century, violence by women was pathologised and women's responsibility for crime was constructed as diminished or circumscribed. In the second dynamic, which has been dominant since the last decades of the twentieth century, the rise to prominence of violence against women – in particular, domestic or family violence – has recast women's violence as responsive – by which I mean comprehensible only by reference to what has already happened – and reconstructed women's responsibility as an amalgam of agency and victimhood/survivorhood. Each of these dynamics has generated atypical responsibility forms that do not fit the unitary story of criminal responsibility, outlined above. I use the term 'atypical' to denote those responsibility forms – formal legal constructions of accountability for crime – that are restricted to particular individuals committing particular offences in particular contexts – and in which elements, such as offence and defence, conduct and fault, and justification and excuse, that are usually separate, are mixed together.[3] It is these two dynamics together with the sets of atypical responsibility forms they produce that determine the formal contours of women's responsibility for crime.

[3] See also A. Loughnan, 'From Carpetbag to Crucible: Reconceptualising Diminished Responsibility Manslaughter', in B. Livings, A. Reed and N. Wake (eds.), *Mental Condition Defences and the Criminal Justice System: Perspectives from Law and Medicine* (Cambridge: Cambridge Scholars Publishing, 2015).

The second main argument advanced in this chapter is that these two dynamics and sets of atypical responsibility forms correspond with different relations of responsibility. Under the first dynamic, in which women's responsibility for crime was constructed as diminished or circumscribed, relations of responsibility centred on the relation of the accused woman with herself, where this relation was oriented around a personalised and psychologised notion of individual integrity. In this way, these atypical responsibility forms represent the reconciliation of developing knowledges and governance practices of the self with the new emphasis on individual responsibility in criminal law. Under the second dynamic, in which women's responsibility is constructed as an amalgam of agency and victimhood/survivorhood, relations of responsibility are oriented around the self in relation to others, encompassing an extended sense of women's autonomy, and implicating other actors, including state actors such as the police, in supporting that autonomy. This change in relations of responsibility reflects the influence of social science and feminist knowledges on social and political discourses, emphasising the structural aspect of violence against women, and rendering such violence a societal and government responsibility as much as an individual responsibility. As this suggests, these relations of responsibility expose the ameliorative tenor of women's responsibility for crime in the current era, with atypical responsibility forms constituting an admission of state failure to protect women from violence.

This chapter makes these arguments via an examination of homicide law reform in Australian criminal jurisdictions since the turn of the twentieth century. This period has seen significant changes in homicide law, with the development of dangerous driving causing death offences, for instance.[4] For my purposes here, the relevant subset of changes concerns responsibility for homicide, that is, those offences and defences that address accountability for unlawful killing. My focus is on legislative reforms, but it would also be possible to track the changes chronicled here through developments in case law. Although an uncommon set of offences, homicide – comprising murder, manslaughter, infanticide and, in some jurisdictions, now also 'one punch' killings[5] – is an apposite focus here, for two main reasons. First, with its gradation of the mental or fault element as a measure of seriousness, the pre-eminent homicide offence – murder – functioned as a model for the structure of modern criminal offences. As Lindsay Farmer argues, the gradation of mental states in murder was taken to be 'paradigmatic for the whole law, producing a theoretical categorization of offences that … required that other crimes distinguish between

[4] On the impact of motoring on the development of criminal law and summary justice in NSW, see T. Mitchell, 'Understanding the Summary Jurisdiction in NSW', PhD thesis, University of Sydney (2017).

[5] Regarding 'one punch' killings, see J. Quilter, 'Criminalisation of Alcohol Fuelled Violence: One-Punch Laws', in T. Crofts and A. Loughnan (eds.), *Criminalisation and Criminal Responsibility in Australia* (Sydney: Oxford University Press, 2015).

actus reus and *mens rea* in their definition'.[6] Second, the law of homicide is an appropriate focus because, as I discuss below, reform in this part of criminal law has attracted high levels of social and political engagement with criminal responsibility which have influenced the development of responsibility principles and practices.

'The Product of the Ordeal that She Had Undergone': Responding to Violence *by* Women

In the period up to the middle of the twentieth century, on the level of the form of the criminal law, women's violence was pathologised and women's responsibility for crime was constructed as diminished or circumscribed. It was women's violence that prompted the creation of a new space of partial responsibility for crime – located between non-responsibility and 'ordinary' or full criminal responsibility – on the face of the criminal law. As I discuss in this section, this construction of women's violence and women's responsibility corresponded with particular relations of responsibility, centred on the relation of the woman accused with herself.

Accommodating Maternal Violence

Criminal legal accommodation of women's violence against their newborn children has cast a long shadow over responses to women's violence and constructions of women's responsibility for crime. Women who killed their newborn children have long been the subjects of special and lenient treatment, but the formalisation of criminal laws (in particular the insanity defence) and criminal process (regularising prosecution and trial) over the nineteenth century circumscribed the space for informal accommodation of these individuals.[7] This formalisation generated pressure for the accommodation of maternal violence in the construction of responsibility for crime, resulting in the creation of atypical responsibility forms.

In the first decades of the twentieth century, in England and Wales, the practice of treating women charged with killing their newborns more leniently than others accused of homicide coalesced into a law of infanticide.[8]

[6] See L. Farmer, 'Bringing Cinderella to the Ball: Teaching Criminal Law in Context' (2012) 58(5) *Modern Law Review* 756–66, 766.

[7] See further A. Loughnan, *Manifest Madness: Mental Incapacity in Criminal Law* (Oxford: Oxford University Press, 2012), ch. 8.

[8] The creation of a distinctive law, carved out from the scope of murder, was prompted in part by legal and political concern about the handing down of death sentences that were imposed but not carried out on women convicted of the murder of their children, as this was thought to be bringing the law into disrepute: see Loughnan, *Manifest Madness*, ch. 8.

The *Infanticide Act 1922* and *Infanticide Act 1938* created and then amended a new homicide provision restricted by perpetrator and victim: only women who killed their newborn children were able to be charged with or convicted of infanticide. The statutes provided that, to be liable for infanticide, a woman must have caused the death of a 'newly born' child, when her 'balance of mind' was 'disturbed' by the effect of childbirth or lactation.[9] As the elements of the provision suggest, the law applies to a mentally incapacitated individual, representing the pathologisation of women's maternal violence. Indeed, infanticide typifies the pathologisation of women's offending because, as Hillary Allen writes, 'mental abnormality is a positive precondition for conviction'.[10] A plea to infanticide or conviction for it was subject to the same penalty structure as manslaughter, attracting discretion in sentencing, rather than the mandatory death penalty that then applied to murder.

In Australian criminal jurisdictions, women's violence against their new born children also attracted a mix of condemnation tinged with compassion for women themselves.[11] Sustained by exculpatory narratives about the physical and mental difficulties of childbirth, the difficult lot of the 'fallen' woman, and the (hidden) part played by the male seducer, infanticidal women were depicted as pitiful subjects in need of help rather than punishment.[12] Expert psychological and psychiatric knowledge – according to which an impulse to kill the child was thought to be a particular feature of 'puerperal mania', a disorder that could follow childbirth[13] – was overlaid onto these social narratives, and, together with the precedent set by England and Wales, prepared the ground for the infanticide provisions adopted in several Australian jurisdictions in the mid-century. The first infanticide provisions, enacted in Victoria in 1949 and in NSW in 1951, were substantially the same as the English provision.[14] The laws made infanticide both a homicide offence (akin to manslaughter) and a partial

[9] *Infanticide Act 1922* (England); *Infanticide Act 1938* (England).

[10] H. Allen, *Justice Unbalanced: Gender, Psychiatry and Judicial Decisions* (Milton Keynes: Open University Press, 1987), p. 27; see also C. Smart, *Women, Crime and Criminology: A Feminist Critique* (London: Routledge, 1976), ch. 6; T. Ward, 'The Sad Subject of Infanticide: Law, Medicine and Child Murder 1860–1938' (1999) 8(2) *Social & Legal Studies* 163–80.

[11] See A. Cossins, *The Baby Farmers* (Sydney: Allen and Unwin, 2013); A. Cossins, 'The Legacy of the Makin Case 120 Years On: Legal Fictions, Circular Reasoning and Some Solutions' (2013) 35 *Sydney Law Review* 731–59; S. Davies, 'Captives of Their Bodies: Women, Law and Punishment, 1880s–1980s', in D. Kirkby (ed.), *Sex, Power and Justice: Historical Perspectives of Law in Australia* (Melbourne: Oxford University Press, 1995), pp. 105–8.

[12] See J. A. Allen, *Sex and Secrets: Crimes Involving Australian Women since 1880* (Melbourne: Oxford University Press, 1990), pp. 31–2.

[13] See further A. Loughnan, 'The Strange Case of the Infanticide Doctrine' (2012) 32(4) *Oxford Journal of Legal Studies* 685–711.

[14] *Crimes Act 1949* (Vic) s 4(1) (subsequently amended by *Crimes (Homicide) Act 2005* (Vic) s 5); *Crimes (Amendment) Act 1951* (NSW) s 2(d).

defence to murder, available to women who kill their biological children when they are suffering from a mental disturbance, as a result of either giving birth or breastfeeding.[15] As in England and Wales, the motive for the reforms seems to have been compassion for the mother who was regarded as 'not in full possession of her mental faculties' after childbirth.[16]

The creation of specific infanticide provisions in Australian jurisdictions authorised the special and lenient treatment of women convicted of killing their new born children. These provisions channelled this group of women homicide defendants away from the law of murder, which, until the second half of the century, attracted a mandatory death penalty.[17] Although women were less likely to be executed than men – the way capital punishment applied to women was affected by gender-based attitudes to matters such as adultery and emancipation, and variables of class and race, as well as formal concern with the severity of the offence[18] – the possibility of the death penalty hung over murder trials. Supported first by the remarkable coincidence between social, medical and legal attitudes to women that characterised the period up to the mid-century,[19] infanticide embedded a cul-de-sac of specialness and leniency in the law of homicide. As Justice Barry stated in the first trial to follow the passage of the Victorian legislation, concerning a 19-year-old woman charged with the murder of her new born baby after having given birth alone in an outside toilet in the early hours of the morning, in such circumstances, the jury may find that her act was 'the product of the ordeal that she had undergone' and that the 'balance' of her mind was disturbed at the time.[20] This cul-de-sac has proved durable, and, despite the discrediting of the 'scientific' basis for the law – in mental disorder following childbirth – infanticide remains on the statute books in some Australian jurisdictions.[21]

15 See, e.g., *Crimes Act 1900* (NSW) s 22A, created by *Crimes (Amendment) Act 1951* (NSW).

16 Hansard, Victoria Legislative Council, col. 1250, 19 May 1949.

17 By contrast with Britain, which had significantly circumscribed the scope of capital punishment in the mid-nineteenth century, several Australian states retained the death penalty for a range of offences, including for rape, carnal knowledge of a girl of less than 10 years, and some forms of robbery and burglary, into the twentieth century: see R. Douglas and K. Laster, 'A Matter of Life and Death: The Victorian Executive and the Decision to Execute 1842–1967' (1991) 24 *Australian & New Zealand Journal of Criminology* 144–60. For a history of the retention of capital punishment in relation to rape, see A. Kaladelfos, 'The Politics of Punishment: Rape and the Death Penalty in Colonial Australia, 1841–1901' (2012) 9(1) *History Australia* 155–75.

18 See K. Laster, 'Arbitrary Chivalry: Women and Capital Punishment in Victoria, Australia 1842–1967' (1994) 6(1) *Women and Criminal Justice* 67–95; see also C. Strange, 'Masculinities, Intimate Femicide and the Death Penalty in Australia, 1890–1920' (2003) 43(2) *British Journal of Criminology* 310–39.

19 See generally Allen, *Sex and Secrets*, pp. 26–40, 245–6.

20 See *R* v. *Hutty* [1953] VLR 338 at 341. The jury acquitted the woman of murder, manslaughter and infanticide.

21 See New South Wales Law Reform Commission, *People with Cognitive and Mental Health Impairments in the Criminal Justice System*, Report No. 135 (2012) (which concluded that

The construction of women's responsibility for the act of infanticide as diminished or circumscribed is achieved via reliance on an atypical responsibility form. The special provision of the offence/defence of infanticide rests on a de facto collapse of conduct and fault into each other. As I have suggested elsewhere, infanticide law has the effect of over-determining the legal significance of the infanticidal woman's act of killing her child, as *caused* or determined, by disorder.[22] As both an offence and a partial defence, the abnormal mental state at the heart of infanticide is both independently inculpatory and (partially) exculpatory. This means that infanticide slides between the categories of offence and defence, making the doctrine itself most accurately understood as both/either partially exculpatory and/or partially inculpatory. This slipperiness is a feature of the atypical responsibility forms that mark the distinctiveness of women's responsibility for crime in the current era, as I discuss below.

Extending the Pathologisation of Lethal Violence

The development of psychological and psychiatric knowledges of mental incapacity that legitimated the law of infanticide also served to underpin the creation of another atypical responsibility form in the mid-century. Diminished responsibility, a partial defence available to murder only, was introduced into the law of England and Wales in 1957, having had a long history in the Scottish criminal law as an informal plea.[23] At this point in time, criticism of the *M'Naghten Rules*, which had governed the common law of insanity since the first half of the nineteenth century, had amplified, and medical and legal organisations had come to advocate the introduction of a defence of diminished responsibility as a remedy for perceived deficiencies in *M'Naghten* (particularly its narrowness).[24] The mid-century was a high point of faith in psychiatric and psychological knowledges to transform legal practices, and the integration of these knowledges into criminal justice, and close involvement of experts in these fields in adjudications of criminal responsibility, seemed to represent the way to modernise and improve the criminal law's approach to mentally incapacitated individuals.[25] I return to this point below.

the 'statutory offence/defence of infanticide affords an appropriate and compassionate criminal law response to the complex and tragic set of circumstances that may result in a mother killing her infant' [5.49]). For the empirical profile of infanticide in Australia, see L. Bartels and P. Easteal, 'Mothers Who Kill: The Forensic Use and Judicial Reception of Evidence of Postnatal Depression and Other Psychiatric Disorders in Australian Filicide Cases' (2013–14) 37 *Melbourne University Law Review* 297–341.

22 See Loughnan, *Manifest Madness*, ch. 8.

23 *Homicide Act 1957* (England) s 2(2); on the Scottish plea, see generally G. H. Gordon, *Criminal Law of Scotland*, 2nd ed. (Edinburgh: W. Green & Son, 1978).

24 See further Loughnan, *Manifest Madness*, pp. 232–3.

25 See for discussion H. Oosterhuis and A. Loughnan, 'Introduction – Madness and Crime: Historical Perspectives on Forensic Psychiatry' (2014) 37(1) *International Journal of Law and Psychiatry* 1–16.

Again following the English reforms, diminished responsibility was introduced in Australia in Queensland in 1961, in NSW in 1974, and subsequently in other states and territories.[26] In each jurisdiction, the defence was drafted broadly along the lines of the English statute, requiring that the defendant suffer from an 'abnormality of mind' (arising from specified set causes) that substantially impaired his or her responsibility for the killing.[27] In both NSW and Queensland, the new defence was thought to be an appropriate reform both because of the flexibility associated with manslaughter (both states had mandatory life imprisonment for murder, as Queensland still does[28]) and because 'the abnormal [as opposed to insane] accused ought to have some degree of protection in law', in the words of the then NSW Minister of Justice.[29] In addition, in Queensland specifically, the defence seems to have been introduced in part in response to concern about the then recent trial of Jack Foy for the murder of his wife, in which the defendant had successfully raised insanity based on his epilepsy, and been acquitted as not criminally responsible at the time of the killing.[30] This catalyst for homicide law reform indicates that the introduction of a new basis for a manslaughter conviction in cases that were 'very close' to insanity was regarded as a tough option,[31] with a conviction for manslaughter more palatable than an acquittal based on insanity.

Although facially or formally non-gendered, in operation, diminished responsibility has something of a gendered cast, and, although not created as a result of a need to accommodate women's violence, the partial defence of diminished responsibility has been sustained by it. Empirical evidence regarding the operation of the defence varies according to its wording, and from jurisdiction to jurisdiction, but there is evidence that women are more likely to have a plea to diminished responsibility accepted by the prosecution or the jury.[32] More generally, diminished responsibility has been sustained in part by the roughly contemporaneous development of the concept of 'battered

[26] *Criminal Code 1899* (Qld) s 304A; *Crimes and Other Acts Amendment Act 1974* (NSW); *Crimes (Amendment) Ordinance No. 2 1990* (ACT); and *Criminal Code Act 1983* (NT) s 37 and (since 2006) s 159.

[27] On differences in the Qld law, see A. Hemming, 'It's Time to Abolish Diminished Responsibility, the Coach and Horses' Defence through Criminal Responsibility for Murder' (2008) 10 *University of Notre Dame Australia Law Review* 1–36.

[28] This has been given as a reason for the introduction of diminished responsibility in NSW: see D. Brown et al., *Criminal Laws: Materials and Commentary on Criminal Law and Process of NSW*, 6th ed. (Sydney: The Federation Press, 2015), p. 867.

[29] Hansard, NSW Legislative Assembly, col. 1356, 13 March 1974.

[30] See *R* v. *Foy* [1960] Qd R 225, which seems to be the 'very recent case' criticised by the Minister for Justice on the introduction of the diminished responsibility provision: see Hansard, Queensland Legislative Assembly, col. 2813, 16 March 1961.

[31] Hansard, Queensland Legislative Assembly, col. 2812, 16 March 1961.

[32] Empirical evidence from England and Wales suggests that there are gender differences in prosecutorial discretion regarding pleas to diminished responsibility manslaughter, conviction of manslaughter, and in sentencing outcomes following conviction: see Law

women's syndrome', which gave a new legitimacy to more long-standing ideas about women's circumscribed responsibility for violence. As is well known, 'battered women's syndrome', which has its origins outside the realm of the law, provides that a psychological state of 'learned helplessness' leads women who are subject to abuse to view 'unreasonable' options (such as killing their abuser) as their only option.[33] Following the landmark Canadian decision of *Lavallee* v. *The Queen* in 1990,[34] 'battered women's syndrome' was first ruled admissible as evidence at trial in South Australia in 1991 and was accepted in other Australian jurisdictions in subsequent cases in that decade.[35] 'Battered women's syndrome' is controversial: as feminist scholars argue, while it has been used successfully by some women, it has serious limitations in that it scopes women's experiences and conduct through a psychological template of disorder (as a 'syndrome'), divorces women from their social, racial and cultural contexts, and obscures the structural nature of violence against women and the gendered nature of the operation of full defences such as self-defence.[36] As this suggests, the pathologisation of women's violence, and the amenability to ascriptions of partial responsibility for crime it facilitates, is a double-edged sword: leniency is achieved for some women, but at the cost of inscribing ideas about women's impaired agency or disordered rationality into criminal responsibility.

In part because of women's amenability to ascriptions of partial responsibility on the basis of diminished responsibility, the defence is controversial, and has been reformulated or abolished in some jurisdictions in recent decades. For example, in NSW, following the high-profile 1993 case of *Chayna* in which a woman who had been subject to serious long-term abuse by her husband was convicted of murdering her sister-in-law and her two daughters,[37] despite raising evidence of diminished responsibility, the

Commission for England and Wales, *Partial Defences to Murder*, Consultation Paper No. 173 (2003), Appendix B. By contrast, the NSW Judicial Commission found that the defence was raised more often by men: see Judicial Commission of New South Wales, *Partial Defences to Murder in NSW 1990–2004* (2006).

33 The concept of 'battered women's syndrome' was developed by Lenore Walker, an American psychologist: see L. Walker, *The Battered Woman* (New York: Harper and Row, 1979).

34 *Lavallee* v. *The Queen* 55 CCC (3d) 397 (1990).

35 See *Runjanjic* v. *R; Kontinnen* v. *R* (1991) 53 A Crim R 362; see also *R* v. *Hickey*, Supreme Court of NSW, Unreported, 14 April 1992; *The Queen* v. *Robyn Kina* [1993] QCA 480; *The Queen* v. *Secretary* [1996] NTCCA 18; *R* v. *Babsek* [1998] QCA 116; *Osland* v. *R* (1998) 197 CLR 316.

36 See, e.g., J. Stubbs and J. Tolmie, 'Race, Gender and the Battered Woman Syndrome: An Australian Case Study' (1995) 8 *Canadian Journal of Women and Law* 122–58; E. Sheehy, J. Stubbs and J. Tolmie, 'Defending Battered Women on Trial: The Battered Woman Syndrome and Its Limitations' (1992) 16(6) *Criminal Law Journal* 369–94.

37 See *R* v. *Chayna* (1993) 66 A Crim R 178.

NSW Law Reform Commission (NSWLRC) was tasked with reviewing the law. Although by this time the mandatory penalty for murder had been abolished in NSW, the NSWLRC recommended that the defence be retained but amended.[38] In NSW, the defence of diminished responsibility was reformulated as 'substantial impairment by reason of abnormality of mind', requiring that a defendant's ability to understand events, or judge right from wrong, or control him or herself be 'substantially' effected by an 'underlying condition' and that the jury conclude that the defendant's liability *ought* to be reduced from murder to manslaughter.[39] The focus of the reformulated defence of substantial impairment remains on individuals with mental incapacity: as the NSWLRC stated, diminished responsibility is an 'intermediate defence' for offenders whose impairment is not so extreme as to warrant the insanity defence, but 'whose mental state is nevertheless such that they should not be convicted of murder'.[40]

Given its gendered cast, and the way in which it has been sustained by women's violence, diminished responsibility has extended the pathologisation of women's violence and the construction of women's responsibility for crime as diminished or circumscribed. Like infanticide, diminished responsibility is an atypical responsibility form. As I have suggested in relation to the law of England and Wales, as diminished responsibility formalised as an exculpatory plea (rather than a plea in mitigation), it was dependent on its restriction to murder, and a tight but unspecified connection between the relevant abnormal mental state and prohibited act.[41] This tight connection between the act and the actor meant that, although somewhat amorphous, the kind of *difference* diminished responsibility denotes resists any neat or sharp division between the actor and act of killing, the excuse and the wrongdoing (in normative terms), or the defence and the offence (in formal terms).[42] Taking into account the ways in which diminished responsibility is proved – via close reliance on expert evidence and clinical diagnoses – I have suggested that this means the sort of difference encoded in diminished responsibility is one of kind, as opposed to one of degree.[43] It is this idea of difference as abnormality that underpins the way in which diminished responsibility slides between a doctrine of (partial) exculpation and one of (partial) inculpation.

[38] See New South Wales Law Reform Commission, *Partial Defences to Murder: Diminished Responsibility*, Report No. 82 (1997).
[39] *Crimes Act 1900* (NSW) ss 23A(1) and (2).
[40] NSWLRC, Partial Defences to Murder, [28].
[41] See Loughnan, *Manifest Madness*, ch. 9.
[42] See further Loughnan, 'From Carpetbag to Crucible'.
[43] See Loughnan, *Manifest Madness*, ch. 9.

Relations of Responsibility I

The dominance of a dynamic of violence by women – under which women's violence was pathologised, and women's responsibility for crime was constructed as diminished or circumscribed – corresponded with particular relations of responsibility, between self, others and the state. These relations centred on the relation of the woman accused with herself, which was oriented around a personalised and psychologised notion of individual integrity. As I discuss in this subsection, the atypical responsibility forms outlined above represent the reconciliation of developing knowledges and governance practices of the self with the new emphasis on individual responsibility in the criminal law.

Over the first half of the twentieth century, major changes in social knowledges meant that the self became both more known and more knowable, within and beyond criminal justice. This development had several dimensions. On the one side, in this period, what Nikolas Rose has called 'psy-knowledge' came to ascendancy, radically reconstituting understandings of the individual and the interaction of mind and body.[44] The growing influence of psychological and psychiatric knowledges in this period reflected changes in political power, and social organisation.[45] On the other side, developing criminological and penological knowledges were enlisted to realise a more effective and more tailored approach to the self in criminal law and process. At the end of the nineteenth century, the rise of the science of criminology (also known as criminal anthropology) gave rise to an era of 'penal modernism', in which crime was regarded as a social problem that could be addressed via a range of different regulatory responses.[46] Central to the innovations advanced by criminologists was the focal conception of the individual criminal – a person who could be studied, assessed and made known to experts and the state. This focus resulted in moves to individualise punishment – with the introduction of indeterminate and future-oriented sentencing, which was informed by expert criminological knowledge and took into account dangerousness – and criticism of the idea that sentences should be fixed at law according to guilt and the seriousness of the offence.[47] As this suggests, developing knowledges of the self were harnessed by states for the extended regulation of collective and individual life: in this mode of governance, the state deployed expertise, scientific research and technological strategies in ways that redefined citizenship, individuality and social integration.[48]

[44] See generally N. Rose, *Inventing Our Selves: Psychology, Power, and Personhood* (Cambridge: Cambridge University Press, 1996).

[45] See Rose, *Inventing Our Selves*, ch. 6.

[46] See D. Garland, 'Penal Modernism and Postmodernism', in T. G. Blomberg and S. Cohen (eds.), *Punishment and Social Control* (New York: Walter de Gruyter, 2003).

[47] See generally M. Pifferi, *Reinventing Punishment: A Comparative History of Criminology and Penology in the Nineteenth and Twentieth Centuries* (Oxford: Oxford University Press, 2016).

[48] See generally D. Garland, *Punishment and Welfare: A History of Penal Strategies* (Aldershot: Gower, 1985).

The major changes that the use of social knowledges and criminology realised in criminal justice were believed by some to also have profound implications for the criminal law. For example, in the context of this emphasis on treatment and prevention, in the mid-century period, the future of the criminal law seemed to some to be likely to involve a move *away* from *mens rea* and fault. The scholar most closely associated with this view is Barbara Wootton, a British sociologist, criminologist and magistrate, who was active in the mid-century in promoting social science and medicine as the basis for criminal justice.[49] Wootton visited Australia in the 1960s, and the influence of ideas about treatment and prevention can be detected in some of Australia's first criminal law textbooks, published in the mid-century.[50] Proceeding from the premise that criminal justice should be (re-)oriented toward prevention of future crime, Wootton's position was that no criminal offences should require proof of fault for conviction, and that sentences for crime should be indeterminate.[51] For Wootton, it was very difficult if not impossible to make a judgment about responsibility, and, in any case, beside the point when the aim of criminal justice is the prevention of crime and treatment of offenders, rather than punishment or condemnation for wickedness.[52]

But, contra Wootton, and as several scholars have pointed out, developments in criminal law in the mid-century were moving in a different direction. As part of a general acceptance of the idea that the criminal law is comprised of a set of general principles of criminal responsibility, in this period, the centrality of *mens rea* and fault to the criminal law was being reinforced. As Nicola Lacey points out, the rise of psychologised understandings of the self enabled the factualisation of *mens rea*, which meant that 'criminal responsibility which could be explicated in legal, technical terms, and hence legitimated as a form of specialist knowledge underpinning an impersonal mode of judgment'.[53] And as Farmer argues with reference to the work of seminal scholars such as Glanville Williams, the first half of the twentieth century was marked by the consolidation of the place of individual responsibility in the criminal law, as moral language around fault came to be replaced by

[49] See B. Wootton, *Crime and the Criminal Law: Reflections of a Magistrate and Social Scientist* (London: Stevens and Sons, 1963), pp. 18–19.

[50] On Wootton's visit to Melbourne, see M. Finnane, '"Irresistible Impulse": Historicizing a Judicial Innovation in Australian Insanity Jurisprudence' (2012) 23(4) *History of Psychiatry* 454–68, 456; on Australia's first criminal law textbooks, see Chapter 4.

[51] See Wootton, *Crime and the Criminal Law*, pp. 40–1, 95–9 and 112–13; for critical discussion see M. Matravers and A. Cocoru, 'Revisiting the Hart/Wootton Debate on Responsibility', in C. G. Pulman (ed.), *Hart on Responsibility* (London: Palgrave Macmillan, 2014), pp. 135–7. Wootton's view was that *mens rea* could be used at sentencing, on the basis that it was evidence about the offender that could be used in his or her treatment (Wootton, *Crime and the Criminal Law*, pp. 52–3).

[52] Wootton, *Crime and the Criminal Law*, p. 51.

[53] See N. Lacey, 'Responsibility and Modernity in Criminal Law' (2001) 9(3) *Journal of Political Philosophy* 249–76, 267–8.

precise terminology.[54] As I discuss in the context of Australian developments in the middle of the twentieth century, explication of principles of criminal responsibility was central to the systematisation of the criminal law offered by judges, commentators and textbook writers.[55] As this suggests, within criminal law, fault and individual responsibility for crime became more, not less, important, in the period up to the mid-century.

The atypical responsibility forms discussed above represent the reconciliation of these developing knowledges and governance practices of the self with the new emphasis on individual responsibility in criminal law. The atypical responsibility forms of infanticide and diminished responsibility, the use of psychological and psychiatric knowledges, which supported tight circumscription around a woman's mental condition (even if the moralised basis of these knowledges permitted some aspects of a women's context to fit within diagnostic categories[56]), constructed women as having a distinctive type of criminal responsibility: as partially exculpatory (and partially inculpatory), these provisions were sustained by the notion that the homicidal woman herself is a victim – of her mental distress and her circumstances – and a less than fully rational subject of the law. These provisions constructed a distinctive subjectivity for criminal women that worked to reinforce the importance of individual responsibility for crime. In mixing together elements of offence and defence, and conduct and fault, these provisions tailored the demands of individual responsibility for crime to the needs of women's responsibility. That is, these provisions operated to reconcile women's criminal responsibility within the frame of individual responsibility in criminal law.

As this discussion indicates, in the period up to the mid-century, violence by women forged a new space of partial responsibility for crime, populated by atypical responsibility forms, which are marked by particularity and specificity: they are restricted to particular individuals committing particular offences in particular contexts, and elements, such as offence and defence, which are usually separate, are mixed together. Through these legal forms, women's violence was pathologised – regarded as the product of, or explicable by reference to, disorder and disease – and women's responsibility for crime was constructed as diminished or circumscribed, less than full or 'normal' (male) responsibility. While these constructions of women's violence and criminal responsibility did not capture all women accused of homicide, as women continued to fall into the general categories of murder and manslaughter,[57] legislative reform of the law of homicide was driven by them. The relations of responsibility corresponding with these constructions were oriented around the relation between

[54] See, e.g., Farmer, *Making the Modern Criminal Law*, pp. 181–8.

[55] See further Chapter 4.

[56] See further Loughnan, *Manifest Madness*, ch. 8.

[57] For contrasting cases, involving women murderers in the mid-century, see C. Scrine, '"More Deadly than the Male": The Sexual Politics of Female Poisoning: Trials of the Thallium Women' (2002) 8 *Limina* 127–43.

the woman accused with herself, reconciling women's criminal responsibility within the frame of individual responsibility for crime. These dynamics – and the constructions of violence and responsibility and the relations of responsibility they generated – changed dramatically in the last decades of the twentieth century, as I now turn to discuss.

'Victims Who Kill': Responding to Violence *Against* Women

Since the last decades of the twentieth century, as a result of the women's movement and feminist activism, the social and political profile of violence against women has risen to prominence, recasting women's violence as responsive and reconstructing women's responsibility as an amalgam of agency and victimhood/survivorhood. The need to accommodate violence against women has generated a new set of responsibility forms characterised by particularity and specificity. As I discuss in this section of the chapter, the relations of responsibility that correspond with these ideas of women's violence and women's responsibility are now oriented around the self in relation to others, stretched across an extended sense of women's autonomy.

Women's Violence as Responsive Violence

While it has long been a crime, in Australia, as elsewhere, violence against women has not long been a prominent social or political issue. In the colonial era, violence against Aboriginal women was part of the frontier violence that marked British colonisation of the continent and which continued until the first decades of the twentieth century.[58] In addition to organised massacres of Aboriginal men, women and children, violence included the sexual enslavement of Indigenous women by white men.[59] From the end of the nineteenth century, Aboriginal women (and men) were subject to protection regimes and other administrative schemes that governed all aspects of their lives (including intimate and family relations).[60] By this time, violence in the home – 'wife battering' – had come to be regarded as criminal, but it was treated as a private or family matter, rather than as something that warranted the public attention encoded in the criminal law.[61] Incest had also became an offence in Australian

[58] On the nature and extent of frontier violence against Indigenous peoples, see H. Reynolds, *Forgotten War* (Sydney: NewSouth Books, 2013).

[59] See for discussion L. Behrendt, 'Consent in a (Neo)colonial Society: Aboriginal Women as Sexual and Legal "Other"' (2000) 15(33) *Australian Feminist Studies* 353–67; H. Robert, 'Disciplining the Female Aboriginal Body: Inter-racial Sex and the Pretence of Separation' (2001) 16(34) *Australian Feminist Studies* 69–81.

[60] See H. Douglas and M. Finnane, *Indigenous Crime and Settler Law: White Sovereignty after Empire* (Basingstoke: Palgrave Macmillan, 2012), ch. 4.

[61] See J. Aitken, '"The Horrors of Matrimony Among the Masses": Feminist Representations of Wife Beating in England and Australia, 1870–1914' (2007) 19(4) *Journal of Women's History* 107–31; see also J. A. Scutt, *Even in the Best of Homes: Violence in the Family* (Ringwood: Penguin Australia, 1983).

jurisdictions by the first decades of the twentieth century, and, in an attempt to increase convictions and enhance protection for women, the penalty for rape had been reduced from death to life imprisonment in almost all states by the same time.[62]

In the years following World War I, Australia's major cities of Sydney and Melbourne experienced crime waves, and violent crime rose to greater public prominence.[63] But, while the problems of violence on the part of returned soldiers raised the profile of violence against women and children in the home,[64] and some women activists and reformers agitated about the situation of Aboriginal women (with activists claiming to speak on behalf of Aboriginal women[65]), violence against women did not attract the same concern as public violence or violence between men. This situation continued into the second half of the twentieth century. Commonly understood as a reaction to the gender ruptures caused by World War II, the post-war era was marked by the re-inscription of traditional sex and gender norms for men and women, organised across separate public and private spheres.[66] As historians suggest, in this period, the family was regarded as the bedrock of society, and the home depicted as a haven from the outside world, which was where 'real' violence occurred: in this context, familial violence was understood as a problem of household morals, with women and children seen to bear some responsibility for the violence of men and fathers.[67]

As in other countries, in Australia, these attitudes began to shift in the 1960s and 1970s, a period marked by profound social turmoil – with gender relations, sexuality and women's position in the home and the workplace the subject of contestation and change. Women's and feminist activism focused on many sites of the oppression of women, with activists demanding to make problems that had been private, visible: the practice of 'speaking out' (consciousness raising) involved sharing problems that had been seen as individual or personal.[68] In Australia in the 1970s, this activist work was assisted by a wave of progressive Labour governments that funded some women's movement activities and

[62] See J. Bavin-Mizzi, 'Understandings of Justice: Australian Rape and Carnal Knowledge Cases, 1877–1924', in D. Kirkby (ed.), *Sex, Power and Justice: Historical Perspectives of Law in Australia* (Melbourne: Oxford University Press, 1995).

[63] See generally S. Garton, *The Cost of War: Australians Return* (Melbourne: Oxford University Press, 1996); see also Allen, *Sex and Secrets*, ch VI.

[64] See E. Nelson, 'Civilian Men and Domestic Violence in the Aftermath of the First World War' (2003) 27 *Journal of Australian Studies* 97–108.

[65] See F. Paisley, 'Citizens of Their World: Australian Feminism and Indigenous Rights in the International Context, 1920s and 1930s' (1998) 58 *Feminist Review* 66–84.

[66] See Allen, *Sex and Secrets*, pp. 218–31.

[67] See L. Featherstone and A. Kaladelfos, 'Hierarchies of Harm and Violence: Historicising Familial Sexual Violence in Australia' (2014) 29(81) *Australian Feminist Studies* 306–24.

[68] See I. B. Meyering, 'Feminism in Sydney's Suburbs: "Speaking Out", Listening and 'Sisterhood' at the 1975 Women's Commissions' (2018) 33(95) *Australian Feminist Studies* 61–80.

also created positions of Women's Advisers to government.[69] A prominent example of this government-activist alliance is the high-profile public inquiry initiated by the newly elected Whitlam Labor Australian government in 1974, the *Royal Commission on Human Relationships*.[70] With its aim of gathering evidence from 'ordinary' people, the Royal Commission represented the *Zeitgeist* of the time – private experiences became the basis for claims about rights and for public and political identities.[71] In and through this activism, feminist movements forged a durable (and controversial) alliance with the state,[72] and, conversely, the involvement of feminists in government ensured that 'femocrats' came to be seen as a distinctively Australian species[73] – heralding the role of feminists, and feminist and activist knowledges, in the new set of relations of responsibility, as I discuss below.

Violence against women (and children) was one private experience that was made visible in this period. Initially, the primary focus of women's and feminist activism was rape and sexual violence. For example, the report of the *Royal Commission on Human Relationships* contained a chapter cataloguing the problems with the law of rape, which was then a sex-specific offence oriented around penetration, and related police and prosecution practices.[74] The report argued for an understanding of rape as an offence of violence rather than a sexual offence, and made recommendations for reform of the law to reduce

[69] See M. Arrow and A. Woollacott, 'Introduction – How the Personal Became Political: The Gender and Sexuality Revolutions in 1970s Australia' (2018) 33(95) *Australian Feminist Studies* 1–8, 6. The world's first Women's Adviser to a head of government was appointed by Prime Minister Whitlam in 1973, and between 1976 and 1986, all Australian states and territories appointed women's advisers.

[70] See Office of the Prime Minister (Gough Whitlam), Royal Commission into Human Relationships, Press Statement No. 306 (Canberra, 21 August 1974). The Royal Commission was spearheaded by Elizabeth Reid, the first Women's Adviser to the Australian Prime Minister.

[71] See M. Arrow, 'Public Intimacies: The Royal Commission on Human Relationships 1974–1977', in L. Featherstone, R. Jennings and R. Reynolds (eds.), *Acts of Love and Lust: Sexuality in Australia from 1945–2010* (Newcastle, UK: Cambridge Scholars Publishing, 2014), pp. 25–6; M. Arrow, 'Making Family Violence Public in the Royal Commission on Human Relationships, 1974–1977' (2018) 33(95) *Australian Feminist Studies* 81–96.

[72] As several feminist scholars have argued, aligning feminist work on violence against women with the state – in calls for changes in the law, but also in demands for resources and other support for women facing violence – has proven costly, as this allowed violence against women to be co-opted by neoliberal agendas (such as 'tough on crime'): see, e.g., D. L. Martin, 'Retribution Revisited: A Reconsideration of Feminist Criminal Law Reform Strategies' (1998) 26 *Osgoode Hall Law Journal* 151–88; see also K. Bumiller, *In an Abusive State: How Neoliberalism Appropriated the Feminist Movement against Sexual Violence* (Durham, NC: Duke University Press, 2008).

[73] Arrow and Woollacott, 'Introduction', 6.

[74] For an overview of the feminist criminological analysis of this period, see N. Naffine, *Feminism and Criminology* (Cambridge: Polity Press, 1997), ch. 4; for an account of the scholarly work to which feminist criminologists were responding, see Smart, *Women, Crime and Criminology*, ch. 4.

the significance of consent and align rape with non-sexual assaults.[75] Feminist activists also turned their attention to violence against women in the home, although it did not initially garner the same high profile as sexual violence.[76] Accordingly, domestic violence was not an express topic of investigation by the Royal Commission. In its public hearings, outreach and extensive consultations on other issues, however, the Commission exposed the prevalence of domestic violence in Australia.[77] As a result, the Commission played a crucial role in naming and defining the problem as a 'product of dysfunctional, narrow gender roles and identities', not personal pathology.[78] In addition, and crucially, women's and feminist activism made it possible to connect rape and domestic violence together as 'violence against women', influencing Federal and state government responses to such violence.[79]

Building on the strategies and techniques employed in relation to rape and rape law, activists and scholars argued that violence between intimate partners was a serious issue of victimisation – not merely 'a domestic', or in the context of family law, insufficiently frequent or serious to provide grounds for divorce.[80] But domestic violence only took on a national profile in the late 1970s and early 1980s, with several high-profile homicide trials of women accused of killing abusive partners. These cases included the South Australian decision of *R* (in which Mrs R was convicted of the murder of her husband hours after discovering he had been abusing their five daughters as well as her[81]), and the NSW cases of Violet Roberts (who, together with her son, was convicted of the murder of her abusive husband[82]) and Georgina

[75] Commonwealth, Royal Commission on Human Relationships, *Final Report* (1977), vol. 5, Part VII, pp. 227–31. The organising mode for these proposed changes was the seriousness of the injury inflicted on the victim in the perpetrators' attempts (successful or not) to effect sexual penetration. For discussion of subsequent reforms to rape law, see J. Quilter, 'Re-framing the Rape Trial: Insights from Critical Theory about the Limitations of Legislative Reform' (2011) 35(1) *Australian Feminist Law Journal* 23–56.

[76] See for discussion A. Genovese, 'The Battered Body' (1997) 12(25) *Australian Feminist Studies* 91–103.

[77] The Commission drew on research conducted by women's refuges, as well as community consultations, and open invitations for individuals to contact the Commission; its discussion of violence against women drew connections to gender inequality and attitudes to women, showing awareness of the cultural nature of violence against women: see Royal Commission on Human Relationships, *Final Report*, vol. 1, pp. 138–9. The Report made fifteen recommendations addressing domestic violence.

[78] Arrow, 'Making Family Violence Public', 82.

[79] See G. Mason, 'Violence', in B. Caine et al. (eds.), *Australian Feminism: A Companion* (Melbourne: Oxford University Press, 1998), pp. 337, 339.

[80] See J. A. Scutt, 'Judicial Bias or Legal Bias? Battery, Women and the Law' (1995) 19(43) *Journal of Australian Studies* 130–43; on family law and violence against women, see S. Swain, *Born in Hope: The Early Years of the Family Court of Australia* (Sydney: UNSW Press, 2012), ch. 5.

[81] See *R* v. *R* (1981) 28 SASR 321.

[82] See *R* v. *Roberts*, Supreme Court of NSW, Unreported, 15 March 1976. Following a grassroots campaign, Roberts and her son were released in 1980.

Hill (who was convicted of the murder of her alcoholic and violent partner[83]). In these cases, the stories of women who had experienced serious long-term abuse attracted sustained public, media and political attention for the first time. These cases set the scene for the appearance of violence against women as a gender rights issue on the agendas of state and Federal governments,[84] and highlighted the inadequacy of existing defences to murder, such as provocation, generating calls for reform of the law of homicide.

Social and political awareness of violence against Indigenous women has followed a different trajectory. In the last decades of the twentieth century, the dismantling of the regimes of protection that had been in place since the nineteenth century brought with it extensive criminalisation of Indigenous peoples, and, as a result, the massive over-representation of Indigenous peoples in the criminal justice system in Australia.[85] As a number of scholars argue, Indigenous women have been subject to both gender and racial stereotypes that have combined to amplify their victimisation, and also worked to deny them the protection of the criminal law.[86] In one particularly egregious case in 1988, in a trial lasting less than a day, Robyn Kina was convicted of the stabbing murder of her de facto husband, Tony Black, who had subjected her to severe long-term physical and sexual abuse. In what would later be revealed as a gross failure in cross-cultural communication, Kina did not call evidence or give her own evidence at trial. Kina appealed to the Queensland Court of Appeal but was unsuccessful.[87] Subsequently, a petition for pardon bought the case back to the Court of Appeal, where a fresh examination revealed the extent of Kina's grounds for defences of provocation, self-defence, and lack of intent to kill, and the court found there had been a miscarriage of justice and quashed Kina's conviction.[88] In recent years, violence against Aboriginal women has come to be treated more seriously, but the issues of over-representation of Indigenous people, and increasingly Aboriginal women, have become even more acute.[89]

[83] See *R* v. *Hill* (1981) 3 A Crim R 397.

[84] See W. Weeks and K. Gilmore, 'How Violence Against Women Became an Issue on the National Policy Agenda', in T. Dalton et al. (eds.), *Making Social Policy in Australia* (Sydney: Allen & Unwin, 1996); see also K. Valentine and J. Breckenridge, 'Responses to Family and Domestic Violence: Supporting Women?' (2016) 25(1) *Griffith Law Review* 30–44.

[85] See, e.g., M. Finnane, 'Aboriginal Violence and State Response: Histories, Policies and Legacies in Queensland 1860–1940' (2010) 43(2) *Australian & New Zealand Journal of Criminology* 238–62; T. Mitchell, ' A Dilemma at the Heart of Criminal Law: The Summary Jurisdiction, Family Violence, and the Over-Incarceration of Aboriginal and Torres Strait Islander Peoples' (2019) 45(2) *University of Western Australia Law Review* 136–165.

[86] See generally Douglas and Finnane, *Indigenous Crime and Settler Law.*

[87] *R* v. *Kina*, Supreme Court of Queensland, Unreported, CA No. 258 of 1988.

[88] See *The Queen* v. *Robyn Kina* [1993] QCA 480; see also K. Pringle, 'R v. Robyn Bella Kina' (1994) 3(67) *Aboriginal Law Bulletin* 14; D. Eades, 'Legal Recognition of Cultural Differences in Communication: The Case of Robyn Kina' (1996) 16(3) *Language & Communication* 215–27.

[89] See Australian Law Reform Commission, Pathways to Justice – An Inquiry into the Incarceration Rate of Aboriginal and Torres Strait Islander Peoples, Report No. 133 (2017), ch. 11.

The rise to prominence of violence against women, and particularly domestic violence, has had a profound effect on both social and political discourses about women's violence: women's violence has been recast as responsive, in both a descriptive and evaluative sense, that is, as reactive to harm or threat of harm from others, particularly men. By this I do not mean that such violence is now see as 'normal' or 'acceptable' in certain conditions; rather, I mean that it is only comprehensible via consideration of what has taken place beforehand. This recasting means that the *context* in which women's violence occurs has become crucial not just to subjective understandings of women's use of violence in particular instances, but to the construction of women's violence in social and political discourses. The significance of context is that women's violence demands more extensive and more thorough consideration of circumstances for its evaluation. As I discuss below, the importance of context has come to the fore through legal institutions other than the criminal trial, in the recent state and Federal inquiries into family and domestic violence. The recasting of women's violence as responsive has displaced (although not eclipsed[90]) the pathologising of women's violence, with its individualised ethos and individualising effects, that was reflected in homicide law reforms taking place up until the middle of the twentieth century.

Women's Responsibility as an Amalgam of Agency and Victimhood/Survivorhood

It has been recognised that the high profile of violence against women, combined with early pioneering criminological research on the disproportionate number of women killed in domestic homicides, has driven reform of the law of homicide in Australia since the 1980s,[91] but the full consequences of the re-casting of women's violence as responsive have not been appreciated. This re-casting has reconstructed women's responsibility as an amalgam of agency and victimhood/survivorhood. Put another way, the identities of women as victims or survivors of violence and identities of women as perpetrators of violence – violence against women and violence by women – have become thoroughly enmeshed: these women are 'victims who kill'. This reconstruction

[90] See P. Easteal et al., 'How Are Women Who Kill Portrayed in Newspaper Media? Connections with Social Values and the Legal System' (2015) 51(1) *Women's Studies International Forum* 31–41.

[91] See J. Morgan, 'Homicide Law Reform and Gender: Configuring Violence' (2012) 45(3) *Australian & New Zealand Journal of Criminology* 351–66, 355; T. Crofts and D. Tyson, 'Homicide Law Reform in Australia: Improving Access to Defences for Women Who Kill Their Abusers' (2013) 39(3) *Monash University Law Review* 864–93; J. Stubbs, 'Murder, Manslaughter and Domestic Violence', in K. Fitz-Gibbon and S. Walklate (eds.), *Homicide, Gender and Responsibility: An International Perspective* (Milton Park, UK: Routledge, 2016), pp. 37–8. On the relevant criminological research, see Brown et al., *Criminal Laws*, pp. 738–40.

of women's responsibility for crime has generated a new set of atypical responsibility forms which can be detected across three strands of homicide law reform, relating to self-defence, excessive self-defence and provocation.

The first strand of law reform reflecting this construction of women's responsibility for crime is self-defence, a general defence available in relation to all criminal offences. Although it has a general remit, self-defence has long been criticised for being inaccessible or less accessible to women.[92] Women have had difficulties satisfying the requirement of the defence that force was used in response to an imminent threat, and that the force was proportionate to that threat. In Australia, the common law of self-defence was reformed in the 1980s to provide that the imminence of the threat has an evidentiary rather than legal significance.[93] Now, in general terms, self-defence provides a full defence to a charge where the defendant believes on reasonable grounds that his or her conduct was a necessary response to a threat to him or herself or others, or to property.[94] While this change was not driven by women's violence, more recent changes to self-defence have been oriented around women – and grounded in an idea that women's violence is responsive. In Victoria, reform to the law in 2005 provided a specific version of self-defence for family violence, which allows the defence to be pleaded where a person is responding to a harm that is not immediate, or the response involves the use of force in excess of the force involved in the harm or threatened harm.[95] To accompany this new provision, a subsidiary provision permits evidence of family violence to be used to prove the elements of this defence (that the person's conduct is necessary in self-defence, and the conduct may be a reasonable response in the circumstances as the person perceives them to be).[96]

This new provision is an atypical responsibility form. It is marked by particularity – it only applies in the context of family violence, meaning it only applies in particular circumstances – and it specifies women's criminal responsibility in novel ways. The provision constructs a version of self-defence – the classic defence of agency as it is thought to involve taking the law into one's own hands[97] – overlaid with a notion of the victimisation entailed in family violence. It is this conjunction that legitimates the extension of self-defence

[92] See, e.g., K. Fitz-Gibbon and J. Stubbs, 'Divergent Directions in Reforming Legal Responses to Lethal Violence' (2012) 45(3) *Australian & New Zealand Journal of Criminology* 318–36, 325.

[93] See *R* v. *Zecevic* (1987) 162 CLR 645.

[94] See, e.g., *Crimes Act 1900* (NSW) s 418(2); for critical discussion, see E. Colvin, 'Abusive Relationships and Violent Responses: The Reorientation of Self-Defense in Australia' (2009) 42 *Texas Tech Law Review* 339–58.

[95] See *Crimes Act 1958* (Vic) s 322M(1).

[96] *Crimes Act 1958* (Vic) s 322M(2).

[97] See, e.g., J. Dressler, 'New Thoughts About the Concept of Justification in the Criminal Law: A Critique of Fletcher's Thinking and Rethinking' (1984–85) 32(1) *University of California Los Angeles Law Review* 61–99.

to circumstances in which the harm is not immediate or the force is not proportionate. While it is open to both men and women, it is the re-casting of women's responsibility for crime as an amalgam of agency and victimhood/survivorhood, which is invoked in this reform. As the Victorian Law Reform Commission stated, in those cases in which women kill their intimate partners, 'the homicide often follows a history of physical abuse at the hands of their male partners'.[98] Now sustained by the enmeshing women's identities – as victims or survivors of violence and as perpetrators of violence – this new version of self-defence shapes women's criminal responsibility as an amalgam of agency and victimhood/survivorhood.

A second, allied strand of law reform reflecting this construction of women's responsibility for crime – as an amalgam of agency and victimhood/survivorhood – is excessive self-defence. Excessive self-defence existed at common law in Australia, but was abolished by the High Court in the 1987 decision of *R* v. *Zecevic*.[99] In the decades since its removal from the law, excessive self-defence has been reintroduced in several Australian jurisdictions.[100] In general terms, the statutory version of excessive self-defence provides a partial defence to murder only, and is available to an accused person who would have relied on self-defence, but could not satisfy the requirement of reasonable grounds for belief in the need for defensive force. Although originally accommodating male violence,[101] in its current form, excessive self-defence now accommodates women's violence, understood as responsive, in particular, in the context of violence following domestic abuse. As the Victorian Law Reform Commission stated in recommending the introduction of a partial defence of excessive self-defence, 'excessive self-defence would seem to better fit the circumstances of women who kill in this [family violence] context than ... provocation or ... diminished responsibility. ... [U]nlike diminished responsibility, women's actions are not treated as if they arise from a mental condition'.[102] As this suggests, women who use excessive force in defending themselves against abusive partners are seen as a particular class of 'deserving accused',[103] and it is appropriate to accommodate them within homicide law.

Excessive self-defence is an atypical legal form – it mixes together elements that are usually separate. In legal-philosophical thinking, self-defence

[98] Victorian Law Reform Commission (VLRC), *Defences to Homicide: Final Report*, Report No. 94 (2004), [1.3].

[99] *R* v. *Zecevic* (1987) 162 CLR 645; see further discussion in Chapter 4.

[100] See, e.g. NSW (*Crimes Act 1900* s 421), South Australia (*Criminal Law Consolidation Act 1935* s 15, introduced in 1991 and amended in 1997) and Western Australia (*Criminal Code Act Compilation Act 1913* sch. 1 s 248).

[101] All the common law cases involved male defendants: see *R* v. *McKay* [1957] VR 560, *R* v. *Howe* [1958] SASR 95, *R* v. *Buffalo* [1958] VR 363, *R* v. *Haley* [1959] WN (NSW) 550, *R* v. *Tikos* (No. 1) [1963] VR 285, *R* v. *Tikos* (No. 2) [1963] VR 306.

[102] VLRC, *Defences to Homicide*, [3.117], Recommendation 9, and ch. 3 more generally.

[103] VLRC, *Defences to Homicide*, [3.83].

is typically regarded as a justification (a defence based on the idea that the defendant had a moral right to do as he or she did), as opposed to an excuse (a defence based on the idea that, in certain circumstances or because of certain characteristics, it is morally inappropriate to hold an individual accountable under the criminal law).[104] On this view, excessive self-defence is a *partial* justification, or perhaps a combination of a justification and an excuse, with aspects of the moral rights of a rational responsible subject mixed with excusing conditions or circumstances. Again, it is the reconstruction of women's responsibility for crime as an amalgam of agency and victimhood/survivorhood that is animating this atypical responsibility form. Thus, according to the Victorian Law Reform Commission, several aspects of the circumstances in which women use violence, such as power imbalances – 'many women who kill in response to family violence use a weapon, often against their unarmed partner' – or affect or emotion – 'women responding to a history of physical and psychological abuse might quite legitimately have feelings of anger towards their abusers, while still acting out of fear for their lives'[105] – may be relevant to excessive self-defence.

As is well known, the Victorian government opted to reject the Law Commission's recommendation to re-introduce excessive self-defence, but, in part in order to accommodate abused women who used lethal violence against their abusers, the government created a new homicide offence of 'defensive homicide'.[106] 'Defensive homicide' applied to an individual who killed a victim under a genuine but unreasonable belief that he or she was using lethal force in self-defence. It was introduced to sit alongside manslaughter and provide a halfway house between an acquittal (via self-defence) and a conviction of murder for women who killed an abusive partner, and for individuals with mental illness who could not fit within the mental illness defence.[107] 'Defensive homicide' was also an atypical legal form, in that it combined elements of offence ('homicide') and defence ('defensive') together. Like infanticide, 'defensive homicide' moved between offence and (partial) defence, but unlike infanticide, it was not sustained by the pathologisation of women's violence, but by the idea that women's violence is responsive – comprehensible only by reference to what has gone before – and the construction of women's responsibility for crime as an amalgam of agency and victimhood/survivorhood. Although it was intended for use by women responding to domestic violence, 'defensive homicide' was not restricted to homicides that occurred in particular circumstances,

[104] See generally G. Fletcher, 'The Nature of Justification', in J. Horder and J. Gardner (eds.), *Action and Value in Criminal Law* (Oxford: Clarendon Press, 1993).

[105] VLRC, *Defences to Homicide*, [3.92] and [3.83] respectively.

[106] See *Crimes Amendment (Abolition of Defensive Homicide) Act 2014* (Vic).

[107] See M. Ulbrick, A. Flynn and D. Tyson, 'The Abolition of Defensive Homicide: A Step Towards Populist Punitivism at the Expense of Mentally Impaired Offenders' (2016) 40 *Melbourne University Law Review* 324–70.

and, before it was abolished in 2014, the majority of individuals convicted of the offence were men who had killed other men.[108]

A third strand of homicide law reform reflecting this construction of women's responsibility for crime – as an amalgam of agency and victimhood/survivorhood – is the partial defence of provocation. Following England and Wales, in Australian common law, provocation is a partial defence that reduces murder to manslaughter where the defendant lost control at the time of the killing (the subjective limb of the defence), in circumstances in which an ordinary person could have done the same (the objective limb of the test).[109] Because of its use by men charged with the murder of their intimate partners, provocation reform has been a centrepiece of law reform campaigns around violence against women.[110] In the 1980s, concerns that provocation was more available to men than women led to reforms to allow for 'slow burn provocation' (taking into account a course of conduct over time in determining what counts as provocative conduct), the type of provocation associated with women who kill a partner after long-term abuse.[111] Despite these changes to accommodate women's violence, empirical studies of Australian cases indicated that provocation was still more likely to be successfully raised by men charged with murder (including for killing their wives and partners) than by women.[112] This, together with the use of the provocation defence in so-called 'homosexual advance defence' homicides,[113] led to wholesale critique of the defence in Australia from the 1990s and, as a result of reforms, in recent years, provocation has been abolished in several states and severely circumscribed elsewhere.[114]

108 See for discussion K. Toole, 'Defensive Homicide on Trial in Victoria' (2013) 39(2) *Monash University Law Review* 473–505; see also R. Hunter and D. Tyson, 'The Implementation of Feminist Law Reforms: The Case of Post-provocation Sentencing' (2017) 26(2) *Social & Legal Studies* 129–65.

109 See S. Bronitt and B. McSherry, *Principles of Criminal Law*, 3rd ed. (Sydney: Thomson Reuters (Lawbook Co.), 2017), [5.10]-[5.75]. On the trajectory of the provocation defence over time see J. Horder, *Provocation and Responsibility* (Oxford: Clarendon Press, 1992).

110 See K. Fitz-Gibbon, *Homicide Law Reform, Gender and the Provocation Defence: A Comparative Perspective* (London: Palgrave Macmillan, 2014), ch. 7.

111 E.g. *Crimes (Homicide) Amendment Act 1982* (NSW), following recommendations contained in the Report of New South Wales Task Force on Domestic Violence to Honourable N. K. Wran QC, MP Premier of New South Wales (New South Wales Task Force on Domestic Violence, New South Wales Premier's Department, 1981): see Stubbs, 'Murder, Manslaughter and Domestic Violence', p. 37.

112 See, e.g., Fitz-Gibbon, *Homicide Law Reform, Gender and the Provocation Defence*.

113 The most high-profile case of this kind is *Green* v. *R* (1997) 191 CLR 334; for analysis of this and other cases, see S. Tomsen and T. Crofts, 'Social and Cultural Meanings of Legal Responses to Homicide among Men: Masculine Honour, Sexual Advances and Accidents' (2012) 45(3) *Australian & New Zealand Journal of Criminology* 423–37.

114 See, e.g., *Criminal Code Amendment (Abolition of Defence of Provocation) Act 2003* (Tas); in 2014, following *Singh* v. *R* [2012] NSWSC 637 and the report *The Partial Defence of Provocation* (Legislative Council Select Committee on the Partial Defence of Provocation, Parliament of New South Wales, 2013), NSW severely circumscribed provocation as 'extreme provocation': see *Crimes Act 1900* (NSW) s 23 and see for discussion T. Crofts and A. Loughnan, 'Provocation, NSW Style: Reform of the Defence of Provocation in NSW' [2014] 2 *Criminal Law Review* 109–25.

Following a high-profile case in which a 28-year-old man killed his 16-year-old girlfriend, and successfully raised provocation, provocation was reviewed by the Queensland Law Reform Commission in 2008.[115] The reforms recommended by the Commission were designed to limit the use of provocation based on words alone to situations of a 'most extreme and exceptional character', with the Commission recommending that the particular circumstances of abuse survivors (such as 'slow burn provocation') be dealt with via a different defence.[116] At around the same time, the Queensland government investigated the option of a specialised defence for victim/survivors of domestic violence. This was enacted as a partial defence of 'killing for preservation in an abusive domestic relationship' in 2010.[117] The 'preservation defence' was intended for any individual responding to domestic violence (understood against a factual backdrop of awareness that the vast majority of victims of domestic violence are women) and designed to avoid the restrictions of existing defences of self-defence and provocation, which required the defendant to respond to a specific assault, or threat, or to an instance of provocation within a particular timeframe.[118] The 'preservation defence' is an atypical legal form in that it brings separate elements together – here, offence and defence as well as justification and excuse ('killing for preservation' – a hallmark of self-defence – but 'in an abusive domestic relationship' – a situation of victimisation) – and is marked by particularity (it is restricted by the context in which it can be raised – a killing of one partner in a 'domestic relationship' by the other). This provision has been used on only a couple of occasions.[119]

Homicide law reform reflects the dominant imperative on states to, in the words of the Australian Law Reform Commission 'ensure that their defences to homicide accommodate the experiences of family violence victims who kill'.[120] The means by which this imperative has been met are bespoke responsibility forms. Each of the three strands of homicide law reform canvassed here has relied on atypical responsibility forms in which separate elements – offence and defence, conduct and fault, and justification and excuse – are mixed together, and which

115 See *R* v. *Sebo*, Supreme Court of Queensland, Unreported, 2007; *R* v. *Sebo, ex parte Attorney-General (Qld)* [2007] QCA 426, and Queensland Law Reform Commission, *A Review of the Excuse of Accident and the Defence of Provocation*, Report No. 64 (2008).

116 For critical discussion, see H. Douglas, 'A Consideration of the Merits of Specialized Homicide Offences for Battered Women' (2012) 45(3) *Australian & New Zealand Journal of Criminology* 367–82, 372.

117 *Criminal Code* 1899 (Qld) s 304B ('the preservation defence'). Queensland also amended the law on provocation at this time.

118 See Douglas, 'A Consideration of the Merits of Specialized Homicide Offences for Battered Women', 375–7.

119 See M. Edgely and E. Marchetti, 'Women Who Kill Their Abusers: How Queensland's New Abusive Domestic Relationships Defence Continues to Ignore Reality' (2011) 13(2) *Flinders Law Journal* 125–76.

120 Australian Law Reform Commission (ALRC) and New South Wales Law Reform Commission (NSWLRC), *Family Violence – A National Legal Response*, ALRC Final Report No. 114, NSWLRC Final Report No. 128 (2010), vol. 1, [14.91].

apply to particular defendants committing particular offences in particular circumstances. While homicide law reforms have varied from jurisdiction to jurisdiction – reflecting the role of localised histories and political campaigns, as well as the specifics of the triggering cases, in reform processes[121] – atypical responsibility forms are an important if hitherto underappreciated formal feature of criminal laws across jurisdictions. These legal forms are not characterised by generality and universalism, but by particularity and specificity: in the current era, they are sustained not by the pathologisation of women's violence, but by the re-casting of women's violence as responsive that the high social and political profile of violence against women has forged. These legal forms represent the subsistence of particularity and specificity in criminal law in the current era, giving distinctive contours to women's responsibility for crime, and undermining the standard story of the generality and universalism of criminal responsibility.

Relations of Responsibility II

The re-casting of women's violence as responsive – comprehensible only by reference to what has gone before, as discussed above – and the reconstruction of women's responsibility as an amalgam of agency and victimhood/survivorhood, corresponds with changed relations of responsibility. These relations of responsibility are now oriented around the self in relation to others, encompassing an extended sense of women's autonomy, and implicating other actors, including state actors such as the police, in supporting that autonomy. As I discuss in this section, these relations of responsibility expose the ameliorative tenor of women's responsibility for crime in the current era, with atypical responsibility forms an admission of state failure to protect women from violence.

The backdrop to these changed relations of responsibility in recent decades is the rise of victims' rights and the more generalised sense of vulnerability that it both represents and enhances.[122] This is a multi-faceted development that is closely connected to changing political dynamics in liberal democracies, in particular, the rise of neoliberalism.[123] As Peter Ramsay argues in the English context, recent decades have witnessed 'the construction of a new subject – the vulnerable subject'.[124] Ramsay argues that the vulnerability of the citizen is now an assumption or baseline of liberal governance, and that it is a paradox of liberalism that its threats – through the criminal law and its sanctions – are premised on its own inadequacy to provide security

[121] See Fitz-Gibbon and Stubbs, 'Divergent directions', 320–2. As Fitz-Gibbon and Stubbs note, legislative change coincided with changes in judicial attitudes in which courts became more receptive to women's victimisation by partners and others.

[122] For critical discussion, see M. D. Dubber, *Victims in the War on Crime: The Use and Abuse of Victims' Rights* (New York: New York University Press, 2006).

[123] See R. Ginsberg, 'Mighty Crime Victims: Victims' Rights and Neoliberalism in the American Conjuncture' (2014) 28(5–6) *Cultural Studies* 911–46.

[124] P. Ramsay, *The Insecurity State: Vulnerable Autonomy and the Right to Security in the Criminal Law* (Oxford: Oxford University Press, 2012), p. 9.

to such citizens.[125] As this suggests, in the current era, the criminal law is regarded as inadequate in the face of the pervasive and constitutive sense of vulnerability suffusing modern constructions of subjectivity.

The notion of vulnerability has particular gender dimensions, and, as crime victims, women are constructed in particular ways. As mentioned above, context has become crucial to the evaluation of women's violence. The enhanced significance of context is the result of the coming together of the activist and feminist knowledges with social-scientific knowledge about violence – covering matters such as incidence, prevalence and the presentation of violence – in social and political discourses. This combination of knowledges underscores the structural aspect of such violence, and renders violence against women a societal and government responsibility as much as an individual responsibility. In some spaces within social and political discourses, awareness of the significance of the context of violence – in intimate relations, and in the home – extends beyond a woman's immediate surroundings, to take into account wider aspects of context – such as the historical failures of police to take domestic violence seriously, or the personal dangers and social stigma that discourages the reporting of abuse. As this suggests, feminist and social-scientific knowledge now competes with traditional legal knowledges of crimes of violence against women. As Peter Rush suggests in an analysis of rape law reform since the 1980s, 'the social scientific presentation of the order and governance of crime' has come to the fore as knowledge of principles and practices of criminal responsibility has receded.[126]

The crucible in which activist and feminist knowledges about domestic violence have come together with social scientific knowledges is the distinctive legal mechanism of the public inquiry. In recent years, large-scale public inquiries into violence against women have been held at both state and Federal levels in Australia.[127] In general terms, public inquiries are inquisitorial rather than adversarial, public independent, ad hoc and future-orientated.[128] Public inquiries into domestic violence have involved wide consultations – with professionals, victim/survivors and others – and have had broad remits that extend to all aspects of domestic violence, including violence prevention, policing practices and family law, as well as the role of the criminal law in prosecuting offenders. For example, the Victorian *Royal Commission into*

125 Ramsay, *The Insecurity State*, p. 9.

126 P. Rush, 'Jurisdictions of Sexual Assault: Reforming the Texts and Testimony of Rape in Australia' (2011) 19(1) *Feminist Legal Studies* 47–73, 59.

127 See, e.g., ALRC and NSWLRC, *Family Violence*; Victoria, Royal Commission into Family Violence, *Report and Recommendations* (2016). The Victorian Commission's terms of reference required it to inquire into and make practical recommendations to improve Victoria's response to family violence and the Victorian government undertook to implement all 227 recommendations made by the Commission.

128 See for discussion A. Burgess, 'The Changing Character of Public Inquiries in the (Risk) Regulatory State' (2011) 6(1) *British Politics* 3–29. I discuss public inquiries further in Chapter 8.

Family Violence was tasked with making 'practical recommendations' for improvements in matters including early intervention, victim support, the coordination of community and government responses, and the measurement of successful policies and programs, as well as making 'perpetrators accountable'.[129] The recommendations of the Victorian Royal Commission were wide-ranging, and included moving family violence matters to specialist courts, which would deal with criminal, civil and family law matters together, greater reliance on restorative justice and improving risk assessment and screening procedures in the health system.[130] As this suggests, these public inquiries traverse a number of discrete legal sub-disciplines and areas of governance, in a way that both recognises and constructs domestic violence as a problem that exceeds the bounds of criminal law, and even law in general, to become a problem of 'public risk'.[131]

In light of this construction of domestic violence, relations of responsibility have changed and the role and responsibility of actors (and institutions) *other* than the individual perpetrator have come to the fore. These actors include state actors such as the police, social services and prosecution agencies, which are now implicated in supporting women's autonomy. Against a backdrop formed by the historical failure of the police to take domestic violence seriously, the policies and practices of the police have come to attract significant attention and the police are seen as the front line in addressing the problem of domestic violence. As the Victorian Royal Commission stated in explaining the reasons it had not recommended new offences, 'whatever laws we have will be only as effective as those who enforce, prosecute and apply them … [i]mproving these practices … is likely to be more effective than simply creating new offences'.[132] Similarly, the social services agencies dealing with families in which violence is occurring have come under scrutiny and criticism.[133] In addition, prosecution services have been encouraged to address attrition rates in domestic violence prosecutions, and to enhance training of legal officers in the dynamics of domestic violence.[134] The increased prominence of actors and institutions other than the individual perpetrator of domestic violence implicates them in cases in which a woman kills an abuser. Within social and

[129] See Royal Commission into Family Violence, *Report and Recommendations*, vol. 1, p. 1. The Commission's report, published in March 2016, covered a wide range of topics including violence against Aboriginal women, information sharing, court practices and experiences of victims.

[130] Royal Commission into Family Violence, *Report and Recommendations*, vol. 1.

[131] Burgess, 'The Changing Character of Public Inquiries in the (Risk) Regulatory State', 14.

[132] Royal Commission into Family Violence, *Report and Recommendations*, vol. 1, p. 27; see also New Zealand Law Commission, *Some Criminal Defences with Particular Reference to Battered Defendants*, Report No. 73 (2001) (recommending against the introduction of partial defences for battered women).

[133] Here, the emphasis has been on sharing relevant information and adopting a whole-of-government approach: see, e.g., ALRC and NSWLRC, *Family Violence*, vol. 2, ch. 20.

[134] See ALRC and NSWLRC, *Family Violence*, vol. 2, Recommendations 26-1 and 26-3, and, more generally, ch. 26.

political discourses, the spectre of women charged with killing their abusers now brings with it the possibility that it is the 'failure' of state actors and agencies to provide protection lead to the woman's use of lethal violence. Put another way, the woman who resorts to violence following abuse – that is, a 'victim who kills' – is or may be a woman who has been failed by the state.[135]

These changed relations of responsibility expose the ameliorative tenor of women's responsibility for crime in the current era: atypical responsibility forms may be understood as an admission of state failure to protect women from violence. With their mix of offence and defence, conduct and fault, excuse and justification, and their restriction to particular homicides committed in particular contexts, these forms do not just generate a particular gendered legal subjectivity for 'victims who kill', but also constitute recognition that, by the time these responsibility forms are in play in a criminal trial of women accused of killing her abusive partner, such women have been left to defend themselves against their violent partners.

In this chapter, I have made the case that, contra the standard legal-philosophical claim that criminal responsibility is marked by generality and universalism, women's responsibility for crime is characterised by particularity and specificity. This particularity and specificity has been the product of two dynamics, relating to violence by women and violence against women. I suggested that the rise of violence against women over the period since the last decades of the twentieth century has recast women's violence as responsive – comprehensible only by reference to what has gone before – and reconstructed women's responsibility for crime as an amalgam of agency and victimhood/survivorhood. As well as creating a new set of atypical responsibility forms designed to accommodate this specificity, this reconstruction of women's responsibility for crime has reconfigured relations of responsibility: such relations were oriented around a woman's relations to herself – understood in a personalised and psychologised idea of individual integrity – but are now oriented around the self in relation to others – where other actors, including state actors, are implicated in women's autonomy. This perspective exposes the ameliorative tenor of women's responsibility for crime in the current era, with atypical responsibility forms an admission of state failure to protect women from violence.

[135] The state actors and agencies that might be regarded as having failed abused women who resort to lethal violence, including the police and social services, are not usually subject to criminal charges for their actions or inaction. While there have been some law suits for negligence in the investigation of domestic violence or the inadequacy of protection provided to victims who have sought police assistance, these matters concern the civil law, and thus revolve around issues of liability, damages and accountability, rather than (individual) responsibility, punishment and blame. Empirical studies indicate it is difficult to succeed in suing the police for failings in relation to domestic violence: for discussion in the context of Queensland, see M. Shircore, H. Douglas and V. Morwood, 'Domestic and Family Violence and Police Negligence' (2017) 39 *Sydney Law Review* 539–67.

7

Others

This chapter presents the second of my investigations into relations of responsibility. As discussed in Chapter 2, the role, and hence, significance of criminal responsibility is that it organises relations of responsibility. Relations of responsibility – between self, others and the state – subtend the principles and practices of criminal responsibility that are now at the heart of the criminal law. Like the other chapters in this Part of the book, the analysis I present traverses each of the three nodes of my tripartite schema of relations of responsibility – between self, others and the state – but foregrounds one of these three nodes: here, I explore the idea and place of individuals or 'others' in relations of responsibility. As I show in this chapter, the broader developments in interpersonal and intersubjective relations that have taken place over the twentieth century have impacted on the way in which criminal responsibility organises relations of responsibility between individuals.

Relations between individuals have not received adequate attention in criminal responsibility scholarship. As outlined in Chapter 2, in the dominant legal-philosophical scholarly tradition, the rational autonomous self of criminal responsibility tends to be treated in isolation from others, and as acting alone in committing criminal conduct. As Alice Ristroph writes, criminal responsibility revolves around the individual offender – 'her acts, her brain, her self-control, her blameworthiness' – examined in isolation.[1] Even within the circumscribed space of complicity or participation in crime, the focus tends to be on the will or intention of the individual perpetrator.[2] But law routinely structures relations between individuals, even if this is not apparent or taken into account by responsibility scholars. Focusing on 'others' in relations of responsibility provides a way of examining relationality in criminal

[1] A. Ristroph, 'Responsibility for the Criminal Law', in R. A. Duff and S. P. Green (eds.), *Philosophical Foundations of Criminal Law* (Oxford: Oxford University Press, 2011), p. 109.

[2] For critical discussion, see C. Kutz, *Complicity: Ethics and Law for a Collective Age* (Cambridge: Cambridge University Press, 2007).

law – broadly, the interconnectedness of individuals and others – and links criminal responsibility to sociality, the realm of collective or shared life.

The idea and place of individuals or 'others' in relations of responsibility could be studied in different ways. With an interest in otherwise ordinary relations between individuals, in this chapter, I focus on the law of consorting. Consorting has been claimed as an 'Australasian contribution to the criminal law',[3] having been pioneered in New Zealand and Australia around the turn of the twentieth century, and returning to prominence on the Australian political and legal landscape in recent decades. The offence of consorting involves the criminalisation of relations between individuals, where one or more of the individuals is a criminal. In broad terms, the offence functions to criminalise an individual who associates (for any reason, not for a criminal purpose) with another individual who is a criminal, and the degree of association is sufficient to be 'habitual'. As this indicates, consorting criminalises conduct, but it is not just a matter of criminalisation. With the standard offence of consorting made out without the association between individuals being for a criminal purpose, consorting is a particularly salient way in which the criminal law regulates otherwise ordinary interpersonal relations, implicating others in the evaluation of the particular individual charged with the offence. Via consorting offences, the individual becomes criminal in his or her relations with others, as that individual's conduct with, and knowledge of, others is the basis for the offence.

I make two main arguments in this chapter. First, I argue that consorting laws fall into two generations. The first generation of laws, which appeared around the turn of the twentieth century, had a distinctive orientation, mode (which denotes the way in which criminal responsibility is expressed) and form. As I discuss, the first generation of consorting laws was oriented around public protection, its mode of responsibility was social – with the legal status of the individual criminal taking meaning from the social status of the individual as 'undesirable' – and the laws took an 'old' legal form, revolving around the manifestly criminal nature of the proscribed conduct. By contrast, the second generation of laws, which developed in the last decades of the twentieth century and the first years of the twenty-first century, is oriented around the security of the state, its mode of responsibility is legal – where the laws rest not on external statuses or meanings but on other legal practices and technologies – and the form or structure of the laws is 'new', conforming to the familiar common law construction of criminal responsibility, across conduct, fault and defences. While my analysis reveals some points of continuity around

[3] *Johanson* v. *Dixon* (1979) 143 CLR 376 at 382–3 per Mason J. While this is a widely held view, the use of vagrancy laws to prohibit association between 'undesirables' has a long history, dating to the sixteenth century: see A. McLeod, 'On the Origins of Consorting Laws' (2013) 37(1) *Melbourne University Law Review* 103–42, 112–13 (referring to statutory provisions making association with 'Egyptians' a felony).

police use of the laws in each generation – in targeting suspect populations and status as much as conduct – overall, the two generations of laws are marked by difference rather than similarity.

The second main argument made in this chapter is that these generations of consorting laws correspond with different relations of responsibility between individuals or 'others'. In my analysis, relations of responsibility between individuals fall into two archetypal patterns. The first generation of laws proscribed 'companionship with thieves', with relations of responsibility reinforcing existing, highly stratified social relations, and the laws operating to keep individuals falling within different categories of 'undesirables' apart from each other. Under these laws, individuals charged with consorting were responsible for causing harm or disorder, or, more accurately, for raising the possibility of the threat of harm or disorder, in certain public contexts, and were responsible to the community rather than the state. The second generation of consorting laws inculcates 'friendship with the state', with relations of responsibility between individuals assuming a flat and standardised structure, and the state brought into the relationship between individuals in a distinct way – as a 'friend'. Individuals charged with consorting are now responsible *to* the state, and what they are responsible *for* in their relations with others has changed, with a more extensive conception of responsibility – encompassing personal attitudes and self-regulation – now sustaining relations of responsibility.

This chapter comprises four main parts. Over the first three parts, I present my analysis comparing and contrasting the two generations of consorting laws. In the fourth part of the chapter, synthesising from the preceding analysis, I assess the relations of responsibility between individuals that correspond with these two generations of laws. In this discussion, I draw on both statute and case law from across Australian jurisdictions.[4]

Orientation: From Protection of the Public to Security of the State

The first and second generations of consorting laws have different orientations. The first generation of laws – low-level offences constituting a subset of the wider category of vagrancy laws – was oriented toward protecting the public and maintaining order, while the second generation of laws – serious stand-alone offences that are linked to a wider group of laws addressing serious and organised crime – is oriented to the security of the state.

[4] A number of consorting charges are dealt with in the summary courts, and, as such, are not reported. In this chapter, I draw on reported judgments, including appeals of unreported first instance decisions.

Australasian Innovations in Vagrancy Laws

The first generation of consorting laws appeared around the turn of the twentieth century, but had deep roots in vagrancy laws, a body of statutory laws focused more on poverty than crime that can be traced to the fourteenth century. In the early modern era, with the disintegration of the feudal system, vagrancy laws were introduced to govern the new phenomenon of the 'masterless man', regulating individuals' free labour and the geographical mobility that came with development of mercantile and then capitalist economic practices, industrialisation and urbanisation.[5] As historians have argued, from the sixteenth century, vagrancy laws were constructed and reconstructed as, gradually and unevenly, the state came to replace the parish in the provision of relief of poverty.[6] In the nineteenth century vagrancy laws acted as a useful vehicle for the more interventionist administrative state, operating as part of a raft of regulations that were designed to inculcate self-reliance on the part of the poor, and prevent dependency on welfare.[7] In the now infamous language of vagrancy laws, members of the 'less desirable classes of the population'[8] were classified either as 'idle and disorderly persons', 'vagabonds and rogues' or 'incorrigible rogues'[9] – a moralised taxonomy that provided the scaffolding for the first generation of consorting laws.

Like other parts of the Commonwealth, including New Zealand, Australian colonies enacted their own vagrancy provisions based on the English *Vagrancy Act 1824*.[10] The vagrancy regime proved flexible and useful in the Australian colonial context. Sitting alongside *Masters and Servants Acts*, which governed labour relations both 'at home' and in the colonies, vagrancy laws governed the unemployed and the itinerant.[11] These colonial vagrancy laws aimed to establish order among the free populations in the colonies, control the movement

[5] There is an enormous scholarly literature on vagrancy laws: see, e.g., W. J. Chambliss, 'A Sociological Analysis of the Law of Vagrancy' (1964) 12(1) *Social Problems* 67–77; A.L. Beier, *Masterless Men: The Vagrancy Problem in England 1560–1640* (London: Methuen, 1985); McLeod, 'On the Origins of Consorting Laws', 106–13; N. Rogers, 'Policing the Poor in Eighteenth Century London: The Vagrancy Laws and Their Administration' (1991) XXIV *Histoire sociale/Social History* 127–47.

[6] See generally Rogers, 'Policing the Poor'.

[7] See generally M. J. Wiener, *Reconstructing the Criminal: Culture, Law and Policy in England, 1830–1914* (Cambridge: Cambridge University Press, 1994).

[8] *Bryan* v. *White* [1962] Tas SR 113 at 116.

[9] This taxonomy first appeared in statutes in the eighteenth century: see McLeod, 'On the Origins of Consorting Laws', 108.

[10] The 1824 Act was the first statute that separated poor relief from the criminalisation of vagrancy, dealing only with the latter: McLeod, 'On the Origins of Consorting Laws', 110.

[11] See, e.g., *Masters and Servants Act 1840* (NSW). On the *Masters and Servants Acts* in Australia, see M. Quinlan, 'Australia, 1788–1902: A Working Man's Paradise?', in D. Hay and P. Craven (eds.), *Masters, Servants, and Magistrates in Britain and the Empire,*

of ex-convicts, and prevent miscegenation.[12] The vagrancy laws included provisions that made it an offence to be in a house frequented by thieves, prostitutes or persons without lawful means of support, and for non-Aboriginal persons to keep company or live with Aboriginal peoples.[13] While the first sort of prohibition had antecedents in English and Scottish law (although it was used for distinctively colonial ends in Australia),[14] prohibitions on association between Aboriginal and non-Aboriginal people were 'novel'.[15] As this suggests, vagrancy laws were 'social policy devices that targeted race as well as "vice"',[16] and they were used to target threats and dangers.[17] These colonial era laws set the scene for the further adaptation of vagrancy laws in the post-colonial period, including meeting the imperative of segregating Aboriginal peoples from others.

The first consorting laws formed an additional limb to the 'traditional gradations of rascality' already enumerated in vagrancy laws.[18] The Australasian innovation lay in the inclusion of the act of consorting as one of several bases for a finding that an individual was 'idle and disorderly' per vagrancy laws; that is, the statutes created a new subset of vagrancy, proscribing mere association between certain individuals. Following the template of the New Zealand *Police Offences Amendment Act 1901*,[19] Australian legislatures criminalised individuals who 'habitually consorted' with 'reputed thieves' or prostitutes. For example, in NSW, following a press and public campaign around the growth of crime gangs in Sydney,[20] and against a backdrop of longer standing concerns with prostitution and gambling, in 1929, the parliament introduced the offence of 'habitually consorting' with 'reputed criminals or known

1562–1955 (Chapel Hill, NC: University of North Carolina Press, 2004), p. 219. Under these laws workers could be sentenced to imprisonment for disobedience, misconduct or misdemeanors. 'Poor laws' were not introduced in Australia: see S. Garton, *Out of Luck: Poor Australians and Social Welfare 1788–1988* (Sydney: Allen and Unwin, 1990).

12 J. Kimber, 'Poor Laws: A Historiography of Vagrancy in Australia' (2013) 11(8) *History Compass* 537–50, 538.

13 See, e.g., *Police Offences Act 1890* (Vic) s 40 and *Police Act 1892* (WA) s 65.

14 These prohibitions were the basis for prosecutions of white women and Chinese men who cohabited: see Jan Ryan, '"She Lives with a Chinaman": Orient-ing "White" Women in the Courts of Law' (1999) 23(60) *Journal of Australian Studies* 149–59.

15 McLeod, 'On the Origins of Consorting Laws', 124.

16 Kimber, 'Poor Laws', 538.

17 Markus Dubber analyses vagrancy as an instance of police power, the power of the state to govern threats and dangers: see generally M. D. Dubber, *The Police Power: Patriarchy and the Foundations of American Government* (New York: Columbia University Press, 2005).

18 *Jolly* v. *Salvitti* [1974] VR 484 at 486.

19 The *Police Offences Amendment Act 1901* (NZ) amended the *Police Offences Act 1884* (NZ) and introduced consorting in New Zealand.

20 See A. Steel, 'Consorting in New South Wales: Substantive Offence or Police Power?' (2003) 26(3) *University of New South Wales Law Journal* 567–602, 582–7; see also G. D. Woods, *A History of the Criminal Law in New South Wales: The New State 1901–1955* (Sydney: Federation Press, 2018), ch. 18.

prostitutes or persons who have been convicted of having no visible lawful means of support'.[21] A few years later, in Victoria, with Melbourne facing the same sort of problems with street gangs and vice crimes, the legislature amended the *Police Offences Act 1928* (Vic) along the same lines.[22] As the then new Australian High Court made clear in its first consideration of vagrancy, in 1907, the laws created only one offence – that of 'being an idle and disorderly person' – with consorting one of the factual bases on which a conviction for vagrancy could be founded.[23]

What is it that brings together prostitutes, those without lawful means of support, and thieves, and what accounts for their prominence in the law of consorting? Each of these groups of individuals was regarded as a threat to the social order, with the precise nature of the threat varying from group to group. Prostitution generated particular concerns about sin and vice, and, in the early twentieth-century Australian context, fears about the moral health of white populations on the continent.[24] Amid concerns about the spread of venereal disease, and the quality of life in city slums, vagrancy laws provided an additional tool for policing street prostitution.[25] Individuals without lawful means of support were a mainstay of vagrancy laws, as 'the person apparently without lawful means of support is in law considered dangerous'.[26] As John Pratt argues in the context of English criminal justice, itinerancy as a way of life threatened the social order because it meant an individual was 'unknowable'.[27] The prominence of thieves in the laws reflects the status of theft as a particularly serious threat. In the first decades of the twentieth century, property crime was associated with recidivism and 'dangerousness',[28] and a thief – 'a person who steals and is prepared to steal, to commit the crime of larceny, should the opportunity offer'[29] – was a socio-legal term with wide currency.[30]

21 *Vagrancy (Amendment) Act 1929* (NSW) s 2(b), amending *Vagrancy Act 1902* (NSW) s 4.

22 *Guider* v. *Walker* [1933] VLR 413 at 415 citing *Police Offences (Consorting) Act 1931* (Vic); see also *Muller* v. *Murphy; ex parte Murphy* [1935] St R Qd 85, referring to *The Vagrants, Gaming and Other Offences Act 1931* (Qld).

23 See *Lee Fan* v. *Dempsey* (1907) 5 CLR 310 at 312 per Griffith CJ (in relation to the *Police Act 1892* (WA)).

24 See S. Davies, 'Captives of Their Bodies: Women, Law and Punishment, 1880s–1980s', in D. Kirkby (ed.), *Sex, Power and Justice: Historical Perspectives on Law in Australia* (Melbourne: Oxford University Press, 1995), pp. 99, 101–5; see also J. A. Allen, *Sex and Secrets: Crimes Involving Australian Women Since 1880* (Melbourne: Oxford University Press, 1990).

25 See H. Golder and J. Allen, 'Prostitution in New South Wales 1870–1932: Restructuring an Industry' (1979–80) 18/19 *Refractory Girl* 17–24, 18–19.

26 *Lee Fan* v. *Dempsey* (1907) 5 CLR 310 at 321 per Isaacs J.

27 See J. Pratt, 'Governing the Dangerous: An Historical Overview of Dangerous Offender Legislation' (1996) 5(1) *Social & Legal Studies* 21–36, 24.

28 Pratt, 'Governing the Dangerous', 29.

29 *Dias* v. *O'Sullivan* [1949] SASR 195 at 204.

30 See A. J. Piper, 'To Judge a Thief: How the Background of Thieves Became Central to Dispensing Justice, Western Australia, 1921–1951' (2017) 4(1) *Law & History* 113–44.

Indeed, the prominence of theft and thieves in consorting laws subsisted for a long time, surviving until the recasting of the offences in the 1970s, as I discuss below.

The miscellaneous collection of people who posed a threat to the social order shared the same socially stigmatic status – as 'undesirable'.[31] In operation, the laws operated like a 'dragnet'[32]: they allowed the police to target a diverse range of suspect populations and low level offenders, including 'stand over men' who intimidated 'bettors, sly grog sellers and other individuals', and friends and thieves.[33] As the High Court commented in *Lee Fan* v. *Dempsey* in 1907, each group falling under vagrancy provisions was 'a menace to society'.[34] In *Lee Fan*, the defendant, who was alleged to frequent 'gambling houses in the Chinese quarter in Perth' and live on his pay as a 'fighting man', was convicted of being 'idle and disorderly' on the basis that he had no lawful means of support.[35] At this time, anti-Chinese racism was feeding into both police practices and campaigns by social reformers and members of the temperance movement for the suppression of betting and opium-smoking, which were widely thought to be linked to sexual exploitation of white women by Chinese men.[36] Although most cases of consorting involved men, women were also prosecuted under the laws, for prostitution and other offences.[37]

As low-level offences, consorting convictions attracted either short prison sentences or fines. While some concerns were expressed about policing practices based on this first generation of laws – including what a Queensland court referred to as 'the danger of what is intended as a provision for the protection of the public, being used as an instrument for harrying individuals even though such individuals fall short of the standards of estimable citizens'[38] – and some prosecutions attracted critical comments from the courts – such as in the Queensland case in which a returned soldier's conviction for consorting was upheld, but the judge noted that the defendant might find it difficult to avoid the company of 'some doubtful characters' because he lived in a boarding house, and warned the police to be careful to avoid 'any suggestion that they are

31 *Byrne* v. *Shearer* [1959] VR 606 at 609 (where the court refers to a 'legislative policy' to keep individuals without means of support from associating with 'undesirable companions').

32 Woods, *A History of Criminal Law in New South Wales*, p. 391.

33 See *Muller* v. *Murphy; ex parte Murphy* [1935] St R Qd 85; *MacDonald* v. *The King* (1935) 52 CLR 739 at 740; *Canino* v. *Samuels* [1968] SASR 303 (Canino argued unsuccessfully that he was not a thief but a false pretender), respectively.

34 *Lee Fan* v. *Dempsey* (1907) 5 CLR 310 at 321 per Isaacs J (referring specifically to persons without lawful means of support).

35 *Lee Fan* v. *Dempsey* (1907) 5 CLR 310. The defendant argued no offence was disclosed but his conviction was upheld.

36 See M. Finnane, 'The Politics of Police Powers: The Making of Police Offences Acts', in M. Finnane (ed.), *Policing in Australia: Historical Perspectives* (Sydney: New South Wales University Press, 1987), p. 99.

37 See, e.g., *Auld* v. *Purdy* (1933) 50 WN (NSW) 218; *Birrell* v. *Astor* [1940] VLR 180.

38 See *Muller* v. *Murphy; ex parte Murphy* [1935] St R Qd 85 at 93 per Macrossan S.P.J.

administering this Act in an oppressive way'[39] – the focus of this criticism was on the use of the laws by the police, rather than the laws themselves. Overall, consorting was regarded as an 'effective weapon for breaking up associations of criminals'.[40]

As this discussion suggests, the first generation of consorting laws was oriented toward the protection of the public and the enforcement of public order through the prevention of low-level crime. As Mark Finnane argues in relation to the larger category of vagrancy laws, of which consorting was a part, they were used by the police as a 'general public order power'.[41] This reflects the core role of the police in exercising a 'generalised peace-keeping function' – preventing and detecting crime and keeping public order – in the first decades of the twentieth century.[42] Significantly, it was the in-person associations between individuals from such stigmatic groups that were regarded as threatening: the associations did not need to be for a criminal purpose to be caught by the laws. In criminalising 'habitual consorting', the laws were intended 'to prevent the regular meeting of congeries of individuals (persons generally regarded by those, who ought to know, as having vicious propensities)'.[43] In the words of one South Australian judge, legislation on consorting is 'a legislative attempt to give legal sanction to St Paul's advice to the Corinthians': '[e]vil communications corrupt good manners'.[44] With the social threat posited by consorting arising from mere association, it did not make sense to limit the reach of the laws to association for a criminal purpose. As the South Australian Supreme Court put it in 1930, consorting governed 'not companionship in thieving, but with thieves'.[45] I return to this point below.

The Rise of Serious and Organised Crime

By contrast with the first generation of laws, the second generation of consorting laws is oriented not to low-level crime but to serious and organised crime. Against the background of the reform of police services, and the development of national law enforcement and justice institutions from the 1970s,[46] Australia introduced laws against organised crime in the 1980s, in response to 'the dangers presented to the Australian community by organised crime and

39 *Codd* v. *Lewis* (1944) 38 QJPR 135 at 139.

40 *Bryan* v. *White* [1962] Tas SR 113 at 116 (discussing the *Police Offences Act 1935* (Tas)).

41 See M. Finnane, *Police and Government: Histories of Policing in Australia* (Oxford: Oxford University Press, 1994), p. 95.

42 Finnane, 'The Politics of Police Powers', p. 98.

43 *Dias* v. *O'Sullivan* [1949] SASR 195 at 199.

44 *Reardon* v. *O'Sullivan* [1950] SASR 77 at 82 per Abbott J.

45 *Gabriel* v. *Lenthall* [1930] SASR 318 at 327; see also *Clarke* v. *Nelson; ex parte Nelson* [1936] QWN 17.

46 I discuss these developments in Chapter 5.

crimes involving sophisticated techniques and methods',[47] and, in the period since then, organised crime has become a notable dimension of serious crime in Australia.[48] In this context, the immediate catalyst for the introduction of a second generation of consorting laws in the early twenty-first century was concern with serious violent offences committed by 'outlaw motorcycle gangs'.[49] Following a series of high profile crimes by members of 'bikie gangs', several states and territories enacted extensive legislative regimes to criminalise association between members of 'criminal organisations'.[50] At around the same time, Australian Attorneys-General agreed that 'organised crime is a national issue requiring a nationally coordinated response by all jurisdictions', and recommended that all states and territories consider introducing legislation that included 'consorting or similar provisions that prevent a person from associating with another person who is involved in organised criminal activity as an individual or through an organisation'.[51] Within a few years, almost all Australian jurisdictions had enacted new consorting offences.[52]

Under this second generation of consorting laws, consorting is not a subset of vagrancy but a stand-alone offence which attracts significant penalties. For example, in 2005, Victoria amended its *Summary Offences Act 1966* to make it an offence to habitually consort with a person who has been convicted of, or is reasonably suspected of, having committed, an organised crime offence, and, in 2012, replaced this offence with an offence of 'unlawful association'.[53] Similarly, in 2006, the Northern Territory added a new section to the *Summary Offences Act 1923* (NT), making it an offence to consort with another person where each person has been convicted of a 'prescribed' offence.[54] In 2012, NSW

[47] See Hansard, Commonwealth House of Representatives, col. 2394–5, 21 October 1982 (introducing the *National Crimes Commission Act 1982* (Cth)).

[48] Organised crime organisations have come to be implicated in a wide range of criminal activities, including drug trafficking and manufacture: see Parliamentary Joint Committee on the Australian Crime Commission, Parliament of Australia, *Inquiry into the Future Impact of Serious and Organised Crime on Australian Society* (2007).

[49] The term 'outlaw motorcycle gangs' has attained quasi-legal status, being used in government policy documents. See, e.g., Parliamentary Joint Committee on the Australian Crime Commission, Parliament of Australia, *Inquiry into the Legislative Arrangements to Outlaw Serious and Organized Crime Groups* (2009); Justice and Community Safety Directorate (ACT), *Discussion Paper: Consorting Laws for the ACT* (2016), p. 5.

[50] See *Serious and Organised Crime (Control) Act 2008* (SA); *Crimes (Criminal Organisations Control) Act 2009* (NSW); *Criminal Organisations Act 2009* (Qld); *Serious Crime Control Act 2009* (NT).

[51] Standing Committee of Attorneys-General, *Communiqué* (16–17 April 2009), p. 8.

[52] Recently the ACT Government conducted a review into the need for a consorting offence in that jurisdiction: see Justice and Community Safety Directorate, *Discussion Paper: Consorting Laws for the ACT* (2016). This review recommended that consorting laws be introduced into the ACT, but, at the time of writing, no such laws have been introduced.

[53] See *Vagrancy (Repeal) and Summary Offences (Amendment) Act 2005* (Vic), s49F, and *Criminal Organisations Control Act 2012* (Vic), s124A, respectively. The maximum penalty for the offence under s 49F was 2 years imprisonment and is 3 years under s124A.

[54] *Summary Offences Act* (NT) s 55A (a prescribed offence is defined as one punishable by 10 years imprisonment). The maximum penalty is 2 years imprisonment.

enacted a new consorting law, making it an offence to associate by any means with at least two convicted offenders on at least two occasions.[55] In the words of the then NSW Parliamentary Secretary on the introduction of the new laws, the legislation 'modernises the offence of consorting as well as extending and clarifying its application'.[56] The NSW offence formed the model for the recent reforms in Queensland, which saw a new offence of 'habitual consorting' introduced on the basis that it was more 'constitutionally robust', fairer, and 'more effective and efficient' than the more extensive anti-association laws that it was to replace.[57] The new Queensland offence attracts a maximum penalty of three years imprisonment.[58]

These stand-alone consorting offences are now linked to serious crime (although, as I discuss below, the laws are still used by police to target low-level offenders). This link is evident in the structural connection between these laws and criminal organisations laws. For example, dovetailing its consorting law with criminal organisation laws, in 2008, South Australia enacted laws to criminalise consorting six or more times within twelve months with a person who is a member of a 'declared organisation', or subject to a control order or between persons with prescribed criminal convictions.[59] Here, consorting rests on another legal process, in which an organisation is classified as a 'declared organisation'.[60] Once an organisation has been made a declared organisation, judges are empowered to issue, on the application of the police commissioner, orders limiting or prohibiting association between members. These criminal organisations laws have been subject to several constitutional challenges,[61] prompting legislatures to make changes to the

[55] *Crimes Amendment (Consorting and Organised Crime) Act 2012* (NSW). This provision survived constitutional challenge: see *Tajjour* v. *New South Wales*; *Hawthorne* v. *New South Wales*; *Forster* v. *New South Wales* (2014) 254 CLR 508.

[56] Hansard, New South Wales Legislative Council, col. 9091, 7 March 2012.

[57] See Queensland Taskforce on Organised Crime Legislation, Queensland Department of Justice and Attorney-General, *Final Report* (2016), pp. 194–5. The Taskforce recommended the repeal of the *Vicious Lawless Association Disestablishment Act 2013* (Qld), which included a range of provisions targeting organised crime and 'bikie' gangs in particular.

[58] See *Criminal Code 1899* (Qld) s 77B(1).

[59] *Serious and Organised Crime (Control) Act 2008* (SA) s 35. The penalty for conviction of this offence is 5 years imprisonment. Some parts of this law were declared invalid by the High Court in *South Australia* v. *Totani* (2010) 242 CLR 1.

[60] In general terms, under criminal organisation laws, a police commissioner or a minister may apply for an organisation to be made a 'declared organisation', an administrative judgment determined on the basis that the members of that organisation associate for the purposes of planning or engaging in serious criminal activity. These applications have been subject to strong criticism: see generally N. Cowdery, 'A Threat to the Rule of Law: The New South Wales Crimes (Criminal Organisations Control) Act 2009' (2009) 21(2) *Current Issues in Criminal Justice* 321–4; A. Loughnan, 'The Legislation We Had to Have? The Crimes (Criminal Organisations Control) Act 2009 (NSW)' (2009) 20(3) *Current Issues in Criminal Justice* 457–65. See also J. Ayling, 'Pre-emptive Strike: How Australia Is Tackling Outlaw Motorcycle Gangs' (2011) 36(3) *American Journal of Criminal Justice* 250–64.

[61] Re the SA legislation, see *South Australia* v. *Totani* (2010) 242 CLR 1; re NSW, see *Wainohu* v. *New South Wales* (2011) 243 CLR 181; re QLD, see *Kuczborski* v. *Queensland* (2014) 254 CLR 51.

laws, and producing what is effectively a pro forma law that seems to have furnished a constitutional challenge-proof model for consorting laws. Thus, as the High Court noted in relation to creation of the new NSW consorting offence, Section 93X of the *Crimes Act 1900* (NSW), it 'adopts language which has been the subject of authoritative judicial exposition'.[62]

The connection between consorting offences and criminal organisations laws exposes the changed orientation of consorting: the second generation of laws is oriented to the security of the state, with the protection of the public and enforcement of public order now serving this new, larger goal, rather than constituting an end in itself. The goal of security, which has both a national and an international aspect, and extends beyond criminal justice, addresses the capacity of the state to provide social goods for its citizens, and, thus, threats to security go to the sovereignty of the state.[63] In this respect, criminal organisations pose a profound threat, including to the state's monopoly on violence, arrogating to themselves rights that belong to the sovereign state.[64] The security orientation of consorting laws now links them with preventive orders (control orders and preventive detention provisions), and non-association orders (a sentencing power), as well as criminal organisations laws, that are utilised in relation to the most serious criminal offences, including terrorism.[65] These links point to broader developments in the security discourse in the current era, in which security has become an all-embracing paradigm and risk has entered security practices.[66] As part of this elaborate arsenal, in their orientation to serious and organised crime, consorting laws are now securing the state.

Mode: From Social Responsibility to Legal Responsibility

The first and second generations of consorting laws reflect different modes of responsibility, that is, responsibility is expressed in different ways. The first generation of laws reflects a social mode of responsibility: under these laws, the legal status of an individual – as criminal – takes meaning from the social status of the individual – as 'undesirable'. By contrast, the second generation of laws reflects a legal mode of responsibility: these laws rest not on external social statuses or meanings, but on *other* legal practices and technologies.

[62] *Tajjour* v. *New South Wales* at 576, [135] per Gageler J. This provision was found not to breach any constitutional protections.

[63] There is a large body of work on criminal justice and security; see, e.g., V. Tadros, 'Crimes and *Security*' (2008) 71(6) *Modern Law Review* 940–70; L. Zedner, 'Too Much Security?' (2003) 31(3) *International Journal of the Sociology of Law* 155–84.

[64] See M. C. Meliá, 'The Wrongfulness of Crimes of Unlawful Association' (2008) 11(4) *New Criminal Law Review* 563–89, 585.

[65] For critical discussion of preventive measures in criminal law, see A. Ashworth and L. Zedner, *Preventive Justice* (Oxford: Oxford University Press, 2014).

[66] See S. Selchow, 'Security Policy and (Global) Risk(s)', in M. Kaldor and I. Rangelov (eds.), *The Handbook of Global Security Policy* (London: Palgrave Macmillan, 2014).

Enforcement of the Social Status Quo

The first generation of consorting laws applied to a range of 'undesirable' persons, and, as discussed above, individuals in each group of persons potentially liable to charges of 'habitual consorting' shared socially marginalised status. The marginalised social status of the individuals – as thieves or prostitutes or other – and the legal status of those individuals – as criminal – reinforced each other. Put another way, the laws targeted 'members of the criminal class',[67] with membership of this legal class having social as well as legal determinants. In the early twentieth-century context of highly stratified social relations characterised by sharp divisions of class, gender and race, each of the groups of 'undesirable' persons was 'undesirable' in its own way. In keeping different individuals within these groups of 'undesirables' apart from each other, the first generation of consorting laws served not just public order but the enforcement of the social status quo. In this respect, the consorting laws dovetailed with other legal and social practices that produced and reproduced existing social relations, aiming to isolate and marginalise individuals who threatened those relations. The consorting laws were designed to 'ensure that "birds of a feather do not flock together"',[68] meaning that, as Julie Kimber has written in relation vagrancy laws more generally, consorting operated to make the convicted person 'friendless'.[69]

A clear illustration of the social mode of responsibility of the first generation of consorting laws is provided by those provisions that criminalised association between Aboriginal peoples and non-Aboriginal peoples. For instance, a Northern Territory ordinance, *Ordinance Relating to Aboriginals* 1918, made it an offence for any non-Aboriginal person to 'habitually consort with a female aboriginal or half-caste'.[70] Here, consorting likely referred to intimate relations rather than association more generally.[71] Similarly, under the Victorian law, it was an offence for a non-Aboriginal person to be 'found lodging or wandering in company with any of the Aboriginal natives of Victoria'.[72] These consorting laws were animated by the fear of miscegenation that was a distinctive feature of the broader racist laws and practices directed towards Aboriginal peoples in Australia. As historians have argued,

[67] *Wilson* v. *Giles* [1966] SASR 361 at 362.

[68] Ibid.

[69] Kimber, 'Poor Laws', 537.

[70] See, e.g., *Aboriginals Ordinance 1918* (Cth) s 53(1)(a); see also *Welfare Ordinance 1953* (Cth) s 64(b) (providing that it was an offence for a male person to 'habitually consort, keep company or associate, with a female ward to whom he is not married': the penalty for a first offence was a fine of 100 pounds or 6 months imprisonment or both). As this provision indicates, Aboriginal people were made wards of the state under the protection system.

[71] See McLeod, 'On the Origins of Consorting Laws', 128.

[72] *Police Offences Act 1957* (Vic) s 69(1)(a).

fear of miscegenation loomed large over the development of the Australian population in the nineteenth and early twentieth centuries. At this time, government policy held that Aboriginal peoples were a 'dying race', and that mixing of Aboriginal and white people would have a degrading influence on the advance of Australian civilisation. What was called 'the half-caste problem' – the idea that 'mixed-bloods' would 'inherit the "vices" of both races and few of their virtues'[73] – was understood as a 'problem of hybridity and degeneration' that threatened the 'racial purity' of white Australia.[74] These fears fed into the protection system, a dense regulatory matrix governing all aspects of the lives of Aboriginal peoples that was only dismantled in the 1960s and 1970s.[75]

The social mode of responsibility of the first generation of consorting laws is also evident in the place of reputation in the offences. Reputation – 'the popular belief of the nature of a man's character'[76] – was the lynchpin of the offences falling into first generation of consorting laws. Reputation, which was distinct from other concepts in use in criminal law, such as bad character and criminal history,[77] revolves around beliefs held about a person, and necessarily has a social dimension, as it depends on what others believe about an individual. In consorting, reputation was regarded as a matter of fact, and generally treated by courts as an unproblematic notion. Indeed, for a South Australian court, it was possible to divide the community into '(i) persons who have the reputation of being thieves, and (ii) those who do not'.[78] While it was acknowledged that someone with an 'unsavoury reputation' may be 'virtuous and law abiding', what mattered was reputation, not character, and, if, 'rightly or wrongly', a person gained a reputation as reputed thief, 'that person becomes a reputed thief'.[79] Similarly, for a Tasmanian court, while companionship with one reputed thief was 'equivocal as an indication of a man's character', the 'inference' that could be drawn from 'persistent companionship' with more than one was 'ordinarily inescapable'.[80] As this indicates, reputation was not a high bar to conviction.

[73] See R. van Krieken, 'The "Stolen Generations" and Cultural Genocide: The Forced Removal of Australian Indigenous Children from Their Families and Its Implications for the Sociology of Childhood' (1999) 6(3) *Childhood* 297–311, 301.

[74] van Krieken, 'The "Stolen Generations" and Cultural Genocide', 303.

[75] See H. Douglas and M. Finnane, *Indigenous Crime and Settler Law: White Sovereignty after Empire* (Basingstoke: Palgrave Macmillan, 2012), ch. 4. I discuss the protection system in the context of state responsibility in Chapter 8.

[76] *Dias* v. *O'Sullivan* [1949] SASR 195 at 203.

[77] See *Berry* v. *Ritchie* [1932] [Vol. IV] NZLR 357 (holding that a conviction for a consorting offence did not require proof of either bad character or 'adoption of a criminal mode of life').

[78] *Dias* v. *O'Sullivan* [1949] SASR 195 at 202. For this judge, if there were conflicting viewpoints on a person's status as a known criminal, he did not have the reputation of a reputed thief because 'there can only be one reputation' (203).

[79] *Dias* v. *O'Sullivan* [1949] SASR 195 at 203–4.

[80] *Porter* v. *Bryan* [1963] Tas SR 41 at 43.

Reputation might amount only to propensity; as the NSW Supreme Court stated in 1938, '"reputed thief" means a person of whom people who know him believe that he steals when he gets the chance'.[81]

For the purposes of a charge of habitual consorting, reputation was treated as self-evident, and a criminal reputation could be proved by police evidence. The evidence of the police detectives and senior officers – 'persons whose business it is to know' – was considered sufficient to establish this aspect of the offence.[82] This meant that a criminal conviction was not required for an individual to have the reputation of a thief or a prostitute, and to make anyone who associated with him or her liable for the offence of consorting. Reputation operated not only as sufficient grounds for conviction but, in addition, as a basis for policing practices, including surveillance of particular individuals and attempts to separate them from others.[83] As such, consorting laws were harnessed by the police in their work regulating towns and cities and delineating social and economic spaces within urban contexts.[84] As this suggests, via then current policing practices, reliance on reputation facilitated a slippage between issues of law and evidence, or elements of the offence and proof of it. With reputation a requirement of the consorting offence, and evidence of reputation furnished by police statements about the individual and his or her conduct with others, these consorting offences were 'effectively proved on charge', which, as Alex Steel argues, made them particularly useful to police.[85]

The place of reputation in this generation of consorting laws reveals the laws' dependency on a relatively stable community for their coherence and operation. The laws rested on the idea that the reputation of certain individuals – as thieves, or prostitutes – was a meaningful notion that revealed the identity of such individuals – as thieves or prostitutes, where those identities were themselves a shorthand for a wider and more diffused social category of 'undesirable' people. Like reputation, 'undesirability' was regarded as manifest or evident. The manifest or evident quality of undesirability reflects the genesis of vagrancy laws in the era of 'manifest criminality', when crimes were those acts that constituted a clear threat to society and were recognised by all as such.[86] Thus, as a Queensland court stated in 1936, 'the [prohibited] association is with persons of a reputation which would ordinarily cause them to be

[81] *Ex parte King; Re Blackley* (1938) 38 SR (NSW) 483 at 491.

[82] *Gabriel* v. *Lenthall* [1930] SASR 318 at 323; see also *Auld* v. *Purdy* (1933) 50 WN (NSW) 218; *O'Connor* v. *Johnston* (1903) 23 NZLR 183 at 184 ('The evidence of a police officer as to whether a man is reputed to be a member of the criminal class, and, if so, of what branch of that class, seems to me to be the best evidence of the man's reputation').

[83] See, e.g., *Guider* v. *Walker* [1933] VLR 413 (Walker was alleged to 'habitually consort' with reputed thieves, and also to be a reputed thief himself).

[84] See Finnane, *Police and Government*, p. 96.

[85] Steel, 'Consorting in New South Wales', 575.

[86] On 'manifest criminality', see G. Fletcher, *Rethinking Criminal Law*, 2nd ed. (Oxford: Oxford University Press, 2000).

avoided by honest men'.[87] As this suggests, what was being criminalised via the laws was criminal 'disposition',[88] or the danger or threat some individuals posed to the stable social system, rather than conduct as such. This focus of criminalisation connects with the relations of responsibility that correspond with this first generation of consorting laws, as I discuss below.

From Reputation to Record

The first evidence of a changed mode of responsibility in consorting – from social to legal – appeared with a recasting of some of the then existing laws, which occurred in the 1970s. In this recasting, the focus of the laws shifted to association with criminals in general as opposed to association with particular socially 'undesirable' individuals. At this time, overtly morally evaluative terms and nebulous provisions, like 'reputation', were replaced with reference to criminal records or convictions. Thus, in NSW, in 1970, the language used in the consorting offence was changed from 'reputed criminals', 'known prostitutes' and 'convicted vagrants', to 'reputed prostitutes', 'reputed drug offenders', 'other reputed criminals', and those who had been convicted of vagrancy, and then, in 1979, each of these categories was replaced with a single category – 'persons convicted of indictable offences'.[89] As this indicates, this change represented greater reliance on criminal records. In addition, also as a result of the 1979 amendment, NSW law came to require that a person convicted of consorting had knowledge that the person he or she was associating with had been convicted of a serious offence.[90] Knowledge was quite hard to prove and these changes rendered the laws less useful to police than they had been,[91] setting the scene for the appearance of new consorting laws in the first decades of the twenty-first century.

The re-casting of some of the consorting laws reflected increased concern with social welfare, and public and political awareness of human rights that arose in Australia, as elsewhere, in the 1960s and 1970s. At this time, consorting laws themselves – as opposed to police practices based on them – became more of a focus for concern, with criticisms levied at the laws on the basis of infringements of rights of individuals to free association and to freedom from state interference. For example, in his dissent in the 1979 High Court decision

87 *Ex parte Finney; Re Miller & Anor* (1936) 50 WN (NSW) 190 at 191.

88 *Wilson* v. *Giles* [1966] SASR 361 at 363 (stating that consorting laws applied to individuals who 'manifest[ed] a disposition to associate with the criminal class').

89 See *Summary Offences Act 1970* (NSW) s 25; *Crimes (Summary Offences) Amendment Act 1979* (NSW) s 4, inserting *Crimes Act 1900* (NSW) s 546A.

90 See *Crimes (Summary Offences) Amendment Act 1979* (NSW) s 4, inserting *Crimes Act 1900* (NSW) s 546A.

91 There is some evidence that the offences continued to be used as a means of gathering intelligence: see Steel, 'Consorting in New South Wales', 592–3.

of *Johanson* v. *Dixon*, which concerned the scope of the consorting offence in the *Vagrancy Act 1966* (Vic), Justice Murphy expressed concern that a person could be imprisoned for associating with others even if the association was 'innocent of an "sinister, illicit or illegal" purpose'.[92] His Honour noted that the consorting legislation contravened human rights standards, giving this as a 'special reason' for construing the laws strictly in favour of the defendant.[93] Similarly, in a South Australian Supreme Court decision in 1983, Chief Justice King sounded a note of concern that a defendant convicted of consorting 'is to be punished not for any harm which he has done to others, but merely for the company which he has been keeping, however difficult and even disloyal it might be to avoid it.'[94] These sorts of concerns prompted the abolition of the then existing offences of consorting in the ACT,[95] and later, in Western Australia.[96] As the Law Reform Commission of Western Australia stated in its 1992 review of the relevant laws in that state, criminalising individuals on the basis that they are 'known to be in a particular category', or 'reputed' to be in such a category, is 'inconsistent with the principles of the criminal law'.[97]

The re-casting of consorting laws around the category of 'criminals', and their organisation around the device of criminal records, or convictions for particular crimes, did not signify a triumph of human rights concerns, however. Rather, the changes that shifted consorting into a different, legal mode reflected the rise of modern liberal governance practices and 'ways of knowing'[98] that had developed over the period since the creation of the first generation of consorting laws in the early twenty-first century. As a number of scholars argue, the development of new technologies and forms of expertise in the formation of the welfare state generated new possibilities for governance of individuals and groups, including future-oriented risk-based analyses.[99] Reliance on criminal records, and ostensibly neutral categories like 'persons convicted of serious indictable offences' in consorting laws shows the greatly

92 *Johanson* v. *Dixon* (1979) 143 CLR 376 at 393.

93 *Johanson* v. *Dixon* (1979) 143 CLR 376 at 392.

94 *Jan* v. *Fingleton* (1983) 32 SASR 379 at 380.

95 *Police Offences (Amendment) Ordinance 1983* (ACT) s 6(2).

96 The Law Reform Commission of Western Australia recommended the abolition of the relevant offences in 1992 and these offences were repealed in 2004: *Criminal Law Amendment (Simple Offences) Act 2004* (WA): see Law Reform Commission of Western Australia (LRC (WA)), *Report on the Police Offences Act*, Project No. 85 (1992) (in relation to ss 65(7) and (9) of the *Police Act 1892* (WA)).

97 See LRC (WA), *Report on the Police Offences Act*; see also N. Morgan, 'Criminal Law Reform 1983–1995: An Era of Unprecedented Legislative Activism' (1995) 25 *University of Western Australia Law Review* 283–300.

98 See generally M. Foucault, *Discipline and Punish: The Birth of the Prison* (New York: Pantheon Books, 1977).

99 See, e.g., D. Garland, *Punishment and Welfare: A History of Penal Strategies* (Aldershot: Gower, 1985); N. Rose, *Governing the Soul: The Shaping of the Private Self*, 2nd ed. (London: Routledge, 1999) and N. Rose, 'Government, Authority and Expertise in Advanced Liberalism' (1993) 22(3) *Economy and Society* 283–99.

extended administrative capacity of Australian states by the last decades of the twentieth century. By this point in time, policing and criminal justice practices had undergone a process of professionalisation, and official records, such as criminal records, were more complete and more reliable.[100] In addition, and crucially, bureaucratic technologies such as convictions and criminal records presented the more acceptable, morally neutral face of criminal justice that was by then necessary for the legitimation of the use of coercive power in criminal law and justice. I discuss legitimation again below.

The most important factor in the changed mode of responsibility of the second generation of consorting laws was the major social changes that took place in Australia in the last decades of the twentieth century. As a result of these changes, the stable, stratified social system on which the first generation of consorting laws depended fell away. Liberal social values, social diversity and moral pluralism radically undercut concepts such as criminal reputation, which were central to the structure and operation of these laws. In this context, and as the South Australian Police commented in a recent parliamentary review of the laws relating to organised crime, 'the classification of persons' as 'reputed thieves', 'prostitutes and the like' became 'petty':[101] such a 'classification of persons' was clearly no longer regarded as stigmatic or effective in enforcing the law. As the social system underpinning the first generation of consorting laws had changed so thoroughly, consorting laws were no longer functioning in the way intended. Indeed, in a wholesale reversal of fortune, via its connection with serious and organised crime, a criminal reputation had become less like an incriminating device, as under the first generation of consorting laws, and more like a business asset, 'no different to goodwill for a legitimate business'.[102]

Legal Form: From 'Old' to 'New' Structures of Accountability

The first and second generations of consorting laws have different legal forms or structures. Consorting laws falling under the first generation of laws are characterised by an older and looser form, revolving around the manifestly criminal nature of the prohibited conduct, while the second generation of laws have a somewhat tighter and 'new' or modern form – conforming with the familiar common law construction of criminal responsibility across conduct, fault and defences – and realised as much via formalised procedures as changes to the component parts of individual responsibility for crime.

[100] On the development of policing in Australia, see Finnane, *Police and Government*.

[101] Government of South Australia, Submission No. 13 to the Parliamentary Joint Committee on the Australian Crime Commission, *Inquiry into the Legislative Arrangements to Outlaw Serious and Organized Crime Groups* (2009), p. 29 (referring to *Summary Offences Act 1953* (SA) s 13).

[102] Government of South Australia, Inquiry into the Legislative Arrangements to Outlaw Serious and Organized Crime Groups, p. 18.

'Manifest Criminality'

Consorting offences in the first generation of laws had a loose, open-textured quality, reflecting the way in which they depended on and reinforced the (marginalised) social status of the individuals whose associations with others they proscribed. Flowing from the status of consorting as a species of vagrancy, laws in the first generation revolved around a manifestly criminal act – associating with 'undesirable' individuals – with the significance of the conduct or behaviour element of the offence far greater than any mental or fault element.[103] The laws did not require that the prosecution prove *mens rea* because 'habitually consorting with reputed thieves is such conduct as *prima facie* to shew [sic] a guilty mind'.[104] While there were some references in the case law to 'the necessary blameworthy condition of mind' required by the offence, this amounted only to knowledge of the reputation of the persons with whom the defendant had been in company, and because of the role of reputation, discussed above, it was possible to infer such knowledge from the absence of proof to the contrary.[105] With police evidence about the reputation of an individual operating to construct a *prima facie* case, knowledge was a thin fault requirement that did not operate as a genuine bar to conviction. As suggested by what appears to be the low success rate of appeals against conviction, it was difficult to argue that the evidence was not sufficient to make out the charge.[106]

This open-textured offence structure supported flexible practices of policing, prosecution and punishment. Like the vagrancy laws of which they were a part, consorting laws were characterised by the high degree of discretion they afforded police and magistrates. The laws enabled police officers to arrest without a warrant an individual suspected of consorting if he or she was alleged to be consorting at the time of the arrest. At least in some cases, accidental meetings between individuals could be the subject of 'bookings' by the police and taken into account for the purpose of supporting a charge of habitual consorting.[107] Arrest for consorting also operated as a backup

103 Under the 'manifest criminality' pattern of criminality, the criminality of the defendant's act is objective, and it manifests the defendant's criminal purpose: see Fletcher, *Rethinking Criminal Law*, p. 89.

104 *Gabriel* v. *Lenthall* [1930] SASR 318 at 324; see also *Ex parte Finney; Re Miller & Anor* (1936) 50 WN (NSW) 190 at 191; *Dias* v. *O'Sullivan* [1949] SASR 195 at 200.

105 *Gabriel* v. *Lenthall* [1930] SASR 318; *Dias* v. *O'Sullivan* [1949] SASR 195 at 204.

106 See, e.g., *Canino* v. *Samuels* [1968] SASR 303 at 304.

107 See, e.g., *Beer* v. *Toms, Ex parte Toms* (1952) 46 QJPR 102 at 111. The only limitation on police powers that emerged sometime in the mid-century was the time period within which the instances of consorting had to occur. In NSW, this was 6 months, based on the requirement that summary proceedings must be commenced not later than 6 months following the alleged offence: see *Justices Act 1902* (NSW) s 56 and *Criminal Procedure Act 1986* (NSW) s 179(1). As a continuing offence, all instances of consorting had to occur within this timeframe: see Steel, 'Consorting in New South Wales', 573.

charge, used when it was not possible to make out a charge for another, more serious offence: indeed, it was possible that consorting provided the means by which to make an arrest once the police had concluded a person was a criminal.[108] The discretion that consorting laws allowed police linked the laws with bribery and corruption, as the threat of a consorting charge could be used to extract 'consideration in cash or kind', as well as to pressure individuals to 'dog' on their associates.[109] Once charged, consorting was tried in the summary jurisdiction, and magistrates also had significant discretion in deciding convictions and penalties. Consorting cases often turned on their facts – in particular, the degree of association required to satisfy the 'habitual' aspect of the offence[110] – and, reflecting widespread judicial support for policing practices, and public support for the laws themselves, rates of conviction seem to have been high. Few defendants had the resources required to appeal,[111] and, even where they may have reached a different conclusion on the facts of a particular case, appellate courts were reluctant to overturn convictions.[112]

Reflecting a debt to the laws of vagrancy, and the manifest nature of the crime, there was no such thing as 'innocent' consorting,[113] and individuals charged with consorting did not have many means by which to defend the charge. Alongside what appears to be the common defence argument that the number of associations did not amount to 'habitual' consorting, some individuals relied on the statutory defence available to a charge of consorting. This defence required that the person charged with the offence give 'to the satisfaction of the court a good account of his lawful means of support and also of his so consorting'.[114] As this indicates, the defendant bore the burden of proving this defence. Just as what constituted consorting was interpreted broadly, so the scope of this defence was interpreted narrowly. The logic of

[108] Steel, 'Consorting in New South Wales', 589.

[109] Woods, *A History of Criminal Law in New South Wales*, p. 392.

[110] See, e.g., *Brealy* v. *Buckley* [1934] Argus LR 371 at 372; *MacDonald* v. *The King* (1935) 52 CLR 739.

[111] The nature of police offences meant that if a person convicted of consorting contested his or her conviction, he or she did so via an action against the senior police officer or detective in charge of the prosecution. This meant that an individual appealing his or her conviction had to obtain an order *nisi* to review the decision, and the appeal court either discharged that order and upheld the conviction (see, e.g., *Brealy* v. *Buckley* [1934] Argus LR 371), or made the order absolute and quashed the conviction (see, e.g., *Guider* v. *Walker* [1933] VLR 413). This feature of police offences also meant that a number of appeals against conviction featured the same police officer: see, e.g., *Codd* v. *Lewis* (1944) 38 QJPR 135; *Codd* v. *Wall* (1944) 38 QJPR 141.

[112] See, e.g., *Patterson* v. *Harrison* [1957] Argus LR 1195.

[113] See *Johanson* v. *Dixon* (1979) 143 CLR 376 at 384 per Mason J (but in his dissent, Justice Murphy argued that this interpretation of the law gives consorting an overly broad scope: at 392–3).

[114] See, e.g., *Police Offences Act 1957* (Vic) s 69(d)(i).

this part of the law was explained by Justice Smith of the Supreme Court of Victoria, in a statement worth extracting in full:

> ... the view of the Legislature would seem to have been this: a person who habitually consorts with criminals and undesirable persons is likely to be supporting himself by preying on the community in some way, or to be under strong temptation to do so. Any such person may therefore be imprisoned for the protection of the community unless he shows he is not in fact a danger ... But such proof of present means cannot be accepted as sufficient, in itself, to show that he is not a danger. Even though he has means he must still be regarded as a danger because of his habitual consorting unless he gives, in addition, a good account of that consorting.[115]

As Justice Smith's comment indicates, providing evidence of lawful means of support undercut the manifest meaning of the act of consorting: that the accused was 'preying on the community in some way'. Thus, for an account of consorting to be a 'good account', it had to operate to excuse the conduct in some way, and not merely show that 'there was habitual consorting but nothing more'.[116]

Procedural Solutions to Substantive Challenges

Under the second generation of consorting laws, the broad contours of the offence have been carried over – associating with proscribed individuals with knowledge of their status – but the conduct and fault elements have been made more robust. In relation to conduct, in light of the potential of the laws for abuse, the requirement of 'habitual consorting' is now strictly defined, meaning that the laws are intended to capture only 'companionship, not mere conversation', and 'casual conversation on the street with an acquaintance' cannot amount to consorting.[117] Reliance on 'numerous instances of reiteration',[118] as required to support convictions for 'habitual consorting' under the first generation of laws, has been replaced with a requirement that the defendant associate with a specified number of individuals on a specified number of occasions. For example, in NSW, the offence provides that a person does not 'habitually consort' with convicted offenders unless he or she consorts with at least two such people and with each convicted offender on at least two occasions.[119] For the purposes of consorting, association now extends beyond in-person communications, to include any type of communication,

[115] See *Byrne* v. *Shearer* [1959] VR 606 at 613 (citing *Police Offences Act 1957* (Vic) s 69(d)(i)).

[116] *Johanson* v. *Dixon* (1979) 143 CLR 376 at 384 per Mason J. A 'good account' could be furnished by evidence that the defendant was associating with 'close relatives, for filial or family reasons, or because his occupation required him so to do' (384).

[117] *Forster* v. *Director of Public Prosecutions* (NSW) [2017] NSWSC 458, [59].

[118] *Dias* v. *O'Sullivan* [1949] SASR 195 at 201.

[119] See, e.g., *Crimes Act 1900* (NSW) s 93X(2). See also *Summary Offences Act 1953* (SA) s 13; Justice and Community Safety Directorate, *Discussion Paper*, p. 13.

including electronic communication, between individuals,[120] a change which has off set the narrowing effect of the stricter conduct requirements of the new laws.

In addition, in an effort to avoid the victimisation of vulnerable people, there have been some attempts to limit the class of people who may be convicted of the offence of consorting. In some jurisdictions, consorting is limited to those who are associating with individuals who have been convicted of serious offences. Thus, in Victoria, the scope of consorting is restricted to associations with those who have committed, or are reasonably suspected of committing, 'organised crime offences'.[121] In South Australia, consorting can only be charged in relation to individuals convicted of an indictable offence.[122] In Western Australia, it is an offence for an individual who has been convicted of certain declared drug offences to associate with another individual convicted of those offences.[123] These limitations on the scope of consorting laws – to serious and organised crime – reflect the changed orientation of the second generation of laws – toward security of the state – discussed above.

The fault element for the offence of consorting – knowledge of the criminal status of the other person – has been made a (more) genuine element of the offence. While, in general, the laws continue to criminalise association in itself, rather than require an intention to associate for a criminal purpose,[124] there have been two developments in relation to the fault element of the offence. The first development clarifies the fault requirement. As discussed above, while there were some references in the case law to 'the necessary blameworthy condition of mind' required by the first generation of laws, this amounted only to knowledge of the reputation of the persons with whom the defendant had been in company, and because of the role of reputation, it was possible to infer such knowledge from the absence of proof to the contrary. Under the second generation of laws, the fault requirement conforms with 'the recognisably modern tripartite division of criminal fault' – intention, recklessness and negligence.[125] For example, under the South Australian laws, it is necessary for the person to know or be reckless as to the status of the person

[120] See, e.g., *Crimes Act 1900* (NSW) s 93X.

[121] See *Criminal Organisations Control Amendment (Unlawful Associations) Act 2015* (Vic).

[122] *Summary Offences Act 1953* (SA) s 13.

[123] *Criminal Law Amendment (Simple Offences) Act 2004* (WA) s 32, inserting *Criminal Code 1913* (WA) s 557J. A similar consorting offence applies to convicted child sex offenders (s 557K); see also *Director of Public Prosecutions (WA) v. McGarry* [No. 9] [2016] WASC 306.

[124] Among the Australian jurisdictions, only the Commonwealth and the Northern Territory laws restrict police officers to issuing consorting warnings only where they believe on reasonable grounds that such a warning will prevent the commission of an offence: see *Criminal Code 1995* (Cth) s 104.2(2) and *Summary Offences Act* (NT) s 55A.

[125] L. Farmer, 'Criminal Responsibility and the Proof of Guilt', in M. D. Dubber and L. Farmer (eds.), *Modern Histories of Crime and Punishment* (Stanford: Stanford University Press, 2007), p. 43.

with whom they consort.[126] The second development relating to fault concerns a change in the procedural scaffolding around the laws, which functions to buttress the knowledge requirement of the offence. Here, a particular instance of association will only count for the purposes of a charge where an individual has already been warned about associating with that individual. Thus, under the Queensland and NSW provisions, an individual must be given either one or two 'official warnings' by a police officer that he or she is associating with a convicted offender, and that consorting with a convicted offender is an offence, before he or she can be convicted of consorting.[127] Changes to the procedural scaffolding around consorting reflect the way in which the state is now brought into relations between individuals, and I pick up on this point below.

Even with the tightening up of the conduct and fault elements of the offences, consorting laws are again a useful tool in the toolbox of police powers. Revealing a degree of continuity in the operation of the first and second generation of laws, and despite the restriction of consorting to serious or indictable offences, police are using consorting as part of 'observations of people spending time together in places open to the public'.[128] This has meant that certain groups, including Aboriginal peoples, have been disproportionately affected by the new consorting laws. A review by the NSW Ombudsman found that the NSW laws are used in relation to vulnerable individuals such as young people and homeless people.[129] As the Supreme Court of NSW noted in hearing an appeal from the first person convicted of the new offence of consorting in that state, police evidence had included a 'disarmingly frank account' of the use of the consorting law to deal with recidivist offenders and 'crime hot spots' in town.[130] This level of continuity indicates that, on an operational level, consorting continues to be used in policing low-level offences and protecting public order, which itself reveals that the main targets of the laws – suspect populations, and status as much as conduct – are common to the first and second generation of laws.

Consistent with the modern structure of criminal responsibility – across conduct, fault and defences – in which limitations on liability have formalised as either restrictions on the scope of offences or as defences, there are now clearer

126 *Serious and Organised Crime (Control) Act 2008* (SA) s 35(2).

127 See *Criminal Code 1899* (Qld) s 77B(1)(b) and *Crimes Act 1900* (NSW) s 93X(3) respectively.

128 New South Wales Ombudsman, The Consorting Law: Report of the Operation of Part 3A, Division 7 of the *Crimes Act 1900* (2016), p. 4.

129 See NSW Ombudsman, *The Consorting Law*. The Ombudsman found that, in the first three years of its operation, 3300 people were either issued with a consorting warning, or had others warned about consorting with them; only 42 people were charged with 46 offences of habitually consorting (p. 3). This report referred to the 'lawful but inappropriate' use of consorting, and recommended the inclusion of an 'objects' clause in the legislation to state that the purpose of the law is to prevent serious criminal offending (pp. 5, 8, and recommendation 19).

130 *Forster* v. *Director of Public Prosecutions (NSW)* [2017] NSWSC 458, [26] (referring to evidence before the Magistrate who had convicted the appellant of consorting).

limits on consorting offences. Under the current laws, these limits are carved out from within the statutory provisions. For example, under the Commonwealth offence of 'associating with terrorist organisations', communication with a 'close family member' about 'a matter of family or domestic concern' cannot form the basis of a consorting charge.[131] In NSW, consorting is not an offence where it is 'reasonable in the circumstances', which includes associating with family members, for employment or education, and consorting in the course of receiving legal advice.[132] In Queensland, particular acts of consorting – with family members and for the purposes of lawful business – are to be 'disregarded' under the law.[133] As this statutory language indicates, these associations are still consorting, but cannot form the basis of a conviction for the offence. The burden of establishing these defences or exclusions is on the person charged with consorting. These provisions delineate a circumscribed legal zone, beyond the reach of the criminal law, for particular types of interpersonal contact.

As this discussion suggests, the tighter and more modern structure of consorting laws in the second generation has been realised in part via the formalisation of procedures as much as by changes to the component parts of the offence. These procedures expose the role of criminal justice institutions and criminal processes in addressing modern demands for legitimation in criminal law. These formalised procedures concern the policing practices – including record-keeping, the use of police discretion and surveillance – that have developed around the offences of consorting (and allied criminal organisation offences). These procedures constitute a significant buttressing of the laws themselves. Thus, the system of police warnings that must precede a charge of consorting in NSW and Queensland jurisdictions 'has the practical effect that a person so warned would find it difficult to say that he or she did not know the persons with whom he or she was thereafter consorting were convicted offenders'.[134] As this indicates, these warnings put an individual on notice about the status of his or her associates. In addition to both requiring and depending on extensive record keeping, these procedural provisions enable consorting laws to meet the enhanced rule of law demands of the current era. As explained by the Queensland Taskforce in advocating for a new consorting law in that state, utilising an offence based on the criminal convictions of the person with whom the individual is now associating is the appropriate way to avoid unfairness to individuals.[135]

[131] *Criminal Code 1995* (Cth) s 102.8(4) (the evidential burden is on the accused).

[132] *Crimes Act 1900* (NSW) s 93Y. The burden is on the defendant to satisfy the court in relation to these defences. The NSW Ombudsman's review of the operation of the NSW laws recommended adding to these defences, and defining 'family members' to ensure recognition of Aboriginal kinship relations: see NSW Ombudsman, *The Consorting Law*, ch. 10.

[133] See *Criminal Code 1899* (Qld) s 77C.

[134] *Tajjour* v. *New South Wales* [26] per French CJ (in relation to the NSW offence).

[135] See Taskforce on Organised Crime Legislation, *Final Report* 2016 (contrasting the laws with the then existing laws targeting criminal organisations).

The role of formalised procedures that have developed around the offence of consorting reveals the changed position of the state in relations of responsibility between individuals, as I discuss in the following section of the chapter.

Relations: From 'Companionship with Thieves' to 'Friendship with the State'

The first and second generation of consorting laws analysed in the preceding sections correspond with different relations of responsibility between individuals or 'others'. According to these different relations of responsibility, *to* whom or what and *for* what individuals are responsible has changed. Under the first generation, the laws proscribed 'companionship with thieves', and individuals were responsible to the community for the threat or danger they posed to public order. By contrast, under the second generation of laws, consorting inculcates 'friendship with the state', according to which individuals are responsible to the state and a more extensive conception of responsibility – encompassing personal attitudes and self-regulation – now sustains relations of responsibility.

The relations of responsibility that correspond with this first generation of laws proscribed 'companionship with thieves', with the laws operating to keep individuals from 'undesirable' groups apart from each other. As discussed above, the first generation of consorting laws was oriented towards public order, its mode of responsibility was social, and it took an older legal form. Under these laws, relations of responsibility reinforced existing, stratified social relations. In this respect, the consorting laws dovetailed with other legal and social practices that produced and reproduced existing social relations, aiming to isolate and marginalise individuals who threatened those relations. Thus, notions such as 'reputation' were technical terms in use in the criminal law, but their meaning was socially derived. As this suggests, the first generation of consorting laws enlisted social meanings – around the racial, classed and gendered identity and status of individuals subject to the laws – for legal and law enforcement ends. In this sense, like the wider category of vagrancy laws of which they were a part, consorting laws operationalised the widely understood and broadly accepted notion of 'the criminal classes' that prevailed at the time, and which reflected the distinction drawn by the police, as well as members of the population between 'the decent citizen and the criminal'.[136]

What individuals were responsible for under these relations of responsibility extended only so far. Under these relations, and against a background of a criminal legal and police focus on the prevention and deterrence of crime,

[136] See Finnane, *Police and Government*, pp. 79, 80.

individuals charged with consorting were responsible for causing harm or disorder, or, more accurately, for raising the possibility of the threat of harm or disorder, in certain public contexts. The emphasis of consorting was on the threat or disorder posed by 'undesirable' individuals congregating (seeking 'companionship') in public space, with such congregations perceived as highly visible signs of deviancy which exposed the limits of social control. It was the public display these marginalised individuals presented that was targeted through consorting laws.[137] In this context, the threat that was posed by these individuals was a threat to the community, where community is understood as a natural realm made up of the interactions of people in particular physical locations, and what was required of individuals was desistance from threatening conduct. Thus, the threat posed by prostitution was to social purity and the health of the population, as well as to the stability of the gender relations and family structures. Similarly, the threat of low-level offending, such as petty theft, was a threat to perceptions of safety and the sanctity of the home. This idea of threats to the community was shot through by class, as those targeted by consorting laws transgressed middle class morality as well as criminal laws.[138] As this discussion suggests, under these relations of responsibility, responsibility was state-defined but was not a responsibility to the state.

Between the first and second generations of consorting laws, relations between individuals underwent thorough reconstruction. In broad terms, this change in relations between individuals is linked to what sociologists and others have conceptualised as the shift to a distinctive phase of modernity,[139] which is variously labelled 'advanced liberal', 'late', 'second', or 'reflexive' modernity.[140] For these scholars, changed relations between individuals are central to this shift, marking out contemporary societies. Interpersonal relations have been thoroughly reconstructed along horizontal lines, itself a nuanced development that encompasses a number of factors, such as the declining significance of class.[141] In the current era, relations between individuals are now characterised by a radical reflexivity, whereby individuals are actively engaged in a constant

137 See J. Kimber, '"A Nuisance to the Community": Policing the Vagrant Woman' (2010) 34(3) *Journal of Australian Studies* 275–293, 279 (in relation to vagrancy laws in general).

138 Kimber, 'A Nuisance to the Community', 276.

139 Modernity is a contested concept: it is used here to denote a distinctive 'mode of life', in which the state, as opposed to local and religious institutions, provides the main framework: see A. Giddens, *The Consequences of Modernity* (Stanford: Stanford University Press, 1990), p. 4.

140 See N. Rose, *Inventing Our Selves: Psychology, Power, and Personhood* (Cambridge: Cambridge University Press, 1998); D. Garland, *The Culture of Control: Crime and Social Order in Contemporary Society* (Chicago: University of Chicago Press, 2001); U. Beck, *Risk Society: Towards a New Modernity* (Mark Ritter trans, London: Sage Publications, 1992); A. Giddens, *The Consequences of Modernity*; A. Giddens, *Modernity and Self-Identity: Self and Society in the Late Modern Age* (Stanford: Stanford University Press, 1991).

141 See, e.g., S. Hall, 'The Meaning of New Times', in D. Morley and K. Chen (eds.), *Stuart Hall: Critical Dialogues in Cultural Studies* (London: Routledge, 1996).

process of self-individualisation.[142] In the context of the increasing complexity of identities, relations with others are a crucial aspect of the reflexivity of the self, and, in this context, choice becomes primary, as relations with others are not fixed but changing, and personal identity is constantly being created and recreated.[143] The shift from modernity to late modernity also entailed changed relations between individuals and the state, as declining trust in political institutions, and rising perceptions of insecurity, has led to a recalibration of politics and political subjectivities.[144]

Against this wider background of reconstructed interpersonal and intersubjective relations, the way in which criminal responsibility organises relations of responsibility has changed. These relations now inculcate 'friendship with the state', with relations of responsibility between individuals assuming a flat and standardised structure, and the state brought into relations between individuals in a distinct way. As discussed above, the orientation of these laws is to the security of the state, their mode of responsibility is legal, and they conform to a 'new' offence structure. These laws rest not on external social statuses or meanings (coalescing around 'undesirability'), as under the first generation of laws, but on *other* legal practices and technologies. Thus, they rely not on overtly moralised concepts such as reputation, but on technical and morally neutral devices such as criminal records, which themselves depend on modern liberal governance practices. In addition, the second generation of laws have a somewhat tighter modern form – conforming with the familiar common law construction of criminal responsibility across conduct, fault and defences – and realised as much via formalised procedures around police practices as changes to the component parts of individual responsibility for crime.

Under these relations of responsibility, what individuals are responsible *for* in their relations with others has changed. In the current era, and against the backdrop of liberal governance practices that characterise collective life in Australia and elsewhere, the individual is *activated* in his or her interpersonal associations: he or she is addressed in his or her community, which is understood as a technique of governance rather than a natural phenomenon, and as an individual who has certain bonds to a surrounding network of individuals.[145] In this context, the significance of the conduct of individuals – the politics of conduct – extends and alters the meaning of criminal behaviour, like associating with criminals. Such conduct is regarded as reflecting back on

[142] See, e.g., U. Beck and E. Beck-Gernsheim, *Individualization Institutionalized: Individualism and Its Social and Political Consequences* (London: Sage, 2002).

[143] See generally N. Rose, *Powers of Freedom: Reframing Political Thought* (Cambridge: Cambridge University Press, 1999).

[144] See A. Giddens, 'Living in a Post-Traditional Society', in U. Beck, A. Giddens and S. Lash, *Reflexive Modernisation: Politics, Tradition and Aesthetics in the Modern Social Order* (Cambridge: Polity Press, 1994).

[145] N. Rose, *Powers of Freedom*, p. 176, and more generally, 176–79.

the subject, representing a reflective moral or ethical position as opposed to a single act at one point in time.[146] As a result, a more extensive conception of responsibility – encompassing personal attitudes and self-regulation – now comes along with relations of responsibility between individuals. Thus, in their orientation to the security of the state, consorting laws implicate individuals' attitudes to practices of securing the state. As this suggests, private or personal mental space, and self-regulation, is now as or more important to consorting as public space and policing by the police.

As per these changed relations of responsibility, the individual is responsible *to* the state, as the state is brought *into* the relationship between individuals in a distinct way. On the level of form, consorting laws encode a nebulous, but meaningful, standardisation of relations between individuals and the state. Here, all individuals are brought into the *same* relation with the state. As indicated by the elaborate system of police warnings about association with criminals, and the extensive formal record keeping that now surrounds the offence of consorting, referred to above, the laws establish a uniform legal relation between the individuals falling under the laws and the state: via consorting, all interpersonal associations can be plotted in relation to wider, state-sanctioned practices around matters such as security. On the level of substance, the nature of the standardised relations between individuals and the state has changed. I suggest that, in these relations, the state is posited as a 'friend', albeit a weak institutional form of a friend. With its hallmarks of mutuality and equality, and correlates of loyalty and allegiance, friendship is a mode of relation characterised by choice: it may be contrasted with unchosen, fixed relations, characterised by role or custom, and with unequal relations, characterised by dominance, vulnerability, or dependency.[147] Friendship is a useful concept for grasping relations between individuals and the state because, in the current era, it has become a privileged type of social relation that corresponds with the current emphasis on self-individualisation, and, in the context of loss of trust in authority, reflects an aspiration for non-hierarchical interpersonal relations.[148] The thick, social notion of friendship helpfully captures the substance of these changed relations between individuals and the state as these relations approximate interpersonal relations.

The significance of the idea that consorting now encodes 'friendship with the state' is that, via consorting, the criminal law is encoding loyalty and

[146] Ibid., pp. 178–9.

[147] There is a large sociological and historical literature on friendship: see, e.g., R. Pahl, *On Friendship* (Cambridge: Polity Press, 2000); G. Allan, 'Friendship, Sociology and Social Structure' (1998) 15(5) *Journal of Social and Personal Relationships* 685–702; M. Peel, 'New Worlds of Friendship: The Early Twentieth Century', in B. Caine (ed.), *Friendship: A History* (London: Equinox Publishing, 2009) and M. Peel, L. Reed and J. Walter, 'The Importance of Friends: The Most Recent Past', in B. Caine (ed.), *Friendship: A History* (London: Equinox Publishing, 2009).

[148] See D. Chambers, *New Social Ties: Contemporary Connections in a Fragmented Society* (Basingstoke: Palgrave Macmillan, 2006), pp. 2–3, and, more generally, Introduction.

allegiance. This is overlaying the older ideas of harm and threat that animated the first generation of consorting laws. Under consorting, the individual subject to the laws is posited as having to choose between (criminal) 'friends' and the state and thus not associating with the 'friends'. Crucially, and reflecting the hallmarks of friendship, this choice transcends obligation and is regarded as reciprocal: there is an equality of exchange across the social goods of freedom and protection, and the interests of the state – around its own security – are rendered equivalent to those of a friend. Thus, even as consorting continues to be used to police low-level threats and public order, the notion of moral wrongness at the heart of the offence has changed: what is now wrong about consorting is less about threats in public space and more about attitudinal disloyalty, or dis-allegiance. In this sense, what is said to be distinctive about organised crime (to which consorting is now allied) – with recognisable leadership, hierarchies, rules, symbolic identification, and codes of silence[149] – when compared with other crime also reveals what it is that the consorting laws are now condemning: loyalty to a person, people, or a group or organisation other than, and set up in opposition to, the state.

This chapter offered an analysis of consorting laws in Australian jurisdictions. Taking into account their orientation, mode (denoting the way in which criminal responsibility is expressed) and form, I argued that the laws fall into two generations. These laws correspond with different relations of criminal responsibility between individuals or 'others'. The first generation of consorting offences proscribed 'companionship with thieves', with relations of responsibility reinforcing existing, highly stratified social relations, with the laws operating to keep different categories of 'undesirables' apart from each other. By contrast, the second generation of laws inculcate 'friendship with the state', with relations of responsibility assuming a flat and standardised structure, according to which the state is brought into the relationship between individuals in a distinct way – as a 'friend'. This revealed that to whom or what, and for what, individuals are responsible in their relations with others has changed over time – from responsibility to the community for causing harm, or the threat of harm, in certain public contexts, to a more extensive conception of responsibility to the state that encompasses personal attitudes and self-regulation.

149 These features of organised crime are recognised as impediments to traditional policing tactics: see Government of South Australia, *Inquiry into the Legislative Arrangements to Outlaw Serious and Organized Crime Groups*, p. 56.

8

State

This chapter provides the third and final of my investigations into relations of responsibility. As argued in Chapter 2, the significance of criminal responsibility arises from the way in which it organises keys sets of relations – between self, others and the state – as relations of responsibility. Like the preceding two chapters, the analysis presented here foregrounds one of the three nodes of my tripartite schema of relations of responsibility: here, I focus on the state, which I understand as a set of institutions coordinating a large set of regulatory and governance practices. My investigation of the state in relations of responsibility entails going behind doctrinal arrangements concerning individual responsibility for crime, and the procedural setting in which these arrangements play out – the criminal trial – to open up the prior issue of the state's position and function in relations of responsibility. As I show in this chapter, the position and function of the state in relations of responsibility is dynamic, reflecting changing social and political norms regarding the role of the state.

A study of the state in relations of responsibility could be undertaken in different ways. I choose to examine these relations through government responses to (allegations of) crimes against children in institutions.[1] This is an apposite focus for three main reasons. First, the broad history of child welfare in Australia exists in 'intimate relation to the history of the state in general', particularly through the criminal law, courts and penal institutions, and welfare services.[2] Thus, although a number of children's institutions are run by charities rather than by governments, each operates within a web of regulation which encompasses welfare, immigration and guardianship laws, licensing systems, and financial payments. Second, and as I discuss in this

[1] It is estimated that over 500,000 Australians spent time in orphanages, industrial schools and other institutions or the care of families other than their own over the twentieth century: see Senate Community Affairs References Committee, Parliament of Australia, *Forgotten Australians: A Report on Australians Who Experienced Institutional or Out-of-Home Care as Children* (2004), xv.

[2] R. van Krieken, *Children and the State: Social Control and the Formation of Australian Child Welfare* (Sydney: Allen & Unwin, 1991), p. 5.

chapter, government responses to crimes against children in institutions intersect with responses to the situation of Aboriginal peoples, a distinctive feature of the Australian story of the state in relations of responsibility. Third, as a result of recent high-profile public inquiries, most notably, the Federal *Royal Commission into Institutional Responses to Child Sexual Abuse*,[3] crimes against children in institutions (now conceptualised as institutional child abuse) have become a prominent part of the criminal justice terrain in Australia, generating unprecedented public discussion of both individual responsibility and state responsibility. This is the case although it is widely acknowledged that the Commission's focus – institutional child sexual abuse – constitutes a 'small fraction' of the total number of child sexual abuse matters, and that child sexual abuse is one of several types of child abuse.[4] With my focus on government responses to crimes against children in institutions, I examine an issue which represents the preeminent collective reckoning with state responsibility in Australia.

To examine government responses to crimes against children in institutions, I break away from the standard scholarly focus on criminal doctrines and criminal trials, and review public inquiries that were conducted into children's institutions over the twentieth century and the first years of the twenty-first century. Here, public inquiries are understood broadly, as those inquiries initiated by governments that are more or less independent of the executive, parliament and judiciary.[5] While the focus of inquiries in the current era is on child abuse – and child sexual abuse in particular – reflecting the current prominence of child abuse on the social and political horizon,[6] historically, public inquiries did not specify crimes so precisely. Indeed, as I discuss below, for a part of the period under discussion in this chapter, crimes against children in institutions were not conceptualised as such. Acknowledging this, public inquiries into children's institutions – examining problems, treatment

[3] Commonwealth, Royal Commission into Institutional Responses to Child Sexual Abuse, *Final Report* (2017) ('Royal Commission into Institutional Responses'). The Commission operated from 2013 to 2017. I take the definition of institution from the letters patent establishing the Royal Commission into Institutional Responses to Child Sexual Abuse – 'any public or private body, agency, association, club, institution, organisation or other entity or group of entities of any kind … and however described', excluding the family: see Royal Commission into Institutional Responses, *Final Report*, vol. 1, Appendix A.

[4] See A. Freiberg, H. Donnelly and K. Gelb, *Sentencing for Child Sexual Abuse in Institutional Contexts*, Report for the Royal Commission into Institutional Responses to Child Sexual Abuse (2015), p. 9; Queensland, Commission of Inquiry into Abuse of Children in Queensland Institutions, *Report* (1999), iv–v, respectively.

[5] See Australian Law Reform Commission (ALRC), *Royal Commissions and Official Inquiries*, Discussion Paper No. 75 (2009), [1.10] (defining public inquiries as inquiries conducted on an ad hoc basis by an entity established by, but external to, the executive arm of government).

[6] On changing meanings and significance of child abuse over time, see I. Hacking, 'The Making and Molding of Child Abuse' (1991) 17(2) *Critical Inquiry* 253–88.

and conditions or crimes as well as allied issues – have been a feature of the Australian political landscape since before the turn of the twentieth century.[7] There is now a long line of such inquiries, including state, territory and Federal parliamentary inquiries, ad hoc inquiries and royal commissions, covering matters of juvenile justice, child welfare, social services, and the law, policy and practice relating to Aboriginal children, as well as what is now identified as institutional child abuse and institutional child sexual abuse.[8] This has led one commentator to label the Australian response to institutional child abuse 'ongoing public investigation'.[9] Over time, as child abuse has risen to prominence, these inquiries have come to attract significant national and international attention.

As a specific mechanism of liberal democratic government, public inquiries are particularly useful for my purposes because they illuminate the state's position in a particular way. Public inquiries do not occur automatically through democratic processes: rather, they are ad hoc and involve political discretion, special authorisation and targeted resources, thus involving the government (and specifically, the executive or parliament) in a self-regulatory or reflexive mode.[10] In general terms, public inquiries tend to be inquisitorial or policy-oriented rather than adversarial, and geared towards establishing factual accounts of incidents or problems that may involve multiple individuals and institutions, and to learning lessons in order to prevent such problems from occurring again in the future.[11] These inquiries are public in a distinctive sense, in that they involve a public engagement with a problem that has attracted the concern of either political leaders and, increasingly over time,

[7] Shurlee Swain lists 83 inquiries into institutions providing care for children between 1852 and 2013, and 57 between 1900 and 2013, including coronial inquiries and inquiries into adult institutions that also housed child residents. Swain develops a taxonomy of these inquiries according to what she identifies as their purpose: inquiries concerned with the development of the child welfare system (1850s to post-World War II period), those established to respond to allegations of abuse (1860s–1990s) and those focused on listening to the testimony of survivors (1990s to present): see S. Swain, *History of Australian inquiries reviewing institutions providing care for children*, Report for the Royal Commission into Institutional Responses to Child Sexual Abuse (2014).

[8] Royal Commissions, which are authorised by state and federal Acts (see, e.g., *Royal Commissions Act 1902* (Cth); *Royal Commissions Act 1923* (NSW)), are 'the highest form of public inquiry in Australia': ALRC, *Royal Commissions and Official Inquiries*, [1.1.7].

[9] See K. Gleeson, 'Responsibility and Redress: Theorising Gender Justice in the Context of Catholic Clerical Child Sexual Abuse in Ireland and Australia' (2016) 39 *University of New South Wales Law Journal* 779–812, 793.

[10] See generally S. Prasser, *Royal Commissions and Public Inquiries in Australia* (Sydney: LexisNexis, 2006), ch. 1.

[11] A. Burgess, 'The Changing Character of Public Inquiries in the (Risk) Regulatory State' (2011) 6(1) *British Politics* 3–29, 6–7. This latter feature of public inquiries leads Burgess to argue that they fit well in the current era of concern about risk, as they revolve around 'how authority responds to demands for protection' (10).

the public itself.[12] Taken together, these formal features of public inquiries construct problems as multifaceted, and adopt a broad approach to possible responses or 'solutions' to such problems. And, crucially for my interest in relations of responsibility underpinning criminal responsibility principles and practices, these inquiries open up, rather than close off, questions about the state in relations of responsibility.

In this chapter, I argue that there are four historic positions of the state in relations of responsibility. As per the first position, prominent in the first decades of the twentieth century, children and children's institutions were linked to the development of the Australian nation, but in the context of limited capacity, the role of governments was restricted to advocating the modernisation of institutions and child welfare practices to deal with perceived problems. The second position of the state, prominent in the middle decades of the century, involves governments in the development of social welfare and criminal justice institutions, with crimes against children in families, and to a lesser extent in institutions, coming to receive greater attention. The third position of the state is prominent in the last decades of the century and early years of the twenty-first century, and is characterised by a complex mix of assuming and denying responsibility for crimes against children in institutions, as Australian governments negotiated their responsibility across the boundary between past and present, and Empire and nation. As per the fourth position of the state, which has been prominent in recent years, governments are (re-)negotiating responsibility in a global context, and embracing responsibility for crimes against children in a more wholesale way, with the civil law as well as the criminal law harnessed to the task of addressing what is now perceived as a serious injustice. Each of these positions of the state in relations of responsibility correlates with a division of responsibility *between* the state and individuals, where such a division is a dynamic outcome of changing norms about the state and individuals.

Responsibility in a New Nation

The first historic position of the state in relations of responsibility links institutions for children with the development of the Australian nation, but, in the context of limited capacity overall, the role of governments was restricted. This position of the state, which was prominent in the first decades of the twentieth century, involves governments encouraging modernisation of children's institutions and child welfare practices, on the basis

[12] See generally Burgess, 'The Changing Character of Public Inquiries in the (Risk) Regulatory State'; Prasser, *Royal Commissions and Public Inquiries in Australia*, ch. 2.

that the benefits of intervention outweigh any particular problems (not typically conceptualised as crimes) occurring in particular institutions at particular times.

Institutions for children were among the first institutions established after colonisation.[13] Mirroring the practice of institutionalisation that was then current in Britain, institutionalisation was regarded as rescuing children from the corrupting influences of their environment.[14] From the mid-1800s century, increased economic activity and population growth in the cities of Melbourne and Sydney made the issue of children living on the streets and in slums a social concern: such children were seen as both a threat to public order and social stability (arising from child prostitution, for instance), and as victims of neglect.[15] From the last decades of the nineteenth century, as demand for child welfare increased and government institutions developed in the now independent colonies, children's departments and separate systems of juvenile courts and corrections were established.[16] These courts dealt with both criminal cases (juvenile offenders) and welfare matters (child neglect), effectively collapsing the distinction between the two in a way that became a hallmark of the juvenile justice system.[17] Children's courts were empowered to place children in industrial schools and reformatory schools – 'workhouses in all but name' – which had been established in each jurisdiction by this time.[18] At this time (and for the first decades of the twentieth century), welfare policy was trained on procedures governing the removal of children and the transfer of guardianship to the state, an administrative process that gave the state extensive powers over the child ('ward').[19] Throughout this period, neglect

[13] See J. Ramsland, *Children of the Back Lanes: Destitute and Neglected Children in Colonial New South Wales* (Sydney: New South Wales University Press, 1986), ch. 1; see also J.F. Forgarty, 'Some Aspects of the Early History of Child Protection in Australia' (2008) 78 *Family Matters* 52–9, 56.

[14] Senate Standing Committee on Social Welfare, Parliament of Australia, *Children in Institutional and Other Forms of Care: A National Perspective* (1985), p. 13; S. Swain, 'Institutional Abuse: A Long History' (2018) 42(2) *Journal of Australian Studies* 153–63, 158, 160.

[15] See Committee of Enquiry into Child Care Services in Victoria, Parliament of Victoria, *Report* (1976), p. 14; see also D. Scott and S. Swain, *Confronting Cruelty: Historical Perspectives on Child Protection in Australia* (Melbourne: Melbourne University Press, 2002), p. 4; see also van Krieken, *Children and the State*, p. 79. Vagrancy laws were used by police to deal with juvenile offenders or with children found begging or homeless.

[16] South Australia was the first jurisdiction to legislate for juvenile courts: see *State Children's Act 1895* (SA) (formalising what was already a practice of separating juvenile cases from the police court cases); see also *Neglected Children and Juvenile Offences Act 1905* (NSW); *Children's Court Act 1906* (Vic): for discussion see M. Finnane *Punishment in Australian Society* (Melbourne: Oxford University Press, 1997), pp. 93–98.

[17] Parliament of Australia, *Forgotten Australians*, [2.93].

[18] Parliament of Australia, *Forgotten Australians*, [3.14], and S. Swain, 'Beyond Child Migration: Inquiries, Apologies and Implications for the Writing of Transnational Child Welfare History' (2016) 13(1) *History Australia* 139–52, 141, respectively.

[19] Parliament of Australia, *Children in Institutional and Other Forms of Care*, p. 13.

and delinquency were perceived to be problems of the working class,[20] and, in their focus on the 'neglect' of children, children's departments and courts utilised a broad, moralised and classed category that encompassed parental immorality and actual or potential juvenile delinquency as well as cruelty.[21]

Following Federation in 1901, child welfare systems and practices were overlaid with a new nation-building rationality, which was underpinned by racialised concerns with the small size of the Australian population and perceived need for the growth of the 'white race'. According to this rationale, (white) children were citizens who would develop the new nation of Australia.[22] As the 1921 Western Australian Royal Commission into the state children's department stated, 'the nation which realises that [the child is its best asset] ... will be truly great'.[23] This nation-building rationality spurred a number of initiatives – including the supervision of mothers of new born infants and the reform of child labour practices, in efforts to reduce infant mortality and improve child welfare[24] – as well as the development of a nascent welfare system (limited to old age and invalidity).[25] At this time, enhanced regulation through child welfare services strengthened government responses to delinquency and family dysfunction, and increased the numbers of children under supervision.[26] These decades also saw increased reliance on the boarding out system, which provided 'family-like care' for children removed from their homes, with children allocated to families viewed as 'more respectable' than their own.[27] Although boarding out did not replace children's institutions, the profile of boarding out across Australia allowed reformers to claim that they were world leaders in child welfare, and that Australia was taking a national rather than philanthropic approach to state care of children.[28] In addition, it was in the context of

[20] See N. Musgrove, 'The Role and Importance of History', in J. Sköld and S. Swain (eds.), *Apologies and the Legacy of Abuse of Children in 'Care': International Perspectives* (Basingstoke: Palgrave Macmillan, 2015), p. 157.

[21] Scott and Swain, *Confronting Cruelty*, pp. 5–6.

[22] Ibid., pp. 54–5.

[23] Western Australia, Royal Commission on State Children and Charities Department, *Report* (1921), p. 13.

[24] See, e.g., *Infant Life Protection Act 1904* (NSW); see for discussion G. D. Woods, *A History of Criminal Law in New South Wales Volume 2: The New State, 1901–1955* (Sydney: The Federation Press, 2018), pp. 71–2; Scott and Swain, Confronting Cruelty, ch. 3. The 'maternalism' of the early twentieth century was influenced by the temperance movement and Christian organisations: see C. Evans, 'Excellent Women and Troublesome Children: State Foster Care in Tasmania, 1896–1918' (2002) 83 *Labour History* 133–148.

[25] The effects of the economic recession of the 1890s, the emergence of the Labor Party at the turn of the century, and the influence of ideas from England that welfare could play a role in 'consolidating the gains of large-scale industrialisation' prepared the way for these early welfare initiatives: see T. Carney and P. Hanks, *Social Security in Australia* (Melbourne: Oxford University Press, 1994), p. 30.

[26] See generally van Krieken, *Children and the State*, ch. 5.

[27] Swain, 'Institutional Abuse', p. 156; van Krieken, *Children and the State*, p. 78, respectively.

[28] Swain, 'Beyond Child Migration', pp. 143–4.

nation-building that the practice of accepting child migrants from Britain began, supported initially by shared goals around European settlement of the spaces of Empire,[29] as I discuss below.

The nation-building rationale sustained particular forms of government intervention into the lives of Aboriginal children and Aboriginal adults. In the colonial and post-colonial period, government responsibility in relation to Aboriginal peoples was thoroughly racialised and paternalistic: borrowing Peter Fitzpatrick's words, it was 'responsibility for' rather than 'responsibility to',[30] meaning that Aboriginal peoples were objects rather than subjects of state intervention. This responsibility – in the language of a 1928 public inquiry, 'for the upliftment of a downtrodden race'[31] – was aimed at 'civilising' Aboriginal peoples for membership of the modern Australian nation and liberal citizenship.[32] This responsibility was embodied in the protection system, which, from its establishment at the end of the nineteenth century until its demise in the second half of the twentieth century, placed Aboriginal peoples under the near-total control of Chief Protectors and Protection Boards through laws governing employment, wages or rations, movement, marriage and all other aspects of life.[33] The racialised paternalism sustaining protection constructed Aboriginal peoples as a burden on governments and the Australia nation. For instance, in public inquiries, Aboriginal peoples were reported as being vulnerable to 'wasting their money', or 'moral abuse' (through prostitution, for example), but the concern this gave rise to was their dependency on government relief, or the 'trouble' caused for 'working natives' or white communities located close to camps (in transmitting venereal disease, for

[29] See generally E. Boucher, *Empire's Children: Child Emigrations, Welfare, and the Decline of the British World, 1869–1967* (Cambridge: Cambridge University Press, 2014), Introduction.

[30] See P. Fitzpatrick, 'Terminal Legality: Imperialism and the (De)composition of Law', in D. Kirkby and C. Coleborne (eds.), *Law, History, Colonialism: The Reach of Empire* (Manchester: Manchester University Press, 2001), p. 22 (analysing colonial state responsibility for native peoples).

[31] Parliament of Australia, *The Aboriginals and Half-Castes of Central Australia and North Australia* (1928), p. 30.

[32] R. van Krieken, 'The 'Stolen Generations' and Cultural Genocide: The Forced Removal of Australian Indigenous Children from Their Families and Its Implications for the Sociology of Childhood' (1999) 6(3) *Childhood* 297–311, 300–2.

[33] See for discussion Human Rights and Equal Opportunity Commission (HREOC), *Bringing Them Home: Report of the National Inquiry into the Separation of Aboriginal and Torres Strait Islander Children from Their Families* (1997), ch. 2. Some Chief Protectors have become notorious in Australian history for their zealous enforcement of the law: e.g. A. O. Neville (Chief Protector, Western Australia, 1915–1936, and Commissioner for Native Affairs, 1936–1940): see A. Haebich and R. H. W. Reece, 'Neville, Auber Octavius (1875–1954)', in G. Serle (ed.), *Australian Dictionary of Biography Volume 11: 1891–1939* (Melbourne: Melbourne University Press, 1988). Even individuals who were regarded as progressive for the time, such as John Bleakley (Chief Protector, Northern Territory, 1914–1942), were thoroughly immersed in the racist ideology of the period: see R. Evans, 'John William Bleakley (1879–1957)', in B. Nairn and G. Serle (eds.), *Australian Dictionary of Biography Volume 7: 1891–1939* (Melbourne: Melbourne University Press, 1979).

example).[34] As the 1928 inquiry put it, the 'disintegration of tribal life' had commenced, and it was the duty of the Protector, mission staff and the government to minister to Aboriginal peoples 'in sickness or distress and generally with a watchful eye on their welfare'.[35]

A core power under the protection system was the power to forcibly remove Aboriginal children from their families, and to place them in government institutions and on church-run missions.[36] Backed by then current ideas about eugenics, and as part of a policy of biological assimilation that targeted lighter skinned Aboriginal peoples (as those who were 'assimilable'), the removal of children was the central activity of a system deliberately designed to eliminate the 'full blood' population and culture.[37] In this context, family situations made little difference to welfare decision-making, because being Aboriginal was itself a reason for regarding children as 'neglected'.[38] In institutions and on missions, the focus was on education and training for menial 'outside situations', such as blacksmithing for boys and laundry work for girls, on the basis that Aboriginal children were 'the stockmen and servants of the future'.[39] Some of these institutions – such as Sister Kate's orphanage in Perth – would later become by-words for cruelty and hardship when subject to public inquiries that drew on the testimony of survivors. At the time, they were praised: for instance, in the 1913 South Australian *Royal Commission* on the Aborigines, the church-run missions in that state are described as having 'a most beneficial effect' on Aboriginal peoples.[40] Similarly, in the inquiry into the 'condition and treatment of Aborigines' by the Western Australian Parliament in 1935, which was triggered by allegations of the enslavement of Aboriginal adults, Sister Kate's was described as being of 'great value' and deserving of more financial support from the government.[41]

As per this first position of the state in relations of responsibility, government responses to crimes against children in institutions were circumscribed examinations of particular cases or particular aspects of institutional procedures that did not implicate the state itself. Public inquiries into harm to (and even death of) children were generally not conceptualised as investigations into crimes, but

34 See Parliament of Australia, *The Aboriginals and Half-Castes*, pp. 6, 10, 12–13.

35 Ibid., p. 24.

36 See, e.g. ,*Aborigines Act 1905* (WA); *Northern Territory Aboriginals Act 1906* (SA).

37 R. Hogg and D. Brown, *Rethinking Law & Order* (Sydney: Pluto Press, 1998), p. 143.

38 See generally HREOC, *Bringing Them Home*, ch. 1.

39 See, e.g., South Australia, Royal Commission on the Aborigines, *Progress Report* (1913), vii–viii; and Parliament of Australia, *The Aboriginals and Half-Castes*, p. 8, respectively.

40 Royal Commission on the Aborigines, *Progress Report*, viii.

41 Western Australia, Royal Commission Appointed to Investigate, Report and Advise Upon Matters in Relation to the Condition and Treatment of Aborigines, *Report* (1935), p. 15; for a critical assessment of the impact of Sister Kate's and other institutions on their 'inmates', see M. D. Jacobs, *White Mother to a Dark Race: Settler Colonialism, Maternalism, and the Removal of Indigenous Children in the American West and Australia, 1880–1940* (Lincoln: University of Nebraska Press, 2009).

as failures of systems and processes. For example, the 1917 NSW inquiry into the State Children Relief Department, which was prompted by allegations of the ill-treatment of children in care, concluded that any ill-treatment occurred 'many years ago', although it nonetheless advocated increases in inspection staff in order to maintain standards.[42] Similarly, the 1921 Western Australian *Royal Commission into the State Children and Charities Department* examined specific allegations that child slavery existed in certain farming communities (for which it found no evidence), as well as the management of matters such as regular payments to widows.[43] In its report, the Royal Commission regarded the placement of a female child from an institution with 'a woman of ill repute' who was living in a 'Chinese den' as an 'extraordinary case' that pointed to a general need for improvement in record keeping.[44] The appropriateness or need for state care for some children was not questioned in government responses, and indeed, even in cases in which problems were identified, the 'splendid work performed by institutions on behalf of helpless children' and the 'care, foresight and humanity' of child guardians was commended.[45]

Where children's institutions were criticised, it was on the basis of the need to modernise institutions and implement modern practices of care, with the role of the governments limited to fostering or advocating such modernisation from a position of distance from the institutions and practices themselves. The then current understanding of modernisation encompassed both moralised and 'scientific' care of children.[46] Thus, the 1921 Western Australian Royal Commission referred to the need for a magistrate to deal with delinquent children who would have the 'essential qualifications' of 'common sense, kindness, firmness, and a good knowledge of children, normal and otherwise'; that same Royal Commission criticised institutions for failing to employ 'expert' staff with 'special training in sociology or psychology', and classify children within the care system according to whether they were delinquent or 'mentally defective', separating these children from others in the institutions.[47] In relation to institutions for Aboriginal children, 'scientific' classification meant the separation of those 'with a preponderance of European or Chinese blood' from 'half-caste children'.[48] Some of these same ideas about modernisation

[42] Parliament of New South Wales, *Report of the Public Service Board into the Working of the State Children Relief Branch Particularly with Reference to the Conditions under Which Children Are Boarded Out* (1917), vi, viii.

[43] Royal Commission on State Children and Charities Department, *Report*, pp. 3, 9–10.

[44] Ibid., pp. 6–7.

[45] Royal Commission on State Children and Charities Department, *Report*, p. 8 and Parliament of New South Wales, *Report of the Public Service Board*, viii, respectively.

[46] van Krieken, *Children and the State*, pp. 131–2.

[47] Royal Commission on State Children and Charities Department, *Report*, pp. 13, 7, 11 respectively.

[48] Parliament of Australia, *The Aboriginals and Half-Castes*, p. 16 (recommending the establishment of separate institutions in different regions of the territory for these groups).

and 'scientific' classification were also being implemented in Australian prisons at around the same time.[49]

As this discussion suggests, through this position of the state in relations of responsibility, child welfare, children's institutions, and (white) children in families were a frontline in the development of the new Australian nation. Problems involving children in families or in institutions were understood as issues for the future of the nation: here, the story about state responsibility was a positive one – Australia, 'with institutions in plastic condition', was 'especially responsive to the demands of the age' to modernise child welfare practices, and to successfully deal with problems because 'they still remain obvious' in the 'new' nation.[50] At the same time, in the first decades of the century, operating in a context of limited capacity, the abiding concerns of the new Federal government were national unity, interstate trade and industrial matters, rather than crime or criminal law, which remained a state sphere of power at Federation.[51] At state level, while crime was attracting increasing public and political attention in the years before and after World War I, the focus was largely on matters such as public disorder, and vice crimes such as prostitution and gambling. Government action in relation to crime revolved around establishing and maintaining state police forces to combat crime, and in legislating to prohibit practices such as street prostitution.[52]

This recessive position and limited function for the state in relations of responsibility came along with a particular division of responsibility between individuals and the state. Against the background of highly moralised attitudes to crime in general, criminal conduct was seen as a moral failing on the part of individuals, and, with the state's role oriented around prevention and deterrence of crime, criminal responsibility was understood to lie squarely with the individual perpetrator. Crimes against children did not have a high profile, however. In general terms, crimes against children in the family were obscured by moralised and classed ideas about childhood and parenting that collapsed them under the broad category of 'neglect', and, in relation to sexual crimes in particular, by connection to a broader category of deviant sexual practices.[53]

[49] See for discussion Finnane *Punishment in Australian Society*, ch. 3.

[50] A. W. Green (President of the State Children's Board, NSW) 'The Baby – The Empire's Asset' in *Report of the Proceedings of the Conference on Infant and Child Welfare* (Sydney: W.C. Penfold & Co. Ltd, Printers, 1917), pp. 78–85, 83.

[51] Woods, *A History of Criminal Law in New South Wales Vol. 2*, pp. 4–6.

[52] See generally J. A. Allen, *Sex and Secrets: Crimes Involving Australian Women Since 1880* (Melbourne: Oxford University Press, 1990); M. Finnane *Police and Government: Histories of Policing in Australia* (Oxford: Oxford University Press, 1994); and H. Golder and J. Allen, 'Prostitution in New South Wales 1870–1932: Restructuring an Industry' (1979–80) 18/19 *Refractory Girl* 17–24.

[53] See T. W. Jones, 'Finding Child Sex Abuse in the Archives: The Treatment of sexually offending clergy in the Church of England, 1871–1960,' in Y. Smaal, A. Kaladelfos and M. Finnane (eds.), *The Sexual Abuse of Children: Recognition and Redress* (Melbourne: Monash University Press, 2016), p. 46.

Beyond the family, child molesters were seen as 'pathetic and innocuous' individuals who were child-like themselves,[54] at the same time as the child who was subject to sexual abuse was seen as sexualised or seductive, and complicit in his or her own fate.[55] With regard to crimes against children in institutions in particular, with institutions such as orphanages and reformatories run along 'regimental, prison-like' lines, complaints from children resulted in disbelief or denial and punishment rather than assistance.[56] Thus, although sexual offences against children were the object of policing and prosecution, indicating that such offending was regarded seriously,[57] in Shurlee Swain's words, such conduct was not 'bought into discourse',[58] meaning that it was not the subject of public debate. This situation, and the division of responsibility between state and individual, changed radically under the second historic position of the state in relations of responsibility, as I discuss in the next section of this chapter.

Responsibility for Responsibility

The second historic position of the state in relations of responsibility involves governments in the development of social welfare and criminal justice institutions, in accordance with the formation of the apparatus of the welfare state, with crimes against children in families, and to a lesser extent in institutions, coming to receive greater attention. As per this position, which is prominent in the middle decades of the century, from the 1940s to the 1970s, government responses to crimes against children in institutions revolved around 'responsibility for responsibility', focusing on regulation, standard-setting and a future-oriented prevention, as well as training and oversight of the professionals increasingly involved in children's institutions.

From the post-World War II period, major changes in expert medical, psychological and psychiatric knowledges come to reconstruct understandings of childhood and crimes against children. In relation to childhood, emerging psychological theories about child development, theories of attachment and the importance of the family shifted attitudes to children, as childhood came to be seen to be characterised by innocence, dependence and vulnerability.[59] This characterisation amplified the importance of parents and the family in the

[54] See S. Angelides, 'The Emergence of the Paedophile in the Late Twentieth Century' (2005) 36 *Historical Studies* 272–95, 278.

[55] Scott and Swain, *Confronting Cruelty*, pp. 69–71.

[56] See Swain, 'Institutional Abuse', p. 159.

[57] See M. Finnane and Y. Smaal, 'Some Questions of History: Prosecuting and Punishing Child Sexual Assault', in Y. Smaal, A. Kaladelfos and M. Finnane (eds.), *The Sexual Abuse of Children: Recognition and Redress* (Melbourne: Monash University Press, 2016).

[58] See S. Swain, 'Narratives of Innocence and Seduction', in Y. Smaal, A. Kaladelfos and M. Finnane (eds.), *The Sexual Abuse of Children: Recognition and Redress* (Melbourne: Monash University Press, 2016), p. 37.

[59] See generally C. Pascoe, 'Be Home by Dark: Childhood Freedoms and Adult Fears in 1950s Victoria' (2009) 40(2) *Australian Historical Studies* 215–31.

growth of children to maturity, and the influence of these knowledges on parenting meant that the gap between the experience of children raised in families and the situation of children in care widened.[60] These psychological knowledges also grounded the early critiques of British child migration schemes that emerged in the 1950s.[61] According to these changes, and by contrast with the broad notion of child 'neglect' – through which a child could be removed from his or her family on the basis that he or she had 'no visible lawful means of support or has no fixed place of abode', or if the child was 'falling into bad associations or is exposed to moral danger'[62] – over the mid-century, moralised ideas about poverty gradually gave way to social and psychological theories of disadvantage.[63]

Emerging expert knowledges also influenced understandings of crimes against children, which came to be focally conceived around child abuse, a superficially technical term that centred on physical violence. Child abuse was medicalised, a development encapsulated by the diagnosis of 'battered child syndrome' which was developed by American medical professionals in the 1960s and oriented around physical abuse.[64] 'Battered child syndrome' was picked up in Australia, with evidence of physical injuries in children who were examined in hospital and in state care in Melbourne prompting the establishment of an inquiry into neglect and maltreatment in Victoria in 1966.[65] Like crimes against children more generally, sexual crimes against children were also understood in terms of physical violence, with stigmatising consequences of pregnancy for girls and 'infection' with homosexuality for boys.[66] Child sexual assault was regarded as a part of child abuse more generally, but was considered rare: reflecting the influence of Sigmund Freud's psychoanalytic theories, children's complaints of

[60] Musgrove, 'The Role and Importance of History', 156.

[61] See Boucher, *Empire's Children*, ch. 5.

[62] See *Child Welfare Act 1939* (NSW) s 72; see also *Child Welfare Ordinance 1957* (ACT) s 5; *Child Welfare Act 1954* (Vic) s 16.

[63] S. Garton, *Out of Luck: Poor Australians and Social Welfare 1788–1988* (Sydney: Allen and Unwin, 1990), p. 142.

[64] See Hacking, 'The Making and Molding of Child Abuse', 266–9.

[65] The Committee of Investigation into Allegations of Neglect and Maltreatment of Young Children issued two reports, in 1967 and 1969. The medical evidence to which the Committee responded was published as R. G. Birrell and J. H. Birrell, 'The "Maltreatment Syndrome" in Children' (1966) 2(24) *Medical Journal of Australia* 1134–8 and D. Bialestock, 'Neglected Babies: A Study of 289 Babies Admitted Consecutively to a Reception Centre' (1966) 2(24) *Medical Journal of Australia* 1129–33. The 'battered child' diagnosis was also the subject of a national conference in Australia in 1975: see Department of Community Welfare (WA), *The Battered Child: Proceedings of the First National Australian Conference, Mt. Lawley Teachers College, Perth, August 25–28, 1975* (1975), and Committee of Investigation into Allegations of Neglect and Maltreatment of Young Children, *Second Report to the Honourable the Chief Secretary and the Honourable to Minister of Health* (1969).

[66] L. Featherstone, '"Children in a Terrible State": Understandings of Trauma and Child Sexual Assault in 1970s and 1980s Australia' (2018) 42(2) *Journal of Australian Studies* 164–76, 171.

incest were not believed by professionals, or if they were, incest was seen as 'a symptom of family dysfunction, not its cause'.[67] Thus, the first report of the 1966 Victorian committee noted that the discovery of a 'battered child' pointed to a 'problem family' that required urgent assistance.[68] As this suggests, at this time, police and criminal justice focus was on abuse within the family or in the home, and institutional child abuse occupied a marginal position – as 'child abuse in other contexts'.[69]

These emerging expert knowledges fed the development of the welfare state over the period of the mid-century, a complex and multifaceted change in liberal governance practices which greatly extended government intervention into individual and collective lives. As Nikolas Rose writes, the welfare state brings governance practices into relation with expertise, 'as a way of codifying a new rationality of social solidarity' in which the role of government is to produce 'healthy, responsible, adjusted social citizens'.[70] In this context, the emphasis is on 'self-government and subjectivity'.[71] Alongside emerging expert knowledges, new professions such as social work enhanced government capacity for regulation, and permitted the tracking individuals who interacted with government services from a distance, meaning that 'public powers of law, regulation and bureaucracy' supported detailed knowledge of individuals, criminals, families and others.[72] At the same time, governance practices became forward-looking or future-oriented, incorporating the prevention of harms like unemployment and poverty through the 'prophylactic' dimensions of social control.[73] The development of the welfare state also radically reformed criminal justice institutions, as social scientific and criminological knowledges were harnessed to the task of preventing crime and administering criminal justice institutions.[74] This reflected a broader change in orientation in criminal law and criminal

[67] See J. Breckenridge, 'Intervention in Child Welfare: An Inflicted Evil or Solicited Response?', in M. Wearing and R. Berreen (eds.), *Welfare & Social Policy in Australia: The Distribution of Advantage* (Sydney: Harcourt Brace, 1994), pp. 143–4, and Featherstone, '"Children in a Terrible State"', 167, 171, respectively.

[68] Committee of Investigation into Allegations of Neglect and Maltreatment of Young Children (Vic), *Report to the Honourable the Chief Secretary and the Honourable to Minister of Health* (1967), [5.2].

[69] Law Reform Commission, *Child Welfare*, Report No. 18 (1981), [405]; see also Swain, 'Why Sexual Abuse? Why Now?', p. 84.

[70] See N. Rose, 'Expertise and the Government of Conduct', in S. S. Silbey and A. Sarat (eds.), *Studies in Law, Politics and Society* (Greenwich, CT: JAI Press, 1994), pp. 359, 375.

[71] See N. Brown, *Governing Prosperity: Social Change and Social Analysis in Australia in the 1950s* (Cambridge: Cambridge University Press, 1995), p. 11.

[72] Rose, 'Expertise and the Government of Conduct', p. 378.

[73] Ibid., p. 376.

[74] See generally D. Garland, *Punishment and Welfare: A History of Penal Strategies* (Aldershot: Gower, 1985); in the Australian context, see Hogg and Brown, *Rethinking Law & Order*, p. 144.

justice, towards future risk, which involves a precautionary logic and focuses on demands for protection and prevention of harm.[75]

In Australia, the development of the welfare state came along with an expanded role for the Federal government in social welfare relative to the role of state governments. At around the same time as taxation powers were centralised to the Commonwealth government, in 1941, child endowment commenced, and reforms to pensions, unemployment and sickness benefits followed in subsequent years.[76] State governments continued to provide social services and govern the distribution of funds, together with church and charitable organisations which continued to be 'vital' to welfare provision.[77] In the 1970s and 1980s, welfare expanded significantly and shifted away from a charity model to a universal, social rights and justice based model.[78] In a way that would have a decisive impact on government responses to crimes against children in institutions at the end of the century, the evolving Commonwealth system and increasing 'centralisation of policy and service design' in social welfare enhanced demands that the Federal government exercise 'clear leadership' on matters of 'national significance and importance', such as institutional child abuse.[79] I pick up on this point again below.

Against the wider background of the development of the welfare state, government responses to crimes against children in institutions were oriented towards regulation and prevention, and, with the greater prominence of professionals in welfare services and institutions, training and oversight. For example, the 1967 report of the *Committee of Investigation into Allegations of Neglect and Maltreatment of Young Children* recommended establishing a voluntary scheme for doctors to report child abuse, registration of child care workers and defining minimum standards for organisations involved in the care of children.[80] Another example is provided by the report of the 1975 NSW *Child Welfare Legislation Review Committee*, which recommended 'greater use' of professionally trained personnel and improved training of residential and field workers and others.[81] Reflecting the emphasis on professionals and

[75] See for discussion L. Zedner, 'Pre-crime and Post-criminology?' (2007) 11(2) *Theoretical Criminology* 261–281.

[76] See Carney and Hanks, *Social Security in Australia*, ch. 2; Garton, *Out of Luck*, ch. 7.

[77] Garton, *Out of Luck*, p. 141.

[78] See P. Smyth 'The Historical Context for Action', in A. McClelland and P. Smyth (eds.), *Social Policy in Australia: Understanding for Action* (Melbourne: Oxford University Press, 2014), p. 86.

[79] Senate Community Affairs References Committee, Parliament of Australia, *Lost Innocents and Forgotten Australians Revisited: Report on the Progress with the Implementation of the Recommendations of the Lost Innocents and Forgotten Australians Reports* (2009), [6.8].

[80] Committee of Investigation into Allegations of Neglect and Maltreatment of Young Children, *Report to the Honourable the Chief Secretary and the Honourable to Minister of Health* (1967), Recommendations 1, 4 and 7.

[81] New South Wales Department of Youth, Ethic and Community Affairs, Child Welfare Legislation Review Committee, *Report* (1975); see also Parliament of Queensland, *Report and recommendations of the Commission of Inquiry into the Nature and Extent of the Problems Confronting Youth in Queensland* (1975), pp. 30–1.

professionalisation, the 1976 *Committee of Enquiry into Child Care Services in Victoria* stated that child welfare must be viewed not 'as a "soft" field for merely well-intentioned people', but as a 'hard' area, requiring professional skills exercised within 'sound' administrative frameworks.[82] In the same vein, and in contrast with the inquiries that would follow in later decades, these public inquiries into the situation of children in institutions tended to hear evidence from government and other staff, and experts in the field, as opposed to those who had been or were currently residents in homes or institutionalised in reformatories or industrial schools.[83]

On the basis that it was inferior to growing up in a family, the institutionalisation of children now came in for criticism in government responses to crimes against children in institutions. The 1956 Victorian *Juvenile Delinquency Advisory Committee* stated that 'institutional life is thoroughly undesirable for young children', and advocated adoption and fostering,[84] and the 1967 report of the *Committee of Investigation into Allegations of Neglect and Maltreatment of Young Children* started from the premise that 'for the normal growth and development of the child there is no satisfactory of replacement for his own family'.[85] In Australia and elsewhere, over the mid-century period, there was a growing move towards 'de-institutionalisation'.[86] This generated calls for improved support services for families. For example, the 1976 *Committee of Enquiry into Child Care Services in Victoria* advocated the further development of 'services aimed at preventing familial disintegration and admission of children to state care', and criticised the antiquated condition of child welfare provision in that state for failing to keep up with the needs of 'contemporary society'.[87] From the 1970s, foster care became 'the placement of

82 Parliament of Victoria, *Report*, p. 10.

83 For instance, in its inquiry into juvenile delinquency in Victoria in 1956, the Juvenile Delinquency Advisory Committee decided not to hold public sittings or hear witnesses because this would not 'add materially to existing information' that could be gained from 'the agencies, governmental, academic and voluntary': Victoria, Juvenile Delinquency Advisory Committee *Report* (1956), p. 7.

84 Juvenile Delinquency Advisory Committee, *Report*, p. 34. This report recommended that a central 'Youth Authority' coordinating child welfare activities be set up in Victoria (p. 79), and a 'special police unit be established with the function of preventing and detecting juvenile delinquency' and training courses provided for Children's Court magistrates (pp. 92–3). Reflecting his extensive involvement in criminal justice, J. V. Barry was the Chair of this Committee: on J. V. Barry's scholarly work on criminal responsibility, see Chapter 4.

85 Committee of Investigation into Allegations of Neglect and Maltreatment of Young Children, *Report to the Honourable the Chief Secretary and the Honourable to Minister of Health* (1967), [5.2]; see also Parliament of NSW, *Children in Need: an Account of the Administration and Functions of the Child Welfare Department, New South Wales, Australia, with an Examination of the Principles Involved in Helping Deprived and Wayward Children* (1956), pp. 19–20.

86 Parliament of Australia, *Children in Institutional and Other Forms of Care*, p. 14.

87 Parliament of Victoria, *Report*, p. 11.

choice' in Australia.[88] As a result, significant numbers of Aboriginal children were fostered or adopted by white families.[89] But, children who were regarded as unsuitable for foster care or adoption, such as those who had committed offences, continued to be sent to institutions, and despite the changed emphasis, throughout this period, there were high numbers of children in institutional care.[90]

Government responses to Aboriginal children in institutions, and the situation of Aboriginal peoples more generally, were characterised by broad continuities with the first historical position of the state in relations of responsibility – which, as discussed above, was marked by a racist paternalism – although, over the mid-century, the distinct policy regimes applying to Aboriginal peoples attracted greater criticism. Reflecting a shift to the assimilation of Aboriginal peoples through welfare and education, as opposed to biological assimilation, there were moves to bring Aboriginal children under general welfare provisions, but, even where this happened, the laws were applied differently, and Aboriginal children continued to be removed in large numbers.[91] Against the background of the rise of civil and human rights movements, in the 1960s and 1970s, Aboriginal peoples' activism around disadvantage, dispossession and land rights galvanised public and political attention. The policies of removing Aboriginal children to missions and homes attracted particular attention, and protests from the *Aborigines Advancement League* and other organisations against child removals eventually led to the repeal of protection legislation across Australian jurisdictions.[92] In a way that directly implicated the Commonwealth government in the institutionalisation of Aboriginal children, during this period, the Commonwealth administered the Northern Territory, with missions in the territory 'accepting responsibilities as agents of the Government in regard to educational, health and economic programmes' for Aboriginal peoples.[93] As a result of the 1967 referendum amending the Australian constitution, the Commonwealth government was granted power to legislate specifically for Aboriginal peoples.[94] This set the

88 Swain, 'Institutional Abuse', p. 156.

89 Parliament of Australia, *Children in Institutional and Other Forms of Care*, p. 17.

90 Scott and Swain, *Confronting Cruelty*, p. 102.

91 For example, the *Welfare Ordinance 1953* (Cth), which applied to the Northern Territory, covered both Aboriginal and non-Aboriginal children: see *Welfare Ordinance 1953* (Cth) and for discussion J. Chesterman and H. Douglas 'Law on Australia's Frontier: The Fall and Rise of Race' (2009) 24 *Canadian Journal of Law and Society* 69–83.

92 See, e.g., *Aborigines and Torres Strait Islander Act 1965* (Qld). The assimilation policy was only officially abandoned by the Federal government in 1973 in favour of Indigenous self-management.

93 See Commonwealth of Australia, *The Northern Territory Report for the Period 1 July 1953, to 30 June 1955* (1956), p. 43.

94 Following the amendment, s 51(xxvi) of the Australian Constitution, the 'race' power', gave the Federal government the same power to legislate for Aboriginal peoples in states as it had for Aboriginal peoples in territories.

scene for the developments at the end of the twentieth century and beginning of the twenty-first century, as I discuss in the next part of this chapter.

As this discussion suggests, this second position of the state in relations of responsibility saw the (institutions of the) state catch up with the (idea of the) nation, as social welfare and criminal justice institutions developed to significantly enhance state regulatory capacity. The enhanced position of, and an amplified function for, the state in relations of responsibility arose from the deployment in criminal justice of expert knowledge, scientific research and technological strategies that came along with the formation of the welfare state. The function of the state now extended to the close analysis of the individual offender – as someone with a particular character ('normal', 'defective') and an 'uncertain degree of rationality'[95] – and to more active prevention of crime into the future. Under these relations of responsibility, individual responsibility for crime also increased, as techniques of liberal governance produced a dynamic of 'responsibilisation'.[96] The medicalisation of offending against children had the effect of profoundly individualising wrongdoing – not now as individual immorality, but as individual pathology, in the form of paedophilia.[97] Like state responsibility, individual responsibility extended forward in time, as individuals were required to take responsibility for the prevention of crime and reduce their future risk of offending.

By the end of the mid-century period, child abuse in families, and to a lesser extent in institutions, had a high public profile. This was in significant part a product of the women's movement of the 1970s. Feminist campaigns enhanced social awareness of, and shifted public and political attitudes to, child abuse, which became increasingly politicised.[98] In this period, as part of wider campaigns, feminists and others were actively engaged in agitating for reforms to child welfare institutions, including the closure of by now notorious institutions such as the Parramatta Girls Home in Sydney.[99] In addition, as an unintended consequence of activism around sexual violence against women, levels of domestic violence and child abuse were exposed. For example, through public meetings, a phone help line and individual correspondence,

95 See D. Garland, *Punishment and Welfare A History of Penal Strategies* (Aldershot: Gower, 1985), pp. 26, 31.

96 See generally D. Garland *The Culture of Control: Crime and Social Order in Contemporary Society* (Chicago: University of Chicago Press, 2001).

97 Alan Norrie argues that law and psychiatry share 'an *individuation* of social problems': see Alan Norrie, *Crime, Reason and History: A Critical Introduction to Criminal Law*, 3rd ed. (Cambridge: Cambridge University Press, 2014), p. 271 (emphasis in original).

98 Breckenridge, 'Intervention in Child Welfare', p. 147; H. Boxall, A. Tomison and S. Hulme, *Historical Review of Sexual Offence and Child Sexual Abuse Legislation in Australia: 1788–2013*, Report prepared by the Australian Institute of Criminology for the Royal Commission into Institutional Responses to Child Sexual Abuse (2014), p. 9.

99 A number of feminist activists were involved in this campaign: see, e.g., S. Bellamy, 'Guthrie, Bessie Jean (1905–1977)', in J. Ritchie (ed.), *Australian Dictionary of Biography Volume 14: 1940–1980* (Melbourne: Melbourne University Press, 1996).

the *Royal Commission into Human Relationships,* which commenced in 1974, revealed the extent of the problem of violence against women and children in the home.[100] As a result of this activism and publicity, and as was the case in relation to violence against women, child abuse came to be recognised as a problem that required prevention strategies and support services from governments.[101] As under the first historic position of the state in relations of responsibility, crimes against children in institutions received less attention: in institutions, 'Victorian' attitudes to children subsisted, rendering children vulnerable to mistreatment and abuse,[102] and, although there was increased concern about, and policing and prosecution of, sex crimes from the 1950s, there was no systematic policing of assaults against children, and few criminal cases of offending in institutions came to the attention of the police or proceeded to charge.[103]

Responsibility Between Past and Present, and Empire and Nation

The third historic position of the state in relations of responsibility is characterised by a complex mix of assuming and denying responsibility across the boundary between Australia's past, as part of the British Empire, and its present, as an independent nation. This position of the state is most prominent in the period from the 1980s to early 2000s, a watershed moment in Australia, with three high-profile and broad-ranging public inquiries into crimes against children in institutions – concerning Aboriginal children, child migrants and children in care – representing and advancing this new position of the state in relations of responsibility, in which responsibility extended backwards as well as forwards in time.

The period from the 1980s witnessed a *fin-de-siècle* rethinking of Australian history and national identity. The bicentenary of colonisation in 1988 and the approaching end of the millennium prompted public debates about and reflection on Australia's past and its future. In these debates, the nature and legitimacy of colonisation, and previously accepted narratives of civilisation and progress, were subject to fundamental re-examination. This period generated what became known as the 'culture wars', as different visions of Australia's colonial and post-colonial history – as a story of violence and dispossession or

[100] I discuss this Royal Commission as part of my analysis of women's responsibility for crime: see Chapter 6.

[101] See Law Reform Commission, *Child Welfare*, p. 371; see also Breckenridge, 'Intervention in Child Welfare', pp. 148–9, 151.

[102] S. Swain, 'Why Sexual Abuse? Why Now?', in J. Sköld and S. Swain (eds.), *Apologies and the Legacy of Abuse of Children in 'Care': International Perspectives* (Basingstoke: Palgrave Macmillan, 2015), p. 93.

[103] L. Featherstone and A. Kaladelfos, *Sex Crimes in the Fifties* (Melbourne University Press, 2016), pp. 81–2.

a story of triumph in adverse conditions – competed for dominance.[104] Against a backdrop of the rise of human rights discourses and enhanced consciousness of the injustices of the past (such as under colonialism), the treatment and condition of Aboriginal peoples was a lightning rod for these debates, with matters such as land rights claims and native title challenging both the legal and political past and present.[105] In addition, the *Royal Commission into Aboriginal Deaths in Custody*, which issued its report in 1991, exposed the histories of institutionalisation of many Aboriginal prisoners as well as the way in which generalised problems of discrimination and disadvantage continued to impact on the lives of Aboriginal peoples.[106] In this context, received wisdom about Australian history was questioned, and new ways of accessing the 'truth' of history emerged, including new histories of colonisation.[107]

Against this background, and as a result of Aboriginal peoples' activism, and strategic alliances with public intellectuals, the policies and practices of forced removals of Aboriginal children from their families became the subject of a high-profile public inquiry. The Human Rights and Equal Opportunity Commission's *National Inquiry into the Separation of Aboriginal and Torres Strait Islander Children from Their Families*, also known as the 'Stolen Generations' Inquiry, issued its report, *Bringing Them Home*, in 1997.[108] The inquiry examined the laws, practices and effects of the policies of forced removal of what was estimated to be between ten and thirty percent of Aboriginal children between 1910 and 1970.[109] The Inquiry involved extensive public consultation and its Report provided detailed analysis of the manifold effects of the practices of forced removal, including psychological trauma, and loss of culture and native title entitlements, on Aboriginal peoples. The focus of the inquiry was the harm of removal in general, although child abuse – in

104 See M. McKenna, 'Metaphors of Light and Darkness: The Politics of 'Black Armband' History' (1998) 25 *Melbourne Journal of Politics* 67–84.

105 See, e.g., *Mabo* v. *State of Queensland* (1988) 166 CLR 186 (Mabo No. 1) and *Mabo* v. *State of Queensland* (No. 2) (1992) 175 CLR 1 (Mabo No. 2).

106 Commonwealth, Royal Commission into Aboriginal Deaths in Custody, *Final Report* (1991).

107 Work by historians Manning Clark and Henry Reynolds exposing the violence of colonisation was labelled the 'black armband' view of Australian history by fellow historian Geoffrey Blainey, and the term was taken up by conservatives including then Prime Minister John Howard: see McKenna, 'Metaphors of Light and Darkness'.

108 HREOC, *Bringing Them Home*. The topic of separation of Aboriginal families was referred to HREOC by the then Attorney-General, Mr Michael Lavarch MP.

109 HREOC, *Bringing Them Home*, p. 37. This practice has been called an attempted genocide of Aboriginal peoples: see generally A. D. Moses, 'An Antipodean Genocide? The Origins of the Genocidal Moment in the Colonization of Australia' (2000) 2(1) *Journal of Genocide Research* 89–106. Despite the manifold harms this policy produced, when the High Court adjudicated claims by members of the Stolen Generations, the lack of intention to do harm meant the policy did not fall under the Genocide Convention 1948: see *Kruger* v. *Commonwealth* (1997) 190 CLR 1; *Cubillo* v. *Commonwealth* (No. 2) (2000) 103 FCR 1.

institutions and foster care – emerged as a theme in this inquiry.[110] Among a suite of recommendations, the *Bringing Them Home* report recommended that Federal and state governments and religious institutions acknowledge their responsibility for forced removals, and issue apologies to those who were taken from their families, and that those individuals who were forcibly removed receive compensation.[111]

Around the same time, and reflecting developments overseas, the historic experience of British migrant children in Australia was coming to attract political and public attention.[112] Between the first years of the twentieth century and the 1960s, Australia received several thousand British child migrants who were expatriated to Australia.[113] Notwithstanding the advent of self-government in Australia, in the first decades of the century, anxieties about the small size of the population, and the genesis of the 'white Australia' policy meant Australia was an enthusiastic recipient of British children.[114] Expatriation was part of a long-term and large-scale process of British child migration to settler colonies such as Canada that was itself part of 'an imperial endeavour of land settlement' – just 'as much about the British race building Empire as rescuing children'.[115] British charitable organisations (such as Barnardos and the Fairbridge Society) determined which children would be sent to Australia and on what terms,[116] and, reflecting the population of care homes in Britain, and because they were valued for their capacity to work in the Australian agricultural economy, the majority of British child migrants were boys.[117] Between them, British and Australian governments

110 Abuse was one of the heads of damage identified as a basis for the compensation the report recommended be awarded to individuals who were forcibly removed: HREOC, *Bringing Them Home*, Recommendation 14.

111 HREOC, *Bringing Them Home*, Recommendations 5a and 14–19. Police forces, churches and others involved in removals were also recommended to acknowledge responsibility and issue apologies: Recommendations 5b, 6.

112 In England, the House of Commons undertook an inquiry into the situation of former British child migrants: see Select Committee on Health, United Kingdom House of Commons, *The Welfare of Former British Child Migrants, Third Report* (1998). As a result of this report, the British government created a fund for child migrants to reunite with family and, later, in 2010, Prime Minister Gordon Brown apologised on behalf of the government. At the time of writing, the British government announced that former child migrants would be given compensation payments.

113 See B. Coldrey, *Good British Stock: Child and Youth Migration to Australia Research Guide* (Canberra: National Archives of Australia, 1999), ch. 1.

114 The *Immigration Restriction Act 1901* (Cth) and the *Pacific Islands Labourers Act 1901* (Cth) severely restricted non-European immigration to Australia until the 1960s; for analysis of the 'white Australia' policy, see M. Lake and H. Reynolds, *Drawing the Global Colour Line: White Men's Countries and the International Challenge of Racial Equality* (Cambridge: Cambridge University Press, 2008).

115 G. Sherington, 'Contrasting Narratives in the History of Twentieth-Century British Child Migration to Australia: An Interpretive Essay' (2012) 9(2) *History Australia* 27–47, 28; see also Swain, 'Beyond Child Migration', 145.

116 See for discussion Coldrey, *Good British Stock*, ch. 1, and Swain, 'Beyond Child Migration', 145.

117 Boucher, *Empire's Children*, p. 95.

managed the expatriation process, with the Federal government assuming responsibility for the medical examination, transportation, and settlement of child migrants.[118] Thus, as was the case with forced removals of Aboriginal children, the Commonwealth government was directly implicated in the practices of British child migration. Australian state governments were also involved as state welfare departments exercised oversight over the institutions hosting child migrants.

Triggered by campaigns on the part of former child migrants,[119] in Australia in the early 2000s, the Federal Parliament referred the issue of British child migrants to a parliamentary committee, which published the *Lost Innocents* report in 2001.[120] Testimony from former child migrants themselves revealed 'shocking physical and sexual abuse and assault' committed by those tasked with caring for migrant children.[121] The report found that the supervision of child migrants in Australia (via official visits to institutions and inspections) was inadequate, and the level of funding host organisations received to cover their costs was 'poor'.[122] The report also found that state welfare departments and agencies running institutions were 'equally at fault', with the Commonwealth government sharing in the responsibility for failing to protect migrant children when it became aware of problems.[123] While acknowledging that 'the individual responsibility of those who were actually in charge of children must never be understated',[124] the *Lost Innocents* report concluded that migration schemes and the 'abuse and assault' of children that went undetected constituted failures of the duty of care owed by British, and Australian Federal and state governments.[125] In this inquiry, the narratives of child rescue and race-building across Empire that had initially sustained the practice of British child migration to Australia were replaced with a narrative of loss – of family, identity and belonging – which in turn generated 'a sense of grievance and the need for redress for past wrongs'.[126] The *Lost Innocents*

118 See *Empire Settlement Act 1922* (England) and *Immigration (Guardianship of Children) Act 1946* (Cth). Under the latter Act, the Minister for Immigration was made the guardian of all child migrants from their arrival in Australia until they reached 21 years, but some of the Minister's powers were delegated to state welfare authorities: see Senate Community Affairs References Committee, Parliament of Australia, *Lost Innocents Righting the Record – Report on Child Migration* (2001), [5.2].

119 The abuses suffered by these children came to light in significant part through the lobbying and advocacy work of social workers and others in Britain and elsewhere who formed advocacy and support groups (such as The Child Migrant Trust) for former child migrants.

120 See Parliament of Australia, *Lost Innocents Righting the Record*.

121 Parliament of Australia, *Lost Innocents Righting the Record*, Prologue.

122 Ibid., [5.4]–[5.14], [5.20].

123 Ibid., [5.29]–[5.30].

124 Parliament of Australia, *Lost Innocents Righting the Record*, [5.72]; see also Parliament of Australia, *Forgotten Australians*, [7.40].

125 Parliament of Australia, *Lost Innocents Righting the Record*, [5.72]. The report concluded that this was 'not only a moral obligation but also a direct responsibility' ([5.106]).

126 Sherington, 'Contrasting Narratives', pp. 36–7.

report recommended the provision of funding of services for former child migrants, rather than individual compensation, as the appropriate means of redress.[127]

The *Bringing Them Home* and the *Lost Innocents* reports prompted advocacy groups representing adults who had been in institutional care as children to mobilise for a public inquiry into the practice of institutionalising children more generally, on the basis that this group constituted 'another lost generation'.[128] This mobilisation resulted in a parliamentary inquiry into children in institutional and foster care, which commenced in 2003 and issued its first report, *Forgotten Australians*, in 2004, and its second report, *Protecting Vulnerable Children*, in 2005.[129] This Inquiry heard testimony about 'neglect, humiliation and deprivation of food, education and healthcare' in children's institutions, and found that there had been 'wide scale unsafe, improper and unlawful care of children'.[130] Like *Lost Innocents*, the *Forgotten Australians* report acknowledged that the isolation and vulnerability of children in institutions, and the lack of government regulation of institutions and inadequate oversight that permitted abuses to continue.[131] The report concluded that, although the Commonwealth government was not directly involved in the administration of children's institutions, it had a 'moral obligation to acknowledge the harm done to many children' in care.[132] The Report recommended that the Federal government establish a national reparations fund for victims of abuse in institutional care.[133]

With their extended timeframes for investigation – stretching beyond specific institutions and incidents – to cover the multiple decades over which laws and policies operated, these three inquiries represented and advanced an idea of state responsibility that extended backwards as well as forwards in time. While the forward-looking aspect of state responsibility was more familiar – as a product of the prevention orientation of welfare state governance practices, discussed above – the backwards looking aspect of state responsibility was novel. In the context of a generalised idea about the Australian state existing over time, state responsibility now came to encompass historic harms and wrongs, on the basis that the effects of these harms and wrongs continue into the present, and might now be understood as crimes although they were not so understood at the time. As the *Bringing Them Home* report noted, 'the actions of the past resonate in the present and will continue to do so in the future' because 'the laws, policies

127 Parliament of Australia, *Lost Innocents Righting the Record*, [5.103], Recommendation 5.

128 Swain, 'Beyond Child Migration', pp. 146–7.

129 Parliament of Australia, *Forgotten Australians*, and Senate Community Affairs References Committee, Parliament of Australia, *Protecting Vulnerable Children: A national challenge* (2005).

130 Parliament of Australia, *Forgotten Australians*, xv, xvi.

131 Ibid., [5.31], [5.15]–[5.17]; see also Commission of Inquiry into Abuse of Children in Queensland Institutions, *Report*, viii.

132 Parliament of Australia, *Forgotten Australians*, [7.105].

133 Ibid., Recommendation 6.

and practices which separated Indigenous children from their families have contributed directly to the alienation of Indigenous societies today.'[134] Similarly, *Lost Innocents* noted that the damage done to former child migrants is 'passed on to subsequent generations'.[135] This extension of responsibility backwards in time significantly expands state responsibility, and, as the profile of institutional child abuse increased, opened up new fronts in government responses to crimes against children in institutions, as I discuss below.

Government responses to the *Bringing Them Home*, *Lost Innocents* and *Forgotten Australians* reports were striking in their similarities. The responses represent both a willingness on the part of governments to assume responsibility *and* an impetus to assign it to others, a mix of taking and denying responsibility that was structured across Australia's mixed identity as part of the British Empire, and as an independent nation. On the one hand, the Commonwealth government response to the findings and recommendations of *Bringing Them Home* was a package of funds to provide finances for matters such as family support and parenting programs and the maintenance of language and culture for Aboriginal peoples.[136] In response to the *Lost Innocents* report, formal apologies were issued to former child migrants by Western Australia, as well as some agencies (such as churches) which had been identified as responsible, and redress schemes were also created by some states.[137] On the other hand, however, government responses reveal an impetus to assign responsibility. Under conservative Prime Minister John Howard, the Commonwealth government sought to defend the policies of removal of Aboriginal children by insisting that they were 'welfare' policies pursued in the interests of Aboriginal peoples by well-intentioned individuals,[138] and, working on the basis that it was not possible to be responsible for the actions of past governments, the Federal government issued a statement of 'deep and sincere regret' rather than a formal apology.[139] Similarly, the Federal government did not make an apology in response to *Lost Innocents*.[140] In response to *Forgotten Australians*, the Federal

134 HREOC, *Bringing Them Home*, ch. 1.

135 Parliament of Australia, *Lost Innocents Righting the Record*, Prologue.

136 J. Herron (Minister for Aboriginal and Torres Strait Islander Affairs), *Bringing Them Home: Commonwealth Initiatives* (Media Release), 16 December 1997.

137 See Parliament of Western Australia, Apology to Former Child Migrants, Hansard, Western Australian Legislative Assembly, col. 214, 13 August 1998.

138 See for discussion R. van Krieken, 'Rethinking Cultural Genocide: Aboriginal Child Removal and Settler-Colonial State Formation' (2004) 75(2) *Oceania* 125–51, 139.

139 See John Howard MP, Prime Minister, Motion of Reconciliation (26 August 1999); this was later eclipsed by an apology given by Labour Prime Minister Kevin Rudd MP (13 February 2008). See for discussion van Krieken 'The 'Stolen Generations' and Cultural Genocide', 299–300, and P. Vines, 'Apologising to Avoid Liability: Cynical Civility or Practical Morality?' (2005) 27 *Sydney Law Review* 483–506, 492–4.

140 Following the publication of a progress report on the implementation of the recommendations of both *Lost Innocents: Righting the Record* and *Forgotten Australians*, the Federal government later issued a formal apology to former child migrants: Kevin Rudd MP, Prime Minister (16 November 2009).

Government issued only a statement of 'sincere regret', stating that 'it would not be appropriate for the Australian Government to issue an apology for a matter for which it does not have responsibility'.[141] And in declining to establish a reparations fund for victims of institutional care, the Commonwealth stated that this was a matter for 'those who managed or funded the institutions, namely state and territory governments, charitable organisations and churches'.[142]

The division of responsibility between the state and individuals that correlates with this third historic position of the state in relations of responsibility exhibits a similar dynamic – in which responsibility was assumed (by the state) and assigned (to individuals). On the one hand, the extension of responsibility backwards in time brought with it a prominent position for the state in relations of responsibility, and an extended function in repairing past harms and wrongs through funding packages addressing wronged groups as a class. On the other hand, firmly demarcating between the charitable organisations and state bodies that managed children's institutions and the state itself represented an attempt to circumscribe the position and function of the state in relations of responsibility. Against a backdrop of high profile criminal trials of individual offenders (including 'paedophile priests' and other religious personnel) for crimes against children during this period,[143] affirming 'the individual responsibility of those who were actually in charge of children'[144] involved holding the individual responsible for crimes against children in institutions. This affirmation rests on the tacit idea that offenders in organisations were merely 'bad apples' in otherwise blameless or neutral institutional contexts,[145] and further implies that some of such individuals exploited state institutions in order to commit offences.

As this discussion indicates, and by contrast with other historic positions of the state in relations of responsibility, considered above, state responsibility in relation to crimes against children in institutions now overshadows its responsibility in relation to children in families, as institutional child abuse has come to reflect back on the state and its capacity to provide social goods such as safety for children. As a result, the ways in which governance practices regulate family life and relations between parents and children, as

141 Senate Community Affairs References Committee, Parliament of Australia, *Australian Government Response to Forgotten Australians* (2005).

142 Parliament of Australia, *Australian Government Response to Forgotten Australians* (2005).

143 See K. Daly, 'Redress for Historical Institutional Abuse of Children,' in A. Deckert and R. Sarre (eds.), *The Palgrave Handbook of Australian and New Zealand Criminology, Crime and Justice* (London: Palgrave Macmillan, 2017), p. 454.

144 Parliament of Australia, *Lost Innocents Righting the Record*, [5.72]; see also Parliament of Australia, *Forgotten Australians*, [7.40].

145 See J. Wangmann, 'Liability for Institutional Child Sexual Assault: Where Does Lepore Leave Australia?' (2004) 28 *Melbourne University Law Review* 169–202, 195–7.

well as specific intrafamilial crimes against children like incest, have been obscured.[146] The focus on institutions *other than* the family reaches a new height under the fourth historic position of the state in relations of responsibility, with the scope of the most high-profile public inquiry to date defined by way of exclusion of the family.[147]

Responsibility in a Global Context

The fourth historic position of the state in relations of responsibility has been prominent in recent years. As per this position of the state, governments are (re-)negotiating responsibility in a global context, and embracing responsibility in relation to crimes against children (including historic cases) in a more wholesale way, with government responses to crimes against children in institutions now representing a collective reckoning with past practices, according to which state responsibility is shared by both governments and the public.

This historic position of the state has emerged against a global backdrop of enhanced public and political receptivity to institutional and state liability for past injustices. In what has been labelled a global phenomenon of 'reparations politics', demands for recognition, compensation and commemoration from governments and other public and private organisations for past wrongs and harms have come to be channelled into juridical form, into claims for monetary compensation.[148] In settler societies such as Canada, such claims – for loss of land and forced institutionalisation – have been made by Aboriginal peoples.[149] In addition, in a number of countries such as Ireland, religious organisations like the Catholic Church have been the target of high-profile public investigations and claims for compensation in relation to past injustices, particularly in relation to crimes against children.[150] Around the world,

[146] See for discussion M. Salter, 'The Privatisation of Incest: The Neglect of Familial Sexual Abuse in Australian Public Inquiries' in Y. Smaal, A. Kaladelfos and M. Finnane (eds.), *The Sexual Abuse of Children: Recognition and Redress* (Melbourne: Monash University Press, 2016); see also Y. Smaal, 'Historical Perspectives on Child Sexual Abuse, Part 1' (2013) 11(9) *History Compass* 702–14 and 'Historical Perspectives on Child Sexual Abuse, Part 2' (2013) 11(9) *History Compass* 715–26.

[147] As discussed above, the definition of 'institutions' in letters patent establishing the Royal Commission into Institutional Responses excludes the family: see Royal Commission into Institutional Responses, *Final Report*, vol. 1, Appendix A.

[148] See J. Torpey '"Making Whole What Has Been Smashed": Reflections on Reparations' (2001) 73 *The Journal of Modern History* 333–58.

[149] In relation to Canada, see, e.g., M. Moran, 'The Role of Reparative Justice in Responding to the Legacy of the Indian Residential Schools' (2014) 64(4) *University of Toronto Law Journal* 529–65.

[150] In relation to Ireland, see A. McAlinden, 'An Inconvenient Truth: Barriers to Truth Recovery in the Aftermath of Institutional Child Abuse in Ireland' (2013) 33(2) *Legal Studies* 189–214, and A. McAlinden and B. Naylor, 'Reframing Public Inquiries as Procedural Justice for Victims of Institutional Child Abuse: Towards a Hybrid Model of Justice' (2016) 38(3) *Sydney Law Review* 277–309.

including Australia, multiple inquiries have examined the way in which the harms of child abuse have been covered up or minimised, and the offending conduct of priests and others deemed to be matters for internal church discipline, rather than state or criminal matters.[151] This has had the effect of amplifying moral condemnation of such conduct and enhancing the broad acceptability of institutional liability for past injustices.

At the same time, and also playing out on a global scale, child sexual abuse has now come to be regarded as a preeminent 'wrong against childhood',[152] and institutional child abuse has been recognised as a serious and widespread problem. Child sexual abuse – both within families and in institutions – now has a distinct political as well as technical identity, separate from other forms of child abuse. As discussed above, the spectre of the paedophile, as the pathologised perpetrator of child abuse came to mark a specific, pathologised psychic identity within a wider category of sex offenders,[153] but, by contrast with earlier eras, children are now seen to lack power in sexual encounters with adults, and legal and policy categories of 'moral danger' have been replaced with terms such as 'sexual exploitation'.[154] In addition, the multifaceted harms, including psychological harms, of child abuse and child sexual abuse have come to be more fully understood.[155] In relation to institutional child abuse, as child abuse is now understood as an issue of power, the context in which abuses occur has come to attract much greater attention,[156] opening the way for the finessing of the division of responsibility between state and individual responsibility, as I discuss below.

Just as public and political receptivity to institutional liability for past injustices has increased, and child abuse and institutional child abuse have come to the fore, the limitations of existing, state-supported options for redress for historic harms and harms committed in institutional contexts have become apparent. The limitations have appeared in both civil law and criminal law. In relation to the civil law, while the long-term expansion of the tort of

151 In the Australian context, see Family and Community Development Committee, Parliament of Victoria, *Betrayal of Trust: Inquiry into the Handling of Child Abuse by Religious and Other Non-Government Organisations, Final Report* (2013), [1.3.2]; for discussion K. Gleeson, 'Exceptional Sexual Harms: The Catholic Church and Child Sexual Abuse Claims in Australia' (2017) 27(6) *Social & Legal Studies* 1–21, and 'Why the Continuous Failures in Justice for Australian Victims and Survivors of Catholic Clerical Child Sexual Abuse?' (2016) 28(2) *Current Issues in Criminal Justice* 239–50.

152 Swain, 'Why Sexual Abuse? Why Now?', p. 83.

153 See generally Angelides, 'The Emergence of the Paedophile in the Late Twentieth Century'.

154 Angelides, 'The Emergence of the Paedophile', 283–4.

155 Breckenridge, 'Intervention in Child Welfare', 149.

156 See L. Farmer, *Making the Modern Criminal Law: Criminalization and Civil Order* (Oxford: Oxford University Press, 2016), p. 289; see also G. Schneebaum, 'Making Abuse Offences in the Modern Criminal Law' (2017) 4(1) *Critical Analysis of Law* 42–52.

negligence has opened up avenues for a private law of institutional wrongs,[157] issues related to unincorporated organisations, vicarious liability and limitation periods have restricted access to justice for victims of historic abuse.[158] In addition, for Aboriginal children, loss of culture and language has proved hard to render into a compensable legal wrong under civil law.[159] In relation to criminal law – and specifically criminal responsibility – difficulties have emerged concerning holding organisations such as corporations to account under the criminal law,[160] and, with limitations on positive duties to act under criminal law, in criminalising failures to act as well as conduct itself.[161] These difficulties are compounded by the evidential and procedural issues that may accompany criminal prosecutions for institutional child abuse, including delayed reporting, and the difficulties that arise in prosecuting and defending historic cases.[162] As the *Royal Commission into Institutional Responses* (discussed below) states, while recognising that criminal justice options are important to survivors and in preventing abuse occurring in the future, 'it must be recognised that the criminal justice system is unlikely ever

[157] On the development of negligence, see M. Moran 'Reshaping Responsibility: The Emerging Private Law of Institutional Wrongs', in K. Barker et al. (eds.), *Private Law and Power* (Oxford: Hart Publishing, 2017), 263–83; on the Australian situation, see generally Gleeson, 'Responsibility and redress'.

[158] Regarding unincorporated organisations; see *Trustees of the Roman Catholic Church for the Archdiocese of Sydney* v. *Ellis* [2007] NSWCA 117 (holding that priests are not employees of the Church, and the Church cannot be held vicariously liable for their actions; the opposite conclusion has been reached in England: see *JGE* v. *The Trustees of the Portsmouth Roman Catholic Diocesan Trust* [2012] 4 All ER 1152). Regarding vicarious liability, see *NSW* v. *Lepore* (2003) 195 ALR 412; *Prince Alfred College Incorporated* v. *ADC* (2016) 258 CLR 134; *Erlich* v. *Leifer & Adass Israel School Inc* [2015] VSC 499: see for discussion Gleeson, 'Exceptional Sexual Harms', 7–9. Regarding limitation periods, see for discussion Wangmann, 'Liability for Institutional Child Sexual Assault', 173–4.

[159] See for discussion R. Graycar 'Compensation for the Stolen Children: Political Judgments and Community Values' (1997) 4(3) *University of New South Wales Law Journal* 24–27; see also M. Moran, 'The Role of Reparative Justice in Responding to the Legacy of the Indian Residential Schools' (2014) 64(4) *University of Toronto Law Journal* 529–65, 542–6.

[160] The classic statement of the failure of the criminal law in such cases has been made by John Coffee: see J. C. Coffee, '"No Soul to Damn: No Body to Kick": An Unscandalized Inquiry into the Problem of Corporate Punishment' (1981) 79(3) *Michigan Law Review* 386–459; for contemporary discussion, see S. Bronitt, 'New Regulatory Paradigms for Preventing Institutional Child Sexual Abuse: Lessons from Corporate Crime and White-Collar Criminals', in Y. Smaal, A. Kaladelfos and M. Finnane (eds.), *The Sexual Abuse of Children: Recognition and Redress* (Melbourne: Monash University Press, 2016); P. Crofts, 'Legal Irresponsibility and Institutional Responses to Child Sex Abuse' (2016) 34(2) *Law in Context: A Socio-Legal Journal* 79–99.

[161] See for discussion A. Ashworth, *Positive Obligations in Criminal Law* (London: Bloomsbury, 2013), ch. 2.

[162] See J. Cashmore, A. Taylor, R. Shackel, and P. Parkinson, *The Impact of Delayed Reporting on the Prosecution and Outcomes of Child Sexual Abuse Cases*, Report for the Royal Commission into Institutional Responses to Child Sexual Abuse (2016); see also Parliament of Australia, *Lost Innocents and Forgotten Australians Revisited*, [6.85].

to provide an easy or straightforward experience for a complainant of institutional child sexual abuse'.[163]

This is the context in which the most recent set of government responses to institutional child abuse have appeared. Government responses have continued to proceed on a broad basis – stretching beyond specific institutions and incidents – but many of the most recent inquiries are squarely focused on child sexual abuse. While sexual abuse was not singled out for special attention in public inquiries into children's institutions taking place in previous eras, it was one of the types of abuse found to be endemic in the institutions subject to examination,[164] and, by the time of the inquiries of the new millennium, sexual abuse had become a 'core subject for investigation'.[165] Sexual abuse was the trigger for, and the exclusive focus of, the Northern Territory *Board of Inquiry into the Protection of Aboriginal Children from Sexual Abuse*, which issued its report in 2007,[166] and of the 2008 South Australian *Children in State Care Commission of Inquiry*.[167] These inquiries centre on personal testimony from survivors, which is now crucial in establishing genuine understandings of institutional care,[168] and operates to undercut previous 'practices of individualising accusations of sexual abuse, discrediting witnesses and minimising reporting in the interests of public morality'.[169] As the profile of personal testimony suggests, adults who survived institutional abuse have become an authority in themselves, and have expectations that their experiences will be included in Australia's national history.[170]

The Federal *Royal Commission into Institutional Responses to Child Sexual Abuse* continues the approach of these current public inquiries. In the face of 'a loss of community faith in the way that governments and institutions had responded, and continued to respond, to child sexual abuse', the *Royal*

[163] Commonwealth, Royal Commission into Institutional Responses to Child Sexual Abuse, *Consultation Paper: Criminal Justice* (2016), 9, 12; see also Parliament of Australia, *Lost Innocents and Forgotten Australians Revisited*, [6.86].

[164] For example, sexual abuse was one of the main categories of abuse (along with emotional, physical and systems abuse, the latter denoting lack of adequate resources for the care of children) identified as occurring in Queensland's institutions in the 1999 inquiry in that state: see Commission of Inquiry into Abuse of Children in Queensland Institutions, *Report*, iv–v.

[165] Swain, 'Why Sexual Abuse? Why Now?', p. 85.

[166] Northern Territory Board of Inquiry into the Protection of Aboriginal Children from Sexual Abuse (NT), *Ampe Akelyernemane Meke Mekarle 'Little Children Are Sacred'*, Report (2007). This report found that child sexual abuse was a significant problem, and was occurring largely because of the breakdown of Aboriginal society and culture.

[167] Parliament of South Australia, Children in State Care Commission of Inquiry: Allegations of sexual abuse and death from criminal conduct (2008).

[168] See, e.g., Parliament of South Australia, *Children in State Care Commission of Inquiry*, xii.

[169] Swain, *History of Australian inquiries*, p. 9; see also K. Wright, 'Challenging Institutional Denial: Psychological Discourse, Therapeutic Culture and Public Inquiries' (2018) 42(2) *Journal of Australian Studies* 177–90, and *The Rise of the Therapeutic Society: Psychological Knowledge and the Contradictions of Cultural Change* (Washington, DC: New Academia, 2011).

[170] Swain, 'Beyond Child Migration', 150.

Commission into Institutional Responses was established by Prime Minister Julia Gillard in 2012.[171] It was tasked with investigating systemic failures in institutional responses to abuse, and making recommendations for policy, practice and law reform, to ensure that institutions were safer places for children in the future.[172] Reflecting political and social awareness of the serious and widespread nature of institutional child sexual abuse, the Royal Commission focused its inquiry on 'systemic failures' by institutions and the identification of 'best practice' to prevent such failures in the future.[173] The Inquiry was conducted on an unprecedented scale, and its final report was published in seventeen volumes.[174] The *Final Report* contained 409 recommendations covering a wide range of matters including civil and criminal laws, government practice and regulation of religious institutions, and support and treatment for survivors. Responses to this report have been prompt and fulsome, with, for example, the Federal government delivering a national apology in 2018, creating a national redress scheme for survivors in which state governments and churches will participate, and pledging to implement all recommendations that concern the government.[175]

As this indicates, governments are embracing responsibility for crimes against children in institutions in a more wholesale manner. Reflecting the profile of institutional child abuse, and the unprecedented public discussion about state responsibility the *Royal Commission into Institutional Responses* in particular has generated, the equivocal responses characterising the previous historic position of the state in relations of responsibility have been replaced with a broad willingness to assume responsibility. The focus of the inquiries of the current era on the systemic and structural issues that are now recognised as making institutional child abuse an intractable problem, and enabling it

[171] Royal Commission into Institutional Responses, *Final Report*, vol. 1, [1.1]. The establishment of a Royal Commission was a recommendation of the *Forgotten Australians Report*: see Parliament of Australia, *Forgotten Australians*, Recommendation 11.

[172] Royal Commission into Institutional Responses, *Final Report*, vol. 1, Appendix A. The *Royal Commission into Institutional Responses* was focused on sexual abuse exclusively, but encompassed both abuse occurring in 'closed' institutions (in which children lived, worked and were educated) and 'open' institutions (which children visited). For discussion, see K. Daly, 'Inequalities of Redress: Australia's National Redress Scheme for Institutional Abuse of Children' (2018) 42(2) *Journal of Australian Studies* 204–16, 205; F. Golding, 'Sexual Abuse as the Core Transgression of Childhood Innocence' (2018) 42(2) *Journal of Australian Studies* 191–203.

[173] Royal Commission into Institutional Responses, *Final Report*, vol. 1, [2.2.2].

[174] The Commission held over 400 days of public hearings, nearly 8000 private sessions with individuals who had been in children's institutions, and released 11 issues papers and five consultation papers: see Royal Commission into Institutional Responses, *Final Report*, vol. 1, [3.1]–[3.3].

[175] Press Conference with the Attorney General and the Minister for Social Services, Office of the Prime Minister Malcolm Turnbull MP, 13 June 2018. A national apology was delivered on 22 October 2018.

to go undetected although widespread, has placed the state at the centre of the frame, and demanded more wide-ranging responses from governments. Government responses to the *Royal Commission into Institutional Responses* include funds for educational programs, the creation of a National Children's Commissioner, and a taskforce to monitor implementation of the recommendations by state governments and churches.[176] Recognising the deep nature of the problem of institutional child abuse, the government referred to the need for 'cultural change in our institutions and society more broadly' to ensure the safety of children.[177] In addition, the redress scheme recommended by the *Royal Commission into Institutional Responses* will allow for individualised payments to survivors of institutional abuse, recognising the individualised nature of victimisation in institutions.

As per this position of the state in relations of responsibility, government responses to crimes against children in institutions now represent a collective reckoning with past practices, according to which state responsibility is shared by both governments and the public. On the basis that 'the pain endured by so many for so long, which had been understood by relatively few, required a community response',[178] these inquiries invoke the public at large in the response, suggesting that governments are responding on behalf of society. Thus in its *Final Report*, the *Royal Commission into Institutional Responses* stated that 'although the primary responsibility for the sexual abuse of a child lies with the abuser and the institution of which they were part, we cannot avoid the conclusion that the problems faced by many people who have been abused are the responsibility of our entire society'.[179] As this suggests, collective responsibility exists in addition to, or alongside, the responsibility of the state and institutions such as children's organisations. In this context, as well as supporting governance institutions and practices that recognise the harms of the past and aim to prevent harm from occurring in the future, as discussed above, the state is taking on the responsibility society bears as a collective.

Against this background, in order to enhance government responses to institutional child abuse, changes to both the civil law and the criminal law have been enacted or recommended. These changes represent a new thrust of criminalisation that encompasses both the state and individuals. For example, in relation to the civil law, limitation periods on prosecution of child abuse have been extended or removed in several Australian jurisdictions,[180] and laws have now been enacted in several jurisdictions to require that all unincorporated organisations working with children make available an entity for

176 Press Conference, Office of the Prime Minister Malcolm Turnbull MP, 13 June 2018.

177 Ibid.

178 Royal Commission into Institutional Responses, *Final Report*, vol. 1, [1.2].

179 Royal Commission into Institutional Responses, *Final Report*, Preface.

180 See, e.g., *Limitations of Actions Amendment (Child Abuse) Act 2015* (Vic).

civil suit.[181] In relation to the criminal law, recommended changes include the wider introduction of third party offences – failure to report and failure to protect – which are based on gross negligence (criminalising a person who knows, suspects or should have known that a child is being or has been sexually abused in an institution).[182] These provisions are intended to sit alongside civil reporting obligations which are imposed on health professionals, police officers and others, and exist in all Australian institutions.[183] While research commissioned by the *Royal Commission into Institutional Responses* had proposed a new offence of 'institutional child sexual abuse' (criminalising an organisation where an individual associated with it is convicted of an offence of child sexual assault and the organisation was reckless as to the commission of the offence[184]), in its *Final Report*, the Royal Commission opted to expand abuse of position of authority offences and to rely on civil liability for institutions.[185] These changes to the legal proscription of child abuse are wide-ranging, and indicate that there is a growing expectation that both the civil and criminal law will be harnessed (and reformed as required) to address institutional child abuse. This represents a comprehensive attempt to ensure that Australia is the kind of nation where such conduct cannot happen again.

As this discussion suggests, this fourth historic position of the state posits an enhanced position and function for both the individual *and* the state. In relation to the individual, the discourse of disease and disorder that emerged to underpin notions of individual responsibility for offending against children has been overlaid by the enhanced moralisation of child abuse.[186] In addition, recent public inquiries have marshalled extensive evidence to indicate that offending against

[181] See, e.g., *Civil Liability Legislation Amendment (Child Sexual Abuse Actions) Act 2018* (WA) and *Legal Identity of Defendants (Organisational Child Abuse) Act 2018* (Vic).

[182] Royal Commission into Institutional Responses, *Final Report*, Recommendations 32–36. In addition to more traditional failure to report offences, offences criminalising failure to report certain serious crimes against children have been enacted in two Australian jurisdictions (see *Crimes Act 1900* (NSW) s 316A(1) and *Crimes Act 1958* (Vic) s 327) (the *mens rea* for these offences is knowledge or belief that the offence has been committed). Specific failure to protect children offences also exist in two jurisdictions (see *Criminal Law Consolidation Act 1935* (SA) s 14 and *Children, Youth and Families Act 2005* (Vic) s 49(3)) (criminalising individuals who have a duty of care to a child and either recklessly or intentionally fail to act that has resulted in harm to the child).

[183] See for discussion B. Mathews, *Mandatory Reporting laws for Child Sexual Abuse in Australia: A Legislative History*, Report for the Royal Commission into Institutional Responses to Child Sexual Abuse (2014). It has been recommended that these reporting obligations be extended to include religious personnel: Royal Commission into Institutional Responses, *Final Report*, Recommendation 7.3.

[184] This provision is modelled on the corporate culture provision of corporate liability in the Commonwealth Criminal Code: see Freiberg, Donnelly and Gelb, *Sentencing for Child Sexual Abuse*, pp. 242–45. I discuss this provision of the Commonwealth Criminal Code in Chapter 5.

[185] Royal Commission into Institutional Responses, *Final Report*, Recommendations 27–9 and 89–93 respectively.

[186] See generally Hacking, 'The Making and Molding of Child Abuse'.

children is not restricted to paedophiles, and that there is no typical offender and no typical offence of institutional child sexual abuse.[187] In relation to the state, the close examination of the institutions in which offences occurred has exposed the ways in which lack of official oversight, inadequate resources and lax organisational controls permitted offences to occur,[188] suggesting that some institutions are themselves criminogenic.[189] As a result, and by contrast with other historic positions of the state, the state is not thought of as an invisible hand or a servant of self-governing individuals, but rather as 'a centralised institutional power that regulates the exercise of sub-institutions of power and authority'.[190] In addition, against a backdrop of extensive media coverage of alleged cover-ups by police, government, churches and charities,[191] the sheer scale and severity of abuse in institutions that has emerged in recent public inquiries has generated a nebulous but palpable sense that responsibility properly rests with the state.

> This report [about children in institutional care] is not just concerned with the past, it is very much about the present and it informs the future of our nation.[192]

This chapter has considered the changing position of the state in relations of responsibility, explored through an examination of government responses to crimes against children in institutions. I argued that there are four historic positions of the state in relations of responsibility, which are prominent at different points across the twentieth century and first decades of the twenty-first century. In these relations of responsibility, the position of the state is less or more prominent, and its function is less or more elaborate – restricted to condemnation and prosecution, extending to prevention and deterrence, and to more elaborate functions concerning reconciliation with the past, preservation of the state and active strategies to avoid recurrence in the future. Each of these historic positions of the state posits a particular relation to individual responsibility for crime, revealing the ways in which criminal responsibility is distributed *between* individuals and the state and showing that such a division is dynamic. In the current era, state responsibility has become more developed, and has come to encompass historic wrongs and harms as well as future or potential harms, and the state has come to take on the responsibility society is understood to bear as a collective. At the same time, the expansion of state responsibility has tracked an enhancement of individual responsibility, as the moralisation of child abuse has overlaid discourses of disease and disorder. In this context, there is a growing awareness of the need to harness all parts of the legal order in attempts to ensure such crimes cannot happen again.

187 See Parliament of Victoria, *Betrayal of Trust*, p. 123.
188 See Commonwealth, Royal Commission into Institutional Responses to Child Sexual Abuse, *Interim Report* (2014), vol. 1, p. 8.
189 Freiberg et al., *Sentencing for Child Sexual Abuse*, p. 7.
190 Schneebaum, 'Making Abuse Offences in the Modern Criminal Law', 47.
191 Daly, 'Redress for Historical Institutional Abuse of Children', p. 454.
192 Parliament of Australia, *Forgotten Australians*, xvii.

Conclusion

This book has re-examined criminal responsibility. In the context of Australian criminal laws, it reassessed the general story told about the rise to prominence of criminal responsibility from around the turn of the twentieth century, paying close and careful attention to the intricacies of developments in criminal responsibility within this period. At the same time, the book reconsidered the role and, hence, significance of criminal responsibility in criminal law, arguing that criminal responsibility organises keys sets of relations – between self, others and the state – as relations of responsibility, and that this is what makes it significant. My analysis generated two main insights. First, it revealed the gradual and distinctive way in which Australian criminal laws came to be organised around criminal responsibility over the twentieth century, and what this makes possible and what it precludes. Second, it exposed the complexity and dynamism of the relations of responsibility that subtend criminal responsibility principles and practices – substituting the still-dominant account of criminal responsibility as singular, general and universal, for an account characterised by multiplicity, specificity and variation across the criminal law field.

My re-examination of criminal responsibility was presented across a socio-historical and a theoretical axis. Exploring the way in which criminal law came to be organised around criminal responsibility, I offered three point-in-time assessments of the part played by criminal responsibility in the organisation of Australian criminal laws. These assessments focused on the state of play at around the turn of the twentieth century, in the mid-century, and in the final decades of the twentieth century, revealing the way in which criminal responsibility moved from a position as one criminal law issue among others, to the centre of the criminal law, as the lens through which issues with the criminal law are refracted. Building on my new account of what makes criminal responsibility significant, and along a theoretical axis, I presented an analysis of relations of responsibility, set out in a tripartite schema – between self, others and the state. This schema allowed me to examine in detail the different sets of relations organised under criminal responsibility. Through my examination, I tracked the ways in which relations of responsibility change over space and time, taking shape in the context of particular systems of criminal law and at particular junctures. My new account of the role and significance of criminal responsibility emerged out of, and contributed to, the critical criminal responsibility scholarship, presenting both a way of understanding and a basis of critique of responsibility in criminal law.

By way of conclusion, in the spirit of scholarly self-reflection central to critical legal studies,[1] I offer a short discussion of some of the implications of my analysis for our understanding of criminal responsibility. First, I consider the implications of my socio-historical analysis of criminal responsibility, and, second, I address the implications of my theoretical argument about the significance of criminal responsibility. Finally, I provide a brief outlook on the possible future research trajectories opened up by the re-examination provided in this book.

Looking Back

The first of the two main arguments advanced in this book relates to the socio-historical development of criminal responsibility over the period since around the turn of the twentieth century. Set in the context of Australian criminal laws, my study revealed that criminal law came to be oriented around criminal responsibility in a gradual and distinctive way over this period.

My socio-historical analysis was grounded in a conviction that space and time are crucial to a deep understanding of criminal responsibility principles and practices. In existing scholarship, space and time have received somewhat uneven treatment in existing studies of criminal responsibility. What I labelled the default northern orientation of criminal responsibility studies operates to homogenise aspects of the different legal systems typically examined by scholars. I suggested that this default orientation carries with it the implication that it is possible to fully grasp the development of criminal responsibility within this circumscribed frame (typically centred on English law), on the basis that other legal systems occupy a lesser or merely derivative position. My own study focused on responsibility principles and practices in Australian criminal laws in the twentieth century. Pitching a critical account of criminal responsibility 'close to the ground' in Australian criminal laws subverted the default northern orientation of existing scholarship, and shed a new light on the topic of responsibility in criminal law. This focus enabled me to introduce a new set of jurisdictions to the criminal responsibility scholarship – Australian criminal

1 See W. Twining, 'Reflections on Law in Context', in P. Cane and Jane Stapleton (eds.), *Essays for Patrick Atiyah* (Oxford: Oxford University Press, 1991).

jurisdictions – and constituted a delimited approach that meant I could to keep space and time in the frame at the same time.

This socio-historical analysis presented in this book has four main implications for scholarly understanding of criminal responsibility. First, the focus on Australia highlighted the relevance of the borrowings and lendings that feature in the development of criminal responsibility in the twentieth century. My analysis revealed the importance of spaces and moments that I labelled 'in between' or interstitial – existing within or between, or perhaps 'in advance of', standard or orthodox legal spaces or moments – for criminal responsibility. The circulation of ideas about criminal responsibility across the interstitial spaces and through the institutions of Empire and its aftermath, and in the context of the development of comparative jurisprudence from the second half of the nineteenth century, impacts on the development of responsibility principles in criminal law. For example, in the major consolidation of criminal laws in NSW at the end of the nineteenth century, as well as in the codification of criminal laws of Queensland, practitioners and legislators drew on the work to codify the English common law of crime, and the draft code developed by James Fitzjames Stephen.[2] Similarly, the development of the central chapter of the *Commonwealth Criminal Code*, on criminal responsibility, at the end of the twentieth century was modelled on the corresponding article of the US *Model Penal and Correctional Code*.[3] Interstitial spaces and moments form a crucial but hitherto neglected dimension of criminal responsibility in that they expose the dynamic ways in which ideas about responsibility in criminal law circulate across space and time. I suggested that Australian criminal responsibility cannot be understood without awareness of these spaces and moments, and borrowings and lendings, and, further, that the story of criminal responsibility in English criminal law would be enhanced by reference to this broader context.

The second main implication of my study of the development of criminal responsibility since around the turn of the twentieth century relates to ideas about the modernisation of criminal law. While the modernisation of the criminal law has been associated with codification,[4] in the Australian context, concerns about the need to modernise criminal law and criminal justice institutions resulted in both codification and consolidation. My examination

[2] See Chapter 3.

[3] See Chapter 5. On the *Model Penal Code*, see M. D. Dubber, 'The Model Penal Code, Legal Process and the Alegitimacy of American Penality', in M. D. Dubber (ed.), *Foundational Texts in Modern Criminal Law* (Oxford: Oxford University Press, 2014).

[4] See, e.g., K. J. M. Smith, 'Macaulay's "Utilitarian" Indian Penal Code: An Illustration of the Accidental Function of Time, Place and Personalities in Law Making', in W. M. Gordon and T. D. Fergus (eds.), *Legal History in the Making: Proceedings from the Ninth British Legal History Conference* (London: The Hambledon Press, 1991), pp. 158–60.

of the *Criminal Law Amendment Act 1883* (NSW) and the Queensland *Criminal Code* enacted in 1899 revealed that each was a product of broad systematising and rationalising law reform efforts: in these efforts, consolidation and the distinctive practice of codification were understood as different options for reform of the criminal law, distinguished in part by pragmatic concerns, and the ambition and scale of the reform. Against a background of the early development of institutions of democratic governance in Australia, and amid concerns with the exercise of government power, the 1883 Act and the 1899 Code represented a commitment to modernisation founded on form – comprehensive legislation or a code – and process – the operation of criminal justice – as much as on principles of criminal responsibility. Thus, although the Act and the Code adopted different approaches to criminal responsibility, the significance of criminal responsibility in the two reforms – in which it was placed onto a legislative platform to make clearer what was considered opaque – was common to each reform. As this indicates, the Australian case suggests that attempts to grasp the modernisation of criminal law should go beyond codification, to take into account other practices of law reform.

The third main implication of my study of the development of criminal responsibility relates to the rise of criminal responsibility to the centre of the criminal law. In Australia, as elsewhere, the idea that the criminal law is comprised of a set of general principles of criminal responsibility took firm hold in the mid-century, when it came to enjoy widespread acceptance among both practitioners and scholars. Such principles are typically understood as the 'grammar' of the criminal law that is shared by common law systems across the world.[5] However, the Australian case demonstrated that criminal responsibility was vital to the development of a sense of *national* criminal law.[6] The principles of criminal responsibility played a key role in the 'birth' of Australian criminal law in the mid-century: through the elucidation and application of these principles by judges, lawyers and scholars, and in the drafting of the first Australian criminal law textbooks, which were published from the late 1940s to the 1960s, in this period it became possible to think about Australian criminal law as such, to conceptualise Australian criminal law as a meaningful idea. In negotiating a position for themselves between the jurisprudence of English courts, and commentaries such as that of Glanville Williams, on the one hand, and US developments such as the *Model Penal Code*, on the other hand, Australian lawyers and commentators came to forge an independent path for the criminal law by reference to criminal responsibility principles: it was with an abiding

[5] See G. Fletcher, *The Grammar of Criminal Law: American, Comparative, and International: Volume 1: Foundations* (Oxford: Oxford University Press, 2007), ch. 1.

[6] See Chapter 4.

ethos of fidelity to these principles that Australian courts and Australian academics came to elaborate a criminal law of Australia, and, as part of that process, to distinguish that law from that of England and Wales, and elsewhere. As this suggests, the Australian case challenges the idea that criminal responsibility can be understood without reference to the positive law contexts in which it operates.

The fourth main implication of my study of the development of criminal responsibility relates to the role of criminal responsibility in criminal law in the last decades of the twentieth century. At this time, a range of problems and challenges combined to generate momentum for, first, a review of Commonwealth law, followed by the development of the *Model Criminal Code*, and then the codification of Commonwealth criminal law via the *Criminal Code Act 1995* (Cth). As a late twentieth century codification, the Commonwealth *Criminal Code* was based on different imperatives from other major codifications. As a legal systematisation, the emphasis in the Commonwealth Code was on the (re-)organisation of criminal laws, and, as a result, aspects of criminal justice such as criminal process or punishment, which had informed the development of the Queensland Criminal Code in the 1890s and the *Model Penal Code* in the mid-century, were left to the side. The emphasis on the (re-)organisation of criminal laws in the codification of Commonwealth criminal law brought with it a particular role for criminal responsibility: as 'the very foundations of any system of criminal justice',[7] the principles of criminal responsibility were fixed at the heart of Australian criminal laws via the codification of Commonwealth law and it was the role of criminal responsibility to provide the integrity of the criminal law, enabling the criminal law to make sense on its own terms. As a late twentieth-century codification, the Australian case of the Commonwealth *Criminal Code* provides a useful counterpoint to more commonly studied codification projects, such as the *Model Penal Code*.

In sum, a study of the development of criminal responsibility set in the context of Australian criminal laws over the twentieth century sheds new light on criminal responsibility. Offering an 'outside-in view of the subject',[8] my examination pointed to the value of situating a study 'close to the ground', in one set of jurisdictions, and over a delimited time period. The scholarly decision to pursue a study with these spatial and temporal parameters allowed me to examine principles and practices of criminal responsibility in their

[7] Criminal Law Officers' Committee (CLOC), Standing Committee of Attorneys-General, *Model Criminal Code Chapters 1 and 2: General Principles of Criminal Responsibility, Final Report* (1992), ii.

[8] M. D. Dubber, 'Colonial Criminal Law and Other Modernities: European Criminal Law in the Nineteenth and Twentieth Century', in H. Pihlajamäki, M. D. Dubber and M. Godfrey (eds.), *The Oxford Handbook of European Legal History* (Oxford: Oxford University Press, 2018), pp. 1062–3.

social, political and institutional context. It opens the way for other similarly close and delimited studies of criminal responsibility set in other contexts and time periods, and for the further exploration of comparative approaches to criminal responsibility, in which the significance of the borrowings and lendings which mark the development of criminal responsibility might be explored.

Looking Around

I now turn to explore the implications of my theoretical analysis of criminal responsibility for existing criminal responsibility scholarship. My theoretical analysis proceeded on the basis that, notwithstanding the value of existing scholarship, a crucial role of criminal responsibility has been overlooked. This hitherto overlooked role of responsibility, and hence, it's significance, necessitated a new account of criminal responsibility.

In my account, criminal responsibility organises key sets of relations – between self, others and the state – as relations of responsibility, and this is what makes it significant. These relations subtend the principles and practices of responsibility in criminal law. While criminal law is generally thought to concern relations between subjects (archetypally, individuals) and objects (harms, wrongs or crimes), I argued that criminal responsibility – something that is primarily an 'artefact' of the criminal law[9] – concerns relations between subjects (and the state). As the basis on which individuals are called to account under criminal law, and the form or structure of the law, criminal responsibility delineates relations between subjects, and plots these relations as relations of responsibility. As such, criminal responsibility concerns the 'people' of criminal law and provides access to the 'social life' of criminal law. I set out these relations of responsibility via a tripartite schema of self, others and the state, and examined the relations that coalesced around each node. My analysis of the role of criminal responsibility exposed its complexity and dynamism, replacing the still-dominant understanding of criminal responsibility as singular, general and universal, with an understanding characterised by multiplicity, specificity and variation across time and across the criminal law field. On my analysis, criminal responsibility is revealed as the means by which matters of subjectivity, relationality and power make themselves felt in the criminal law in particular ways.

There are three main implications of my analysis of relations of responsibility for scholarly understanding of criminal responsibility. The first of these relates to the role of the self in responsibility in criminal law. The self occupies a preeminent place in criminal law and scholarly thinking about

[9] See L. Farmer, *Making the Modern Criminal Law: Criminalization and Civil Order. Series: Criminalization* (Oxford: Oxford University Press, 2016), p. 165.

criminal law,[10] but the self of criminal responsibility is conceptualised in a limited or partial way – as an autonomous rational individual.[11] As Ngaire Naffine writes, reflecting the dominance of the tradition of legal-philosophical scholarship on criminal responsibility – which draws on normative philosophical thinking – the rational agent is the '*sine qua non* of much criminal law theory'.[12] But there is more to the self: he or she exists in context, and he or she has an embodied and material life, and is situated in relations with him or herself, others and the state. Taking my cue from the critical criminal responsibility scholarship, I approached the self or legal subject in this more fulsome way. This approach required taking seriously various aspects of the contexts in which subjects are located, and acknowledging the relevance of social norms, institutions and practices for subjectivity.

In my analysis of the self in relations of responsibility, I focused on the gendered self and examined women's responsibility for crime. I argued that, on the level of legal form, women's responsibility for crime is marked by particularity and specificity – as opposed to the generality and universalism claimed for criminal responsibility under the dominant legal-philosophical account.[13] This particularity and specificity is evident in the two sets of atypical responsibility forms – those forms that are restricted to particular individuals committing particular offences in particular contexts, and in which elements, such as offence and defence, conduct and fault, that are usually separate, are mixed together – that determine the contours of women's responsibility for crime. I also argued that two sets of atypical responsibility forms correspond with different relations of responsibility between self, others and the state: over the twentieth century, changing ideas about violence by women, and violence against women, have generated changes in relations of responsibility, according to which the individual is positioned differently in relation to herself, to others and to the state.

This analysis revealed the relevance of public and political debates for subjectivity in criminal law. These debates have forged a particular configuration of what Lindsay Farmer has referred to as a combination of 'moral and social responsibilities'.[14] In part as a result of changing public and political discourses relating to women's responsibility for crime – particularly what has become a strong societal and moral condemnation of violence against women – women's responsibility for crime has been reconstructed. While the

[10] See N. Lacey, 'Philosophical Foundations of the Common Law: Social not Metaphysical', in J. Horder (ed.), *Oxford Essays in Jurisprudence* (Oxford: Oxford University Press, 2000), p. 25.

[11] See Chapter 2.

[12] N. Naffine, *Law's Meaning of Life: Philosophy, Religion, Darwin and the Legal Person* (London: Hart Publishing, 2009), p. 70.

[13] See Chapter 6.

[14] Farmer, *Making the Modern Criminal Law*, p. 192.

reconstruction of the field of suffering and victimisation as a result of greater public recognition of the harm of domestic violence has been well recognised – and is reflected in the creation of new offences such as stalking and attempted strangulation[15] – the impact of these changed dynamics on responsibility for crime has attracted less attention. The influence of social science and feminist knowledges on social and political discourses has emphasised the structural aspect of violence against women, and rendered such violence a societal and government responsibility as much as an individual responsibility. This has meant that women's responsibility for crime now has an ameliorative tenor, with the atypical responsibility forms that now populate the criminal law constituting an admission of state failure to protect women from violence.

The second of the three main implications of my analysis of relations of responsibility for scholarly understanding of criminal responsibility concerns relations between individuals or 'others'. Just as the self at the centre of criminal responsibility principles and practices is an abstract and abstracted individual, so he or she is typically treated in isolation from others, and as acting alone in committing criminal conduct. As I discussed in Chapter 2, where relations between individuals, or selves and others, are taken into account in the context of criminal responsibility, it tends to be within a circumscribed subspace of criminal responsibility scholarship – that concerned with complicity or participation in crime. Individuals' relations with others impact on criminal responsibility beyond the bounds of complicity, however, even if this is not apparent or taken into account by responsibility scholars.[16] Working on the basis that law routinely structures relations, in my analysis of others as one node of my schema of relations of responsibility, I choose to focus on individuals in otherwise ordinary relations with each other.

This interest led me to focus on the offence of consorting – broadly, the offence of association with criminals – which implicates individuals in ordinary relations with each other. I suggested that, under consorting, the individual becomes meaningful to the criminal law in his or her relations with others, whereby that individual's conduct with, and knowledge of, the other are the basis for the offence. In my analysis, consorting laws fall into two generations, and relations of responsibility between individuals or 'others' fall into two corresponding archetypal patterns – 'companionship with thieves' and 'friendship with the state'.[17] Under the first generation of laws, relations of responsibility reinforced existing, highly stratified social relations, and individuals charged with consorting were responsible for threatening harm or disorder in certain

[15] See, e.g., *Crimes (Domestic and Personal Violence) Act 2007* (NSW) s 13 (offence of stalking or intimidation with intent to cause fear) and *Criminal Code 1899* (Qld) s 351A (offence of strangulation, suffocation and choking in a domestic setting) respectively.

[16] See J. Nedelsky, 'Reconceiving Rights as Relationship' (1993) 1(1) *Review of Constitutional Studies* 1–26, 14.

[17] See Chapter 7.

public contexts, and were responsible to the community rather than the state. Under the second generation of laws, relations of responsibility assume a flat and standardised structure, in which all individuals are brought into the same relation with each other and the state. As I suggested, this relation now looks like 'friendship' – with the responsibility individuals bear to the state equated with their responsibility to each other. Individuals charged with consorting are now responsible *to* the state, and what they are responsible *for* in their relations with others has changed, with a more extensive conception of responsibility – encompassing personal attitudes and self-regulation – now sustaining relations of responsibility.

This analysis revealed the impact that changed ideas about relationality – broadly, the connections between persons, and 'community rather than individuality, sociability rather than the solidary self'[18] – have had on criminal law. Flowing from the shift to 'late' modernity,[19] in the current era, relations between individuals are now characterised by a radical reflexivity, and 'responsibilities for conduct' are assembled in a new way, with the individual located in a network of other individuals making up community.[20] Under these conditions, what individuals are responsible *for* in their relations with others has changed: conduct is regarded as reflecting back on the subject, representing a reflective moral or ethical position as opposed to a single act at one point in time. In addition, the individual is now responsible *to* the state, as the state is brought *into* the relationship between individuals in a distinct way. The individual is *activated* in his or her interpersonal associations: via consorting, all interpersonal associations can be plotted in relation to wider, state-sanctioned practices around matters such as security. And as a result, through relations of responsibility that represent 'friendship with the state', the criminal law is encoding loyalty and allegiance. So, while the relations between individuals that are posited by criminal responsibility principles and practices are sometimes assumed to be singular and static – reduced to a conflict between wrongdoer and wronged, offender and victim, with the state as the prosecutor of the former on behalf of the latter[21] – such relations

[18] G. Lloyd, 'Individuals, Responsibility and the Philosophical Imagination', in C. Mackenzie and N. Stoljar (eds.), *Relational Autonomy: Feminist Perspectives on Autonomy, Agency, and the Social Self* (Oxford: Oxford University Press, 2000), p. 112.

[19] See N. Rose, *Inventing Our Selves: Psychology, Power, and Personhood* (Cambridge: Cambridge University Press, 1998); D. Garland, *The Culture of Control: Crime and Social Order in Contemporary Society* (Chicago: University of Chicago Press, 2001); U. Beck, *Risk Society: Towards a New Modernity* (Mark Ritter trans, London: Sage Publications, 1992); A. Giddens, *The Consequences of Modernity* (Stanford: Stanford University Press, 1990); A. Giddens, *Modernity and Self-Identity: Self and Society in the Late Modern Age* (Stanford: Stanford University Press, 1991).

[20] N. Rose, *Powers of Freedom: Reframing Political Thought* (Cambridge: Cambridge University Press, 1999), p. 176, and more generally, ch. 5.

[21] For critical discussion, see C. Lernestedt, 'Victim and Society: Sharing Wrongs, but in Which Roles?' (2014) 8 *Criminal Law and Philosophy* 187–203.

are multiple and dynamic, and my analysis illuminated the impact of such relations on responsibility in criminal law.

The third of the three main implications of my analysis of relations of responsibility for scholarly understanding of criminal responsibility concerns the state. The state is foundational to criminal responsibility: reflecting modern democratic beliefs about the authority of legal institutions, through principles and practices of criminal responsibility, a person is prosecuted for criminal conduct in the name of the state or community. As discussed in Chapter 2, on this understanding of the state, it is an enforcement agency, and the criminal law is a system of official censure and sanction or punishment for certain types of conduct. Here, the state is understood in a minimal or 'thin' way – in terms of democratic norms, political legitimacy and as an authority for punishment. The ways in which the state is implicated criminal responsibility goes far beyond these boundaries, however. Approaching the state as a set of institutions coordinating a large set of regulatory and governance practices relating to all aspects of social, political and economic life, exposes the different ways in which the state is implicated in relations of responsibility. My examination of the state in relations of responsibility entailed going behind doctrinal arrangements concerning individual responsibility for crime, and the procedural setting in which these arrangements play out – the criminal trial – to open up the prior issue of the state's position and function in relations of responsibility.

This approach led me to examine the role of the state in what has become a particularly prominent aspect of state responsibility in Australia: Australian state responses to child abuse occurring in institutions.[22] I explored state responses to institutional child abuse via a self-consciously reflective aspect of state governance – public inquiries – which opened up, rather than closed off, questions about state responsibility. I argued that there are four historic positions of the state in relations of responsibility, which are prominent at particular times across the twentieth century and in the first years of the twenty-first century. I suggest that, as per these four historic positions, state responsibility is negotiated across dynamics of the modernisation of children's institutions and child welfare practices, the development of institutions associated with the welfare state and the professionalisation of welfare, and across the boundary between past and present, and Empire and nation and in a global context. My study revealed that, since the turn of the twentieth century, state responsibility in relation to crime has become more developed, and has come to encompass historic wrongs and harms as well as future or potential harms, and the state has come to take on the responsibility society is understood to bear as a collective.

[22] See Chapter 8.

This analysis exposed the importance of power in criminal law. Although typically obscured in studies of criminal responsibility, particular power relations structure the allocation or distribution of responsibility between the state and individuals. As I show in my analysis of state responsibility in relation to crimes committed against children in institutions, the division of responsibility between the state and individuals is not a simple zero-sum game in which more of one type of responsibility corresponds with less of the other. Rather, relations of responsibility are structured or patterned according to wider dynamics, including the formation of the apparatus of the welfare state, development of expert psychological and social-scientific knowledges about individuals and systems, and the moral condemnation that now attaches to child abuse. My analysis also opens the way for exploration of other ways in which the state is implicated in relations of responsibility, such as through changes in justificatory defences like self defence, which 'help tie the criminal law to political surroundings',[23] or in the changing position and function of the state embedded in offences like misconduct in public office.[24]

Approaching criminal responsibility as organising relations of responsibility in criminal law helps to develop a nuanced understanding of the part played by criminal responsibility in criminal law. This is the inverse of Farmer's point that criminal responsibility is 'primarily a legal artefact'.[25] According to my analysis, the significance of criminal responsibility is that what is 'primarily a legal artefact' carries with it wide relational resonance. My study suggested that scholars must recognise what we can think of as the social life of criminal responsibility: appreciating this social life deepens our understanding of criminal responsibility, exposing the complexity and dynamism of responsibility in criminal law.

Looking Forward

Finally, I consider the possible future research trajectories opened up by the re-examination of criminal responsibility provided in this book. These trajectories are outlined here with the aim of stimulating further critical scholarly work on criminal responsibility.

One possible trajectory for future research relates to enhancing our understanding of the social dimensions of holding people to account in criminal law. Responsibility occupies a key place in the wider social order of which the legal order is a part. As such, responsibility is central to our personal and collective lives – in particular, in ordering judgments of ourselves and others[26] – and is

23 See C. Lernestedt, 'Vertical, Horizontal, Backwards, Forwards' (2017) 4(1) *Critical Analysis of Law* 22–30, 26.

24 See J. Horder, *Criminal Misconduct in Office* (Oxford: Oxford University Press, 2018).

25 Farmer, *Making the Modern Criminal Law*, pp. 165, 170.

26 See M. Matravers, *Responsibility and Justice* (Cambridge: Polity Press, 2007), p. 1.

also an axis across which social structures – including relations between self and others, family, and state – and social change are measured, meaning that criminal responsibility is an aspect of the organisation of social systems. In the current era, social meanings around responsibility for crime appear increasingly complex and such meanings may be hidden or obscured rather exposed by the neat, familiar and stable categories (offences and defences) beloved by law and legal scholars,[27] and by an overly sharp division of labour between criminal law theory and criminology.[28] The complexity of social relations in the current era has produced calls among social scientists for the development of methods sensitive to 'the complex and the elusive', and the use of slippery non-unit units of analysis, 'units that are not'.[29] Thinking creatively about how such units might be employed in the study of criminal responsibility will open up new avenues for research that better grasps the social dimensions of holding people to account in criminal law.

A second possible trajectory for future research relates to the intellectual history of the concept of responsibility. The language of responsibility may be found in politics and social policy, as well as in political theory, social science, philosophy and elsewhere, and it attracts multiple meanings across these spaces.[30] In the current era, responsibility has come to be intimately associated with political discourses ('rights and responsibilities') and with various governance practices operating in modern liberal democracies such as Australia.[31] As Yascha Mounk argues, the language of responsibility may be found across the political spectrum, with those on the left of politics accepting 'the key normative assumptions of the punitive conception of responsibility' promoted by those on the right, and merely seeking to deny the imposition or applicability of responsibility in particular instances.[32] For Mounk, the transformation of political rhetoric along these lines was grounded in a new consensus in philosophy and social science, whereby the notion of responsibility-as-duty gave way to responsibility-as-accountability.[33] Given the recency of this 'consensus',

27 See A. Loughnan, 'From Carpetbag to Crucible: Reconceptualising Diminished Responsibility Manslaughter', in B. Livings, A. Reed and N. Wake (eds.), *Mental Condition Defences and the Criminal Justice System: Perspectives from Law and Medicine* (Cambridge: Cambridge Scholars Publishing, 2015).

28 Lacey comments on the 'unhelpful' character of the division of labour between criminal law scholars and criminologists: see N. Lacey, 'Legal Constructions of Crime,' in M. Maguire, R. Morgan and R. Reiner (eds.), *The Oxford Handbook of Criminology*, 4th ed. (Oxford: Oxford University Press, 2007), p. 181.

29 See J. Law and J. Urry, 'Enacting the Social' (2004) 33(3) *Economy and Society* 390–410, 404.

30 See Y. Mounk, *The Age of Responsibility: Luck, Choice and the Welfare State* (Cambridge, MA: Harvard University Press, 2017), pp. 4–5.

31 Matravers, *Responsibility and Justice*, pp. 5–11. For a philosophical discussion of some of the possible relations between rights and responsibilities, see J. Deign, 'On Rights and Responsibilities' (1988) 7 *Law and Philosophy* 147–78.

32 Mounk, *The Age of Responsibility*, p. 14, and pp. 13–18 more generally.

33 Mounk, *The Age of Responsibility*, pp. 64–9.

an intellectual history of the concept of responsibility might bring to light now marginal political and social dimensions of responsibility, permitting scholars to imagine different intellectual futures for responsibility in criminal law.

Last, and relatedly, a possible trajectory of future research might consider the ways in which the study of criminal responsibility might be connected to other bodies of work on responsibility, and included in a wider, interdisciplinary 'politics of responsibility'. While, to date, theoretical scholarship on criminal responsibility has been primarily focused on its role in criminal law (in the different ways discussed in Chapter 2), indicating the centrality of responsibility as an aspect of the coherence and rationality of the modern criminal law, there is scope to open out the discussion, moving beyond disciplinary boundaries. Connecting criminal responsibility to other bodies of work on responsibility entails bringing criminal legal scholarly efforts with those of scholars in the humanities and social sciences, and places legal responsibility practices in a wider frame of social practices. This holds out the possibility of exploring other disciplinary traditions for the development of ideas about responsibility.

Criminal responsibility is more than one topic among many, and critical criminal responsibility scholarship is a vibrant scholarly field. My analysis offered both a way of understanding and a basis of critique of criminal responsibility. With the introduction of a new set of jurisdictions and a new account of the significance of responsibility in criminal law, this book sought to push the boundaries of scholarly understanding of criminal responsibility.

Bibliography

Aitken, J. '"The Horrors of Matrimony Among the Masses": Feminist Representations of Wife Beating in England and Australia, 1870–1914' (2007) 19(4) *Journal of Women's History* 107–31.

Allan, G. 'Friendship, Sociology and Social Structure' (1998) 15(5) *Journal of Social and Personal Relationships* 685–702.

Allen, C. K. *Law in the Making* (London: Clarendon Press, 1927).

Allen, H. *Justice Unbalanced: Gender, Psychiatry and Judicial Decisions* (Milton Keynes: Open University Press, 1987).

Allen, J. A. *Sex and Secrets: Crimes Involving Australian Women since 1880* (Melbourne: Oxford University Press, 1990).

Angelides, S. 'The Emergence of the Paedophile in the Late Twentieth Century' (2005) 36 *Historical Studies* 272–95.

Arrow, M. 'Making Family Violence Public in the Royal Commission on Human Relationships, 1974–1977' (2018) 33(95) *Australian Feminist Studies* 81–96.

Arrow, M. 'Public Intimacies: The Royal Commission on Human Relationships 1974–1977', in L. Featherstone, R. Jennings and R. Reynolds (eds.), *Acts of Love and Lust: Sexuality in Australia from 1945–2010* (Newcastle: Cambridge Scholars Publishing, 2014), pp. 23–43.

Arrow, M. and Woollacott, A. 'Introduction – How the Personal Became Political: The Gender and Sexuality Revolutions in 1970s Australia' (2018) 33(95) *Australian Feminist Studies* 1–8.

Ashworth, A. 'Interpreting Criminal Statutes: A Crisis of Legality?' (1991) 107 *Law Quarterly Review* 419–49.

Positive Obligations in Criminal Law (London: Bloomsbury, 2013).

'The Making of the English Criminal Law (4) Blackstone, Foster and East' [1978] *Criminal Law Review* 389–99.

'Towards a Theory of Criminal Legislation' (1989) 1(1) *Criminal Law Forum* 41–63.

Ashworth, A. and Horder, J. *Principles of Criminal Law*, 7th ed. (Oxford: Oxford University Press, 2013).

Ashworth, A. and Zedner, L. *Preventive Justice* (Oxford: Oxford University Press, 2014).

Ayling, J. 'Pre-emptive Strike: How Australia Is Tackling Outlaw Motorcycle Gangs' (2011) 36(3) *American Journal of Criminal Justice* 250–64.

Bagaric, M. 'The High Court on Crime in 2010: Analysis and Jurisprudence' (2011) 35 *Criminal Law Journal* 5–20.

Banivanua-Mar, T. 'Consolidating Violence and Colonial Rule: Discipline and Protection in Colonial Queensland' (2005) 8(3) *Postcolonial Studies* 303–19.

Barry, J. V. *Alexander Maconochie of Norfolk Island: A Study of a Pioneer in Penal Reform* (Melbourne: Oxford University Press, 1958).

'Criminal Law: The General Part' (1954) 27 *The Australian Law Journal* 736–7.

'Criminal Law, The General Part' (1962) 35 *The Australian Law Journal* 352.

'Insanity in the Criminal Law in Australia' (1943) 21 *Canadian Bar Review* 427–39.

Insanity in the Criminal Law in Australia (English Studies in Criminal Science) (London: Macmillan, 1943).

'The Defence of Insanity and the Burden of Proof' [1939] *Res Judicatae* 42–9.

Barry, J. V. and Paton, G. W. (with Sawer, G.), *An Introduction to the Criminal Law in Australia* (London: Macmillan, 1948).

Bartels, L. and Easteal, P. 'Mothers Who Kill: The Forensic Use and Judicial Reception of Evidence of Postnatal Depression and Other Psychiatric Disorders in Australian Filicide Cases' (2013–14) 37 *Melbourne University Law Review* 297–341.

Bavin-Mizzi, J. 'Understandings of Justice: Australian Rape and Carnal Knowledge Cases, 1877–1924', in D. Kirkby (ed.), *Sex, Power and Justice: Historical Perspectives of Law in Australia* (Melbourne: Oxford University Press, 1995), pp. 19–32.

Bayly, C. A. 'European Political Thought and the Wider World During the Nineteenth Century', in G. S. Jones and G. Claeys (eds.), *Cambridge History of Nineteenth Century Political Thought* (Cambridge: Cambridge University Press, 2011), pp. 835–63.

Beck, U. *Risk Society: Towards a New Modernity*, trans. Mark Ritter (London: Sage Publications, 1992) [*Risikogesellschaft: Auf dem Weg in eine andere Moderne*] (first published 1986).

Beck, U. and Beck-Gernsheim, E. *Individualization Institutionalized: Individualism and Its Social and Political Consequences* (London: Sage Publications, 2002).

Behrendt, L. 'Consent in a (Neo)colonial Society: Aboriginal Women as Sexual and Legal "Other"' (2000) 15(33) *Australian Feminist Studies* 353–67.

Beier, A. L. *Masterless Men: The Vagrancy Problem in England 1560–1640* (London: Methuen, 1985).

Bell, D. 'Empire and Imperialism', in G. S. Jones and G. Claeys (eds.), *Cambridge History of Nineteenth Century Political Thought* (Cambridge: Cambridge University Press, 2011), pp. 864–92.

Bell, V. 'Keeping the Criminal Law in "Serviceable Condition": A Task for the Courts or the Parliament?' (2016) 27(3) *Current Issues in Criminal Justice* 335–44.

Bellamy, S. 'Guthrie, Bessie Jean (1905–1977)', in J. Ritchie (ed.), *Australian Dictionary of Biography Volume 14: 1940–1980* (Melbourne: Melbourne University Press, 1996).

Bennett, C. 'The Emergence of Australia's National Campaign Against Drug Abuse: A Case-Study in the Politics of Drug Control' (2008) 32(3) *Journal of Australian Studies* 309–21.

Benson, P. 'Feeling Crazy: Self-Worth and the Social Character of Responsibility', in C. Mackenzie and N. Stoljar (eds.), *Relational Autonomy: Feminist Perspectives on Autonomy, Agency, and the Social Self* (Oxford: Oxford University Press, 2000), pp. 72–93.

Benton, L. A. *Law and Colonial Cultures: Legal Regimes in World History, 1400–1900* (Cambridge: Cambridge University Press, 2002).

Bialestock, D. 'Neglected Babies: A Study of 289 Babies Admitted Consecutively to a Reception Centre' (1966) 2(24) *Medical Journal of Australia* 1129–33.

Birrell, R. G. and Birrell, J. H. 'The "Maltreatment Syndrome" in Children' (1966) 2(24) *Medical Journal of Australia* 1134–8.

Blackstone, W. *Commentaries on the Laws of England in Four Books*, Book 1 (Philadelphia: J.B. Lippincott Co., 1893 [first published in 1768]).

Blumenthal, S. L. *Law and the Modern Mind: Consciousness and Responsibility in American Legal Culture* (Cambridge, MA: Harvard University Press, 2016).

Borick, K. 'Report on the Brisbane Seminar' (1991) *Criminal Law Forum* 515–25.

Boucher, E. *Empire's Children: Child Emigrations, Welfare, and the Decline of the British World, 1869–1967* (Cambridge: Cambridge University Press, 2014).

Breckenridge, J. 'Intervention in Child Welfare: An Inflicted Evil or Solicited Response?', in M. Wearing and R. Berreen (eds.), *Welfare & Social Policy in Australia: The Distribution of Advantage* (Sydney: Harcourt Brace, 1994), pp. 137–53.

Brett, P. *An Inquiry into Criminal Guilt* (Sydney: Law Book Co., 1963).

Brett, P. and Waller, P. *Cases and Materials in Criminal Law* (Oxford: Butterworths, 1962).

Bronitt, S. 'Australia', in K. J. Heller and M. D. Dubber (eds.), *Handbook of Comparative Criminal Law* (Stanford, CA: Stanford Law Books, 2011).

'New Regulatory Paradigms for Preventing Institutional Child Sexual Abuse: Lessons from Corporate Crime and White-Collar Criminals', in Y. Smaal, A. Kaladelfos and M. Finnane (eds.), *The Sexual Abuse of Children: Recognition and Redress* (Melbourne: Monash University Press, 2016), pp. 178–92.

Bronitt, S. and Gani, M. 'Criminal Codes in the 21st Century: The Paradox of the Liberal Promise', in B. McSherry, A. Norrie and S. Bronitt (eds.), *Regulating Deviance: The Redirection of Criminalisation and the Futures of Criminal Law* (Oxford: Hart, 2009), pp. 235–60.

Bronitt, S. and McSherry, B. *Principles of Criminal Law*, 4th ed. (Sydney: Thomson Reuters, 2017).

Brown, D. 'Constituting Physical and Fault Elements: A NSW Case Study', in T. Crofts and A. Loughnan (eds.), *Criminalisation and Criminal Responsibility in Australia* (Melbourne: Oxford University Press, 2015), pp. 13–32.

'Criminalisation and Normative Theory' (2013) 25(2) *Current Issues in Criminal Justice* 605–25.

Brown, D., Farrier, D., McNamara, L. et al. *Criminal Laws: Materials and commentary on Criminal Law and Process of NSW*, 6th ed. (Sydney: The Federation Press, 2015).

Brown, D. H. *The Genesis of the Canadian Criminal Code of 1892* (Toronto: University of Toronto Press, 1989).

Brown, N. *Governing Prosperity: Social Change and Social Analysis in Australia in the 1950s* (Cambridge: Cambridge University Press, 1995).

Bumiller, K. *In an Abusive State: How Neoliberalism Appropriated the Feminist Movement against Sexual Violence* (Durham, NC: Duke University Press, 2008).

Burgess, A. 'The Changing Character of Public Inquiries in the (Risk) Regulatory State' (2011) 6(1) *British Politics* 3–29.

Burton, K., Crofts, T. and Tarrant, S. *Principles of Criminal Law in Queensland and Western Australia*, 2nd ed. (Sydney: Thomson Reuters, 2016).

Bush, B. 'A Model Code?' (2009) 7(2) *Of Substance: The National Magazine on Alcohol, Tobacco and Other Drugs* 18–19.

Byran, M. 'The Modern History of Law Reporting' (2012) 11 *University of Melbourne Collections* 32–36.

Byrne, P. J. *Criminal Law and Colonial Subject, New South Wales, 1810–1830* (Cambridge: Cambridge University Press, 1993).

Cadoppi, A. and Cullinane, K. 'Translation: The Zanardelli Code and Codification in the Countries of the Common Law' (2000) 7 *James Cook University Law Review* 119–90.

Cairns, D. J. A. *Advocacy and the Making of the Adversarial Criminal Trial, 1800–1865* (Oxford: Clarendon Press, 1998).

Cairns, J. W. 'Development of Comparative Law in Great Britain' in M. Reimann and R. Zimmermann (eds.), *The Oxford Handbook of Comparative Law* (Oxford: Oxford University Press 2006), pp. 132–73.

Cane, P. *Controlling Administrative Power: An Historical Comparison* (Cambridge: Cambridge University Press, 2016).

Responsibility in Law and Morality (Oxford: Hart Publishing, 2002).

Carney, T. and Hanks, P. *Social Security in Australia* (Melbourne: Oxford University Press, 1994).

Carter, R. *Criminal Law of Queensland* (Melbourne: Butterworths, 1958).

Castles, A. *An Australian Legal History* (Sydney: Law Book Co., 1982).

Chalmers, J., Leverick, F. and Shaw, A. 'Is Formal Criminalisation Really on the Rise? Evidence from the 1950s' [2015] *Criminal Law Review* 177–99.

Chambers, D. *New Social Ties: Contemporary Connections in a Fragmented Society* (Basingstoke: Palgrave Macmillan, 2006).

Chambliss, W. J. 'A Sociological Analysis of the Law of Vagrancy' (1964) 12(1) *Social Problems* 67–77.

Chappell, D. 'A Review of Federal Law Enforcement Arrangements', in D. Chappell and P. Wilson (eds.), *Australian Policing*, 2nd ed. (Sydney: Butterworths, 1996), pp. 126–46.

Chesterman, J. and Douglas, H. 'Law on Australia's Frontier: The Fall and Rise of Race' (2009) 24 *Canadian Journal of Law and Society* 69–83.

Chiao, V. 'Making Modern Criminal Law Theory: Reflections on Farmer' (2017) 4(1) *Critical Analysis of Law* 1–10.

Christman, J. *The Politics of Persons: Individual Autonomy and Socio-historical Selves* (Cambridge: Cambridge University Press, 2009).

Clark, D. S. 'Nothing New in 2000? Comparative Law in 1900 and Today' (2000) 75 *Tulsa Law Review* 871–912.

Clough, J. 'Bridging the Theoretical Gap: The Search for a Realist Model of Corporate Criminal Liability' (2007) 18(3–4) *Criminal Law Forum* 267–300.

Coffee, J. C. '"No Soul to Damn: No Body to Kick": An Unscandalized Inquiry into the Problem of Corporate Punishment' (1981) 79(3) *Michigan Law Review* 386–459.

Coldrey, B. *Good British Stock: Child and Youth Migration to Australia Research Guide* (Canberra: National Archives of Australia, 1999).

Collier, J. F. Maurer, B. and Suarez-Navaz, L. 'Sanctioned Identities: Legal Constructions of Modern Personhood' (1995) 2(1–2) *Identities: Global Studies in Culture and Power* 1–27.

Columbia Law Review Association, 'Journal of the Society of Comparative Legislation' (Book Review) (1916) 16(4) *Columbia Law Review* 365–6.

Colvin, E. 'Abusive Relationships and Violent Responses: The Reorientation of Self-Defense in Australia' (2009) 42 *Texas Tech Law Review* 339–58.

'Criminal Responsibility under the South Pacific Codes' (2002) 26 *Criminal Law Journal* 98–113.

'Unity and Diversity in Australian Criminal Law: A Comment on the Draft Commonwealth Code' (1991) 15 *Criminal Law Journal* 82–94.

Connell, R. W. 'The State, Gender and Sexual Politics: Theory and Appraisal' (1990) 19 *Theory and Society* 507–44.

Cotterrell, R. *Sociological Jurisprudence: Juristic Thought and Social Inquiry* (London: Routledge, 2018).

Cossins, A. *Female Criminality: Infanticide, Moral Panics and The Female Body* (London: Palgrave Macmillan, 2015).

The Baby Farmers (Sydney: Allen and Unwin, 2013).

'The Legacy of the Makin Case 120 Years On: Legal Fictions, Circular Reasoning and Some Solutions' (2013) 35 *Sydney Law Review* 731–59.

Cowdery, N. 'A Threat to the Rule of Law: The New South Wales Crimes (Criminal Organisations Control) Act 2009' (2009) 21(2) *Current Issues in Criminal Justice* 321–4.

Craies, W. F. 'Criminal Law in New South Wales' (1901) 3(1) *Journal of the Society of Comparative Legislation* 95–7.

Cranston, R. 'Law and Society: A Different Approach to Legal Education' (1978–79) 5 *Monash University Law Review* 54–69.

Crofts, P. 'Legal Irresponsibility and Institutional Responses to Child Sex Abuse' (2016) 34(2) *Law in Context: A Socio-Legal Journal* 79–99.

Crofts, P., Crofts, T., Gray, S. et al. *Waller and Williams Cases and Materials in Criminal Law*, 13th ed. (Sydney: LexisNexis, 2015).

Crofts, T. 'Two Degrees of Murder: Homicide Law Reform in England and Western Australia' (2008) 8(2) *Oxford University Commonwealth Law Journal* 187–210.

Crofts, T. and Loughnan, A. 'Provocation, NSW Style: Reform of the Defence of Provocation in NSW' [2014] 2 *Criminal Law Review* 109–25.

'Provocation: The Good, the Bad and the Ugly' (2013) 37(1) *Criminal Law Journal* 23–37.

Crofts, T. and Tarrant, S. 'Criminal Law Pedagogy and the Australian State Codes', in K. Gledhill and B. Livings (eds.), *The Teaching of Criminal Law: The Pedagogical Imperatives* (Abingdon: Palgrave MacMillan, 2016), pp. 83–92.

Crofts, T. and Tyson, D. 'Homicide Law Reform in Australia: Improving Access to Defences for Women Who Kill Their Abusers' (2013) 39(3) *Monash University Law Review* 864–93.

Cross, G. 'Labour in Settler-State Democracies: Comparative Perspectives on Australia and US, 1860–1920' (1996) 70 *Labour History* 1–24.

Cross, R. 'The Making of the English Criminal Law (5) Macaulay' [1978] *Criminal Law Review* 519–28.

'The Making of the English Criminal Law (6) Sir James Fitzjames Stephen' [1978] *Criminal Law Review* 652–61.

Cullinane, K. 'Preface: The Zanardelli Code and Codification in the Countries of the Common Law' (2000) 7 *James Cook University Law Review* 116–18.

Currey, C. H. 'The Influence of the English Law Reformers of the Early Nineteenth Century on the Law of New South Wales' (1937) XXIII *Royal Australian Historical Society* 227–41.

Curthoys, A. 'Indigenous Subjects', in D. M. Schreuder and S. Ward (eds.), *Australia's Empire* (Oxford: Oxford University Press, 2008), pp. 79–103.

Daly, K. 'Inequalities of Redress: Australia's National Redress Scheme for Institutional Abuse of Children' (2018) 42(2) *Journal of Australian Studies* 204–16.

'Redress for Historical Institutional Abuse of Children', in A. Deckert and R. Sarre (eds.), *The Palgrave Handbook of Australian and New Zealand Criminology, Crime and Justice* (London: Palgrave Macmillan, 2017), pp. 449–66.

Davies, S. 'Captives of Their Bodies: Women, Law and Punishment, 1880s–1980s', in D. Kirkby (ed.), *Sex, Power and Justice: Historical Perspectives on Law in Australia* (Melbourne: Oxford University Press, 1995), pp. 99–115.

'Women War and the Violence of History: An Australian Perspective' (1996) 2 *Violence Against Women* 359–77.

Deign, J. 'On Rights and Responsibilities' (1988) 7 *Law and Philosophy* 147–78.

Denning, A. T. 'Foreword' (1952) 1(1) *International & Comparative Law Quarterly* 1–2.

Diehl, J. B. S. 'R. v. Wheat and Stocks. R. I. P.' (1968) 31(5) *The Modern Law Review* 576–80.

Dixon, O. 'A Legacy of Hadfield, McNaghten and Maclean' (1957) 31 *The Australian Law Journal* 255–66.

'Response to Questions' (1957) 31 *Australian Law Journal* 265–6.

'Science and Judicial Proceedings', in J. V. Barry and A. E. Coates (eds.), *The Proceedings of the Medico-Legal Society of Victoria During the Years 1933–1934 and 1935–1936* (Melbourne: Brown, Prior, Anderson Pty. Ltd., 1937), pp. 1–31.

'The Development of the Law of Homicide' (1935) 9 *Australian Law Journal (Supplement)* 64–72.

Dolinko, D. 'Punishment', in J. Deigh and D. Dolinko (eds.), *The Oxford Handbook of Philosophy of Criminal Law* (Oxford: Oxford University Press, 2011), pp. 403–28.

Donovan, B. H. K. 'The Committee for the Review of the Commonwealth Criminal Law' (1992) 66 *Australian Law Journal* 732–7.

Dorsett, S. and Hunter, I. (eds.), *Law and Politics in British Colonial Thought* (London: Palgrave MacMillan, 2010).

Dorsett, S. and McVeigh, S. 'Just So: "The Law Which Governs Australia Is Australian Law"' (2002) 13 *Law and Critique* 289–309.

Douglas, H. 'A Consideration of the Merits of Specialized Homicide Offences for Battered Women' (2012) 45(3) *Australian & New Zealand Journal of Criminology* 367–82.

'Customary Law, Sentencing and the Limits of the State' (2005) 20(1) *Canadian Journal of Law and Society/Revue canadienne Droit et Société* 141–56.

'Justice Kriewaldt, Aboriginal Identity and the Criminal Law' (2002) 26 *Criminal Law Journal* 204–22.

'The Cultural Specificity of Evidence: The Current Scope and Relevance of the Anunga Guidelines' (1998) 21 *University of New South Wales Law Journal* 27–54.

Douglas, H.and Finnane, M. *Indigenous Crime and Settler Law: White Sovereignty after Empire* (Basingstoke: Palgrave Macmillan, 2012).

Douglas, R. and Laster, K. 'A Matter of Life and Death: The Victorian Executive and the Decision to Execute 1842–1967' (1991) 24 *Australian & New Zealand Journal of Criminology* 144–60.

Douglas-Scott, S. *Law after Modernity. Series: Legal Theory Today* (Oxford: Hart Publishing, 2013).

Dressler, J. 'New Thoughts About the Concept of Justification in the Criminal Law: A Critique of Fletcher's Thinking and Rethinking' (1984–1985) 32(1) *University of California Los Angeles Law Review* 61–99.

Dubber, M. D. 'Alan W. Norrie Punishment Responsibility and Justice: A Relational Critique' (2002) 65(2) *Modern Law Review* 309–11.

An Introduction to the Model Penal Code (New York: Oxford University Press, 2015).

'Colonial Criminal Law and Other Modernities: European Criminal Law in the Nineteenth and Twentieth Century', in H. Pihlajamäki, M. D. Dubber and M. Godfrey (eds.), *The Oxford Handbook of European Legal History* (Oxford: Oxford University Press, 2018), pp. 1052–73.

'Historical Analysis of Law' (1998) 16(1) *Law and History Review* 159–62.

'New Historical Jurisprudence: Legal History as Critical Analysis of Law' (2015) 2(1) *Critical Analysis of Law* 1–18.

'Paradigms of Penal Law', in M. D. Dubber and T. Hörnle (eds.), *The Oxford Handbook of Criminal Law* (New York: Oxford University Press, 2014), pp. 1017–39.

'Penal Panopticon: The Idea of a Modern Model Penal Code' (2000) 4(1) *Buffalo Criminal Law Review* 53–100.

'Policing Possession: The War on Crime and the End of Criminal Law' (2001) 91(4) *The Journal of Criminal Law and Criminology* 829–996.

'The Model Penal Code, Legal Process and the Alegitimacy of American Penality', in M. D. Dubber (ed.), *Foundational Texts in Modern Criminal Law* (Oxford: Oxford University Press, 2014), pp. 239–62.

The Police Power: Patriarchy and the Foundations of American Government (New York: Columbia University Press, 2005).

Victims in the War on Crime: The Use and Abuse of Victims' Rights (New York: New York University Press, 2006).

Dubber, M. D. and Farmer, L. 'Introduction: Regarding Criminal Law Historically', in M. D. Dubber and L. Farmer (eds.), *Modern Histories of Crime and Punishment* (Stanford: Stanford University Press, 2007), pp. 1–14.

Duff, R. A. *Answering for Crime: Responsibility and Liability in the Criminal Law* (London: Hart Publishing, 2007).

Punishment, Communication, and Community (Oxford: Oxford University Press, 2001).

'Responsibility, Citizenship and Criminal Law', in R. A. Duff and S. Green (eds.), *Philosophical Foundations of Criminal Law* (Oxford: Oxford University Press, 2011), pp. 125–48.

Trials and Punishment (Cambridge: Cambridge University Press, 1986).

Duff, R. A., Farmer, L., Marshall, S. and Tadros, V. *The Trial on Trial: Volume 3: Towards A Normative Theory of the Criminal Trial* (London: Hart Publishing, 2007).

Duxbury, N. 'English Jurisprudence Between Austin and Hart' (2005) 91(1) *Virginia Law Review* 1–91.

Dyson, M. 'Shorn-Off Complicity' (2016) 75(2) *The Cambridge Law Journal* 196–9.

Eades, D. 'Legal Recognition of Cultural Differences in Communication: The Case of Robyn Kina' (1996) 16(3) *Language & Communication* 215–27.

Easteal, P., Bartels, L., Nelson, N. and Holland, K. 'How Are Women Who Kill Portrayed in Newspaper Media? Connections with Social Values and the Legal System' (2015) 51(1) *Women's Studies International Forum* 31–41.

Edgely, M. and Marchetti, E. 'Women Who Kill Their Abusers: How Queensland's New Abusive Domestic Relationships Defence Continues to Ignore Reality' (2011) 13(2) *Flinders Law Journal* 125–76.

Editor, 'Malice Aforethought' (1924) 33(5) *Yale Law Journal* 528–36.

Edney, R. and Bagaric, M. *Australian Sentencing: Principles and Practice* (Cambridge: Cambridge University Press, 2007).

Edwards, E. J., Hayes, R. A. and O'Regan, R. S. *Cases on the Criminal Code: Being Cases and Material on the Criminal Law in Queensland, Western Australia and Papua and New Guinea* (Sydney: Law Book Co., 1969).

Emsley, C. *Crime and Society in England 1750–1900*, 3rd ed. (Harlow, UK: Pearson, 2005).

Evans, C. 'Excellent Women and Troublesome Children: State Foster Care in Tasmania, 1896–1918' (2002) 83 *Labour History* 133–48.

Evans, C. L. 'Persons Dwelling in the Borderland: Responsibility and Criminal Law in the Late-Nineteenth-Century British Empire', PhD thesis, Princeton University (2016).

Evans, R. 'John William Bleakley (1879–1957)', in B. Nairn and G. Serle (eds.), *Australian Dictionary of Biography Volume 7: 1891–1939* (Melbourne: Melbourne University Press, 1979).

Fairall, P. 'The Reform of the Criminal Law', in D. Chappell and P. Wilson (eds.), *Crime and the Criminal Justice System in Australia: 2000 and Beyond* (Sydney: Butterworths, 2000).

Farmer, L. 'Bringing Cinderella to the Ball: Teaching Criminal Law in Context' (2012) 58(5) *Modern Law Review* 756–66.

'Codification', in M. D. Dubber and T. Hörnle (eds.), *The Oxford Handbook of Criminal Law* (New York: Oxford University Press, 2014), pp. 379–98.

Criminal Law, Tradition and Legal Order: Crime and the Genius of Scots Law, 1747 to the Present (Cambridge: Cambridge University Press, 1997).

'Criminal Responsibility and the Proof of Guilt' (Working Paper, University of California Center for the Study of Law and Society Faculty, 2005).

'Criminal Responsibility and the Proof of Guilt', in M. D. Dubber and L. Farmer (eds.), *Modern Histories of Crime and Punishment* (Stanford: Stanford University Press, 2007), pp. 42–65.

'Criminal Wrongs in Historical Perspective', in R. A. Duff, L. L. Farmer, S. E. Marshall, M. Renzo and V. Tadros (eds.), *The Boundaries of the Criminal Law* (Oxford: Oxford University Press, 2010), pp. 214–37.

'Of Treatises and Textbooks: The Literature of Criminal Law in Nineteenth Century Britain', in M. Dubber and A. Fernandez (eds.), *Law Books in Action: Essays on the Anglo-American Legal Treatise* (Oxford: Hart Publishing, 2012), pp. 145–64.

'Making the Modern Criminal Law: A Response' (2017) 4(1) *Critical Analysis of Law* 53–60.

Making the Modern Criminal Law: Criminalization and Civil Order. Series: Criminalization (Oxford: Oxford University Press, 2016).

'Reconstructing the English Codification Debate: The Criminal Law Commissioners, 1833–45' (2000) 18(2) *Law and History Review* 397–426.

'Territorial Jurisdiction and Criminalization' (2013) 63 *University of Toronto Law Journal* 225–46.

'The Modest Ambition of Glanville Williams', in M. D. Dubber (ed.), *Foundational Texts in Modern Criminal Law* (Oxford: Oxford University Press, 2014), pp. 263–77.

'The Obsession with Definition: The Nature of Crime and Critical Legal Theory' (1996) 5 *Social & Legal Studies* 57–73.

'Time and Space in Criminal Law' (2010) 13(2) *New Criminal Law Review* 333–56.

Featherstone, L. '"Children in a Terrible State": Understandings of Trauma and Child Sexual Assault in 1970s and 1980s Australia' (2018) 42(2) *Journal of Australian Studies* 164–76.

Featherstone, L. and Kaladelfos, A. 'Hierarchies of Harm and Violence: Historicising Familial Sexual Violence in Australia' (2014) 29(81) *Australian Feminist Studies* 306–24.

Sex Crimes in the Fifties (Melbourne: Melbourne University Press, 2016).

Finn, J. 'Codification of the Criminal Law: The Australasian Parliamentary Experience', in B. Godfrey and G. Dunstall (eds.), *Crime and Empire, 1840–1940: Criminal Justice in Local and Global Context* (Cullompton: Willan Publishing, 2005), pp. 224–37.

Finn, P. *Law and Government in Colonial Australia* (Oxford: Oxford University Press, 1987).

Finnane, M. 'Aboriginal Violence and State Response: Histories, Policies and Legacies in Queensland 1860–1940' (2010) 43(2) *Australian & New Zealand Journal of Criminology* 238–62.

'"Irresistible Impulse": Historicizing a Judicial Innovation in Australian Insanity Jurisprudence' (2012) 23(4) *History of Psychiatry* 454–68.

JV Barry: A Life (Sydney: UNSW Press, 2007).

'Law as an Intellectual Vocation' (2015) 38(3) *Melbourne University Law Review* 1060–79.

Police and Government: Histories of Policing in Australia (Oxford: Oxford University Press, 1994).

Punishment in Australian Society (Melbourne: Oxford University Press, 1997).

'The Limits of Jurisdiction: Law, Governance and Indigenous Peoples in Colonized Australia', in S. Dorsett and I. Hunter (eds.), *Law and Politics in British Colonial Thought* (London: Palgrave Macmillan, 2010), pp. 149–68.

'The Origins of Criminology in Australia' (2012) 45(2) *Australia & New Zealand Journal of Criminology* 157–78.

'The Politics of Police Powers: The Making of Police Offences Acts', in M. Finnane (ed.), *Policing in Australia: Historical Perspectives* (Sydney: New South Wales University Press, 1987), pp. 88–113.

Finnane, M. and Smaal, Y. 'Some Questions of History: Prosecuting and Punishing Child Sexual Assault', in Y. Smaal, A. Kaladelfos and M. Finnane (eds.), *The Sexual Abuse of Children: Recognition and Redress* (Melbourne: Monash University Press, 2016), pp. 7–19.

Fisse, B. and Braithwaite, J. *Corporations, Crime and Accountability* (Cambridge: Cambridge University Press, 1993).

Fitzpatrick, P. 'Terminal Legality: Imperialism and the (De)composition of Law', in D. Kirkby and C. Coleborne (eds.), *Law, History, Colonialism: The Reach of Empire* (Manchester: Manchester University Press, 2001), pp. 9–26.

Fitz-Gibbon, K. *Homicide Law Reform, Gender and the Provocation Defence: A Comparative Perspective* (London: Palgrave Macmillan, 2014).

Fitz-Gibbon, K. and Stubbs, J. 'Divergent Directions in Reforming Legal Responses to Lethal Violence' (2012) 45(3) *Australian & New Zealand Journal of Criminology* 318–36.

Fletcher, G. *Rethinking Criminal Law*, 2nd ed. (Oxford: Oxford University Press, 2000).

The Grammar of Criminal Law: American, Comparative, and International: Volume 1: Foundations (Oxford: Oxford University Press, 2007).

'The Nature of Justification', in J. Horder and J. Gardner (eds.), *Action and Value in Criminal Law* (Oxford: Clarendon Press, 1993), pp. 175–86.

Ford, L. *Settler Sovereignty: Jurisdiction and Indigenous People in America and Australia 1788–1836* (Cambridge, MA: Harvard University Press, 2010).

Forgarty, J. F. 'Some Aspects of the Early History of Child Protection in Australia' (2008) 78 *Family Matters* 52–9.

Foucault, M. *Discipline and Punish: The Birth of the Prison* (New York: Pantheon Books, 1977).

Fox, R. 'New Crimes or New Responses?: Future Directions in Australian Criminal Law' (2002) 28 *Monash University Law Review* 103–25.

Fricke, G. *Judges of the High Court* (Melbourne: Hutchinson, 1986).

Friedland, M. L. 'R. S. Wright's Model Criminal Code: A Forgotten Chapter in the History of the Criminal Law' (1981) 1 *Oxford Journal of Legal Studies* 307–46.

Gani, M. 'Codifying the Criminal Law: Implications for Interpretation' (2005) 29 *Criminal Law Journal* 264–80.

Gans, J. *Modern Australian Criminal Law* (Melbourne: Cambridge University Press, 2012).

Gardner, J. 'On the General Part of Criminal Law', in R. A. Duff (ed.), *Philosophy and the Criminal Law: Principle and Critique* (Cambridge: Cambridge University Press, 1998), pp. 205–56.

Gardner, J. 'The Mark of Responsibility' (2003) 23(2) *Oxford Journal of Legal Studies* 157–71.

Garland, D. 'Penal Modernism and Postmodernism', in T. G. Blomberg and S. Cohen (eds.), *Punishment and Social Control* (New York: Walter de Gruyter, 2003), pp. 45–73.

Punishment and Welfare: A History of Penal Strategies (Aldershot: Gower, 1985).

The Culture of Control: Crime and Social Order in Contemporary Society (Chicago: University of Chicago Press, 2001).

Garran, R. R. and Quick, J. *Annotated Constitution of the Australian Commonwealth* (Sydney: Angus & Robinson, 1901).

Garton, S. *Out of Luck: Poor Australians and Social Welfare 1788–1988* (Sydney: Allen and Unwin, 1990).

The Cost of War: Australians Return (Melbourne: Oxford University Press, 1996).

Genovese, A. 'The Battered Body' (1997) 12(25) *Australian Feminist Studies* 91–103.

Gerangelos, P., Lee, H. P., Aroney, N. et al. *Winterton's Australian Federal Constitutional Law: Commentary and Materials*, 4th ed. (Sydney: Thomas Reuters, 2017).

Getzler, J. 'Law, History and the Social Sciences: Intellectual Traditions of the Late Nineteenth- and Early Twentieth-Century Europe', in A. Lewis and M. Lobban (eds.), *Law and History: Current Legal Issues Volume 6* (London: University College of London, 2003), pp. 215–63.

Giddens, A. 'Living in a Post-Traditional Society', in U. Beck, A. Giddens and S. Lash, *Reflexive Modernisation: Politics, Tradition and Aesthetics in the Modern Social Order* (Cambridge: Polity Press, 1994), pp. 56–109.

Modernity and Self-Identity: Self and Society in the Late Modern Age (Stanford: Stanford University Press, 1991).

The Consequences of Modernity (Stanford: Stanford University Press, 1990).

The Third Way: The Renewal of Social Democracy (Cambridge: Polity Press, 1999).

Giddens, T. 'Criminal Responsibility and the Living Self' (2015) 9 *Criminal Law and Philosophy* 189–206.

Ginsberg, R. 'Mighty Crime Victims: Victims' Rights and Neoliberalism in the American Conjuncture' (2014) 28(5–6) *Cultural Studies* 911–46.

Gleeson, K. 'Exceptional Sexual Harms: The Catholic Church and Child Sexual Abuse Claims in Australia' (2017) 27(6) *Social & Legal Studies* 1–21.

'Responsibility and Redress: Theorising Gender Justice in the Context of Catholic Clerical Child Sexual Abuse in Ireland and Australia' (2016) 39 *University of New South Wales Law Journal* 779–812.

'Why the Continuous Failures in Justice for Australian Victims and Survivors of Catholic Clerical Child Sexual Abuse?' (2016) 28(2) *Current Issues in Criminal Justice* 239–50.

Golder, H. and Allen, J. 'Prostitution in New South Wales 1870–1932: Restructuring an Industry' (1979–1980) 18/19 *Refractory Girl* 17–24.

Golding, F. 'Sexual Abuse as the Core Transgression of Childhood Innocence' (2018) 42(2) *Journal of Australian Studies* 191–203.

Goldsmith, A. 'Seeing Red: Legal Indifference on a Field of Pain and Death' (2009) 34 *Australian Journal of Legal Philosophy* 228–33.

Goode, M. 'An Evaluation of Judicial Interpretations of the Australian Model Criminal Code', in W. C. Chan, B. Wright and S. Yeo (eds.), *Codification, Macaulay and the Indian Penal Code: The Legacies and Modern Challenges of Criminal Law Reform* (Surrey: Ashgate Publishing, 2011), pp. 313–36.

'Codification of the Australian Criminal Law' (1992) 16(1) *Criminal Law Journal* 5–19.

'Codification of the Criminal Law' (2004) 28 *Criminal Law Journal* 226–36.

'Constructing Criminal Law Reform and the Model Criminal Code' (2002) 26 *Criminal Law Journal* 152–66.

'Fault Elements' (1991) 15 *Criminal Law Journal* 95–108.

'The Model Criminal Code Project' (1997) 5(4) *Australian Law Librarian* 265–77.

Gordon, G. H. *Criminal Law of Scotland*, 2nd ed. (Edinburgh: W. Green & Son, 1978).

Grabosky, P. *Sydney in Ferment: Crime, Dissent and Official Reaction, 1788 to 1973* (Canberra: ANU Press, 1977).

Gray, A. 'Freedom of Association in the Australian Constitution and the Crime of Consorting' (2013) 32 *University of Tasmania Law Review* 149–83.

Graycar, R. 'Compensation for the Stolen Children: Political Judgments and Community Values' (1997) 4(3) *University of New South Wales Law Journal* 24–7.

Green, A. W. 'The Baby – The Empire's Asset', in *Report of the Proceedings of the Conference on Infant and Child Welfare* (Sydney: W.C. Penfold & Co. Ltd, Printers, 1917), pp. 78–85.

Green, T. A. *Freedom and Criminal Responsibility in American Legal Thought* (Cambridge: Cambridge University Press, 2014).

'The Jury and Criminal Responsibility in Anglo-American History' (2015) 9(3) *Criminal Law and Philosophy* 423–42.

Verdict According to Conscience: Perspectives on the English Criminal Trial Jury (Chicago, IL: University of Chicago Press, 1985).

Green, P., Ward, T. and Lasslett, K. 'The Advance of State Crime Scholarship' (2012) 1(1) *State Crime Journal* 1–7.

Griffin, T. 'A Retrospective – Policy and Legislative Reform Themes in the Attorney-General's Areas of Responsibility, 1991–2001' (2003) 6(2) *Flinders Journal of Law Reform* 263–83.

Griffith, S. 'Criminal Responsibility: A Chapter from a Criminal Code', in *Report of the Seventh Meeting of the Australasian Association for the Advancement of Science* (Sydney: Australasian Association for the Advancement of Science, 1898), pp. 895–903.

Hacking, I. 'The Making and Molding of Child Abuse' (1991) 17(2) *Critical Inquiry* 253–88.

Haebich, A. and Reece, R. H. W. 'Neville, Auber Octavius (1875–1954)', in G. Serle (ed.), *Australian Dictionary of Biography Volume 11: 1891–1939* (Melbourne: Melbourne University Press, 1988).

Hall, R. 'The New Politics of the High Court: Breaking with Constitutional Tradition or Securing a Political Future?' in P. Boreham, G. Stokes, and R. Hall (eds.), *The Politics of Australian Society: Political Issues for the New Century* (Sydney: Pearson Longman, 2000).

Hall, S. 'The Meaning of New Times', in D. Morley and K. Chen (eds.), *Stuart Hall: Critical Dialogues in Cultural Studies* (London: Routledge, 1996), pp. 222–36.

Hamilton, H. M. *Hamilton and Addison, Criminal Law and Procedure, N.S.W.* (Sydney: Law Book Co., 1921).

Harel, A. 'The Triadic Relational Structure of Responsibility: A Defence', in R. Cruft, M. H. Kramer, and M. R. Reiff (eds.), *Crime, Punishment and Responsibility: The Jurisprudence of Antony Duff* (Oxford: Oxford University Press, 2011), pp. 103–22.

Hart, H. L. A. *Punishment and Responsibility* (Oxford: Oxford University Press, 1968).

Punishment and Responsibility: Essays in the Philosophy of Law, 2nd ed. (Oxford: Oxford University Press, 2008).

The Concept of Law, 3rd ed. (Oxford: Oxford University Press, 2012).

Heathcote, G. *Feminist Dialogues on International Law* (Oxford: Oxford University Press, 2019).

Hemming, A. 'It's Time to Abolish Diminished Responsibility, the Coach and Horses' Defence Through Criminal Responsibility for Murder' (2008) 10 *University of Notre Dame Australia Law Review* 1–36.

Herlihy, J. M. and Kenny, R. G. *An Introduction to Criminal Law in Queensland* (Melbourne: Butterworths, 1978).

Hirst, J. 'Empire, State, Nation', in D. M. Schreuder and S. Ward (eds.), *Australia's Empire* (Oxford: Oxford University Press, 2008), pp. 142–62.

Hogg, R. and Brown, D. *Rethinking Law and Order* (Sydney: Pluto Press, 1998).

Hogg, R. and Golder, H. 'Policing Sydney in the Late Nineteenth Century', in M. Finnane (ed.), *Policing in Australia: Historical Perspectives* (Sydney: New South Wales University Press, 1987), pp. 59–73.

Horder, J. *Ashworth's Principles of Criminal Law*, 9th ed. (Oxford: Oxford University Press, 2019).

'Criminal Law', in P. Cane and M. Tushnet (eds.), *The Oxford Handbook of Legal Studies* (Oxford: Oxford University Press, 2003), pp. 226–49.

Criminal Misconduct in Office (Oxford: Oxford University Press, 2018).

Provocation and Responsibility (Oxford: Clarendon Press, 1992).

'Rethinking Non-fatal Offences against the Person' (1994) 14(3) *Oxford Journal of Legal Studies* 335–51.

Hostettler, J. *The Politics of Criminal Law Reform in the Nineteenth Century* (Southampton, UK: Barry Rose Law Publishers, 1992).

Howard, C. 'An Australian Letter – The Meaning of Accident' [1965] *Criminal Law Review* 516–22.

Howard, C. *Australian Criminal Law* (Sydney: Law Book Co., 1982).

Howie, R. 'Letter to the Editor' (1996) 14 *Australian Bar Review* 87–9.

Hunter, I. 'Global Justice and Regional Metaphysics: On the Critical History of the Law of Nature and Nations', in S. Dorsett and I. Hunter (eds.), *Law and Politics in British Colonial Thought* (London: Palgrave MacMillan, 2010), pp. 11–29.

Hunter, I. and Dorsett, S. 'Introduction', in S. Dorsett and I. Hunter (eds.), *Law and Politics in British Colonial Thought* (London: Palgrave MacMillan, 2010), pp. 1–8.

Hunter, R. 'Contesting the Dominant Paradigm: Feminist Critiques of Liberal Legalism', in M. Davies and V. E. Munro (eds.), *The Ashgate Research Companion to Feminist Legal Theory* (Farnham: Routledge, 2016), pp. 13–30.

Hunter, R. and Tyson, D. 'The Implementation of Feminist Law Reforms: The Case of Post-provocation Sentencing' (2017) 26(2) *Social & Legal Studies* 129–65.

Husak, D. *Overcriminalization: The Limits of the Criminal Law* (Oxford: Oxford University Press, 2008).

Ibawoh, B. *Imperial Justice: Africans in Empire's Court* (Oxford: Oxford University Press, 2013).

Irving, H. 'New South Wales', in H. Irving (ed.), *The Centenary Companion to Australian Federation* (Cambridge: Cambridge University Press, 1999), pp. 19–92.

Jacobs, M. D. *White Mother to a Dark Race: Settler Colonialism, Maternalism, and the Removal of Indigenous Children in the American West and Australia, 1880–1940* (Lincoln: University of Nebraska Press, 2009).

Jain, N. *Perpetrators and Accessories in International Criminal Law: Individual Modes of Responsibility for Collective Crimes* (London: Bloomsbury Publishing, 2014).

James, J. C. H. 'Modes of Legislation in the British Colonies: Western Australia' (1899) 1(1) *Journal of the Society of Comparative Legislation* 70–4.

Jones, T. W. 'Finding Child Sex Abuse in the Archives: The Treatment of Sexually Offending Clergy in the Church of England, 1871–1960', in Y. Smaal, A. Kaladelfos and M. Finnane (eds.), *The Sexual Abuse of Children: Recognition and Redress* (Melbourne: Monash University Press, 2016), pp. 45–57.

Joyce, R. B. 'Griffith, Sir Samuel Walker (1845–1920)', in B. Nairn and G. Serle (eds.), *Australian Dictionary of Biography Volume 9: 1891–1939* (Melbourne: Melbourne University Press, 1983).

Kadish, S. H. 'Codifiers of the Criminal Law: Wechsler's Predecessors' (1978) 78 *Columbia Law Review* 1098–144.

Kaladelfos, A. 'The Maliciousness of Rape' (2016) 40 *Criminal Law Journal* 230–2.

'The Politics of Punishment: Rape and the Death Penalty in Colonial Australia, 1841–1901' (2012) 9(1) *History Australia* 155–75.

Kayman, M. A. 'A Memorial for Jeremy Bentham: Memory, Fiction and Writing the Law' (2004) 15 *Law and Critique* 207–29.

Keith, K. J. 'The Unity of the Common Law and the Ending of Appeals to the Privy Council' (2005) 54 *International & Comparative Law Quarterly* 197–210.

Kelman, M. 'Interpretive Construction in the Substantive Criminal Law' (1981) 33 *Stanford Law Review* 591–673.

Kennedy, C. 'Lindsay Farmer: Making the Modern Criminal Law: Criminalization and Civil Order' (2017) 11 *Criminal Law and Philosophy* 637–44.

Kercher, B. 'Alex Castles on the Reception of English Law' (2003) 7 *Australian Journal of Legal History* 37–45.

An Unruly Child: A History of Law in Australia (Sydney: Allen & Unwin, 1995).

'R v. Ballard, R v. Murrell and R v. Bonjon' (1998) 3(3) *Australian Indigenous Law Report* 410–25.

'Recovering and Reporting Australia's Early Colonial Case Law: The Macquarie Project' (2000) 18(3) *Law and History Review* 659–65.

Kerr, L. 'The Legitimate Scope of the Criminal Law: A Question for Legal History?' (2017) 4(1) *Critical Analysis of Law* 11–21.

Kimber, J. '"A Nuisance to the Community": Policing the Vagrant Woman' (2010) 34(3) *Journal of Australian Studies* 275–93.

'Poor Laws: A Historiography of Vagrancy in Australia' (2013) 11(8) *History Compass* 537–50.

Kirby, M. 'Criminal Law Futurology' (2005) 17(1) *Current Issues in Criminal Justice* 122–36.

'Editorial' (2001) 25 *Criminal Law Journal* 181–3.

'Why Has the High Court Become More Involved in Criminal Appeals?' (2002) 23 *Australian Bar Review* 4–23.

'Recollections of Sir Harry Gibbs' (2005) 49(9) *Quadrant* 54–7.

Kirkby, C. 'Review Article: Henry Maine and the Re-Constitution of the British Empire' (2012) 75(4) *Modern Law Review* 655–73.

Kociumbas, J. 'Azaria's Antecedents: Stereotyping Infanticide in Late Nineteenth-Century Australia' (2001) 13(1) *Gender & History* 138–60.

Kolsky, E. 'Codification and the Rule of Colonial Difference: Criminal Procedure in British India' (2005) 23(3) *Law and History Review* 631–83.

Kriewaldt, M. 'The Application of the Criminal Law to the Aborigines of the Northern Territory of Australia' (1960–1962) 5(1) *University of Western Australia Law Review* 1–50.

Kryger, M. 'Compared to What?' (2009) 34 *Australian Journal of Legal Philosophy* 241–7.

Kutz, C. *Complicity: Ethics and Law for a Collective Age* (Cambridge: Cambridge University Press, 2007).

'Responsibility', in J. Coleman and S. Shapiro (eds.), *The Oxford Handbook of Jurisprudence and the Philosophy of Law* (Oxford: Oxford University Press, 2004), pp. 548–87.

Lacey, N. *A Life of H.L.A. Hart: The Nightmare and the Noble Dream* (Oxford: Oxford University Press, 2006).

'Character, Capacity, Outcome: Towards a Framework for Assessing the Shifting Pattern of Criminal Responsibility in Modern English Law', in M. D. Dubber and L. Farmer (eds.), *Modern Histories of Crime and Punishment* (Stanford: Stanford University Press, 2007), pp. 14–41.

'Contingency, Coherence and Conceptualism: Reflections on the Encounter between "Critique" and "Philosophy of the Criminal Law"', in A. Duff (ed.), *Philosophy and the Criminal Law* (Cambridge: Cambridge University Press, 1998), pp. 9–59.

'Feminist Legal Theory beyond Neutrality' (1995) 48(2) *Current Legal Problems* 1–38.

'Historicising Criminalisation: Conceptual and Empirical Issues' (2009) 72(6) *Modern Law Review* 936–60.

'Institutionalising Responsibility: Implications for Jurisprudence' (2013) 4(1) *Jurisprudence* 1–19.

In Search of Criminal Responsibility: Ideas, Interests, and Institutions (Oxford: Oxford University Press, 2016).

'In Search of the Responsible Subject: History, Philosophy and Social Sciences in Criminal Law Theory' (2001) 64(3) *Modern Law Review* 350–71.

'Jurisprudence, History and the Institutional Quality of Law' (2015) 101 *Virginia Law Review* 919–45.

'Legal Constructions of Crime', in M. Maguire, R. Morgan and R. Reiner (eds.), *The Oxford Handbook of Criminology*, 4th ed. (Oxford: Oxford University Press, 2007), pp. 179–200.

'Philosophical Foundations of the Common Law: Social Not Metaphysical', in J. Horder (ed.), *Oxford Essays in Jurisprudence* (Oxford: Oxford University Press, 2000), pp. 17–39.

'Philosophy, History and Criminal Law Theory' (1998) 1 *Buffalo Criminal Law Review* 295–328.

'Responsibility and Modernity in Criminal Law' (2001) 9(3) *Journal of Political Philosophy* 249–76.

'Scott Veitch: Law and Irresponsibility: On the Legitimation of Human Suffering' (2009) 18(2) *Social & Legal Studies* 270–2.

'Space, Time and Function: Intersecting Principles of Responsibility Across the Terrain of Criminal Justice' (2007) 1(3) *Criminal Law and Philosophy* 233–50.

'The Resurgence of Character: Responsibility in the Context of Criminalization', in R. A. Duff and S. Green (eds.), *Philosophical Foundations of Criminal Law* (Oxford: Oxford University Press, 2011), pp. 151–78.

'Thomas Andrew Green: Freedom and Criminal Responsibility in American Legal Thought' (2016) 79(6) *Modern Law Review* 1137–41.

Unspeakable Subjects: Feminist Essays in Legal and Social Theory (Oxford: Hart Publishing, 1998).

'Violence, Ethics and Law: Feminist Reflections on a Familiar Dilemma', in S. James and S. Palmer (eds.), *Visible Women: Essays on Feminist Legal Theory and Political Philosophy* (London: Hart Publishing, 2002), pp. 117–36.

Lake, M. and Reynolds, H. *Drawing the Global Colour Line: White Men's Countries and the International Challenge of Racial Equality* (Cambridge: Cambridge University Press, 2008).

Landa, D. and Lewis, C. 'Making the Police Accountable for Their Conduct', in D. Chappell and P. Wilson (eds.), *Australian Policing*, 2nd ed. (Sydney: Butterworths, 1996), pp. 12–25.

Langbein, J. H. *The Origins of the Adversary Criminal Trial* (Oxford: Oxford University Press, 2003).

Torture and the Law of Proof: Europe and England in the Ancient Regime (Chicago, IL: University of Chicago Press, 1977).

Laster, K. 'Arbitrary Chivalry: Women and Capital Punishment in Victoria, Australia 1842–1967' (1994) 6(1) *Women and Criminal Justice* 67–95.

Lavi, S. and Schneebaum, G. 'Criminal Law and Sociology', in M. D. Dubber and T. Hörnle (eds.), *The Oxford Handbook of Criminal Law* (New York: Oxford University Press, 2014), pp. 152–72.

Law, J. and Urry, J. 'Enacting the Social' (2004) 33(3) *Economy and Society* 390–410.

Leader-Elliott, I. 'Australian Letter' [1969] *Criminal Law Review* 511–23.

'Benthamite Reflections on Codification of the General Principles of Criminal Liability: Towards the Panopticon' (2006) 9(2) *Buffalo Criminal Law Review* 391–452.

'Elements of Liability in the Commonwealth Criminal Code' (2002) 26 *Criminal Law Journal* 28–42.

'The Australian Criminal Code: Time for Some Changes' (2009) 37 *Federal Law Review* 205–36.

Lernestedt, C. 'Vertical, Horizontal, Backwards, Forwards' (2017) 4(1) *Critical Analysis of Law* 22–30.

'Victim and Society: Sharing Wrongs, but in Which Roles?' (2014) 8 *Criminal Law and Philosophy* 187–203.

Lloyd, G. 'Individuals, Responsibility and the Philosophical Imagination', in C. Mackenzie and N. Stoljar (eds.), *Relational Autonomy: Feminist Perspectives on Autonomy, Agency, and the Social Self* (Oxford: Oxford University Press, 2000), pp. 112–23.

Lobban, M. *The Common Law and English Jurisprudence 1760–1850* (Oxford: Clarendon Press, 1991).

'Sociology, History and the "Internal" Study of Law', in R. Nobles and D. Schiff (eds.), *Law, Society and Community: Socio-Legal Essays in Honour of Roger Cotterrell* (Farnham: Ashgate Publishing, 2014), pp. 39–59.

Loughnan, A. 'Asking (Different) Responsibility Questions: Responsibility and Non-Responsibility in Criminal Law' (2016) 4(1) *Bergen Journal of Criminal Law and Criminal Justice* 24–46.

'From Carpetbag to Crucible: Reconceptualising Diminished Responsibility Manslaughter', in B. Livings, A. Reed and N. Wake (eds.), *Mental Condition Defences and the Criminal Justice System: Perspectives from Law and Medicine* (Cambridge: Cambridge Scholars Publishing, 2015), pp. 339–64.

'Historicizing Criminal Responsibility', in C. Flanders and Z. Hoskins (eds.), *The New Philosophy of Criminal Law* (Lanham: Rowman and Littlefield, 2015), pp. 133–51.

'In Accordance with Modern Notions: Criminal Responsibility at the Turn of the Twentieth Century', in T. Crofts and A. Loughnan (eds.), *Criminalisation and Criminal Responsibility in Australia* (Melbourne: Oxford University Press, 2015), pp. 157–75.

Manifest Madness: Mental Incapacity in Criminal Law (Oxford: Oxford University Press, 2012).

'M'Naghten's Case (1843)', in P. Handler, H. Mares and I. Williams (eds.), *Landmark Cases in Criminal Law* (London: Hart Publishing, 2017), pp. 125–45.

'"Society Owes Them Much": Veteran Defendants and Criminal Responsibility in Australia in the Twentieth Century' (2015) 2(1) *Critical Analysis of Law* 106–34.

'The Legislation We Had to Have? The Crimes (Criminal Organisations Control) Act 2009 (NSW)' (2009) 20(3) *Current Issues in Criminal Justice* 457–65.

'The Meta-Significance of Criminal Responsibility' (2017) 4(1) *Critical Analysis of Law* 31–41.

'The Strange Case of the Infanticide Doctrine' (2012) 32(4) *Oxford Journal of Legal Studies* 685–711.

'"The Very Foundations of Any System of Criminal Justice": Criminal Responsibility in the Australian Model Criminal Code' (2017) 6(3) *International Journal for Crime, Justice and Social Democracy* 8–24.

Loughnan, A. and Gless, S. 'Understanding the Law on Intoxicated Offending: Principle, Pragmatism and Legal Culture' (2016) 3(2) *Journal of International and Comparative Law* 345–73.

MacCormick, N. 'Taking Responsibility Seriously' (2005) 9(1) *Edinburgh Law Review* 168–75.

MacDonald, E. and Williams, G. 'Combating Terrorism: Australia's Criminal Code Since September 11, 2001' (2007) 16(1) *Griffith Law Review* 27–54.

MacIntyre, S. *Australia's Boldest Experiment: War and Reconstruction in the 1940s* (Sydney: NewSouth Publishing, 2015).

Mackenzie, G. 'An Enduring Influence: Sir Samuel Griffith and his Contribution to Criminal Justice in Queensland' (2002) 2(1) *Queensland University of Technology Law and Justice Journal* 53–63.

Mantena, K. *Alibis of Empire: Henry Maine and the Ends of Liberal Imperialism* (Princeton, NJ: Princeton University Press, 2010).

Martin, D. L. 'Retribution Revisited: A Reconsideration of Feminist Criminal Law Reform Strategies' (1998) 26 *Osgoode Hall Law Journal* 151–88.

Mason, A. 'Changing the Law in a Changing Society' (1992) 18 *Commonwealth Law Bulletin* 1166–72.

Mason, G. 'Violence', in B. Caine, M. Gatens, E. Grahame, J. Larbalestier, S. Watson and E. Webby (eds.), *Australian Feminism: A Companion* (Melbourne: Oxford University Press, 1998), pp. 337–44.

Matravers, M. 'Responsibility and Choice' (2002) 5(2) *Critical Review of International Social and Political Philosophy* 77–92.

Responsibility and Justice (Cambridge: Polity Press, 2007).

Matravers, M. and Cocoru, A. 'Revisiting the Hart/Wootton Debate on Responsibility', in C. G. Pulman (ed.), *Hart on Responsibility* (London: Palgrave Macmillan, 2014), pp. 129–53.

Matthews, J. J. *Good and Mad Women: The Historical Construction of Femininity in Twentieth-Century Australia* (Sydney: Allen and Unwin, 1984).

Mayall, J. 'Nationalism and Imperialism', in T. Bell and R. Bellamy (eds.), *Cambridge History of Twentieth Century Political Thought* (Cambridge: Cambridge University Press, 2003), pp. 104–22.

McAlinden, A. 'An Inconvenient Truth: Barriers to Truth Recovery in the Aftermath of Institutional Child Abuse in Ireland' (2013) 33(2) *Legal Studies* 189–214.

McAlinden, A. and Naylor, B. 'Reframing Public Inquiries as Procedural Justice for Victims of Institutional Child Abuse: Towards a Hybrid Model of Justice' (2016) 38(3) *Sydney Law Review* 277–309.

McHugh, P. G. *Aboriginal Societies and the Common Law: A History of Sovereignty, Status, and Self-determination* (Oxford: Oxford University Press, 2004).

McKenna, J. *Supreme Court of Queensland: A Concise History* (Brisbane: University of Queensland Press, 2012).

McKenna, M. 'Metaphors of Light and Darkness: The Politics of "Black Armband" History' (1998) 25 *Melbourne Journal of Politics* 67–84.

McKenzie, G. 'An Enduring Influence: Sir Samuel Griffith and his Contribution to Criminal Justice in Queensland' (2002) 2(1) *Queensland University of Technology Law Journal* 53–64.

McLeod, A. 'On the Origins of Consorting Laws' (2013) 37(1) *Melbourne University Law Review* 103–42.

McNamara, L. 'Criminalisation Research in Australia: Building a Foundation for Normative Theorising and Principled Law Reform', in T. Crofts and A. Loughnan (eds.), *Criminalisation and Criminal Responsibility in Australia* (Melbourne: Oxford University Press, 2015), pp. 33–51.

McSherry, B. 'Terrorism Offences in the Criminal Code: Broadening the Boundaries of Australian Criminal Laws' (2004) 27(2) *UNSW Law Journal* 354–72.

Meliá, M. C. 'The Wrongfulness of Crimes of Unlawful Association' (2008) 11(4) *New Criminal Law Review: An International and Interdisciplinary Journal* 563–89.

Mewett, A. W. 'The Canadian Criminal Code, 1892–1992' (1993) 72(1) *The Canadian Bar Review* 1–27.

Meyering, I. B. 'Feminism in Sydney's Suburbs: "Speaking Out", Listening and 'Sisterhood' at the 1975 Women's Commissions' (2018) 33(95) *Australian Feminist Studies* 61–80.

Mitchell, T. 'A Dilemma at the Heart of Criminal Law: The Summary Jurisdiction, Family Violence, and the Over-Incarceration of Aboriginal and Torres Strait Islander Peoples' (2019) 45(2) *University of Western Australia Law Review* 136–165.

'Understanding the Summary Jurisdiction in NSW', PhD thesis, University of Sydney (2017).

Moore, M. S. *Placing Blame: A General Theory of the Criminal Law* (Oxford: Clarendon Press, 1997).

Moore, W. H. 'The Australian Commonwealth Constitution' (1903) 5(1) *Journal of the Society of Comparative Legislation* 115–31.

Moran, M. 'Reshaping Responsibility: The Emerging Private Law of Institutional Wrongs', in K. Barker, S. Degeling, K. Fairweather and R. Grantham (eds.), *Private Law and Power* (Oxford: Hart Publishing, 2017), pp. 263–84.

'The Role of Reparative Justice in Responding to the Legacy of the Indian Residential Schools' (2014) 64(4) *University of Toronto Law Journal* 529–65.

Morgan, J. 'Homicide Law Reform and Gender: Configuring Violence' (2012) 45(3) *Australian & New Zealand Journal of Criminology* 351–66.

Morgan, N. 'Criminal Law Reform 1983–1995: An Era of Unprecedented Legislative Activism' (1995) 25 *University of Western Australia Law Review* 283–300.

Morris, N. 'A New Qualified Defence to Murder' (1960) 1(1) *Adelaide Law Review* 23–52.

'An Australian Letter' [1957] *Criminal Law Review* 389–94.

'An Australian Letter' [1958] *Criminal Law Review* 520–8.

'The Slain Chicken Thief' (1958) 2(3) *Sydney Law Review* 414–35.

Morris, N. and Hawkins, G. *The Honest Politician's Guide to Crime Control* (Chicago, IL: University of Chicago Press, 1970).

Morris, N. and Howard, C. *Studies in Criminal Law* (Oxford: Clarendon Press, 1964).

Moses, A. D. 'An Antipodean Genocide? The Origins of the Genocidal Moment in the Colonization of Australia' (2000) 2(1) *Journal of Genocide Research* 89–106.

Mounk, Y. *The Age of Responsibility: Luck, Choice and the Welfare State* (Cambridge, MA: Harvard University Press, 2017).

Mulqueeny, K. 'Fault Elements from a Code Perspective' (1991) 15 *Criminal Law Journal* 109–12.

Munday, R. 'Annual Survey of Commonwealth Law 1977' (1980) 39(2) *Cambridge Law Journal* 398–9.

Musgrove, N. 'The Role and Importance of History', in J. Sköld and S. Swain (eds.), *Apologies and the Legacy of Abuse of Children in 'Care': International Perspectives* (Basingstoke: Palgrave Macmillan, 2015), pp. 147–58.

Naffine, N. 'Can Women be Legal Persons?' in S. James and S. Palmer (eds.), *Visible Women: Essays on Feminist Legal Theory and Political Philosophy* (London: Hart Publishing, 2002), pp. 69–90.

'Criminal Conversations: Farmer, Lacey and the New Social Scholarship' (2016) 38(4) *Sydney Law Review* 505–17.

Criminal Law and the Man Problem (London: Hart Publishing, 2019).

Feminism and Criminology (Cambridge: Polity Press, 1997).

'Human Agents in Criminal Law and Its Scholarship' (2011) 35 *Criminal Law Journal* 51–6.

'In Defence of the Responsible Subject' (2009) 34 *Australian Journal of Legal Philosophy* 222–7.

Law's Meaning of Life: Philosophy, Religion, Darwin and the Legal Person (London: Hart Publishing, 2009).

'Who Are Law's Persons? From Cheshire Cats to Responsible Subjects' (2003) 66(3) *Modern Law Review* 346–67.

Naffine, N. and Owens, R. (eds.), *Sexing the Subject of Law* (Sydney: Allen and Unwin, 1997).

Neal, D. *The Rule of Law in a Penal Colony: Law and Power in Early New South Wales* (Cambridge: Cambridge University Press, 1991).

Nedelsky, J. *Law's Relations: A Relational Theory of Self, Autonomy, and Law* (Oxford: Oxford University Press, 2011).

'Reconceiving Autonomy: Sources, Thoughts and Possibilities' (1989) 1 *Yale Journal of Law and Feminism* 7–36.

'Reconceiving Rights as Relationship' (1993) 1(1) *Review of Constitutional Studies* 1–26.

Nelken, D. 'Critical Criminal Law' (1987) 14(1) *Journal of Law and Society* 105–17.

Nelson, E. 'Civilian Men and Domestic Violence in the Aftermath of the First World War' (2003) 27 *Journal of Australian Studies* 97–108.

Neville Brown, L. 'A Century of Comparative Law in England: 1869–1969' (1971) 19(2) *The American Journal of Comparative Law* 232–52.

Norrie, A. *Crime, Reason and History: A Critical Introduction to Criminal Law*, 3rd ed. (Cambridge: Cambridge University Press, 2014).

'Justice on the Slaughter-Bench: The Problem of War Guilt in Arendt and Jaspers' (2008) 2 *New Criminal Law Review* 187–231.

'Legal Form and Moral Judgement: Euthanasia and Assisted Suicide', in R. A. Duff, L. Farmer, S. E. Marshall, M. Renzo and V. Tadros (eds.), *The Structures of Criminal Law* (Oxford: Oxford University Press, 2011), pp. 134–57.

'Simulacra of Morality?: Beyond the Ideal/Actual Antinomies of Criminal Justice', in A. Duff (ed.), *Philosophy and the Criminal Law: Principle and Critique* (Cambridge: Cambridge University Press, 1998), pp. 101–56.

Punishment, Responsibility and Justice: A Relational Critique (Oxford: Oxford University Press, 2000).

Odgers, S. 'Conspiracy to Commit a Commonwealth Offence' (2010) 34 *Criminal Law Journal* 240–9.

Principles of Federal Criminal Law, 4th ed. (Sydney: Thomson Reuters, 2019).

Oliver, P. C. *The Constitution of Independence: The Development of Constitutional Theory in Australia, Canada and New Zealand* (Oxford: Oxford University Press, 2005).

Oosterhuis, H. and Loughnan, A. 'Introduction – Madness and Crime: Historical Perspectives on Forensic Psychiatry' (2014) 37(1) *International Journal of Law and Psychiatry* 1–16.

O'Regan, R. S. *New Essays on the Australian Criminal Codes* (Sydney: Law Book Co., 1988).

'Law Reform and Politics' (1996) 14 *Australian Bar Review* 1–5.

'Sir Samuel Griffith's Criminal Code' (1991) XIV(8) *Royal Historical Society of Queensland Journal* 305–17.

Pahl, R. *On Friendship* (Cambridge: Polity Press, 2000).

Paisley, F. 'Citizens of Their World: Australian Feminism and Indigenous Rights in the International Context, 1920s and 1930s' (1998) 58 *Feminist Review* 66–84.

Palmer, B. 'Nineteenth-Century Canada and Australia: The Paradoxes of Class Formation' (1996) 71 *Labour History* 16–36.

Parker, A., Sarat, A. and Umphrey, M. M. 'Introduction', in A. Parker, A. Sarat and M. M. Umphrey (eds.), *Subjects of Responsibility: Framing Personhood in Modern Bureaucracies* (New York: Fordham University Press, 2011), pp. 1–18.

Parker, G. 'The Origins of the Canadian Criminal Code', in D. H. Flaherty (ed.), *Essays in the History of Canadian Law Volume 1* (Toronto: University of Toronto Press, 1981), pp. 249–81.

Parker, R. S. 'Garran, Sir Robert Randolph (1867–1957)', in B. Nairn (ed.), *Australian Dictionary of Biography Volume 8: 1891–1939* (Melbourne: Melbourne University Press, 1981).

Pascoe, C. 'Be Home by Dark: Childhood Freedoms and Adult Fears in 1950s Victoria' (2009) 40(2) *Australian Historical Studies* pp. 215–31.

Pasquino, P. 'Criminology: The Birth of a Special Saviour', in P. Beirne (ed.), *The Origins and Growth of Criminology: Essays on Intellectual History, 1760–1945* (Aldershot, UK: Dartmouth Publishing, 1994), pp. 17–32.

Peel, M. 'New Worlds of Friendship: The Early Twentieth Century', in B. Caine (ed.), *Friendship: A History* (London: Equinox Publishing, 2009), pp. 279–316.

Peel, M., Reed, L. and Walter, J. 'The Importance of Friends: The Most Recent Past', in B. Caine (ed.), *Friendship: A History* (London: Equinox Publishing, 2009), pp. 317–56.

Peelo, M., Francis, B., Soothill, K., Pearson, J. and Ackerley, E. 'Newspaper Reporting and the Public Construction of Homicide' (2004) 44 *British Journal of Criminology* 256–75.

Perkins, R. M. 'A Re-Examination of Malice Aforethought' (1934) 43(4) *Yale Law Review* 537–70.

Philip, R. F. B. 'Criminal Responsibility at Common Law and under the Criminal Code – Some Comparisons' (1948–51) 1(2) *University of Queensland Law Journal* 1–13.

Pifferi, M. 'Criminal Responsibility and Its Histories: New Perspectives for Comparative Legal History' (2017) 4(2) *Critical Analysis of Law* 222–32.

Reinventing Punishment: A Comparative History of Criminology and Penology in the Nineteenth and Twentieth Centuries (Oxford: Oxford University Press, 2016).

Piper, A. J. 'To Judge a Thief: How the Background of Thieves Became Central to Dispensing Justice, Western Australia, 1921–1951' (2017) 4(1) *Law & History* 113–44.

Postema, G. J. *Bentham and the Common Law Tradition* (Oxford: Clarendon Press, 1986).

Prasser, S. *Royal Commissions and Public Inquiries in Australia* (Sydney: LexisNexis, 2006).

Pratt, J. 'Governing the Dangerous: An Historical Overview of Dangerous Offender Legislation' (1996) 5(1) *Social & Legal Studies* 21–36.

Pringle, K. 'R v. Robyn Bella Kina' (1994) 3(67) *Aboriginal Law Bulletin* 14.

Quilter, J. 'Criminalisation of Alcohol Fuelled Violence: One-Punch Laws', in T. Crofts and A. Loughnan (eds.), *Criminalisation and Criminal Responsibility in Australia* (Sydney: Oxford University Press, 2015), pp. 82–104.

'Re-framing the Rape Trial: Insights from Critical Theory about the Limitations of Legislative Reform' (2011) 35(1) *Australian Feminist Law Journal* 23–56.

Quinlan, M. 'Australia, 1788–1902: A Working Man's Paradise?' in D. Hay and P. Craven (eds.), *Masters, Servants, and Magistrates in Britain and the Empire, 1562–1955* (Chapel Hill, NC: University of North Carolina Press, 2004), pp. 219–50.

Rabin, D. *Identity, Crime, and Legal Responsibility in Eighteenth-Century England* (London: Palgrave Macmillan, 2004).

Ramsay, P. *The Insecurity State: Vulnerable Autonomy and the Right to Security in the Criminal Law* (Oxford: Oxford University Press, 2012).

'The Responsible Subject as Citizen: Criminal Law, Democracy and the Welfare State' (2006) 69(1) *Modern Law Review* 29–58.

Ramsland, J. *Children of the Back Lanes: Destitute and Neglected Children in Colonial New South Wales* (Sydney: New South Wales University Press, 1986).

With Just but Relentless Discipline: A Social History of Corrective Services in New South Wales (Sydney: Kangaroo Press, 1996).

Re, L. 'Moore, Sir William Harrison (1867–1935)', in B. Nairn (ed.), *Australian Dictionary of Biography Volume 10: 1891–1939* (Melbourne: Melbourne University Press, 1986).

Reynolds, H. *Forgotten War* (Sydney: NewSouth Books, 2013).

The Other Side of the Frontier: Aboriginal Resistance to the European Invasion of Australia (London: Penguin Books, 1982).

Richter, M. 'The Comparative Study of Regimes and Societies', in M. Goldie and R. Wokler (eds.), *Cambridge History of Eighteenth Century Political Thought* (Cambridge: Cambridge University Press, 2006), pp. 145–71.

Ristroph, A. 'Responsibility for the Criminal Law', in R. A. Duff and S. P. Green (eds.), *Philosophical Foundations of Criminal Law* (Oxford: Oxford University Press, 2011), pp. 107–24.

Robert, H. 'Disciplining the Female Aboriginal Body: Inter-racial Sex and the Pretence of Separation' (2001) 16(34) *Australian Feminist Studies* 69–81.

Robinson, P. H. and Dubber, M. D. 'The American Model Penal Code: A Brief Overview' (2007) 10(3) *New Criminal Law Review* 319–41.

Rodensky, L. *The Crime in Mind: Criminal Responsibility and the Victorian Novel* (Oxford: Oxford University Press, 2003).

Rogers, N. 'Policing the Poor in Eighteenth Century London: The Vagrancy Laws and Their Administration' (1991) XXIV *Histoire sociale/Social History* 127–47.

Rose, A. 'Developments in Criminal Law and Criminal Justice: 1995 Australian Criminal Code Act: Corporate Criminal Provisions' (1995) 6(1) *Criminal Law Forum* 129–47.

Rose, N. 'Expertise and the Government of Conduct', in S. S. Silbey and A. Sarat (eds.), *Studies in Law, Politics and Society* (Greenwich, CT: JAI Press, 1994), pp. 359–97.

Governing the Soul: The Shaping of the Private Self, 2nd ed. (London: Routledge, 1999).

'Government, Authority and Expertise in Advanced Liberalism' (1993) 22(3) *Economy and Society* 283–99.

Inventing Our Selves: Psychology, Power, and Personhood (Cambridge: Cambridge University Press, 1998).

Powers of Freedom: Reframing Political Thought (Cambridge: Cambridge University Press, 1999).

'The Biology of Culpability: Pathological Identity and Crime Control in a Biological Culture' (2000) 4(1) *Theoretical Criminology* 5–34.

Rosen, F. 'Utilitarianism and the Reform of the Criminal Law', in M. Goldie and R. Wokler (eds.), *Cambridge History of Eighteenth Century Political Thought* (Cambridge: Cambridge University Press, 2011), pp. 547–72.

Rowbotham, J. and Stevenson, K. 'Societal Dystopias and Legal Utopias? Reflections on Visions Past and the Enduring Ideal of Criminal Codification' (2000) 9(25) *Nottingham Law Journal* 25–38.

Rush, P. 'Jurisdictions of Sexual Assault: Reforming the Texts and Testimony of Rape in Australia' (2011) 19(1) *Feminist Legal Studies* 47–73.

Ryan, J. '"She Lives with a Chinaman": Orient-ing 'White' Women in the Courts of Law' (1999) 23(60) *Journal of Australian Studies* 149–59.

Salter, M. 'The Privatisation of Incest: The Neglect of Familial Sexual Abuse in Australian Public Inquiries', in Y. Smaal, A. Kaladelfos and M. Finnane (eds.), *The Sexual Abuse of Children: Recognition and Redress* (Melbourne: Monash University Press, 2016), pp. 108–20.

Schneebaum, G. 'Making Abuse Offences in the Modern Criminal Law' (2017) 4(1) *Critical Analysis of Law* 42–52.

Schloenhardt, A. 'Mafias and Motorbikes: New Organised Crime Offences in Australia' (2007) 19 *Current Issues Criminal Justice* 259–82.

'Organised Crime and the Business of Migrant Trafficking: An Economic Analysis' (1999) 32(3) *Crime, Law and Social Change* 203–33.

Scott, D. and Swain, S. *Confronting Cruelty: Historical Perspectives on Child Protection in Australia* (Melbourne: Melbourne University Press, 2002).

Scott, G. 'A Model Criminal Code' (1992) 16 *Criminal Law Journal* 350–2.

Scrine, C. '"More Deadly than the Male": The Sexual Politics of Female Poisoning: Trials of the Thallium Women' (2002) 8 *Limina* 127–43.

Scutt, J. A. 'Judicial Bias or Legal Bias? Battery, Women and the Law' (1995) 19(43) *Journal of Australian Studies* 130–43.

Even in the Best of Homes: Violence in the Family (Ringwood: Penguin Australia, 1983).

Selchow, S. 'Security Policy and (Global) Risk(s)', in M. Kaldor and I. Rangelov (eds.), *The Handbook of Global Security Policy* (London: Palgrave Macmillan, 2014), pp. 68–84.

Shaw, A. G. L. 'British Policy Towards the Australian Aborigines, 1830–1850' (1992) 25(99) *Australian Historical Studies* 265–85.

Sheehy, E., Stubbs, J. and Tolmie, J. 'Defending Battered Women on Trial: The Battered Woman Syndrome and Its Limitations' (1992) 16(6) *Criminal Law Journal* 369–94.

Sherington, G. 'Contrasting Narratives in the History of Twentieth-Century British Child Migration to Australia: An Interpretive Essay' (2012) 9(2) *History Australia* 27–47.

Shircore, M., Douglas, H. and Morwood, V. 'Domestic and Family Violence and Police Negligence' (2017) 39 *Sydney Law Review* 539–67.

Simester, A. P. and Shute, S. 'On the General Part in Criminal Law', in S. Shute and A. P. Simester (eds.), *Criminal Law Theory: Doctrines of the General Part* (Oxford: Oxford University Press, 2002), pp. 1–12.

Skinner, Q. 'A Genealogy of the Modern State' (2009) 162 *Proceedings of the British Academy* 325–70.

Skuy, D. 'Macaulay and the Indian Penal Code of 1862: The Myth of the Inherent Superiority and Modernity of the English Legal System Compared to India's Legal System in the Nineteenth Century' (1998) 32(3) *Modern Asian Studies* 513–57.

Smaal, Y. 'Historical Perspectives on Child Sexual Abuse, Part 1' (2013) 11(9) *History Compass* 702–14.

'Historical Perspectives on Child Sexual Abuse, Part 2' (2013) 11(9) *History Compass* 715–26.

Smart, C. *Women, Crime and Criminology: A Feminist Critique* (London: Routledge, 1976).

Smith, K. 'Subjectivity, Hegemony and the Subaltern in Sydney, 1870–1900' (2007) 19(2) *Rethinking Marxism* 169–79.

Smith, K. J. M. 'General Principles of Criminal Law', in W. Cornish, J. S. Anderson, R. Cocks, M. Lobban, P. Polden and K. Smith (eds.), *The Oxford History of the Laws of England Volume XIII: 1820–1914 Fields of Development* (Oxford: Oxford University Press, 2010), pp. 217–320.

'Macaulay's "Utilitarian" Indian Penal Code: An Illustration of the Accidental Function of Time, Place and Personalities in Law Making', in W. M. Gordon and T. D. Fergus (eds.), *Legal History in the Making: Proceedings from the Ninth British Legal History Conference* (London: The Hambledon Press, 1991), pp. 145–64.

'The Sources and Form of the Criminal Law: The Medium of Change and Development: Consolidation or Codification?' in W. Cornish, J. S. Anderson, R. Cocks, M. Lobban, P. Polden and K. Smith (eds.), *The Oxford History of the Laws of England Volume XIII: 1820–1914 Fields of Development* (Oxford: Oxford University Press, 2010), pp. 180–216.

Smyth, P. 'The Historical Context for Action', in A. McClelland and P. Smyth (eds.), *Social Policy in Australia: Understanding for Action* (Melbourne: Oxford University Press, 2014), pp. 81–94.

Steel, A. 'Consorting in New South Wales: Substantive Offence or Police Power?' (2003) 26(3) *University of New South Wales Law Journal* 567–602.

Stephen, J. F. *A History of the Criminal Law of England Volume 2* (London: Macmillan and Co., 1883).

Stevens, R. B. *Law School: Legal Education in America from the 1850s to the 1980s* (Clark, NJ: The Lawbook Exchange, Ltd., 2001).

Stewart, J. G. 'Complicity', in M. D. Dubber and T. Hörnle (eds.), *The Oxford Handbook of Criminal Law* (New York: Oxford University Press, 2014), pp. 534–59.

Strange, C. 'Masculinities, Intimate Femicide and the Death Penalty in Australia, 1890–1920' (2003) 43(2) *British Journal of Criminology* 310–39.

Stubbs, J. 'Murder, Manslaughter and Domestic Violence', in K. Fitz-Gibbon and S. Walklate (eds.), *Homicide, Gender and Responsibility: An International Perspective* (Milton Park, UK: Routledge, 2016), pp. 36–52.

Stubbs, J. and Tolmie, J. 'Race, Gender and the Battered Woman Syndrome: An Australian Case Study' (1995) 8 *Canadian Journal of Women and Law* 122–58.

Sugarman, D. '"A Hatred of Disorder": Legal Science, Liberalism and Imperialism', in P. Fitzpatrick (ed.), *Dangerous Supplements: Resistance and Renewal in Jurisprudence* (London: Pluto Press, 1991), pp. 34–67.

Swain, S. 'Beyond Child Migration: Inquiries, Apologies and Implications for the Writing of Transnational Child Welfare History' (2016) 13(1) *History Australia* 139–52.

Born in Hope: The Early Years of the Family Court of Australia (Sydney: UNSW Press, 2012).

'Institutional Abuse: A Long History' (2018) 42(2) *Journal of Australian Studies* 153–63.

'Narratives of Innocence and Seduction', in Y. Smaal, A. Kaladelfos and M. Finnane (eds.), *The Sexual Abuse of Children: Recognition and Redress* (Melbourne: Monash University Press, 2016).

'Why Sexual Abuse? Why Now?' in J. Sköld and S. Swain (eds.), *Apologies and the Legacy of Abuse of Children in 'Care': International Perspectives* (Basingstoke: Palgrave Macmillan, 2015), pp. 83–94.

Tadros, V. 'Crimes and Security' (2008) 71(6) *Modern Law Review* 940–70.

Criminal Responsibility (Oxford: Oxford University Press, 2005).

Tarrant, S. 'Building Bridges in Australian Criminal Law: Codification and the Common Law' (2012) 39(3) *Monash University Law Review* 838–63.

Tarrant, S. and Blake, M. 'Introduction to the UWA Law Review Special Issue' (2019) 45(2) *University of Western Australia Law Review* (forthcoming).

Taylor, G. 'Dr Pennefather's Criminal Code for South Australia' (2002) 31(1) *Common Law World Review* 62–102.

'The Victorian Criminal Code' (2004) 23 *University of Queensland Law Journal* 170–204.

Thornton, M. *Privatising the Public University: The Case of Law* (London: Routledge, 2012).

Tomsen, S. and Crofts, T. 'Social and Cultural Meanings of Legal Responses to Homicide Among Men: Masculine Honour, Sexual Advances and Accidents' (2012) 45(3) *Australian & New Zealand Journal of Criminology* 423–37.

Toole, K. 'Defensive Homicide on Trial in Victoria' (2013) 39(2) *Monash University Law Review* 473–505.

Torpey, J. '"Making Whole What Has Been Smashed": Reflections on Reparations' (2001) 73 *The Journal of Modern History* 333–58.

Turner, J. W. C. 'The Mental Element in Crimes at Common Law' (1936) 6(1) *Cambridge Law Journal* 31–66.

Twining, W. 'Reflections on Law in Context', in P. Cane and J. Stapleton (eds.), *Essays for Patrick Atiyah* (Oxford: Oxford University Press, 1991), pp. 1–30.

Ulbrick, M., Flynn, A. and Tyson, D. 'The Abolition of Defensive Homicide: A Step Towards Populist Punitivism at the Expense of Mentally Impaired Offenders' (2016) 40 *Melbourne University Law Review* 324–70.

Urbas, G. and Bronitt, S. 'Courts, Criminal Law and Procedure', in A. Graycar and P. Grabosky (eds.), *The Cambridge Handbook of Australian Criminology* (Cambridge: Cambridge University Press, 2002), pp. 73–93.

Valentine, K. and Breckenridge, J. 'Responses to Family and Domestic Violence: Supporting Women?' (2016) 25(1) *Griffith Law Review* 30–44.

Valverde, M. 'As If Subjects Existed: Analyzing Social Discourses' (1991) 28(2) *Canadian Review of Sociology and Anthropology* 173–87.

van Krieken, R. *Children and the State: Social Control and the Formation of Australian Child Welfare* (Sydney: Allen & Unwin, 1991).

'Rethinking Cultural Genocide: Aboriginal Child Removal and Settler-Colonial State Formation' (2004) 75(2) *Oceania* 125–51.

'The 'Stolen Generations' and Cultural Genocide: The Forced Removal of Australian Indigenous Children from Their Families and Its Implications for the Sociology of Childhood' (1999) 6(3) *Childhood* 297–311.

Veitch, S. *Law and Irresponsibility: On the Legitimation of Human Suffering* (London: Routledge, 2007).

Vincent, N. A. 'A Structured Taxonomy of Responsibility Concepts', in N. A. Vincent, I. van de Poel, and J. van den Hoven (eds.), *Moral Responsibility: Beyond Free Will and Determinism* (New York: Springer, 2011), pp. 15–35.

Vines, P. 'Apologising to Avoid Liability: Cynical Civility or Practical Morality?' (2005) 27 *Sydney Law Review* 483–506.

Walker, L. *The Battered Woman* (New York: Harper and Row, 1979).

Walker, R. 'The New South Wales Police Force, 1862–1900' (1984) 8(15) *Journal of Australian Studies* 25–38.

Wangmann, J. 'Liability for Institutional Child Sexual Assault: Where Does Lepore Leave Australia?' (2004) 28 *Melbourne University Law Review* 169–202.

Ward, D. 'Imperial Policy, Colonial Government, and Indigenous Testimony in South Australia and New Zealand in the 1840s', in S. Dorsett and I. Hunter (eds.), *Law and Politics in British Colonial Thought* (London: Palgrave Macmillan, 2010), pp. 229–47.

Ward, T. 'The Sad Subject of Infanticide: Law, Medicine and Child Murder 1860–1938' (1999) 8(2) *Social & Legal Studies* 163–80.

Weeks, W. and Gilmore, K. 'How Violence Against Women Became an Issue on the National Policy Agenda', in T. Dalton, M. Draper, W. Weeks and J. Wiseman (eds.), *Making Social Policy in Australia* (Sydney: Allen & Unwin, 1996), pp. 141–53.

Wells, B. 'Criminal Codes for the Commonwealth and the States?' (1991) 62 *Reform* 108–10.

Wells, C. *Corporations and Criminal Responsibility* (Oxford: Oxford University Press, 2001).

'Swatting the Subjectivist Bug' [1982] *Criminal Law Review* 209–20.

Wheare, K. C. 'Allen, Sir Carleton Kemp (1887–1966)', in B. Nairn (ed.), *Australian Dictionary of Biography Volume 7: 1891–1939* (Melbourne: Melbourne University Press, 1979).

White, R. 'War and Australian Society', in M. McKernan and M. Brown (eds.), *Australia: Two Centuries of War and Peace* (Canberra: Allen & Unwin, 1988), pp. 391–424.

White, S. 'The Making of the New Zealand Criminal Code Act of 1893: A Sketch' (1986) 16 *Victoria University of Wellington Law Review* 353–76.

Whitman, J. Q. 'The Case for Penal Modernism: Beyond Utility and Desert' (2014) 1(2) *Critical Analysis of Law* 143–81.

'The Transition to Modernity', in M. D. Dubber and T. Hörnle (eds.), *The Oxford Handbook of Criminal Law* (New York: Oxford University Press, 2014), pp. 84–110.

Wiener, M. J. *Reconstructing the Criminal: Culture, Law and Policy in England, 1830–1914* (Cambridge: Cambridge University Press, 1994).

Williams, G. *Textbook of Criminal Law* (London: Stevens, 1978).

Criminal Law: The General Part (London: Stevens, 1953).

Wills, D. 'One Nation: Nine Codes', *The Bulletin*, 16 October 1990.

Wilson, W. F. and Graham, A. D. (eds.), *The Criminal Code of Queensland and the Criminal Practice Rules of 1900* (Brisbane: Government Printer, 1901).

Winterton, G. 'Comparative Law Teaching' (1975) 23(1) *The American Journal of Comparative Law* 69–118.

Woods, G. D. *A History of Criminal Law in New South Wales Volume 1: The Colonial Period: 1788–1900* (Sydney: Federation Press, 2002).

A History of Criminal Law in New South Wales Volume 2: The New State, 1901–1955 (Sydney: The Federation Press, 2018).

Wootton, B. *Crime and the Criminal Law: Reflections of a Magistrate and Social Scientist* (London: Stevens and Sons, 1963).

Wright, B. 'Criminal Law Codification and Imperial Projects: The Self-Governing Jurisdiction Codes of the 1890s' (2008) 12 *Legal History* 19–49.

'Self-Governing Codifications of English Criminal Law and Empire: The Queensland and Canadian Examples' (2007) 26(1) *University of Queensland Law Journal* 39–65.

Wright, K. 'Challenging Institutional Denial: Psychological Discourse, Therapeutic Culture and Public Inquiries' (2018) 42(2) *Journal of Australian Studies* 177–90.

The Rise of the Therapeutic Society: Psychological Knowledge and the Contradictions of Cultural Change (Washington, DC: New Academia, 2011).

Wright, N. E. 'The Problem of Aboriginal Evidence in Early Colonial New South Wales', in D. Kirkby and C. Coleborne (eds.), *Law, History, Colonialism: The Reach of Empire* (Manchester: Manchester University Press, 2001), pp. 140–55.

Yeo, S. 'Revisiting Excessive Self-Defence' (2000) 12 *Current Issues in Criminal Justice* 39–57.

'Revitalising the Penal Code with a General Part' [2004] *Singapore Journal of Legal Studies* 1–19.

'The New Developments in the Law of Self-Defence in Australia' (1987) 7 *Oxford Journal of Legal Studies* 489–96.

Zedner, L. 'Pre-crime and Post-criminology?' (2007) 11(2) *Theoretical Criminology* 261–81.

'Too Much Security?' (2003) 31(3) *International Journal of the Sociology of Law* 155–84.

Reports and Other Sources

American Law Institute, *Model Penal and Correctional Code: Official Draft and Explanatory Notes* (adopted 24 May 1962) (Philadelphia, PA: The American Law Institute, 1985).

Attorney-General's Department (Cth), *Guide to Framing Commonwealth Offences, Civil Penalties and Enforcement Powers* (2007).

Attorney-General's Department (SA), *First Interim Report to the Attorney-General of South Australia on Reform of the Criminal Law in South Australia, Consistency in Criminal Law Reform at a National Level, and Progress Toward a Model Penal Code for Australia* (1991).

Australian Law Reform Commission, *Pathways to Justice – An Inquiry into the Incarceration Rate of Aboriginal and Torres Strait Islander Peoples*, Report No. 133 (2017).

Australian Law Reform Commission, *Recognition of Aboriginal Customary Laws*, Report No. 31 (1986).

Australian Law Reform Commission, *Royal Commissions and Official Inquiries*, Discussion Paper No. 75 (2009).

Australian Law Reform Commission and New South Wales Law Reform Commission, *Family Violence – A National Legal Response*, ALRC Final Report No. 114, NSWLRC Final Report No. 128 (2010).

Boxall, H., Tomison, A. and Hulme, S. *Historical Review of Sexual Offence and Child Sexual Abuse Legislation in Australia: 1788–2013*, Report prepared by the Australian Institute of Criminology for the Royal Commission into Institutional Responses to Child Sexual Abuse (2014).

Cashmore, J., Taylor, A., Shackel, R. and Parkinson, P. *The Impact of Delayed Reporting on the Prosecution and Outcomes of Child Sexual Abuse Cases*, Report for the Royal Commission into Institutional Responses to Child Sexual Abuse (2016).

Cockburn, Lord Chief Justice, Letter containing comments and suggestions in relation to the Criminal Code (Indictable Offences) Bill, 12 June 1879, H.C. Papers, 1878–79, vol. 59.

Cockburn, Lord Chief Justice, Letter to the Attorney General on the Criminal Code, 7 February 1880 (1880) 22 *Law Journal* 184–8, 202–8.

Committee of Enquiry into Child Care Services in Victoria, Parliament of Victoria, *Report* (1976).

Committee of Investigation into Allegations of Neglect and Maltreatment of Young Children (Vic), *Report to the Honourable the Chief Secretary and the Honourable to Minister of Health* (1967).

Committee of Investigation into Allegations of Neglect and Maltreatment of Young Children, *Second Report to the Honourable the Chief Secretary and the Honourable to Minister of Health* (1969).

Commonwealth of Australia, Australian Royal Commission of Inquiry into Drugs, *Report* (1980).

Commonwealth of Australia, Department of Justice, *Introduction of Criminal Code Bill Is Legal History in the Making Says Minister for Justice*, Press Release (1 July 1994).

Commonwealth of Australia, New South Wales, Victoria and Queensland, Royal Commission of Inquiry into Drug Trafficking (1981–1983).

Commonwealth of Australia, Office of the Prime Minister (Gough Whitlam), Royal Commission into Human Relationships, Press Statement No. 306 (Canberra, 21 August 1974).

Commonwealth of Australia, Office of the Prime Minister (Malcolm Turnbull), Press Conference with the Attorney General and the Minister for Social Services (13 June 2018).

Commonwealth of Australia, Parliament of Australia, *The Aboriginals and Half-Castes of Central Australia and North Australia* (1928).

Commonwealth of Australia, Parliament of Australia, Explanatory Memorandum, *Criminal Code Bill 1994* (Cth).

Commonwealth of Australia, Royal Commission into Aboriginal Deaths in Custody, *Final Report* (1991).

Commonwealth of Australia, Royal Commission into Institutional Responses to Child Sexual Abuse, *Consultation Paper: Criminal Justice* (2016).

Commonwealth of Australia, Royal Commission into Institutional Responses to Child Sexual Abuse, *Final Report* (2017).

Commonwealth of Australia, Royal Commission into Institutional Responses to Child Sexual Abuse, *Interim Report* (2014).

Commonwealth of Australia, Royal Commission on Human Relationships, *Final Report* (1977).

Commonwealth of Australia, *The Northern Territory Report for the Period 1st July, 1953, to 30th June, 1955* (1956).

Criminal Law and Penal Methods Reform Committee of South Australia, *Special Report: Rape and Other Sexual Offences* (1976).

Criminal Law Officers' Committee, Standing Committee of Attorneys-General, *Model Criminal Code Chapters 1 and 2: General Principles of Criminal Responsibility, Final Report* (1992).

Criminal Law Officers' Committee, Standing Committee of Attorneys-General, *Model Criminal Code Chapter 2: General Principles of Criminal Responsibility, Discussion Draft* (1992).

Department of Community Welfare (WA), *The Battered Child: Proceedings of the First National Australian Conference, Mt. Lawley Teachers College, Perth, August 25–28* (1975).

Easterbrook, M. 'Moves Begin Toward National Criminal Code', *The Age*, 9 September 1993.

Editorial, 'Consent Laws Barriers to Reform', *The Australian*, 21 December 1996.

Editorial, 'Consent Question Should Be Faced', *The Australian*, 17 December 1996.

Family and Community Development Committee, Parliament of Victoria, *Betrayal of Trust: Inquiry into the Handling of Child Abuse by Religious and Other Non-Government Organisations, Final Report* (2013).

Family Law Council, Parliament of Australia, *Child Sexual Abuse Report* (1988).

Freiberg, A., Donnelly, H. and Gelb, K. *Sentencing for Child Sexual Abuse in Institutional Contexts*, Report for the Royal Commission into Institutional Responses to Child Sexual Abuse (2015).

Gleeson, M. 'The Privy Council: An Australian Perspective' (Address delivered at the Anglo-Australasian Lawyers Society, The Commercial Bar Association and Chancery Association, 18 June 2008).

Government of South Australia, Submission No. 13 to the Parliamentary Joint Committee on the Australian Crime Commission, *Inquiry into the Legislative Arrangements to Outlaw Serious and Organized Crime Groups* (2009).

Griffith, S. W. Digest of the Statutory Criminal Law in Force in Queensland on the first day of January, 1896 (which it is within the competence of the Parliament of Queensland to Repeal or Amend) (Brisbane: Government Printer, 1896).

'Introductory Letter', 29 October 1897, xi, vii.

Letter to the Queensland Attorney-General, 1 June 1896 (Brisbane: Government Printer, 1896), iii–viii.

Letter to the Queensland Attorney-General, 29 October 1897 (Brisbane: Government Printer, 1897), iii–xiv.

Herron, J. (Minister for Aboriginal and Torres Strait Islander Affairs), *Bringing Them Home: Commonwealth Initiatives* (Media Release), 16 December 1997.

Human Rights and Equal Opportunity Commission, *Bringing Them Home: Report of the National Inquiry into the Separation of Aboriginal and Torres Strait Islander Children from Their Families* (1997).

Judicial Commission of New South Wales, *Partial Defences to Murder in NSW 1990–2004* (2006).

Justice and Community Safety Directorate (ACT), *Discussion Paper: Consorting Laws for the ACT* (2016).

Law Commission for England and Wales, *Criminal Law: A Criminal Code for England and Wales Volumes 1 and 2*, Law Com. No. 177 (1989).

Law Commission for England and Wales, *Criminal Law: Codification of the Criminal Law*, Law Com. No. 143 (1985).

Law Commission for England and Wales, *Criminal Liability in Regulatory Contexts: A Consultation Paper*, Consultation Paper No. 195 (2010).

Law Commission for England and Wales, *Partial Defences to Murder*, Consultation Paper No. 173 (2003).

Law Commission for England and Wales, *Partial Defences to Murder: Final Report*, Law Com. No. 290 (2004).

Law Reform Commission, *Child Welfare*, Report No. 18 (1981) (Australia).

Law Reform Commission, *Evidence Law Reform Stage 2*, Discussion Paper No. 23 (1985) (Australia).

Law Reform Commission of Canada, *Recodifying Criminal Law*, Report No. 31 (1987).

Law Reform Commission of Western Australia, *A Review of the Law of Homicide: Final Report*, Project No. 97 (2007).

Law Reform Commission of Western Australia, *Report on the Police Offences Act*, Project No. 85 (1992).

Legislative Council Select Committee on the Partial Defence of Provocation, Parliament of New South Wales, *The Partial Defence of Provocation* (2013).

Mathews, B. *Mandatory Reporting Laws for Child Sexual Abuse in Australia: A Legislative History*, Report for the Royal Commission into Institutional Responses to Child Sexual Abuse (2014).

Model Criminal Code Officers' Committee, Standing Committee of Attorneys-General, *Discussion Paper* (1998).

Model Criminal Code Officers' Committee, Standing Committee of Attorneys-General, *Report on Blackmail, Forgery and Bribery; Non-fatal Offences against the Person* (1994).

Model Criminal Code Officers' Committee, Standing Committee of Attorneys-General, *Report on Conspiracy to Defraud* (1997).

Model Criminal Code Officers' Committee, Standing Committee of Attorneys-General, *Report on Offences against the Administration of Justice* (1998).

Model Criminal Code Officers' Committee, Standing Committee of Attorneys-General, *Report on Public Order Offences* (1998).

Model Criminal Code Officers' Committee, Standing Committee of Attorneys-General, *Report on Serious Drug Offences* (1998).

Model Criminal Code Officers' Committee, Standing Committee of Attorneys-General, *Report on Sexual Offences* (1996).

Model Criminal Code Officers' Committee, Standing Committee of Attorneys-General, *Report on Theft, Fraud and Related Offences* (1995).

New South Wales, Royal Commission into the New South Wales Police Service *Final Report* (1995–97).

New South Wales Department of Youth, Ethic and Community Affairs, Child Welfare Legislation Review Committee, *Report* (1975).

New South Wales Law Reform Commission, *Partial Defences to Murder: Diminished Responsibility*, Report No. 82 (1997).

New South Wales Law Reform Commission, *People with Cognitive and Mental Health Impairments in the Criminal Justice System: Criminal Responsibility and Consequences*, Report No. 138 (2013).

New South Wales Law Reform Commission, *People with Cognitive and Mental Health Impairments in the Criminal Justice System: Diversion*, Report No. 135 (2012).

New South Wales Ombudsman, *The Consorting Law: Report of the Operation of Part 3A, Division 7 of the Crimes Act 1900* (2016).

New South Wales Task Force on Domestic Violence, New South Wales Premier's Department, *Report of New South Wales Task Force on Domestic Violence to Honourable N.K. Wran Q.C., M.P. Premier of New South Wales* (1981).

New Zealand Law Commission, *Some Criminal Defences with Particular Reference to Battered Defendants*, Report No. 73 (2001).

Northern Territory Board of Inquiry into the Protection of Aboriginal Children from Sexual Abuse (NT), *Ampe Akelyernemane Meke Mekarle 'Little Children Are Sacred'*, Report (2007).

Parliament of New South Wales, *Children in Need: An Account of the Administration and Functions of the Child Welfare Department, New South Wales, Australia, with an Examination of the Principles Involved in Helping Deprived and Wayward Children* (1956).

Parliament of New South Wales, *Report of the Public Service Board into the Working of the State Children Relief Branch Particularly with Reference to the Conditions under Which Children Are Boarded Out* (1917).

Parliament of Queensland, *Report and Recommendations of the Commission of Inquiry into the Nature and Extent of the Problems Confronting Youth in Queensland* (1975).

Parliament of South Australia, *Children in State Care Commission of Inquiry: Allegations of Sexual Abuse and Death from Criminal Conduct* (2008).

Parliamentary Joint Committee on the Australian Crime Commission, Parliament of Australia, Inquiry into the Future Impact of Serious and Organised Crime on Australian Society (2007).

Parliamentary Joint Committee on the Australian Crime Commission, Parliament of Australia, Inquiry into the Legislative Arrangements to Outlaw Serious and Organized Crime Groups (2009).

Queensland, Commission of Inquiry into Abuse of Children in Queensland Institutions, *Report* (1999).

Queensland, Commission of Inquiry into Possible Illegal Activities and Associated Police Misconduct (1987–89).

Queensland Law Reform Commission, *A Review of the Excuse of Accident and the Defence of Provocation*, Report No. 64 (2008).

Queensland Taskforce on Organised Crime Legislation, Queensland Department of Justice and Attorney-General, *Final Report* (2016).

Review of Commonwealth Criminal Law (Australia), *Final Report* (1991).

Review of Commonwealth Criminal Law (Australia), *Interim Report [i.e. third]: Principles of Criminal Responsibility and Other Matters* (1990).

Select Committee on Health, United Kingdom House of Commons, *The Welfare of Former British Child Migrants, Third Report* (1998).

Senate Community Affairs References Committee, Parliament of Australia, *Australian Government Response to Forgotten Australians* (2005).

Senate Community Affairs References Committee, Parliament of Australia, *Forgotten Australians: A Report on Australians Who Experienced Institutional or Out-of-Home Care as Children* (2004).

Senate Community Affairs References Committee, Parliament of Australia, *Lost Innocents and Forgotten Australians Revisited: Report on the Progress with the Implementation of the Recommendations of the Lost Innocents and Forgotten Australians Reports* (2009).

Senate Community Affairs References Committee, Parliament of Australia, *Lost Innocents Righting the Record – Report on Child Migration* (2001).

Senate Community Affairs References Committee, Parliament of Australia, *Protecting Vulnerable Children: A National Challenge* (2005).

Senate Standing Committee on Social Welfare, Parliament of Australia, *Children in Institutional and Other Forms of Care: A National Perspective* (1985).

Sentencing Advisory Council, Attorney-General's Department (SA), *A Discussion Paper Considering the Operation of Part 8A of the Criminal Law Consolidation Act 1935* (SA) (2013).

South Australia, Children in State Care Commission of Inquiry, *Children in State Care Commission of Inquiry: Allegations of Sexual Abuse and Death from Criminal Conduct* (2008).

South Australia, Royal Commission on the Aborigines, *Progress Report* (1913).

Standing Committee of Attorneys-General, *Communiqué* (2009).

Swain, S. *History of Australian Inquiries Reviewing Institutions Providing Care for Children*, Report for the Royal Commission into Institutional Responses to Child Sexual Abuse (2014).

Sydney Morning Herald, 'In Parliament', 7 September 1900.

Victoria, Juvenile Delinquency Advisory Committee, *Report* (1956).

Victoria, Royal Commission into Family Violence, *Report and Recommendations* (2016).

Victoria, Royal Commission into Family Violence, *Summary and Recommendations* (2016).

Victorian Government, *Victorian Government Response to the Report of the Family and Community Development Committee Inquiry into the Handling of Child Abuse by Religious and Other Non-government Organisations 'Betrayal of Trust'* (2014).

Victorian Law Reform Commission, *Defences to Homicide: Final Report*, Report No. 94 (2004).

Western Australia, Royal Commission Appointed to Investigate, Report and Advise Upon Matters in Relation to the Condition and Treatment of Aborigines, *Report* (1935).

Western Australia, Royal Commission on State Children and Charities Department, *Report* (1921).

Willox, I. 'Keating Strives for National Law Reform', *The Age*, 22 September 1994.

Index